Liturgical Theology
after Schmemann

LITURGICAL THEOLOGY
THE CHURCH AS WORSHIP

ORTHODOX CHRISTIANITY AND CONTEMPORARY THOUGHT

SERIES EDITORS
George E. Demacopoulos and Aristotle Papanikolaou

This series consists of books that seek to bring Orthodox Christianity into an engagement with contemporary forms of thought. Its goal is to promote (1) historical studies in Orthodox Christianity that are interdisciplinary, employ a variety of methods, and speak to contemporary issues; and (2) constructive theological arguments in conversation with patristic sources and that focus on contemporary questions ranging from the traditional theological and philosophical themes of God and human identity to cultural, political, economic, and ethical concerns. The books in the series explore both the relevancy of Orthodox Christianity to contemporary challenges and the impact of contemporary modes of thought on Orthodox self-understandings.

LITURGICAL THEOLOGY AFTER SCHMEMANN

An Orthodox Reading of Paul Ricoeur

BRIAN A. BUTCHER

FORDHAM UNIVERSITY PRESS
New York • 2018

Fordham University Press has no responsibility for the persistence or accuracy of URLs for external or third-party Internet websites referred to in this publication and does not guarantee that any content on such websites is, or will remain, accurate or appropriate.

Fordham University Press also publishes its books in a variety of electronic formats. Some content that appears in print may not be available in electronic books.

Visit us online at www.fordhampress.com.

Library of Congress Cataloging-in-Publication Data

Names: Butcher, Brian A., author.
Title: Liturgical theology after Schmemann : an orthodox reading of Paul Ricoeur / Brian A. Butcher.
Description: First edition. | New York, NY : Fordham University Press, 2018. | Series: Orthodox Christianity and contemporary thought | Includes bibliographical references and index.
Identifiers: LCCN 2017041269 | ISBN 9780823278275 (cloth : alk. paper) | ISBN 9780823278756 (pbk. : alk. paper)
Subjects: LCSH: Liturgics. | Orthodox Eastern Church—Doctrines. | Shmeman, Aleksandr, 1921–1983. | Ricoeur, Paul.
Classification: LCC BX350 .B873 2018 | DDC 264/.019001—dc23
LC record available at https://lccn.loc.gov/2017041269

Printed in the United States of America

20 19 18   5 4 3 2 1

First edition

CONTENTS

PART IV: "THE VOICE OF THE LORD CRIES OUT UPON THE WATERS"

FOREWORD

Andrew Louth

It is generally recognized that "liturgical theology," as a notion or a discipline, owes its existence to the great Orthodox theologian of the last century, Fr. Alexander Schmemann. Liturgical theology, as Fr. Alexander understood it, is distinct from liturgiology, the study of the history and development of liturgical rites through (primarily) liturgical texts, and from a theology of liturgy, understood as a fundamental dimension of theology of worship. Both these disciplines are important—indeed liturgical theology depends upon them—but liturgical theology, as Fr. Alexander understood it, is theology derived from, or validated by, the liturgical practice of the Church. Fr. Schmemann's own practice of liturgical theology was powerful and influential. The changes in the way in which the Orthodox liturgical rites have been celebrated in the course of the last fifty years or so bear out Fr. Schmemann's influence. These changes can, however, be seen (as can Schmemann's liturgical theology) as growing out of the experience of the Russian émigrés in exile who, robbed of the splendor they were accustomed to in "Holy Russia," had to make do with the bare essentials in makeshift places of worship: there they came to discern the true shape of the liturgy.

To see liturgical theology as Fr. Schmemann did is to enter into a commanding vision with profound entailments for the nature of theology, although the way he practiced liturgical theology is not without its critics. Christians of the Eastern Rite rejoice in their possession of a premodern liturgy. In his search for the true liturgical *ordo*, Schmemann could be seen, with some justice, as undermining the very liturgy he knew and experienced.

By trying to get behind the traditional form of the Orthodox liturgy in search of some supposedly pristine form, he could in turn be accused of betraying a cast of mind formed by Western critical standards with its yearning for the original, and thus failing to grasp what is truly *originary* in authentic Orthodox liturgical experience. Furthermore, like most Orthodox theologians in the last century, he had a tendency to be descriptive, rather than analytical, leading to a somewhat "take it or leave it" manner of exposition. Part of the reason for this latter tendency was a fear, or shyness, of any kind of engagement with contemporary philosophy, partly due (no doubt) to an aversion to what Schmemann himself characterized as the "ponderous theological edifice" of the greatest of his teachers, Fr. Sergei Bulgakov. This reluctance to engage philosophically with theological concepts is perhaps the greatest weakness of what became the dominant strand of Orthodox theology (at least in the diaspora) in the last century—the so-called neo-patristic synthesis, that set its face against what it perceived as the corruption of Orthodox theology by the philosophical intuitions of the Russian Religious Renaissance. In this book, Brian Butcher seeks to reconnect Orthodox theology with significant currents in contemporary Western European philosophy.

Dr. Butcher does this by adopting a double strategy. The first element of this strategy is engagement with the thought of the great French philosopher, Paul Ricoeur. Ricoeur stood in the traditions of phenomenology and hermeneutics that have dominated European philosophical reflection since Husserl, Heidegger, and Gadamer. In Ricoeur, Butcher finds a congenial analysis of symbolic structures and a sense of philosophy as, not so much an individual quest, but a search for and exploration of meaning that involves dialogue, exchange, even, might we say, communion? Ricoeur, he demonstrates, provides a sufficiently ample hermeneutic with which to interpret the richly layered symbolism of Orthodox liturgical practice. The communal dimension of Ricoeur's hermeneutic—which inevitably envisages human beings as embodied and thus communicating through gesture, tone of voice, even song and music, rather than simply exchanging mental concepts—enables Butcher to treat liturgical performance as precisely *performance*, rather than merely a text. The other element of the author's strategy—explicit in the final chapter, but evoked throughout the book—is the liturgical rite of the Great Blessing of the Waters, performed at the Feast of Theophany (focused, in the Byzantine Rite, on the Baptism of the Lord), at the center of which is a prayer, one of the richest in its multilayered symbolism of water and light, in which water is blessed—a prayer ascribed (with some likelihood) to the great seventh-century patriarch of Jerusalem, Sophronios.

This book is a remarkable achievement, both in conception and execution. Dr. Butcher establishes liturgical theology as the central mode of Orthodox theology, not as a whim or a preference, but by the way in which, through engagement with modern hermeneutical reflection, it achieves the liturgical consummation of philosophy. It is humbling for me, as a priest of the Russian Orthodox Church, to acknowledge in this work of a theologian of the Ukrainian Greco-Catholic Church the inauguration of an enterprise that all Christians using the Eastern (Byzantine) Rite need to take if we are to share the treasures that we have in our liturgical worship with other, less fortunate, Christians.

Liturgical Theology
after Schmemann

INTRODUCTION

Several years ago, Pantelis Kalaitzidis issued a clarion call to fellow Orthodox theologians to renew their dialogue with contemporary philosophy, lamenting that such an enterprise has in recent times been commonly held in disfavor in the Christian East—a perhaps unintended result, he suggests, of the twentieth-century "neo-patristic synthesis" promoted by the renowned Georges Florovsky (1893–1979). In "From the 'Return to the Fathers' to the Need for a Modern Orthodox Theology" Kalaitzidis cites approvingly the following exhortation of Alexander Schmemann (1921–83):

> Orthodox theology must keep its patristic foundations, but it must also go "beyond" the Fathers if it is to respond to a new situation created by centuries of philosophical development. And in this new synthesis or reconstruction, *the western philosophical tradition* (source and mother of the Russian "religious philosophy" of the 19th and 20th centuries) *rather than the Hellenistic* [*sic*], must supply theology with its conceptual framework. An attempt is thus made to "transpose" theology into a new "key," and this transposition is considered as the specific task and vocation of Russian theology.[1]

Now I would contend that such a "transposition" is incumbent not only on Russian theologians but on *all* who seek to reflect upon, and from within, the matrix of Eastern Christianity—at least all those who espouse "the necessity of a theological synthesis of Eastern and Western traditions, without which there is no real catholicity."[2]

For its part, Schmemann's own oeuvre arguably exemplifies the most significant and successful modern effort at putting Orthodox thought on the relationship between *liturgy* and theology into a new "key."[3] Michael Plekon judges that with Schmemann, "there was an entirely different approach to liturgy as the *theologia prima*. Worship is not just the locus of symbolism and rubrics but the very source of theology. And it is through this enactment in liturgy, in the 'corporate action' of the Church, that theology thereafter becomes mission in the lives of Christians."[4] But for those who appreciate his legacy—"an unparalleled liturgical and ecclesial renewal that reached far beyond Orthodox borders"—there have in turn emerged further avenues for exploration.[5] Hence the present book: an attempt to chart the territory "beyond Schmemann," as it were, guided by Paul Ricoeur (1913–2005), one of the twentieth century's foremost philosophers. Although Schmemann does not appear to have ever engaged Ricoeur directly, I propose that the latter can enable Orthodox liturgical theology to productively "respond to a new situation created by centuries of philosophical development."[6]

What kind of pertinent issues animate this new situation? Inter alia, the attributes and functions of symbol, metaphor and narrative; the conflict engendered by interpretive pluralism; the dialectic between history and historiography; the manner in which personal and communal identity develops in time; and the dynamics operative in the act of translation. Ricoeur's thought addresses all of the above and more—in short, almost every aspect of how *meaning* is made, communicated and received. Inasmuch as liturgy unfolds the content of Orthodox faith, in keeping with the time-worn adage *lex orandi, lex credendi*, Ricoeur thus offers liturgical theology a plethora of resources.[7] As I shall demonstrate throughout this book, such is the case even if the philosopher reflected explicitly on liturgy only rarely and had but a modest personal connection to the Christian East.[8] Such reflections as there are remain deeply suggestive, warranting a more thorough investigation of his work in this respect. In an interview near the end of his life, for instance, conducted on the occasion of a visit to the ecumenical community of Taizé, he mused:

> We are overwhelmed by a flood of words, by polemics, by the assault of the virtual, which today create a kind of opaque zone. But goodness is deeper than the deepest evil. We have to liberate that certainty, give it a language. And the language given here in Taizé is not the

language of philosophy, not even of theology, but the language of the liturgy. And for me, the liturgy is not simply action; it is a form of thought. There is a hidden, discreet theology in the liturgy that can be summed up in the idea that "the law of prayer is the law of faith."[9]

One of Ricoeur's foremost interpreters confirms the value of applying his thought to the study of liturgy, noting as well the attention it pays to apophaticism—a further convergence with Orthodox theology.[10] John van den Hengel limns the features of a theology in the wake of Ricoeur, terming it at once hermeneutical, biblical, metaphorical, ontological, practical (narrative) and reflexive. The essential point in the final modifier is that the self that engages in theology is what Ricoeur has elsewhere called a "summoned self": one aware of being constituted by its response to the initiative of the Other, an initiative extended as *gift*. And here van den Hengel draws attention to the paradoxical inspiration behind the present work:

> Theology's task is [to] let the superabundance of the gift—the excess that is articulated in "God is love"—the hyperbole of the language and its forms, find its release in human action . . . [in] acts that reorient human action in response to the excess, disproportion or extravagance of the Naming of God, such as *proclamation, liturgy, praise*. For theology this has far-reaching repercussions. It would mean to give priority in our theological enterprise to the praxis of faith-life rather than to theoretical disclosure of meaning.[11]

What is the paradox here? That we will be pursuing what can no doubt be considered, at one level, a "theoretical discussion of meaning": Reflection *on* liturgy is, after all, incommensurate with the *theologia prima* mentioned above—i.e., the "theological work of the liturgical assembly" as found "in the structure of the rite, in its *lex orandi*." Books *about* liturgy, "the work done by an academic upon liturgical material," are in this sense always *theologia secunda*.[12] Nonetheless, my intention is less to provide new theories, so much as to promote *theoria*: In keeping with the etymology of the term, I hope to contribute to a new way of "seeing" what transpires in liturgical events, so as to enrich what van den Hengel calls the "the praxis of faith-life."

The power of liturgy to "reorient human action"—and the importance of sketching how this should be "seen"—is further illustrated in van den

Hengel's consideration of the implications of Ricoeur's monumental *Time and Narrative* for contemporary Christology: Worship proves itself to be the site par excellence for an appropriation of the "historical intentionality" of the Gospels. (As we will see, the question of historicity is one that readily arises in the interpretation of the Byzantine festal hymnography, with its dramatic magnification of, and exponential elaboration upon, the events in the life of Christ.) The Gospel genre configures the life of Christ by means of fictive devices, with a view to the "refiguration of the field of human action and temporality."[13] Such a refiguration does not obtain, in the first instance, in the sphere of a reader's privacy; rather, since the very inscription of the Gospel attests to "a worldview and life pattern of an ecclesial community," the reception of its message requires an analogous context. The performative arena of liturgy plausibly constitutes just such a context, since it is there that narrative time can interact with what Ricoeur calls chronological or cosmic time, compelling a return "from text to action," a passing from a narrative mediation of the temporal to a temporal mediation of the narrative: "In line with Ricoeur's concept of history, a liturgical appropriation that makes use of the symbols of nature, regeneration, sustenance, covenanting, space and time is more attentive to the cosmic pole of temporality. It transcends the narrative identity and appropriation and is a freer testing of the real."[14]

Ricoeur thus seems in many ways an ideal interlocutor, one who should be welcomed, so to speak, to the Eastern Christian hearth. In the first chapter, after introducing Schmemann's legacy—which I take to represent the *point de départ* in regard to contemporary Orthodox liturgical theology[15]—I consider the implications of the Ricoeurian opus for liturgical theology broadly conceived. In the subsequent chapters I lay the groundwork for applying a Ricoeurian hermeneutic to the study of a given service, the Byzantine Rite's "Great Blessing of Water" for Theophany (henceforth, *GBW*). This task is taken up in the final chapter. Because of its structure and content, the *GBW* (celebrated annually on the eve and/or day of the feast of Theophany/Epiphany[16]) is paradigmatic of the Byzantine liturgical tradition as a whole. While not formally regarded as a sacrament it is explicitly imitative of the two central sacraments of Baptism and the Eucharist. Although only one of a myriad of blessing rites, its significance in the church year as well as its role as the sacramental prerequisite for many other liturgical blessings (inasmuch they routinely employ holy water) give it both a theological as well as a practical preeminence among them.

In keeping with the thrust of the series to which this book belongs, my intent is to explore the significance of one contemporary theorist for the elaboration of Orthodox theology in our day. In this respect I consciously adhere to English Catholic theologian Nicholas Lash's prescription that "each [contemporary] theology must genuinely be a 'particular' theology, expressive of some particular context and circumstance, seeking to mediate between that context and some other particular 'place' or places of experience, meaning and value."[17] What follows, therefore, is proposed as a theological mediation between the context of the Eastern Orthodox tradition and the "place" represented by the manifold of Ricoeur's thought.[18]

It is perhaps telling that Ricoeur ended his career with a text that itself concludes by means of a meditation on the ceremonial exchange of gifts.[19] One wishes the philosopher had taken the opportunity to weave together the threads of his insights into ritual. Would he have eventually plotted the course of hermeneutics, so to speak, through the high seas of liturgical experience? The interview at Taizé quoted above intimates an affirmative answer. Ricoeur's observation that liturgy is a kind of language implies in turn that it invites a distinct mode of interpretation. Liturgy is irreducible to the biblical "form of thought" to which it is nonetheless related: a form he regards as an authentic, though "non-philosophical manner of thinking and being." I will argue below that this irreducibility does not merely derive from liturgy employing idioms other than the linguistic—to state the obvious. Rather it is because liturgical language incorporates a potent level of *speculative* discourse, raising in turn numerous interpretative issues. Anyone who has prayed at length in the Byzantine tradition realizes that it is saturated with such discourse that, though nascent in the Bible itself reaches maturation in the patristic attempt to reconcile the biblical witness with philosophical reason. We shall see that the *GBW* provides an exemplary case study in this respect, not least in its appropriation of the apophatic terminology of Pseudo-Dionysius the Areopagite within a narrative context.[20]

The present analysis does not pretend to an exhaustive appropriation of Ricoeur but rather an evaluation and application of select texts, chosen for their pertinence to the topic at hand. I have favored texts that seem to me to both address the concerns of Schmemann and yet point beyond them, by probing the terminology and themes hitherto conventional in liturgical theology. Hopefully, the reader already familiar with Ricoeur will discover in the course of our inquiry new detours for which the philosopher may act as guide; and the reader interested in liturgical theology, new criteria by which to reflect on the meaning of the Orthodox *lex orandi* and its corollary *lex credendi*.

PART

I

"How Will the Lamp Enlighten the Light?"

1

"AFTER SCHMEMANN": INTRODUCING RICOEUR INTO THE CONVERSATION

"Liturgical Theology"

We may begin with the commonplace premise that in Orthodox tradition the primary meaning of theology has been taken to be *prayer* itself—the knowledge and experience of God acquired through participating in a relationship with him. Only secondarily does it imply (as the etymology indicates) "words *about* God."[1] Hence the notion of *liturgical* theology, the *theologia prima* discussed above, whose elaboration was, of course, the goal of Fr. Alexander Schmemann's life work.[2] It is no exaggeration to say that for him the liturgy itself is *the* fundamental object of interpretation. Regarding Schmemann's approach to the Eucharist, for example, Peter Galadza states, "It is a mystagogy of the actual celebration. For him—as for the Fathers—the meaning of the sacrament is not 'behind,' 'above,' or 'beyond' the rite, but *in* it and *through* it."[3] Indeed, it is the gestalt of the liturgy that arguably enables the very perception of Scripture as the Word of God; through the manner in which it is treated in liturgical celebration, the faithful come to experience the Bible as *Holy* Scripture. One must therefore give a certain methodological, if not theological, primacy to the interpretation of the liturgical event—especially for Schmemann as communicated via its *texts*. In other words, the liturgy is at once the experiential site of all authentic theology, as well as an inscribed phenomenon itself in need of interpretation.

Consequently we see, early on in his career, Schmemann identifying the "problem of the Ordo" and the corollary imperative to discern the logic

according to which the liturgical tradition is to be understood and performed. More eventful than the historical development of the liturgy itself, he explains, are the vicissitudes of its theological interpretation down
through the centuries. In the commentaries of the Fathers we hear a harmonization of three distinct potentially dissonant hermeneutics: the early
ecclesiological-eschatological, the secondary historicist-mysteriological and
the tertiary ascetical-pietistic.[4] Salient in Schmemann's rehearsal of
this commentary tradition is his deployment of a Hegelian model of thesis, antithesis, and synthesis.[5] For he asserts that ultimately "within the
Byzantine synthesis the original 'emphases' and categories of both contrasting liturgical traditions [i.e., the monastic-ascetic and the secular-
mysteriological] were interwoven and their contradictions removed." And
again, "From the Areopagite down to Cabasilas we see the elaboration of
one and the same theology—a theology simultaneously monastic (ascetical) and mysteriological in its whole spirit and movement."[6] His *Introduction* thus concludes on an optimistic tone.

Schmemann's ostensible appreciation of this "Byzantine synthesis" is intriguingly qualified, however, fifteen years later—only two years before
his death—in his article "Symbols and Symbolism in the Byzantine Liturgy:
Liturgical Symbols and Their Theological Interpretation." There he decries a
"radical discrepancy between the *lex orandi* as expressed and embodied in
the liturgy itself and its symbolic interpretation, which nevertheless is
commonly held to be an organic part of the Orthodox tradition."[7] He
proceeds to critique the manner in which a correct understanding of the
Eucharist has been obfuscated by the figurative readings of patristic commentators, alleging that these present the discrete actions as well as the
totality of the rite as "symbolic representations, i.e., acts 'representing,' 'signifying,' and thus 'symbolizing,' something else, be it an event of the past,
an idea, or a theological affirmation." Why is this problematic? Due to
"the absence of virtually any reference to such symbols and symbolic
meanings in the liturgy itself, and this means primarily in *the prayers* in
which the different rites and liturgical actions *are given their verbal expression and thus their meaning*."[8] If Schmemann concedes that in certain instances the *lex orandi* does indeed appear to countenance what he terms
an "illustrative symbolism," he nevertheless contends that this is so only
in regard to "secondary rites and representations" that should be set aside
on account of their late reception into the liturgy and their thematic in-

congruence with it. His panacea is a recovery of "eschatological symbolism": none other than the neglected "genuine liturgical theology" of the
early Christian community.[9]

An analysis of Schmemann's views in this respect, therefore, encounters
a perplexing, even vexing ambivalence. Does he esteem Holy Tradition
after the fashion of Vladimir Lossky, "the life of the Holy Spirit in the
Church, communicating to each member of the Body of Christ the faculty of hearing, of receiving, of knowing the Truth in the Light which
belongs to it, and not according to the natural light of human reason"?[10]
Or is he culpable rather of a kind of archaeologism, an a priori privileging
of the earliest stratum of Christian experience as the most authentic site of
"the faith of the Church as expressed, communicated and preserved by the
liturgy"?[11] Stig Frøyshov, in analyzing the discrepancies in Schmemann's
thought with respect to both the issue of liturgical symbolism and the
related question of how the liturgy expresses eschatology, argues that
Schmemann unwittingly eschewed the issue of whether he too, not unlike
his predecessors, did not also *bring* meaning to the liturgy (while naively
believing that he was simply *discovering* it there):

> The method of interpretation that Schmemann aspired to practice,
> but that he did not, I think, follow, shows itself to be very close to
> that of the theologians whom he critiques for having, from the
> eleventh century onwards . . . destroyed the authentic symbolism:
> [this method involves] a rejection of every "imposed" meaning,
> especially allegorical ones, those characteristic of patristic and me-
> dieval exegesis. Schmemann wishes to find the meaning and the
> symbolism of the liturgy itself, its inherent vision. . . . [There is a]
> lack of awareness of the interpreting subject and of the act of
> interpretation.[12]

In the quest for this "inherent vision," Schmemann would appear to
engage in a kind of circular reasoning: The liturgical commentary tradition is not to be trusted because it does not respect the meaning of the liturgical text; where it does so, the liturgical text is in turn not to be trusted
inasmuch as it reifies meanings already determined to be illicit. Moreover,
one cannot avoid the implicit, perennial question of *how* exactly primary
and secondary "rites and representations" are to be distinguished from
one another.[13]

Liturgy and the "Anxiety of Influence"

I think we see here an instance of what Ricoeur calls the invidious "conflict of interpretations"—a kind of conflict his thought seeks rather to negotiate than to quell.[14] The argument of "Symbols" is that the Divine Liturgy has consistently been misunderstood throughout Orthodox history, not only by the common participants in the rite but also, more egregiously, by those charged with explicating it. Nevertheless, Schmemann considers the rite per se to be transparent, affording an immediacy of access to its "essential symbolism" across time and space.

To probe this dilemma, we may adduce a seminal article of Orthodox theologian Anton Ugolnik, to which we will return at length below. For the moment I would like to simply note the author's optimistic estimation that Orthodox have, by maintaining a liturgical frame of reference, been able to avoid the hermeneutical crisis engendered in the West by its recalcitrant individualism and concomitant "anxiety of influence":

> Its own history has given the West a dynamic and particularly "anxious" relationship to its own past. . . . [I]n contemplating the classic text it seeks to restore or revive, or even in seeking to recover the oral, communal emphasis on gospel proclamation that had been lost, western inquiry loops back upon a record of its own identity, confronts a "text" and proceeds forward through the encounter. In this "figurative knot" of critical encounter, we find a crisis of identity hidden in the quest for meaning.[15]

By contrast, the author argues that Orthodoxy is characterized by a profound sense of *continuity* with the past. Not perceiving its own history as punctuated by the caesurae axiomatic to Western historiography, such as the Renaissance or Reformation, it has not felt, in turn, the corollary burden of retrieving something lost. The past has instead been seen as perennially flowering in the on-going life of the Church. For Ugolnik, the process by which this occurs is not passive: Each generation must assume afresh responsibility for the transmission of tradition. And yet, this handing on of what has been handed down does not display the kind of atavistic struggle to which the West seems ever prone.

But *pace* Ugolnik, I would suggest that Schmemann appears to be compelled by just such a stereotypically Western "anxiety" in his own quest to identify a singular interpretation of the Ordo, convinced as he was that the liturgy lauded by Ugolnik (and countless others) as the sine qua non of authentic Orthodox theologizing had itself been subject to distortion. There has been, according to Schmemann, a "discontinuity in the comprehension, i.e., in the understanding and, deeper, in the experience of the liturgy by the ecclesial society at large."[16] It appears in turn that the hermeneutical foundation constituted by the liturgy must actually be regarded as a *task*, and not simply a *given*—a frame of reference that does not simply abide but is continually under construction, as it were, vulnerable to weathering by the elements of history.[17]

By way of example, we can consider Schmemann's treatment of the Prayer of the (Little) Entrance, which he regards as a "primary" layer of the *lex orandi*. Curiously, he avoids the question of whether the same historical-critical method invoked to identify what he terms the ancient, "eschatological" import of the Entrance (in contradistinction to the interpretations subsequently given it by patristic commentaries) might not result in a reductio ad absurdum. That is, why not conclude that the prayer in question is itself *also* secondary: an ancillary, symbolic interpretation of what was originally merely the *practical*—untheologized, so to speak— action of entering the church building to commence the service?[18] Furthermore, Schmemann evades the fact that the rite's allegedly authentic meaning (namely, that "the liturgy, we may say, happens to us. The liturgical entrance is our, or rather, the Church's entrance to heaven"[19]) is no longer borne out by the *lex orandi*, since today it is only the *clergy* who (re) enter the altar, and not the whole congregation that together enters the church building to begin its common worship, as in former times.[20]

Nevertheless, Schmemann is adamant that the classical liturgical commentators—many of whom, of course, are canonized saints in the Orthodox Church—have, in interpreting what *is* actually happening, illegitimately "imposed" *their* own meaning upon the Divine Liturgy (subsequently impressed upon the minds of the faithful) such that "even to question it is, in the eyes of an overwhelming majority, tantamount to subversion and heresy."[21] Schmemann's indictment of the commentators, however, invites the obvious question of why such a pantheon proved unable to grasp the liturgy's "own" meaning, while he himself can so readily achieve this herculean task; why, that is, his perspective is not to be reckoned as but one more idiosyncratic interpretation foisted upon the believing community.

Is Schmemann in this instance perhaps mimicking Ugolnik's stereotypical "*Western* inquiry," which "loops back upon a record of its own identity, confronts a 'text' and proceeds forward through the encounter," in whose "'figurative knot' of critical encounter, we find a crisis of identity hidden in the quest for meaning"? Indeed, Schmemann appears here to succumb to the same vice he elsewhere abjures: "It is indeed the 'original sin' of the entire Western theological development that it made 'texts' the only *loci theologici,* the extrinsic 'authorities' of theology, disconnecting theology from its living source: liturgy and spirituality."[22] For he himself insists upon the liturgical text as the privileged bearer of meaning vis-à-vis the received tradition of popular, allegorical, or mystagogical interpretation—less concerned as this is with *texts*, than with, inter alia, choreography, gestures, and appointments.

I wonder if it is even apropos to suggest a parallel here between Schmemann's view of Tradition and the classically Protestant concern to establish the perspicuousness of Scripture, to unburden it from any necessary connection to the patristic and subsequent medieval accrual of "senses,"—i.e., the *Quadriga* comprising the literal, allegorical, tropological, and anagogical modes of exegesis.[23] Galadza, while quite appreciative of the substance of Schmemann's critique of the commentary tradition, chides him for "a kind of philosophical idealism":

> For some reason, Schmemann is unwilling to accept the obvious fact that it is not only thought that engenders action, but action that engenders thought as well. This, coupled with a kind of Platonic historiography, leads him to make the following (outrageous) statement: "In the tradition of the Church nothing has changed. What has changed is the perception of the eucharist, the perception of its very essence."[24]

I would build on Galadza's analysis by adding that if it is manifestly false that nothing has changed in the history of the liturgy, this does not in turn entail that we must consider liturgical change as resulting only in net *losses*—although Schmemann often implies as much.[25] Surely the Tradition might be expected rather to show some hermeneutical returns for centuries of devotional investment?

Ricoeur and the "Surplus of Meaning"

Here we can begin to see how Ricoeur can serve to lead us "beyond Schmemann." To anticipate the fuller discussion that will follow below, we can recall the oft-quoted conclusion of *The Symbolism of Evil,* where Ricoeur observes: "'The symbol gives rise to thought.' That sentence . . . says two things: the symbol gives; but what it gives is occasion for thought, something to think about. . . . After the gift, positing. The aphorism suggests at the same time that everything has already been said enigmatically and yet that it is always necessary to begin everything and to begin it again in the dimension of thinking."[26] He elaborates elsewhere that this does not mean that symbols mean *anything*; there are more and less plausible interpretations, given the "bound" character of a symbol—i.e., the constraints exercised upon its disclosive power by the specificity of its form: Water, for example, will suggest many things—washing, cleansing, birth, death, and so forth—but not *everything*. What is crucial is the idea that symbols will tend to mean *all that they can*, to "throw together," as the etymology of the word indicates, as much as possible: They proffer, in Ricoeur's evocative phrase, a "surplus of meaning" (*surcroît du sens*).[27]

In this vein, the classical liturgical commentators whom, as indicated above, Schmemann habitually denigrates, may instead be esteemed for exemplifying the power of symbols to *connote*, and not simply *denote*. To stay with the example of the Little Entrance: Even as the practical act of passing through the church doors originally evoked an analogous crossing the threshold into the celestial liturgy, the later, posticonoclastic reduction of the Little Entrance into a "symbolic" clerical circumambulation quite naturally gave rise to further, discrete interpretations. Ricoeur invites us to consider that it is arguably not a matter of a right or wrong "reading" of this, or any other, rite, but rather of a recognition that it pertains to the very essence of symbolism, liturgical or otherwise, to engender *nolens-volens* a multiplicity of meanings. This is so because symbols, particularly as represented verbally through the work of metaphor, do not merely adorn a meaning equally accessible in a nonsymbolic, or nonmetaphorical manner. Instead, they give rise *ex opere operato*, so to speak, to *original* thinking, to a creative redescription of the world—charged, as we will see below, with "ontological vehemence."[28]

Thus, contrary to Schmemann's critique of the commentary tradition for its alleged misinterpretation of the Little Entrance, said tradition at least engages what actually *happens*: namely, a reflection on what Galadza calls that "semiotic of descent and revelation" with which the Byzantine Eucharist, as it stands today (and for centuries hitherto), begins. In other words, symbols are not exhausted by a one-to-one correspondence of signified and signifier; rather, they have the capacity to attract to themselves a battery of significations, complementary or even contradictory. Meaning does not obtain purely in the symbol itself, but rather in what Gadamer famously called the "fusion of horizons" between that which is encountered and the agent encountering it.[29] That the commentators have found *any* meaning in a rite that less imaginative souls might readily deem perfunctory, not to say inane, is perhaps to be admired; do we not see at work that theological imagination whose very élan caused the erstwhile physical entry of the clergy and faithful to itself be interpreted as supra-functional?

Moreover, the symbolism of descending, processing, and entering is surely a species of what Ricoeur calls "root metaphors," which "have the power to bring together the partial metaphors borrowed from the diverse fields of our experience and thereby to assure them a kind of equilibrium. On the other hand, they have the ability to engender a conceptual diversity, I mean, an unlimited number of potential interpretations at a conceptual level."[30] After all, the "semiotic of descent and revelation" referred to by Galadza surely serves as an index to that Christianized Neoplatonic schema of *exitus* and *reditus* that is already presented in liturgical terms in the sixth-century Pseudo-Dionysian corpus, and that will become elemental to the Byzantine liturgy's *Erscheinungsbild*—i.e., the "unique impact created by the sensible splendors of the Byzantine Rite," involving an "intimate symbiosis of liturgical symbolism (ritual celebration), liturgical setting (architecture/iconography), and liturgical interpretation (mystagogy)."[31] The patristic interpretation of the Little Entrance is therefore but one example of how the encounter with a classic text, artifact, ritual, etc., generates a dialogical interaction between what David Tracy, following Ricoeur, calls the "power of disclosure and concealment" of such an object, and the interpreting subject's "experience of recognition."[32]

Such an "experience of recognition" is a phenomenon that itself attracted the attention of Ricoeur, and one that, on account of its pertinence for liturgical theology, will also be developed throughout the course of this book. It is in terms of fundamental capacities for agency that the philosopher locates the fruition of (self-)recognition.[33] Such capacities, simultaneously reflexive and oriented toward alterity, include speaking, acting, and narrating—i.e., attributing to oneself one's actions and thereby assuming responsibility for them. He reserves his choice reflections, however, for the capacities of remembering and promising, which "have the virtue of revealing the temporal dimension of each of the powers considered." Memory allows for an extension of oneself into the past, promising, into the

future, and both faculties carry the connotation of alterity: memories solicit the corroboration of another, while promising implies "standing before another person."[34] We can link Ricoeur's discussion of capacities to the
liturgical "surplus of meaning" and "ontological vehemence" mentioned
above, by proposing that the illustrative symbolism of the liturgical commentators, characteristic of the historicizing inclinations of the Antiochene
school of exegesis, has true *existential* significance: Does it not enjoin upon
the worshipper the arduous labor of *remembering,* a task frequently under-
estimated and neglected?[35] Remaining with our example of the Little Entrance, we might venture that to "remember" the Incarnation, to effectively
call it to mind *at any level,* is no small endeavor, given the unique status of
the event at issue. If we factor in the role Ricoeur attributes to symbols of
providing a representative "figure" to work with, when considering historical phenomena that elude the categories of our everyday experience, we
might deem it salutary that the commentary tradition has sought to charge
nearly every liturgical item, utterance and gesture with "double-duty," so
to speak, by making them serve as ciphers.

Conversely, might it not be possible to appreciate the Alexandrian-style
mystagogical symbolism as nourishing our capacity for *promising,* inasmuch as the genre focuses on *theōsis,* that existential transformation of the
human person through prayer and ascesis that is, after all, a way of grasping the teleology of the liturgy as whole? To ponder, in the moment of the
Little Entrance, "the advent of the '*logos* of spiritual contemplation (*gnōstikē
theōria*)' descending from heaven like a High Priest to discipline 'carnal'
understanding and initiate the worthy in the holy mysteries,"[36] as Maximus the Confessor would have it—is this not somewhat comparable to
Ricoeur's standing-before-another, in this case the divine Other, in whom
one is summoned to profess belief and before whom, to promise fidelity?[37]

Indeed, in the liturgical context, we presumably invoke an additional
capacity—or better, a metacapacity—transformative of those capacities
itemized by Ricoeur in a manner analogous to how root metaphors, in his
estimation, "assemble" other metaphors and "scatter" them again at a higher
level. For the "capable human being" is showcased in the liturgy as one
who is *capax Dei,* "capable of God." Coming full circle, such a description
would surely content Schmemann, for whom the primary definition for
humankind ought not to be *homo sapiens* or *homo faber* (their merit notwithstanding), but rather *homo adorans.* This is because he views the primordial vocation of the human person as doxological, encompassing the

blessing of God on behalf of the world, and the world, on behalf of God.[38] Such a vocation is iconified in the liturgy wherein one is invited to become capable of God: to speak to him, to act in his presence, to remember his mighty deeds, and to promise to live in the light of them.

The liturgical actant may be thus held up as a paragon of what Ricoeur calls the "summoned subject,"—i.e., a self "constituted and defined by its position as respondent to propositions of meaning issuing from the symbolic network [of the tradition]."[39] This subject imputes to him- or herself a personal responsibility for what is attested in common—a responsibility that is exercised at once to others and to the Other inasmuch as to take onto one's lips and into one's hands the words and gestures of the rite is to entertain the respective ethical demands that may ensue. As proposed, liturgical celebration likewise induces an augmentation of both memory and promising: What emerges is the moral imperative to retrieve for one's own the truthful memories of the community ensconced in the rite, as also to genuinely appropriate the promises ritually uttered.[40]

All of these trajectories will be developed in the subsequent chapters. Here my only aim has been to establish that Schmemann's legacy, for all its richness and significance, invites as many questions as it answers—and that Ricoeur may be an ideal dialogue partner in the ongoing conversation. Let us proceed now to explore this possibility in greater detail.

Does Orthodox Theology Need a "Handmaiden"?

Especially in Orthodox circles, the question may well arise: Why privilege the work of *any* particular philosopher in the project of interpreting the Church's worship?[41] As I will discuss momentarily, it is well known that Orthodox thinkers have not infrequently been chary of the explicit harnessing of philosophy lest it cause theology, to paraphrase 2 Cor. 6:14, to become "unequally yoked." At first glance, ecclesiastical ritual might not seem to warrant even the minimal service of philosophy admittedly required by, say, theological ethics or systematic theology. As a prolegomenon then to our project of integrating Ricoeur into an Eastern Christian liturgical theology, we should first touch on the perennial question of the rapport between theology per se and philosophy.

Max Charlesworth helpfully schematizes the history of this relationship in five phases, only one of which (the medieval Thomistic tradition) thematizes it in terms of the complementarity evoked by the familiar analogy of the "handmaiden to theology" (*ancilla theologiae*). In classical antiquity, he explains, philosophy was rather considered as comprehending religion itself; in the wake of the Enlightenment, it has been seen consecutively as "making room for faith," serving the "analysis of religious discourse" and fostering the "postmodernist critique of the religious domain."[42] But Ricoeur's oeuvre is in this respect challenging to locate, as its panorama features all three of the post-Enlightenment enterprises mentioned. Indeed, as I hope to demonstrate, it is arguable that his approach ultimately (if unsystematically) fulfills the threefold theological task assigned philosophy by Aquinas. Charlesworth summarizes these as follows: "First, philosophy helps faith to express and systematise its truths; second, philosophy justifies the preambles or presuppositions of faith; and, third, philosophy defends the truths of faith from skeptical objections."[43]

Dominican Aidan Nichols can thus express due appreciation for Ricoeur's thought, regarding it as well-suited to the contemporary service of theology:

> Concern with the manner in which Christian truth descends through time has [recently] been enlivened by the stimulus of hermeneutical philosophy—the philosophical investigation of the process of interpretation as represented by, most notably, Paul Ricoeur [inter alia]. . . . [Such thought is] clearly pertinent to Christian theology, since that theology can be thought of as the continuous interpretative reappropriation of a religious tradition, a tradition which sees itself as the carrier of a divine revelation, for which our primary metaphor is the Word, precisely, of God.[44]

Nichols also praises the contribution of Emmanuel Lévinas as a "highly original philosophy [being] worked out in our lifetime," whose significance for theology has yet to be fully determined. Ricoeur, however, is surely peer to the latter: As a Christian who was always careful to distinguish his primary philosophical work from his avocation to biblical exegesis (and his occasional forays into theology), it is similarly true of him that "revelation directs the philosopher's interests but not the methods or ideas."[45] Indeed, there is a growing consensus that Ricoeur's interests, as well as his methods and ideas, are in fact quite germane to theological inquiry, not least because of Ricoeur's constant endeavor to occupy a "mediating position"— Nichols's term for the role played by the great philosophical systems upon which Christian theologians have drawn over the centuries.

While the Ricoeurian corpus does not form a unified system or contain a definitive magnum opus, consisting rather of a diffuse collection of texts composed over almost three-quarters of a century, its variegated strands have been woven into a tapestry by several interpreters.[46] What it displays, alternatively termed "hermeneutical phenomenology" and "philosophical anthropology," does not perhaps aspire to the status of a *philosophia perennis*, in the vein of Aquinas; Ricoeur, indeed, would likely have regarded such an achievement as chimerical. Nonetheless, oriented as it is to comprehending both epistemology and ontology, the realms of both thought and life, the work of Ricoeur does hold out the promise of contributing substantially to the elaboration of a contemporary perennial philosophy, a "fundamental way of reading the structure of the universe . . . [into which] we can then go on to insert extra elements drawn from alternative philosophies."[47]

Among theologians at large, the one who has probably done the most to mine the riches of Ricoeur's thought is Dan Stiver, a Baptist scholar specializing in systematic theology and the role of philosophy within it. Both his *Theology after Ricoeur* and his more recent *Ricoeur and Theology* are invaluable. Stiver's appraisal is that Ricoeur furnishes "as comprehensive a philosophy as any in the twentieth century."[48] This philosophy, moreover, is particularly respectful of the irreducibility of the discourses of faith, seeking as it does to illumine by its own lights the phenomena elucidated otherwise by theology. Hence, "Ricoeur's notion of philosophy as at best being able to 'approximate' affirmations of theology is a promising model. It allows for a relationship that is one of neither absolute domination nor absolute distinction."[49] It forms, therefore, what could perhaps be regarded as a sixth category in the taxonomy of Charlesworth adduced above: In it we find a dialectical relationship between the philosophical and the religious domains in which each contributes to exploiting the full potential of the other.

As an aside, I would like to conclude this part by probing the similarities of Ricoeur to a figure from a very different time and place; if the comparison has any worth, it may serve to further clarify why I see such potential in a Ricoeurian "handmaiden." St. Maximus the Confessor, Father of the Church revered in both the Latin and Greek traditions, is a thinker possessing several character traits and methodological protocols in common with our philosopher. According to the portrait of the Confessor drawn by Hans Urs von Balthasar, Maximus is notable for having theologized in cosmopolitan style, mediating between various traditions and contexts.[50] Several readers of Ricoeur have observed that he too is a profoundly synthetic scholar, spanning the speculative divide between the continental and analytic philosophical traditions (as also, in his professional appointments, oscillating between their respective precincts: continental Europe and America).

Moreover, in the search for a fuller understanding of the Gospel, Maximus engaged in criticism through appropriation, rather than vilification, incorporating the influences of his interlocutors by transposing and recombining them in a higher key. For von Balthasar, the Confessor's genius is displayed in his unusual "freedom of mind": "What makes Maximus a genius is that he was able to reach inside, and open up to each other, five or six intellectual worlds that seemingly had lost all contact; he was able to bring out of each a light that illumined all the rest, leading to new connections that gave rise, in turn, to unexpected similarities and relationships."[51] Such a generosity of thought is also readily observable in Ricoeur. Surveying his work, one is immediately struck by the manner in which he carefully reads and reflects upon the work of others before forging his own argument, which emerges as an alloy that exhibits the best properties of different elements. There is a sense, therefore, in which one may read Ricoeur as a historian of philosophy and not simply as a philosopher in his own right, such is the extent to which he attends to his predecessors in treating a given topic. As Maximus critiqued Origen or Pseudo-Dionysius out of his very esteem for their accomplishments, so also Ricoeur returns time and again to his mentor Husserl and "favorite philosopher" Kant, if only to demonstrate the need to transcend them.

One may also note that Ricoeur like Maximus intended to do full justice to both revelation and critical reflection, to provide for what we might call in Chalcedonian terms an "unconfused union" of divine mystery and human reason. This is evident in his methodological determination to distinguish, while never separating, the tasks of philosophy and biblical exegesis; he was unwilling to allow either to subsume the other, insisting nonetheless on a certain *communicatio idiomatum* between them. Neither should their "natures" be severed, as it were, in a Nestorian schizophrenia, nor again rendered indistinct in a Monophysite fusion. It was surely the "ontological vehemence" Ricoeur discerned in language, its capacity to effectively redescribe reality, which inspired Maximus to argue and ultimately suffer for his convictions concerning the nomenclature (natures, wills, operations, etc.) acceptable for speaking of Christ. Both men would likely have concurred with von Balthasar that "the power of thought is the force that transforms the world."[52]

A common commitment to the important of language accounts for why in Ricoeur, as in Maximus, one encounters an "exaggerated precision" that could be mistaken for obscurity. Such conceptual rigor, however, does not detract from shared "concern for the 'realization' of theoretical knowledge," for the transformation of the world, expressed in terms of a concern to convert the resources of contemplation into the action of love.[53] Unlike Origen, who according to von Balthasar disparaged nature, Maximus was "world-affirming," sanguine regarding the potential of created reality as redeemed in Christ. *Mutatis mutandis*, we may perhaps see in the refusal of nihilism on the part of Ricoeur—his determination to not let the "masters of suspicion" have the final word—a parallel optimism. Indeed, Leonard Lawlor posits such optimism to be a distinguishing characteristic of Ricoeur:

> While hermeneutics opposes the most confining type of metaphysical mastery, it nevertheless attempts to recover Western metaphysics' original project. . . . The difference, therefore, between Ricoeur and Derrida, between hermeneutics and deconstruction, between distanciation and *différance*, is a difference between imagination and chance, between presence and absence, between zigzag circulation and spiraling circularity, and finally between revived philosophy and perverted philosophy.[54]

Finally, when exercising his theological "will" and "operations," Ricoeur like Maximus was principally an exegete. Here we may note a marked difference, however, inasmuch as one cannot say of Ricoeur (as von Balthasar does of Maximus) that "[his] whole philosophical undertaking" is ordered to a "synthesis, which is purely biblical."[55] Of Ricoeur one would rather say the opposite, that even in his work in biblical exegesis, he remained first and foremost a philosopher, committed to holding metaphysical assumptions in abeyance and to interrogating the biblical text with the same rigor as any other. To sustain the Christological metaphor: If there is an "asymmetrical union" in Ricoeur, it falls rather on the side of philosophy than on theology.[56]

I have indulged in this perhaps peculiar comparison only to further posit the relevance of Ricoeur to the task at hand. As the treatment of the Pseudo-

Dionysian corpus in Maximus's *Mystagogy* illustrates, the symbiosis between philosophy and liturgical theology is long-standing. Hermeneutics may arguably be said to have the ascendancy in current philosophy that Neoplatonism did in the time of the Areopagite and Maximus, and hence warrant a similar appropriation.

Eastern Theology, Western Philosophy

Although several Western scholars have endeavored to map the relevance of Ricoeur for theology in general, and liturgy in particular, Eastern Christians have yet to really join the discussion. As the latter become ever more rooted in a Western context, however, it would seem imperative that they adapt to its intellectual ecology, if indeed the transplantation of their traditions is to succeed. This process impels a coming to terms with the full spectrum of postmodern thought. Rowan Williams, for instance, applauds the efforts of certain Orthodox to engage in dialogue with twentieth-century philosophy, especially contemporary Greek theologians Christos Yannaras and Metropolitan John Zizioulas:[57]

> On the philosophical front, Zizioulas's recent work suggests the possibility of useful interaction between this kind of ecclesiology [i.e., one involving "new possibilities for interchange"] and various Western attempts at "postmodern" or "postliberal" schemes, in its critique of a metaphysic of unrelated substances and an epistemology based on the myth of a detached or neutral subjectivity. Orthodox theologians have shown willingness to engage with Heidegger, but it is perhaps time for a comparable engagement with Gadamer on the one hand and Wittgenstein on the other.[58]

While Williams does not explicitly mention Ricoeur, the latter certainly fits in the cohort of thinkers commended. Yannaras and Zizioulas follow in the wake of several generations of Russian theologians committed to the enterprise of religious philosophy. Williams singles out Ivan Vasilievich Kireevsky (1806–56) and his canvassing of Pascal and Schleiermacher as well as Eastern monastic writers, "for a perspective neither intellectualist nor voluntarist, for a doctrine of the formation of historical persons in action and relation, an integral view of the human." One almost hears a description of Ricoeur in the former Archbishop of Canterbury's observation that Kireevsky, whose reasoning "is concrete and committed, not ahistorical," presents a figure "something like Kierkegaard as well as something like Heidegger."[59]

The upshot of Williams's survey is that the mavericks like Yannaras and Zizioulas point to the kind of work that can and remains to be done. And yet he concludes with a caveat: "For this sort of development to go forward, Orthodox theology at large has to overcome a certain suspicion of (at worst, contempt for) the world of Western philosophy, a suspicion that is part of the inheritance of the debates in the Russian emigration earlier in this century."[60] That such a suspicion continues to cloud the dialogue between theology and philosophy within Orthodox precincts is vividly illustrated in the lively debate generated by the work of David Bentley Hart. John McGuckin, in a generally appreciative review of the former's magisterial *The Beauty of the Infinite*,[61] advances the startlingly brusque, captious accusation that "though the book is written by an Orthodox theologian, it is not Orthodox theology; rather one of the best examples to date of Euro-American neo-orthodoxy *redivivus*."[62] To this cavil, Hart responds with customary pertness:

> I do, I confess, take exception to the claim that the book "is not Orthodox theology." Of course it is. Admittedly it does not much resemble the sort of "neo-Palamite," "neo-patristic" books which have dominated Eastern theology since the middle of the last century, when the great *ressourcements* movement that has done so much to define modern Orthodoxy was inaugurated. But Orthodox theology has taken many forms over the centuries—mystical, scholastic, mystagogical, idealist, neo-patristic, even "Sophiological"—all of which have been perfectly legitimate expressions of the Eastern Church's mind. And frankly, I think that the theological idiom to which Orthodox theology has been confined for the last fifty years or so has largely exhausted itself and has become tediously repetitive. It has also, to a very great extent, done much to distort the Orthodox understanding of the traditions of both East and West.[63]

In the spirit of Hart's *apologia* the present work seeks to be a genuine exercise of Orthodox theology, if perhaps in a novel idiom.[64]

"An Orthodox Hermeneutic in the West"

One who like Hart has taken up Williams's summons for an irenic engagement with Western philosophy (and whose work discloses an awareness of

Ricoeur) is Orthodox theologian Anton Ugolnik, introduced above. Here the question of hermeneutics serves as a foil for methodological reflection upon the inculturation of Orthodox theology:

> Largely because our historical development has caused us to perceive time somewhat differently, Eastern Christians have not dealt with the problem on the same terms. Hermeneutics in general . . . has not engaged the Eastern Orthodox mind. The hermeneutical issue, perhaps more than any other, brings the question of differences in methodology into sharp focus. Contemporary Orthodox tend to assert or imply that we differ in methodology from the West, even from our Roman Catholic counterparts. As many of us become, geographically speaking, westerners ourselves, we will be challenged to view this hermeneutical question from an Orthodox perspective.[65]

The hermeneutical enterprise for Ugolnik is thus fundamentally bound up with the questions of identity and the nature of our being in time: With this Ricoeur would surely agree. And the locus of hermeneutics? Here we apprehend more precisely the crux of the supposed difference between East and West.

The Orthodox tradition, according to Ugolnik, coheres within a liturgical *Sitz im Leben.* That is to say, it is the worshipping assembly that provides the normative context for an encounter with Scripture, which he deems the principal object of hermeneutical inquiry.[66] In the liturgy the "icon" of the bejewelled Gospel book manifests the Word of God as it is carried in procession, offered homage in the form of kisses, candles and incense, and welcomed by the prostrations and sung acclamations of the faithful:

> Thus, our engagement with the gospel is *dialogic,* realized in the context of *pravoslavie,* the "right praise" which is the liturgical heart of our communally realized faith. . . . Our Orthodox hermeneutic is thus not a private quest constituted in critical response, but a communal search for meaning, expressed anthropologically in socially organized prayer. The text loses all autonomy. The self-sufficient "reader" is no more. Our vision of the gospel centers it literally and figuratively amidst the people to whom the Word is addressed and among whom, in their common assent, the Word is reconstituted.[67]

The reference to *pravoslavie,* the conventional Slavonic term for "orthodoxy," should be clarified. Jaroslav Pelikan explains that the traditional

Greek term lying behind *pravoslavie* was itself ambivalent, its polysemy being only intensified in the calque created by St. Cyril and St. Methodios in the ninth century:

> The noun *doxa* means "opinion," and the noun *orthotēs* means "correctness." Therefore Aristotle . . . without actually using the relatively rare term *orthodoxia*, can propound the definition: "Correctness of opinion is truth [*doxēs orthotēs alētheia*]." But when the opinion of others about someone is favorable, *doxa* already in classical Greek has the meaning of "good reputation" or "honor," and therefore of "glory." . . . In Church Slavonic, and then in the other Slavic languages, *doxa* . . . is translated with *slava*, and *Orthodoxia* becomes *Pravoslavie*. It means simultaneously the right way of believing or teaching and the right way of rendering glory to God, for ultimately the two are seen as identical.[68]

"Ultimately the two are seen as identical": It is because of this very perception that Ugolnik can freight the liturgical experience with such theological import.

The purported equivalence between doctrine and worship is illustrated most dramatically—to the point of having become a topos in Orthodox theology—in that remarkable episode drawn from the founding narrative of Slavic Christianity: During a tenth-century visit to the Church of Holy Wisdom in Constantinople, the emissaries of Prince Vladimir of Kiev experience what can only be termed an "aesthetic conversion." The object of their hitherto unfulfilled quest was evidently to determine which of the great religions espoused by the rival powers of the day was true, in order that Vladimir and his people might in turn become adherents. Disappointed successively by their previous experience with Judaism, Islam and Latin Catholicism, the emissaries are overwhelmed by the beauty of the worship they witness in Hagia Sophia, this liturgical epiphany serving in turn as the catalyst for their embrace of Orthodoxy.[69] Ugolnik is thus rehearsing a venerable pattern in his defense of a liturgical hermeneutic—if not yet of a hermeneutics of the liturgy—resulting from a putative unity between the content of faith and the form of its expression. As we have seen above in our introductory review of Schmemann's legacy, however, the actual coherence of this content and form is perhaps naively presupposed.

Nevertheless, Pelikan concurs with the thrust of Ugolnik's presupposition, affirming just such a principled unity in his discussion of the "symbolical books" of Orthodox Christianity. He asserts that despite its genre, the text of the Divine Liturgy of St. John Chrysostom (the usual eucharistic formulary of the Byzantine Rite) finds itself included in collections of these "books" (the creeds and canons of church councils as well as the "confessions" of Orthodox hierarchs) because it stands as a criterion of the faith.[70] Quoting Paul Meyendorff, Pelikan explains that Orthodox revere the Divine Liturgy as a veritable source of revelation, a datum in a certain sense equivalent to the Scriptures themselves.[71] Its text thus constitutes a "compendium of doctrine" even as it irreducibly denotes an *event*: "The liturgy is intended not primarily to be read or even sung but to be celebrated in action as *leitourgia*. Therefore its constant point of reference is the setting provided by the sacred space in which the celebration is being carried on, as defined by the iconostasis and the icons."[72]

Ugolnik appears to be on firm ground then, in stressing the essential role played by the liturgical gestalt within which the "communal search for meaning" unfolds. This context is contrasted with the dominant motif of the Western tradition in which a "self-sufficient reader" engages a text in solitude: the image par excellence being St. Augustine, mysteriously beckoned to "take and read" (*tolle, lege*).[73] The author considers that such a model remains regnant, being espoused by Ricoeur himself; moreover, Ricoeur is seen to stand in an auspicious line of thinkers following upon Augustine (Luther, Kierkegaard, Bultmann, Barth) for whom the text engenders an individual, not to say solipsistic, striving after meaning. Such a striving—in which community as such plays a tangential, even detrimental role—is unreservedly on display, according to Ugolnik, in Ricoeur's famous claim that "the right of the reader and the right of the text converge in an important struggle that generates the whole dynamic of interpretation."[74]

If Ugolnik does concede that Orthodoxy might profitably take account of the Western hermeneutical tradition, he remains apprehensive lest it eclipse the distinctive "audience" of its Eastern counterpart. Hence he warns that hermeneutics implies "adopt[ing] as normative a particular model of human being. . . . Ours is a dynamic, dramatically defined relationship between a community of interrelated 'selves' and a text. It is anthropologically rather than psychologically centered."[75] Yet it seems to me that the author still paints with too wide a brush, descrying a monolithic ontology amidst the "terms born in the West." For the model of human being that Ricoeur has elaborated over the course of his philosophical itinerary has actually been marked precisely by an anthropological rather than psychological orientation. It is surely something of a straw man to construe the Western paradigm as defined simply by figures like Schleiermacher and Hegel when their contributions have been subject to thorough critique, not least by Ricoeur himself.[76]

In fairness Ugolnik, at the time of writing, did not have our current advantage of being able to take the entirety of Ricoeur's work into consideration. Suggestively, Gerhard Ebeling and Ernst Fuchs, the two modern Western exegetes who do receive Ugolnik's explicit approbation as akin in spirit to the Orthodox, both figure prominently in Ricoeur's own biblical hermeneutics, one that is markedly in favor of a communitarian perspective. As the introduction to *Thinking Biblically* categorically declares: "The text exists, in the final analysis, thanks to the community, for the use of the community, with a view to giving shape to the community."[77] Indeed, in this same volume's discussion of the Song of Songs, Ricoeur demonstrates a remarkable sensitivity to the "dynamic, dramatically defined relationship between a community of interrelated 'selves' and a text" promoted by liturgical celebration:

> The liturgy makes use of a dialogical structure, where the participation of the worshippers is constitutive of the working of the liturgical action under the imprint of a convocation that generates a new "us." The practice of language within the liturgical framework has one specific intention, that of drawing near to a "mystery" that is as much enacted as said. Consequently, when the liturgy cites the texts of Scripture, the participants reassume the movement of involvement and commitment through the words and in the dialogue of the protagonists of the originary dialogue. In this way, the liturgy becomes a privileged place for the reproduction of the text.[78]

This is not to say that Ricoeur's hermeneutics does not also stress a *critical* stance toward tradition—as Ugolnik rightly recognizes—but merely that such a stance must not inescapably end in a "fundamentally private struggle."[79] Ricoeur's mature thinking on this matter emerges in the series of interviews published in 1998. Although his fundamental paradigm does remains the act of *reading*, he unequivocally intends thereby a much more holistic activity than ordinary use of the term might imply: "I know [the biblical] word because it is written, this writing because it is received and read; and this reading is accepted by a community, which, as a result, accepts to be deciphered by its founding texts; and it is this community that reads them."[80] Happily, Ricoeur thus seems to portend more for Orthodox theology than one might at first glance expect.

The wager of the present study is that the Orthodox "theological persona" is not by necessity placed in contradistinction to the "interpreting self" of the Western tradition: Ricoeur's later works actually articulate a form of selfhood that can be attained *only* via a peregrination across *social* landscapes. Indeed, the full extent of the otherness of the Orthodox "theological persona" may prove to be discoverable only along the course of the "interpreting self." We shall see whether it is not a matter of choosing between one or the other, but rather of finding a mediation between them and perhaps discerning their mutual dependence.

In summary, if an *Orthodox* hermeneutic in the West will rightly privilege the role the liturgy can play as the matrix in which the interpretation of Scripture—and by extension of faith itself—can be conducted, it is nonetheless true that an Orthodox hermeneutic in the *West* will have to reckon with a critique of that very matrix. It will need to confront the prospect that the liturgy, as what Ricoeur would call a "document of human life," is susceptible like any text to the crucible of interpretation. The liturgy, that is, is itself in need of a hermeneutical interrogation; it does not simply obtain as a context for the "reading" of Scripture but also must be taken as an datum to be interpreted in its own right—one that does not necessarily yield the univocal sense that Schmemann claimed on its behalf.[81] For while it is easy to sympathize with Ugolnik's complaint that "it is the post-Enlightenment era in the West that finally isolates the 'interpreting self' so completely that to the Orthodox mind the theological persona becomes an exile, cut off by its very methodology from the very community it once sought to address"; and his conclusion that "existential isolation can identify that exile from contemporary community with an acutely estranging 'historical distance'"[82]—for as Ricoeur himself has acknowledged, "beyond the desert of criticism, we wish to be called again"[83]— it is facile to presume that Eastern Christians are immune to similar challenges. As Schmemann's critique of the commentary tradition implies, there has already occurred within the Orthodox mind a certain scission between the liturgy and those who pray it: a negative distanciation between the originary tradition and its historical transmission. It would seem that even in Orthodoxy one cannot abide in a "first naïveté" but must rather assume the arduous itinerary of the "interpreting self"—if not, to be sure, on one's own.

2

WESTERN PERSPECTIVES

Overview

In the previous chapter we set the stage for a Ricoeurian reading of liturgy: After considering the centrality of the Church's *lex orandi* within the Orthodox Weltanschauung, we explored the potential role of philosophy in further developing a liturgical theology "after Schmemann." We also probed the challenges of integrating stereotypically Western forms of thought into Eastern Christian reflection, concluding that although liturgy figures as a sine qua non in Orthodox thinking, it is yet in need of being subjected to a hermeneutical analysis. The next step of our inquiry will be to situate the appropriation of Ricoeur hitherto by other scholars interested in his pertinence for liturgical studies. Then we will be in a position to develop our own application of his thought to the specificity of the Orthodox tradition. In this chapter, therefore, we converse with those who have already employed Ricoeur in the course of their investigations, to learn from what has (not) already been done.[1]

A Roman Catholic Appropriation: Joyce Ann Zimmerman

Over the span of several works, Joyce Ann Zimmerman has given sustained attention to the implications of Ricoeur's thought for liturgical theology. She has consistently argued that while diachronic methods have until recently prevailed—and rightly so, given the rich fruits they have yielded—there are certain problematics to which diachronic methods cannot by their very nature respond. The findings of the social sciences favor a synchronic approach to texts such as those afforded by the pathways of structuralism, semiotics, and reader-response criticism.[2] In her first book on the topic, *Liturgy as a Language of Faith*, Zimmerman makes a case for the relevance of Ricoeur based on his ability to incorporate various "analytics" into the explanatory moment of the "hermeneutical arc," itself conceived in tripartite terms as *participation, distanciation,* and *appropriation*.[3] It is the *form* of Ricoeur's hermeneutics that proves compelling to the author; recognizing texts as documents of life, as repositories of the sediment of human action, he is able to conceive of the movements leading up to and away from the engagement with a text as equally germane to the task of interpretation.

A brief description of Ricoeur's "hermeneutical arc": *Participation* refers to the phenomenon of preunderstanding, or belonging, that enables one to bring a certain prescience to the reading of a text; *distanciation* by contrast indicates the role played by analysis in attempting to explain the text qua text—to engage it objectively using any number of analytical devices; finally, *appropriation* is the act of incorporating the insights gained through *distanciation*, as a refinement of the antecedent preunderstanding, into one's existential situation—i.e., to allow the import of a text to bear upon the redescription of one's own experience of reality.[4] The use of the terms "explanation" and "understanding" have a technical meaning in the field of hermeneutics, referring to what have been construed as the different methodologies appropriate to the natural and human sciences respectively. Yet Ricoeur is not content with this dichotomy, which he rather sees as a productive dialectic.

Accordingly, liturgy for Zimmerman is a structure fixed by tradition through a written text that shapes the worshipping community; this text is both *descriptive* inasmuch as it is the trace of the liturgical action of the past, and *prescriptive* in serving as a script that worshippers follow in order to place themselves in continuity with the past. The emphasis on *action* is key and results from the following conviction:

Shaped by tradition, the text itself also gives shape to the liturgical tradition: it molds the present historical community which, in turn, becomes part of the shaping tradition for subsequent generations. Liturgical texts are not isolated bodies of literature. They have an *arche* and *telos* derived from their relationship to Christian tradition which is normative for liturgical action. This relationship originates from the fact that liturgical texts are a *fixation* of worshipping communities' liturgical *action. Thus liturgical action is primary, but it gives rise through cumulative tradition to fixed texts which, in turn, shape a present liturgical action.* The dynamism is action—written text—action.[5]

Zimmerman echoes Jaroslav Pelikan's appraisal of the (text of the) Divine Liturgy in noting that while the fullness of liturgy is only evident in its celebration, access to the *meaning* of what is celebrated is afforded by the liturgical text itself. After all, it is the text's rubrics that indicate its "action-context," thereby directing the reader "outside," to the world beyond the margin of the page.[6]

Zimmerman continues by providing a helpful review of Ricoeur's early approach to hermeneutics, specifically the manner in which he favored combining the objective focus on the code of language with a subjective concern for its use in discourse by persons; this discussion is framed in terms of the distinction between *langue* (language) and *parole* (speech) made famous by pioneering Swiss linguist Ferdinand de Saussure (1857–1913). Where structural analysis is limited by its concentration on words as individual signs within an ahistorical system, Ricoeur points toward the creativity of words as composed into a *sentence* by a given person; as he would continually insist, language is first and foremost "someone saying something to someone about something." Zimmerman explains:

> The shift in focus from word to sentence is crucial for the process of the recovery of meaning. This shift implies that recovering meaning from a system of signs capitalizes on only one aspect of language. In actuality, language does not begin with signs. We do not begin saying words by consulting a dictionary. We begin to use language because we have something to say, something to communicate.[7]

The author highlights some of the critical dialectics employed by Ricoeur—namely, *event* and *meaning; identification* and *predication;* the three levels of linguistic performativity (which Ricoeur derives from speech-act theorists such as J. L. Austin[8]): the locutionary, illocutionary, and perlocutionary; and *sense* and *reference.* Subsequently, she examines the way in which Ricoeur understands the difference between a discourse and a text, on the one hand, and a text and a *written* text, on the other. Here the key point is that Ricoeur has brought to light the peculiar features of different kinds of speech: (1) as it occurs spontaneously between two interlocutors; (2) as a discourse configured according to an intended structure; and (3) as a discourse that, having been written, is separated from its originary context, author, and audience, and hence subject in a way that oral discourse is not to the "conflict of interpretations." The upshot is that a liturgical text is an entity sui generis: As a written text destined for repeated performance—"the 'reading' of a liturgical text is, in actuality, its celebration"[9]—it begs the question of the degree to which its meaning is *inherent*, as opposed to being brought to it by the particular community by which it comes to life.

Liturgy as a Language of Faith concludes by developing a highly technical "theoretical analytic" intended for application in the explanatory moment of the interpretative process. Zimmerman adduces Ricoeur's semantics of action, and fuses them with the "factors" and "functions" of Roman Jakobson's (1896–1982) communication theory. This taxonomy allows for a text to be analyzed in terms of its addresser, addressee, context, message, contact, and code. Zimmerman molds Jakobson's criterology to suit the analysis of a liturgical text by incorporating certain correctives suggested by Ricoeur's semantics. What emerges is a pattern for schematizing a liturgical text so as to assess the total act of communication engendered by it, all the while assuming an ideal performance. This model is, in turn, applied to the *Novus Ordo* Mass—i.e., the "Ordinary Form" of the Eucharist of the Roman Rite—elucidating the communication dynamics of the rite and critiquing them in regard to their coherence and consistency. A useful comparison to Zimmerman's enterprise may be found in Mark Searle's structuralist treatment of the Roman Rite's blessing of water.[10]

Despite the scope of her study, the author is also well aware of the lacunae in her approach:

> While the results of our specific analytic are promising, we admit that the method is limited by the choice of analytic tools. Other aspects important for a fuller explication of the meaning of the eucharistic rite cannot be addressed without going outside our chosen analytic. Thus, our method does not take into account the full dynamic of an actual celebration nor does it evaluate what is done with a text in that celebration. It brackets the text's historical development with its inherent theological and pastoral weaknesses. It brackets the thematic content of the text and the sources for the content and it does not capitalize on the richness of the text's metaphoric prayer language.[11]

In this list of omissions, Zimmerman has effectively offered a program for further research. She prudently places implicit parentheses around the kind of qualitative research done by anthropologists and others who conduct empirical studies of given ritual events; such field work has the merit of assessing the "full dynamic of an actual celebration" in all its observable dimensions but suffers the corresponding demerit of being defined by that very particularity.

By contrast, a focus on the liturgical text is a methodological decision to privilege rather the universal—i.e., that which is ostensibly common to diverse performances of a given tradition, all things being equal. As we will see below, even studies focused on "actual" celebrations cannot aspire to tell the whole story, since the "dynamic" in question is uniquely constituted anew in every instance in respect of the irreducible particularity of the given community of worshippers. At the limit, their internal disposition remains a phenomenon opaque to any attempt at exhaustive examination, even if it can be gauged to some degree. Surely the adage, "One never steps into the same river twice," is here apropos: Every liturgical celebration is unique. Fieldwork of even the most rigorous sort could thus only ever but comment upon the specific features of the celebration under consideration and the manner in which a common text or tradition is concretized in a particular context.

Zimmerman also notes that her study does not treat the "thematic content" of the rite nor the sources of this content, nor again the "metaphoric prayer language" in which this content is expressed. Unlike her concern with capturing the "full dynamic of an actual celebration," these issues would seem to lend themselves readily to further elaboration through recourse to Ricoeur. Metaphor has been a recurrent theme in his philosophical journey and will hence figure prominently in our present endeavor. Moreover, inasmuch as the thematic content of liturgical celebrations inevitably raises questions of the nature and operation of symbols as well as questions concerning the relationship between history and fiction, between the originary events of a tradition and their ritual representation—all matters to which Ricoeur has also devoted no small amount of attention—there would appear to be ample scope for further reflection.

Another issue unmentioned in Zimmerman's agenda but taken up in her later work is the problem of selfhood. What is the nature of the liturgical subject as conceived in the light of Ricoeur's hermeneutics? One reviewer of *Liturgy as a Language of Faith* suggests that "the major difficulty in the final analysis . . . as other critics of liturgical theology's use of Ricoeur have pointed out, is whether his anthropology and his accompanying view of the self is adequate."[12] Although Zimmerman's book was completed before the publication of Ricoeur's *Oneself as Another*,[13] consecrated to this very topic, she usefully probes the relevance of this seminal work in a subsequent article, "Liturgical Assembly: Who Is the Subject of Liturgy?"[14] The treatment of *Oneself as Another* in Chapter 5 will incorporate the fecund but undeveloped concepts delineated therein.

Liturgy and the "Paschal Mystery"

Zimmerman also has produced a second monograph on the topic at hand, which sets out to consider liturgical spirituality: It treats not only the Eucharist but also Baptism and the principal hours of the Divine Office (Lauds and Vespers), from the perspective of how their *structure* corresponds to the shape of the "Paschal Mystery"—taken as the common referent of both liturgy and Christian life as a whole.[15] The goal of her "postcritical methodological exercise" is to overcome a perceived dualism between liturgy and life, showing how what are often taken to be discrete domains are in fact part of a single hermeneutical continuum.[16] Most important for our purposes are the third and fourth chapters of the book, which shift gears from the preceding historical reflections to the delineation of a postcritical method serviceable for sounding the depth structure of texts.[17] This is carried out through dialogue with language philosophy, hermeneutics and scriptural exegesis—particularly the thought of Ricoeur.

Zimmerman first rehearses Ricoeur's tripartite "hermeneutical arc," described above—i.e., participation, distanciation, and appropriation—but introduces here an intriguing variation on how she sees it connecting to liturgy. Could liturgical celebration itself become the moment of distanciation, a reflective/critical moment vis-à-vis a continuous commitment to Christian living?[18] She proposes in a Schmemannesque vein that liturgy is a moment "out of time," one that allows for a critique of the way we live the Christian mystery: "The celebration of liturgy presents the meaning of our whole Christian living to us in a concrete and manageable ritual moment. To discover the inner dynamic—the deep structure—of Christian liturgy is to discover the inner dynamic—the deep structure—of Christian living. We see ourselves in the liturgy both as we are and as we can become."[19] In this connection Zimmerman also outlines Ricoeur's application of the paradigm of the text to *action*—i.e., "meaningful human activity"—which in this respect has a fourfold quality of (1) pertaining to the ethical-political sphere; (2) manifesting of human freedom; (3) being the object of interpretation according to "ideology"; and (4) inviting schematization in terms of "praxis."

Part 2 of Zimmerman's book conducts an investigation of particular rites in light of the three moments of the hermeneutical arc by applying the concept of meaningful action to the liturgical domain. Thus Chapter 5 explores the basis of *participation*—namely, the self-understanding of Christians as members of the Body of Christ. The sixth through eighth chapters are pastoral interpretations of the "moments of distanciation" constituted by Lauds and Vespers, Sunday Eucharist, and the liturgical year, respectively. Chapter 9 treats the moment of *appropriation*, that is, of choosing between new existential possibilities. Although Zimmerman's interpretation of these elements of the Roman Rite as well as her foregoing scriptural exegesis are insightful and evocative, the overall project of elaborating a liturgical spirituality does not appropriate Ricoeur's thought as much as one might expect, employing instead one cardinal feature (the hermeneutical arc) as an organizing principle.[20] Two principal criticisms emerge, which will shape our own approach to developing a liturgical application of the Ricoeurian oeuvre.

The first concerns the notion of what constitutes a "postcritical method." Explaining this concept, Zimmerman contends as follows: "Critical methods are limited in that they cannot search beyond the context in which a text was produced. Postcritical methods bracket (set aside) original contexts to focus on meaning in a new context."[21] Given this premise, one would expect a privileging of the matter of the liturgical text, what Ricoeur calls the "world of the text" opening out in front of it. Instead, the surprising argument is made that the praying of the Psalms in a liturgical setting should *not* be Christologically focused: "To pray the psalms Christologically is to distort them because we have taken them out of their cultural context. It also shortchanges us because Israel's history stands on its own as our history."[22] This is a curious interpretation not least because the recitation of the Psalms in classical liturgical usage in both East and West almost invariably concludes with a trinitarian doxology, while the content of the Psalter is consistently interpreted typologically—i.e., Christologically—in its attendant hymnography (antiphons in the West, for example, or stichera and troparia in the Byzantine tradition).[23] Indeed, as indicated above,

Ricoeur for his part regards the liturgical "reproduction" of Scripture as a positive function of the "surplus of meaning" inherent in it as a poetical text. In keeping with Zimmerman's thesis that the Paschal Mystery is not simply a past event but one that actively refigures our present, it seems a non sequitur to suggest that "Israel's history stands on its own as our history." Surely, it is "our history"—and expressly does *not* "stand on its own"— precisely because the Church, following the example of Christ, has interpreted it in light of the Paschal Mystery.[24]

Zimmerman's discussion of the Psalms in fact manifests an assimilation of them to the structural analysis of the Paschal Mystery afforded by her reading of the Lucan Last Supper. The eschatological-soteriological dialectic she uncovers in this analysis seems to be imposed upon the Psalms with the effect of reducing the specificity of the genre (and subgenres) in question:

> Psalmody—an idealized and comprehensive recitation of the relation-
> ship between God and God's people—captures an eschatological
> moment in which we liturgically experience the fullness of God's love
> and fidelity. Psalmody is a reassuring moment of hope in which we
> identify with all the promises God has already fulfilled. Their narra-
> tive genre, therefore, is essential to grasping the eschatological char-
> acter of the psalms. By drawing us into God's story of relationship
> with God's people, the psalms bracket chronological time and en-
> able us to enter into liturgical time during which God's past, present
> and future deeds on our behalf are all experienced as "at hand" and
> fulfilled. The eschatological hope that can be released by the psalms
> has as its basis the witness to God's unwavering love and fidelity.[25]

There are several issues here. Firstly, the notion that the Psalms render God's future deeds "at hand" surely implies, in a Christian liturgical con- text, the inclusion of the kind of Christological/typological referent that Zimmerman has already contested. Secondly, Ricoeur would not agree that the Psalms should be categorized as "narrative"; to the contrary, he finds them to exemplify the lyric form and be irreducible to another form. Hence he writes:

> The praise addressed to God's prodigious accomplishments in nature
> and history is not a movement of the heart which is added to narrative
> genre without any effect on its nucleus. In fact, celebration elevates
> the story and turns it into an invocation. . . . [U]nder the three figures

of praise, supplication, and thanksgiving human speech becomes invocation. It is addressed to God in the second person, without limiting itself to designating him in the third person as in narration, or to
speaking in the first person in his name as in prophecy.[26]

While Zimmerman is undoubtedly correct to suggest that the Psalms
may "captur[e] an eschatological moment in which we liturgically experience the fullness of God's love and fidelity," this cannot be the whole of
the matter: As Ricoeur notes, the Psalter also contains the genre of supplication (a category inclusive also of psalms of deprecation). It is baffling
that such texts are presented as offering a "reassuring moment of hope,"
given that they present the voice of one caught in medias res—i.e., in a
soteriological flux as yet unresolved. In this connection, it would have been
helpful for the author to have developed her distinction between chronological and liturgical time, a theme to which Ricoeur has devoted much
reflection, the complexities of which do not emerge in Zimmerman's treatment of the portentous "eschatological moment."[27]

Distanciation vs. Configuration

A further criticism concerns Zimmerman's overall application of Ricoeur's
hermeneutical arc. Dan Stiver has suggested that many interpreters of
Ricoeur unwittingly conflate his hermeneutical and narrative arcs, despite
the fact that the second moments of each (distanciation and configuration)
involve opposite epistemological operations.[28] It would seem that Zimmerman is complicit in this regard inasmuch as she situates liturgical celebration as a moment of distanciation between the moments of *belonging*
to the Christian tradition (participation), and of reconstituting that belonging through transformative praxis (refiguration). Liturgical celebration
functions in her estimation as a *critical* moment challenging the first naïveté of Christian identity and propelling it to rediscover itself as a dynamic
becoming. Hence, "Tradition refers to the moment of participation. When
we critique that tradition [i.e., by participating in liturgy], we have entered
a reflective moment of distanciation."[29]

And yet it is not at all clear that liturgical celebration provides for such
distanciation as understood by Ricoeur; he appears instead to regard the
"religious moment" as one of profound *conviction*, intercalated with the moment of critique offered by the philosophical enterprise:

The religious moment as such [is not] a critical moment; it is the moment of adhering to a word reputed to have come from farther and from higher than myself, and this occurs in a kerygmatic reading within a profession of faith. At this level, one finds, then, the idea of a dependence or a submission to an earlier word. . . . What seems to me to be constitutive of the religious is, therefore, the fact of crediting a word, in accordance with a certain code and within the limits of a certain canon.[30]

One could well argue *pace* Zimmerman that it is the existential critique posed by pluralism or by the experience of suffering or other "limit-experiences," if not the less common route of avowed philosophical reflection, that issues the challenge to a mature appropriation of faith (expressed in a renewed commitment to liturgical praxis). In place of Zimmerman's model of "life-liturgy-life," we could formulate the process as "liturgy-life-liturgy": In this latter, liturgy grounds the moment of participation in which Zimmerman's "visages" of Christian identity come into focus; life in turn is the arena where recognition of oneself in these "visages" is tested. To return to liturgy is to pass from doubt to faith.

Incidentally, Ricoeur's hermeneutic arc typically takes the reader and text as its starting point. Worship, by contrast, may be better understood not principally as a *work* that we encounter as a discrete phenomenon but rather, like language and culture more broadly, something that interprets us *before* we come to the act of interpretation. Certainly in the case of those raised in a given tradition, reflection on that tradition and on the cumulative effect of its constituent elements (e.g., cultic events) occurs "too late." As Ricoeur underscores: "To be a religious subject is to agree to enter or *to have already entered* into this vast circuit involving a founding word, mediating texts, and traditions of interpretation." He muses further concerning his own faith journey that it is an instance of "chance transformed into destiny by continuous choice. . . . I would agree to say that a religion is like a language into which one is either born or has been transferred by exile or hospitality; in any event, one feels at home there, which implies a recognition that there are other languages spoken by other people."[31] The distinction between being born *into* a tradition and entering it as an adult is perhaps significant: Does the religious moment and hence liturgical celebration function differently in each case?

Aside from the two major texts treated above, Zimmerman has explored the pertinence of Ricoeur for liturgical studies in several articles. In "Paschal Mystery, Whose Mystery?," we see a reprise of the contours of the life-liturgy-life arc elaborated in *Liturgy as Living Faith*. But here it is the narrative arc elaborated in *Time and Narrative* rather than his earlier hermeneutical arc that provides the interpretive paradigm.[32] The narrative arc involves a tripartite variation upon the Aristotelian concept of the rede-scription of human action in poetry, mimesis: Ricoeur's $mimesis_1$ (prefiguration); $mimesis_2$ (configuration); and $mimesis_3$ (refiguration). This promising model lends itself much more readily to Zimmerman's application, in its movement from an initial "guess" at meaning, through a "following" of a story, to a transformation of action in the light of the world proposed in front of the "text" (i.e., the event of liturgical celebration).

Zimmerman's principal questions are, "How do we participate in a historical event that is past and not yet come?" and "How do we live this mystery today?"[33] She discerns in Ricoeur's narrative theory a response to the temporal aporias implied by these questions:

> This narrative approach directly addresses the recurring challenge of the relationship of liturgy and life. As Ricoeur remarks, "narrative has its full meaning when it is restored to the time of action and of suffering in $mimesis_3$," (*Time and Narrative*, 1:70). Liturgy, then, from the purview of narrative theory, has its fullest meaning only when the emplotment of action that liturgy celebrates actually refigures the lives of those who celebrate. In such a way is Christ's mystery *our* mystery.[34]

As the reader's response contributes to the mediation of narrative, so also liturgy cannot be understood as such without including our appropriation of its story in our lives. Zimmerman elsewhere reiterates that liturgy merely "ritualizes what, in fact, Christian living is all about,"[35] reaching fulfillment beyond the assembly in Ricoeur's "just institutions." Such ethical engagement, moreover, is not only the currency of refiguration but also the stock on which further prefiguration trades, in a continuous mimetic economy leading back to ritual configuration.

We will have occasion below to reflect further on this trajectory. At present it suffices to note what does not feature in Zimmerman's interpretation: namely, the question of the very followability of the narrative at hand. That is, there seems to be a presumption that the story of Christ's Paschal Mystery

is itself readily comprehensible, and an optimism that any resulting interpretations will be effectively free of conflict. Anglican theologian Graham
Hughes is apprehensive of such an approach, which he finds to be the
hallmark of what he terms the "church theology" method of liturgical
theology. Contrarily, he contends that postmodern (in Hughes's lexicon:
"late modern") worshippers actually suffer from an impaired capacity to
grasp liturgical meaning, straining to follow the narrative presented by
liturgy. He thus chides Schmemann (as well as Aidan Kavanaugh and
Geoffrey Wainwright) for their misplaced confidence that "the church's traditional liturgical formulations . . . when joined with an appropriate performance of them, may confidently be relied upon to effect their own
meanings."[36] Instead, Hughes argues that "the precepts of modernity have
seriously undermined for vast numbers of people in the western world . . .
their confidence in a theistic reading of reality." We suffer from a "religious
disenchantment"; our societies "function without recourse to religion"; and
for many people's existence, "the question of belief or disbelief is simply
not an issue."[37] The thrust of his analysis is that those who practice "church
theology" need to be disabused of their naïveté; the problem of the retrieval
of meaning is acute, and cannot be resolved simply by a repristination of
the liturgical status quo ante.[38] And yet Schmemann was well aware that
the due celebration of liturgy did not lead automatically to its proper
interpretation, not to say, appropriation; hence his chagrin at the long-
standing discrepancy between the liturgy and the conventional understanding accompanying it. Taken as a whole, Zimmerman's work also makes a
valuable contribution to a nuanced perspective on the matter: She is certainly cognizant of the difficulties bedeviling attempts to "make sense of
liturgical significations in a culture of religious disenchantment."[39] We
will thus have occasion to dialogue with her further as subsequent chapters unfold.

An Anglican Appropriation: Bridget Nichols

While Zimmerman is the only liturgist to have given sustained attention
to Ricoeur over the course of several works, there are a few other figures
whose work should be noted. Some of these will be engaged in the chapters that follow. At this stage it is important to consider Bridget Nichols's
monograph *Liturgical Hermeneutics: Interpreting Liturgical Rites in Performance,* which undertakes a similar project of discerning how hermeneutics

(particularly the work of Gadamer and Ricoeur) applies to the interpretation of liturgy. Nichols's subtitle is used advisedly: "interpreting liturgical rites *in performance*" expresses her conviction that liturgical hermeneutics has hitherto privileged the interpretation of the liturgical *text*. She intends rather to comprehend the manner in which meaning obtains in and through the *enactment* of the ritual script. Nichols treats three services in the Anglican liturgical tradition (the Eucharist, Baptism, and the funeral service) and looks to account for both the liturgical text and the spatio-temporal implications of rubrics.

Interpreting Liturgy as "Performance"?

At the outset Nichols points to a discrepancy that will recur like a leitmotif in the course of her study:

> The distinctive duality in the nature of liturgy has engendered a clear division between theory and practice. On the one hand, there are the professional liturgists who have traced the history and origins of rites, and whose findings continue to enrich the understanding of liturgical practice as it has developed over the course of the centuries. On the other hand, there are countless Christians who have conducted their worship according to prescribed forms over the same period, and whose lives are directly affected as a result. Their awareness of the processes they engage in represents another potentially illuminating approach to ritual.[40]

The author's concern is to balance the critical study of liturgical texts with reflection upon the meaning they have as celebrations in the life of actual people—in other words, to mediate between a deductive, quantitative methodology and an inductive, qualitative. What does it mean to interpret a liturgy as a "performance" as opposed to focusing on the liturgical text (i.e., the default approach of Schmemann discussed above)?

Nichols sees in the early twentieth-century Anglican Benedictine Dom Gregory Dix a movement from a historical-critical to a hermeneutical approach to the study of liturgy—a "pioneering achievement" that "shift[ed] the ground of liturgical research." For "instead of dwelling on considerations of the meaning of liturgy, he paves the way for an investigation of what it is that makes liturgy a meaningful practice."[41] Nichols contends that the meaning of liturgy obtains in a personal negotiation between one's own faith and the propositions of the Christian Faith itself, these latter being dynamically presented through the process of the liturgical event. She begins with a review of the origins of hermeneutics and an exposé of the thought of Gadamer (particularly his well-known idea of the "fusion of horizons") as it is developed by Ricoeur. Here she observes that Romantic hermeneutics, which sought to connect the reader with the authorial genius behind a given text, proves particularly fruitless where *anonymous* texts are concerned. Following Ricoeur she asserts that the original context and audience of a text are similarly tangential to its contemporary potential for proposing a world that can be appropriated by the reader, and that can transform his or her own life situation.

The author proceeds to establish a dialectic, which will govern her interpretation of the rites in question, between two senses of the term "faith" (depending on whether it is written with a majuscule or miniscule "f"). The former is the tradition "handed down through the medium of scriptural writing, and distancing the congregation of the present time from the original producer of the biblical utterance. It is understood here as a credal position based on biblical evidence, and amplified by the Church's doctrinal pronouncements. These are summed up, for example, in the tenets of the Apostles' and Nicene Creeds." In contrast, the latter "evades confident definition. It belongs instead to each individual worshipper and has its being in the individual's appropriation of the community's proclamation of the Faith."[42] "The Faith" and "faith" subsist in codependent relationship brought to light in the liturgical act: "Liturgy is therefore a discourse, or better, a practice, generated by the tension between faith and the Faith. This is a version of the hermeneutic circle to the extent that neither can properly be identified as the origin of the discourse."[43] Moreover, the liturgical setting is a locus of "risk": The structural divisions in the services reveal a recurring pattern of "separation, transition, and incorporation" through which participants confront the existential challenge of trusting in the world proposed.[44]

Early on in *Liturgical Hermeneutics* Nichols issues a peculiar dismissal of Zimmerman's work, accusing the latter of "misappropriat[ing] Ricoeur's theory of the text by implying strongly that liturgical texts carry an implicit and predetermined meaning, which is rendered explicit in performance." Hence, "Zimmerman's structural-semiotic interest predisposes her to find objective meaning in the liturgical text. Treating liturgy as a 'closed system of discourse' with its beginning and end connected by an 'internal logic,' she identifies the task of hermeneutics as being to '[uncover] this inner logic as a structure unique to that text.'"[45] What is perplexing about this criticism is that Zimmerman's approach actually mirrors Ricoeur's own, in its effort to cede due place to the structural moment of explanation that can compass the range of objective meanings constituted by the formal features of a text.[46] Even more surprisingly, Nichols tends to describe her own project in the very terms with which she castigates Zimmerman by proposing, for example, that "a *structural* method related to eucharistic language in its role as a threshold language opens up a route toward the hermeneutical concerns of the ASB rite"[47] or insisting that "the liturgical rite is itself a *closed system*, comprising a variety of religio-literary genres that includes prayer, psalmody, prose narrative, prophecy, exegetical and homiletic forms, and credal statements."[48] Nichols then elaborates upon her initial objection:

> Zimmerman derives a whole metaphor of liturgical interpretation from the primacy of the text: "The 'reading' of a liturgical text is, in actuality, its celebration. From this, certain questions arise: Is the recovery of the meaning of a liturgical text a wholly subjective venture depending on its particular celebration by a local worshipping community? Or is there an objectivity about its meaning that threads its way into each celebration, minimizing the conflict of interpretations?" Such a distortion shows how easily misappropriations might occur and how little resistance Ricoeur's textual hermeneutics offers to an ideal of objective meaning.[49]

Nichols does not seem to appreciate the irony of accusing Zimmerman of misappropriating the meaning of Ricoeur's texts while also suggesting that texts do *not* in fact contain an "objective meaning"; if there is no objective meaning, one might counter, on what basis is Zimmerman's said misappropriation—i.e., misinterpretation—of Ricoeur to be judged? And rather than Zimmerman it is Ricoeur himself who has posited the text as a metaphor for the interpretation of "meaningful action."[50] In any event Zimmerman is not speaking metaphorically as such in this context but rather—again, ironically, given the gravamen of Nichols's own work— arguing that liturgical texts are not meant to be read privately as literature but enacted corporately, even as a dramatic script is intended to be realized in theatrical production. Indeed, she is effectively making *precisely the same point* as Nichols—namely, that a liturgical rite, strictly speaking, ought to be interpreted as a *performance*. Furthermore, Zimmerman's query regarding the way in which meaning is negotiated between the shape of the text and its reproduction within a range of possible celebrations, along with her acknowledgement of what Ricoeur calls the specter of the "conflict of interpretations," gives further evidence that she *does not* regard the text as having a univocal, ideal meaning. She is aware that the text is plurivocal, proposing not only a "world" but "worlds"—in virtue of the plurality of liturgical participants.[51]

Ultimately, Nichols appears to also cede primacy to the liturgical text, offering the disclaimer that she has been obliged for sake of methodological economy to "be content with a notion of the 'ideal performance.'"[52] Said performance, of course, is derived from none other than the written rite itself: text and rubrics. She does not conduct empirical research into *actual* performances nor even—less excusably—endeavor to analyze the constituent components of an ideal setting (architecture, vesture, music, choreography, etc.) for the rites under consideration; nor does she weigh how these variables might affect the transaction of meaning accomplished in the performance. It is true that in one instance—namely, a comparison of the 1552 and 1662 orders for the Eucharist—Nichols demonstrates convincingly how an alteration in the arrangement of the altar-table and seating of congregants could condition the interpretation given to the rite, but this inclusion of nontextual factors is far from consistently practiced. In fact, the author acknowledges that she is not in a position to take account of the "other features of liturgical performance which have equally important structural claims, preeminently music and physical gesture," and thus adheres to the liturgical text as given in the *editio typica* of the Anglican rites in question. Revealingly she describes her own approach as follows: "The trend in the methodology which this thesis establishes, with its reliance on Ricoeur, Gadamer, and in due course, Derrida and Austin, is toward issues of language. This dictates the scope of its considerations."[53]

In this light, Nichols's caveat concerning the serviceability of an "ideal performance" seems counterproductive. She warns, "Always, it must be emphasised that little profit will accrue from treating services as illustrative models for the methodological hypotheses of liturgical hermeneutics," yet does not explain why this is so.[54] To the contrary, this quote aptly describe Nichols's own program: On the hypothesis that Ricoeur and Gadamer can tender a richer comprehension of the nature of liturgical performance, she scrutinizes a series of Anglican rites to determine how they mediate between "the Faith" and "faith" by placing worshipers in a "threshold po-sition" wherein they can encounter the world of "the Kingdom." Indeed, I would advise that liturgical hermeneutics, unlike the historical-critical practice of *Liturgiewissenschaft*, for example, adheres precisely to this pattern—at once embraced and disavowed by Nichols. Where the latter discipline, being deductive, begins with the collation and codification of liturgical manuscripts (alongside other relevant data), the former starts with a heuristic and proceeds inductively, testing it upon extant liturgical material with a view to elaborating a new mode of understanding. Nichols seems to cut off the branch upon which she sits, in resisting the notion that liturgical hermeneutics *should* involve precisely the application of a given method to a liturgical text/performance, in order to indicate how it augments the intelligibility of the rite.

A final matter merits comment—namely, Nichols's ambiguous notion of "faith." While challenging Zimmerman for alleging that there *is* mean-ing in the liturgical text itself, she approvingly cites Ricoeur's observation that "what in theological language is called 'faith' is constituted, in the strongest sense of this term, by the new being that is the 'thing' of the text."[55] It is the "threshold" quality of this "new being" in turn that pro-vides the guiding thread for her reading of the select Anglican services, in which she seeks to identify how the given ritual configuration of texts and actions does or does not successfully promote its appropriation. She accepts as a given, in other words, Ricoeur's understanding of biblical faith (the "new being" generated by the Scriptures), saying that it provides the "ground" of liturgy.[56] The biblical text in this instance is evidently taken to have a meaning of its own. And yet she alternatively claims that it is important to progress from "questions of the meaning *of* liturgy, to a con-cern with what makes liturgy a meaningful action," and then to determine "the ground or referent for meaningful action, as distinct from an endorse-ment of reified meaning."[57] One wonders why the biblical text is seen to possess an atomistic meaning—i.e., the "faith" that will serve as the ground for liturgy—while the liturgy must be defended against a similar eisegesis. Is the acquisition of biblical faith not a performative enterprise in its own right, similarly subject to the dynamics of action?

Certainly an Eastern Christian perspective would not see biblical faith as conveyed apart from its cultivation within the liturgical act. Our con-siderations in Chapter 1 illustrated how liturgy is characteristically seen as the very arena within which the Bible is encountered. Nichols perhaps be-

trays a Protestant bias in her presumption that the liturgical subject has an
a priori biblical frame of reference.[58] This presumption is further exacer-
bated in her attempt to posit "the Faith" as one of the poles between which
the negotiation of liturgical meaning unfolds, on the basis of the Creeds;
if meaning is not to be found *in* texts, how can the Creeds (apart from a
performative context) serve as monuments of "the Faith"? Again, within
an Eastern Christian context the Creed functions as a *prayer*, an element
within the liturgical performance rather than a discrete site of meaning;
but Nichols inconsistently assumes the Creed to have a meaning (i.e., the
representation of "the Faith") instead of asking what makes it meaningful. It is at least questionable that the meaning of Creed should be isolated
from its performance, especially when it also features as a segment of the
liturgy in the Anglican eucharistic rites covered by Nichols.[59]

Entering the Interpretive Circle

Notwithstanding the discrepancies just mentioned, Nichols does offer valuable insight into the way in which the liturgy provides for self-interpretation,
in keeping with Ricoeur's insistence that interpretation has an "ontological
vehemence." For Nichols, the limit-expression of "the Kingdom"—all the
more salient for an Orthodox liturgical theology because of its privileged
status in Schmemann's own lexicon[60]—promotes a Ricoeurian "reorientation
through disorientation" by being incorporated as the reference point for the
liturgical services under consideration. She stresses that this is a dynamic
process occurring over time as congregants are repeatedly exposed to the
narrative of the liturgy, producing a hermeneutical circle:

> We now enter an interpretative circle that denies any one point of ori-
> gin for the practice of liturgy. The matter of whether worshippers con-
> tinue to participate in liturgical action because they believe in the
> textually enshrined promise of the Kingdom, or whether they gain
> glimpses of the Kingdom as a consequence of their belief in the validity
> of the act of worship is not a case for decision, but for an act of faith.[61]

Several further aspects of Nichols's work should be also retained. Firstly,
her treatment of J. L. Austin's categories of "speech acts" resumes the important discussion concerning the manner in which speech and action are
related; just as Ricoeur sees "meaningful action" as amenable to being
treated as "text" so Austin's work brings into relief the fact that speech is

never simply propositional (the *locutionary* act), but results from an *illocutionary* impetus, conveying *perlocutionary* effects in its wake. As we will see further on, this reciprocal construal of text and action according to each other's criteria proves an important theme in Ricoeur's work. Nichols's invocation of Derrida's concept of the "written performative" is a welcome cross-reference in this discussion.[62]

Secondly, Nichols makes a valuable observation regarding Ricoeur's analysis of the polyphonic discourse of Scripture (the varied voices with which it speaks in respect of its plurality of genres); this polyphony is compounded exponentially by being situated in a liturgical context, inclusive as this is of both verbal and nonverbal forms of expression. As mentioned earlier, Ricoeur exhibits an awareness of how Scripture's surplus of meaning is compounded exponentially by liturgical configuration; the challenge is to avoid a homogenization of the scriptural/liturgical discourse such that its polyphony is reduced to a monophony, while also recognizing the potential interpretive gain resulting from a harmonization of the voices. Nichols persuasively argues:

> Each time a passage from the Bible is incorporated as a reading within an act of worship, or referred to in a prayer, a double movement takes place. The new situation draws, first of all, on the force of the borrowed utterance in its original position to give power to its reference. This calls upon the whole range of background knowledge of biblical contexts which participants in liturgy are presumed to bring with them. In the next stage of the movement, the original force undergoes a transformation brought about by its new relationships with other utterances which might resonate with it typologically, thematically, or even by the seeming inappropriateness of the enforced proximity.[63]

We might add that in an Eastern Christian context this movement is typically reversed, since (as discussed above) the Bible is principally encountered *within* the liturgy, and only secondarily (if at all) as a discrete "closed system." The liturgy is seen to be the "original position" of biblical texts, its dynamics the source of their "original force." Thus Orthodox Scripture theologian John Breck can insist that following patristic precedent, "every proper (i.e., 'orthodox-catholic') reading of Scripture [is] an ecclesial act. The liturgy is the first and most basic context within which the Word of God comes to expression. While personal meditation on the Biblical texts is essential, there is no such thing as a 'private' reading. This is because every reading must be governed by Church Tradition, with its particular dogmatic and liturgical stance."[64]

Thirdly, Nichols's contention that liturgy shows itself to be receptive to interpretation under the sign of "threshold, appropriation and risk" is well founded. As we shall see in our examination of the *GBW*, the liturgical idiom explicitly acknowledges the kinds of temporal aporias that according to Ricoeur render all interpretation provisional. Inasmuch as the liturgy opens out onto an eschatological horizon—it is designed to be repeated (short of the Lord's parousia) indefinitely—its meaning can never be said to be fully attained; paradoxically, this is so until the epiphany of that by which it will be entirely eclipsed. Nichols summarizes:

> So, because of the essentially promissory nature of liturgical meaning, there is no "exhaustively definable context" for acts of worship. There is always an element of incompleteness, in that the Kingdom will come, but not yet. Liturgical action is therefore provisional, conducted on that threshold which marks its responsibility to the demands of the present, and to the demands of an order which must still come into being. Since the rite can be repeated, and indeed must be repeated "in memory of [Christ]" and "until his coming again," it is never total. Thus there can be no "free consciousness present for the totality of the operation," and fully in possession of an intention for that operation. Finally, the "full meaning" of the rite cannot be achieved until rites themselves are no longer performed.[65]

In this light, Austin's categories for "speech acts" also acquire a certain tentativeness. Who can measure, after all, the full extent of liturgical language's perlocutionary import? How may one gauge the ultimate result of prayer? Ricoeur concedes that the perlocutionary aspect of language is not simply that which is least amenable to inscription; it also presents language's fundamental dynamic as a kind of parabola whose trajectories are conceivable if not necessarily measurable.

Finally (and related to the previous remark), Nichols ably demonstrates that liturgical hermeneutics has a fundamentally praxeological orientation. The performance of liturgy is not a singular event, not even one bound to a self-contained cycle of repetition, but rather an agora in which the sacred and secular transact their affairs.[66] For Nichols the marriage rite exemplifies such commerce, as a human reality upon which liturgy confers a divine dimension. The principle applies generally:

In worship, the horizons of ordinary contemporary experience are continually encountering the horizons of Christian tradition, so that ordinary life is newly evaluated under the proposals of ritual action, while the terms of Christian tradition are carried out into the everyday world at each liturgical gathering.[67]

Nichols admits that liturgy is vulnerable; an exclusive focus on the future and one trained solely on the present can be equally paralyzing. Yet the ritual domain remains a viable site for contemporary utopian discourse, which can subsequently translate into a critique of the ideological status quo—although liturgy itself must be open to critique. It opens up the possibility of a productive tension with potential to refigure the public sphere.[68]

Text vs. Performance

Before concluding this chapter, we need to turn our attention briefly to the trenchant critique of Nichols's project in Martin Stringer's "Text, Context and Performance: Hermeneutics and the Study of Worship,"[69] in which he also addresses her summary criticism of his own earlier work in the area. Following this critique will assist us in situating our own project amid the text-vs.-performance debate that (as we have already found with Zimmerman and Nichols) is both necessary and nettlesome. We began this book by establishing the importance of liturgical theology as theology *from* the liturgy, so to speak: theology as rooted in the liturgy itself. The overarching question, however—which has hopefully by now become clear—is that of *where* precisely to locate "the liturgy": Do we follow Schmemann by taking the liturgical text as the representative source of all potential "performances"? Or must we follow a deductive approach, gathering empirical data that can then be integrated into our interpretation of what "the liturgy" means? Our excursus through the debate attending this question is important for discerning what can and cannot be accomplished in our own appropriation and application of Ricoeur.

The Limits of Hermeneutics

Like Nichols, Stringer begins with a criticism that the method used to interpret liturgy hitherto (based as it has been on the liturgical text) has proven unequal to the task at hand—namely, the evaluation of what is fundamentally a *performative* phenomenon: "It treats the liturgy as a literary/ theological text and ignores the fact that the liturgical text is only one small part of a much wider act of worship."[70] Nichols is singled out as representative of those scholars endeavoring to alter the status quo, although acknowledgment is made of the work of Joyce Ann Zimmerman as also of Kieran Flanagan.[71] Stringer indicates that his own approach has been ethnographic and diagnostic: in researching the experiences of several Manchester congregations, he determined that ordinary people "did not 'understand' the liturgy in theological terms at all. Their understanding was instead based on very different criteria pertaining to visual and performative aspects of the rite, their own life problems, and their personal relations with other people taking part."[72] Liturgical meaning in consequence is to be found rather in the minds of those participating in a rite than in the rite itself. This finding insinuates that hermeneutics can only be of limited significance in the enterprise of liturgical interpretation since it is by nature focused on the *text*.

Having reviewed the hermeneutical tradition up to and including Ricoeur, Stringer then moves on to his critique of Nichols. He first takes issue with the Ricoeurian notion that a text projects a "world," and that it is this world that transforms the reader who encounters it. Below I shall indicate why Stringer seems to misunderstand Ricoeur. His principal objection as it emerges at this point is to how Nichols claims to attend to the world of the text as manifest in performance, all the while prescinding from the variables implied by an actual performative environment. As mentioned in my own critique above, Nichols restricts herself to the model of an "ideal" performance. Stringer phrases his concern thus:

Each new order [i.e., each actual instance of an order of service] would clearly change the dynamic of a specific reading, along with the nature of the world projected by that text. . . . The same is true for hymns, sermons and other interpolated texts that Nichols also puts to one side for ease of analysis. However, the actions and setting of the rite are also overlooked in Nichols' conception of the "ideal" performance and this cannot be dealt with quite so easily. A liturgy can be conceived of that has no hymns, no sermon and sticks slavishly to the order of the text. No act of worship, however, can be imagined that has no setting and no action (i.e., does not involve the participation of real people). Setting and action make worship a performance.[73]

If real people are essential to any consideration of liturgy as performance, reasons Stringer, then it is consequently implausible to suggest that the "world" projected by the rite is not in some respect a function of its participants. Stringer cogently draws a parallel with the notorious anthropological dilemma concerning the participant-observer: To wit, there can be no strictly objective ethnographic account of a given culture inasmuch as the prejudices of the anthropologist necessarily condition the interpretation, even the determination, of the data in question.

Furthermore, Stringer objects to the ideal worshipper presupposed as a corollary of Nichols's ideal performance; he doubts that the average participant in liturgy actually keeps to the itinerary of meaning mapped out in an order of service. Hermeneutics is therefore bound to eventually implode under pressure of the variables of a performance-based model of liturgical interpretation; there are simply too many factors to consider. Hence his reprimand to Nichols for her unwitting neglect of the "perlocutionary" aspect of liturgical language—that is to say, the manner in which, when re-realized as discourse, it results in the production of effects in the world that radiate beyond the context of the rite itself.[74] For Stringer, hermeneutics cannot hope to capture the penumbra of *action*, working as it does with a textual brush:

> [Nichols] has to construct an "ideal" performance of the liturgies she is discussing in order to apply hermeneutical interpretative methods to them. However, this is a "textual" construction. It is the "writing" of the original discourse or action of the rite, the "performance," into "text" in order to interpret it. This illusion can be created because the liturgy as performance is based on a text (the text which Nichols actually chooses to use). In its use within performance, however, that text is, we might say, "unwritten," and moves back along Ricoeur's journey from discourse to writing, to become discourse once again, with all the locutionary, illocutionary and perlocutionary force of that discourse.[75]

The import of the preceding statement is that each performance is unique and so too, a fortiori, the "world" encountered by each participant. As Stringer admits, his critique "taken to its logical conclusion would suggest that each individual attending the liturgy—each with their own context, their own perspective, their own levels of engagement with the rite and so on—will have their own interpretation of, or construct their own meaning for, the rite in question. This would suggest that there are as many interpretations, or 'meanings,' for any liturgical act as there are people attending."[76]

Only a methodology willing to venture forth into the empirical deep will be able to construe with any adequacy the meaning that lies on the horizon of the liturgical performance; standing on the shore will not suffice.

Stringer's argument amounts to an apologia on behalf of the ethnographic approach taken by those sociologists and anthropologists (and liturgists) who have compassed the field of ritual studies in search of an adequate vantage point from which to survey their own terrain.[77] For Stringer is understandably unwilling to allow his "logical conclusion" to become a solipsistic reductio ad absurdum. While maintaining that liturgical meaning as such can never be determined apart from the experience of a given participant, he nevertheless grants that "the different strategies by which that meaning is derived, negotiated or constructed" *can* be, and that these are thus the proper object of liturgical study.[78] One wonders if this is an obscurantist instance of making a "distinction without a difference," because it is not at all apparent why such strategies should prove any less idiosyncratic and inscrutable than the meaning they treat. It seems doubtful, moreover, that Stringer would be willing to extend his radical perspectivism to other forms of communication. Why, for example, may liturgy effectively mean anything, while the experience of, say, Stringer's own essay not be similarly plurivocal?

As Graham Hughes has noted, "questions might be directed to Stringer about the selective use of Ricoeur on which he bases (some at least) of his criticisms."[79] Hughes does not itemize these, but the following come to mind. Firstly, Stringer does not seem to properly understand how Ricoeur conceives of the deployment of the "world of the text." If Ricoeur did indeed hold to the notion that the text univocally proposes a world—i.e., without the reader bringing his or her own situation to bear upon the act of reading—it is difficult to see how he would conclude that hermeneutics cannot eschew the "conflict of interpretations." Rather, because a text means all that it can, there will always be a plurality of interpretations reflecting the fusion of horizons between the world of the text and the world of the given reader, with the result that the meaning that obtains is *not* singular. Yet this does not signal "to each his own" because every interpretation must reckon with the exigencies of a work's structure. Stringer seems to miss Ricoeur's emphasis that texts (including liturgies) are structured works; while interpretations may be legion, it is reasonable to compel them to appear before the tribunal convoked by the *sense* of the work.

In other words, Stringer's liturgical participant seems to pass directly from the moment of prefiguration, of a guess at the meaning of the act, to refiguration, the moment of appropriating a meaning for his or her own life; what is missing is the moment of configuration wherein he or she is summoned to follow the narrative presented. If the modes of prefiguration and refiguration are indisputably all but limitless—as Stringer has it, the site of meanings "too personal to be expressible in a form that people could communicate to the analyst"[80]—surely this is not the case in regard to the mode of configuration, subject as it is to the canons of rationality. As Hughes observes, "There cannot be a response without something to respond to (in this case [i.e., in liturgy], the pattern of the 'typical story') which thus makes [the construction of meaning in liturgy] a collaborative arrangement."[81]

Hughes insists that while Stringer does acknowledge (in his actual ethnographic studies) how meaning is forged from both the world proposed by the liturgy and the worlds adduced by its participants, his theoretical predilection is to situate meaning firmly within the minds of the latter. One sees this ambiguity in the conclusion to "Text, Context and Performance" where the author declares, "The meaning of the rite is situated in the minds of the participants rather than in the liturgical text. Or to rephrase this in a way that Nichols might approve priority in the relationship surrounding the negotiation of meaning lies not with the text but with each individual participant. If this is true then we can never state the 'meaning' of the liturgical performance in any generalised, official or objective sense."[82] On the premise that the discernment of meaning of liturgical rites *in performance* is thus something of a quixotic quest, one is seemingly faced with the option of adopting in toto the methods of ritual studies. Is there no room then for liturgical hermeneutics?

Ritual Studies or Liturgical Hermeneutics?

What is at stake in the debate covered in this chapter is the question of how best to take account of what Zimmerman calls the "full dynamic of an actual celebration." In this regard, Martin Stringer is not alone in questioning the pertinence of Ricoeur's thought. Margaret Mary Kelleher remarks, "Although Ricoeur's influence has been widespread, there are some who point to the inadequacies of using the notion of the text as a model for studying human action. They express concern about the loss of the acting subject, the inability of the text analogue to deal adequately with the nonverbal and affective dimensions of human action, and the ease with which the sociocultural context of the action can be ignored." Since "bodily movements, sound, facial expressions, interactions, use of space" are also "mediators of meaning," Kelleher holds that "it is necessary to explore models beyond that of the text when searching for principles of interpretation that will do justice to the complexity of performance."[83]

Yet it is arguable that the terra incognita of "models beyond the text," is inexorably destined to become, as it were, a colony of hermeneutics. Why? Even an anthropological methodology eventually has to face the challenge of interpretation with respect to the *writing* by which its perception of the ritual reality is communicated: It involves, literally, "ethno-graphy,"[84] a perennial challenge recognized by none other than the pioneer and doyen of modern anthropology himself, Clifford Geertz. According to Kelleher, "Interpretation plays a major role in [Geertz's] understanding of ethnographic description and his presentation of the ethnographer as one who 'inscribes' social discourse and then tries to rescue and fix the 'said' of such discourse discloses the influence of . . . Ricoeur."[85] Kelleher notes further that the "turn to the subject" within anthropology has generated controversy concerning the perception/description of Otherness, the subjectivity of the ethnographer and the role of prejudice and ideology in the writing of ethnography, although she does not mention of Ricoeur's critical reflections on these matters.[86] If we think of the potent influence of the proto-ethnography recorded in the *Primary Chronicle* discussed above—i.e., the immense importance of the alleged account of the Kievan emissaries' experience of Hagia Sophia's liturgy—we can readily appreciate how ethnography occupies no neutral position.

As explained above, Ricoeur considers any text to have a "surplus of meaning." This is not simply a matter of counterposing textual univocity to performative plurivocity, since a performance passes away—being by nature an event, like an instance of discourse—while the text, as the referent for performance, abides for further reactualization. Thus the liturgical text is a witness to performance in its own right inasmuch as it exhibits a sedimentation of past action. Not only is the very existence of a liturgical text in some respect a witness to a tradition (whether actual or provisional) of performance, but its rubrics inscribe traces of the "meaningful action" by which it is recognizable as a *liturgical* text, as available and suitable for potential ritual enactment.[87] To explore the "world" that opens out "in front" of liturgical texts is thus arguably *already* to consider "liturgical rites in performance"—or rather, to consider liturgical performance as transcribed in its rite, "meaningful action" in its textual inscription. As Stiver assesses, concerning the great events of salvation history: "What we have in these events is a rich interplay between actions and texts that interpret the events. Actions already involve meaning." In turn "the interpretation of an action is, as such, a text that calls for its own history of interpretation."[88]

Furthermore, given Ricoeur's understanding of narrative as mimesis (i.e., the representation of action/passion), a consideration of the narrative shape of a liturgical text affords an entry into its configuration of past divine and human "performance"—that very "meaningful action" whose repercussions are felt along the historical continuum constituted by a given liturgical tradition. To quote Stiver again, "Hermeneutics . . . cannot be understood apart from action. Likewise, hermeneutics enriches the understanding of action."[89] With respect to liturgy we could here substitute "performance" for "action." If hermeneutics as such is typically defined precisely by its orientation toward the interpretation of texts, Ricoeur's work demonstrates that the hermeneutical operation is not for that reason isolated from the world of action. In a certain sense one could argue that a liturgical text subsumes the horizon of all possible performances for which it serves as script; while any individual celebration of a rite is by nature a phenomenon that goes beyond the text, this transcendence is in principal already countenanced by the liturgical contours of the "world" proposed by it.

Finally, it is worth remembering that there is a peculiar "textuality" to *Christian* liturgy as such. Recall the observation of Jaroslav Pelikan above concerning the status of the Divine Liturgy of St. John Chrysostom as one of the "symbolical books" of Orthodoxy.[90] It is surely not the case that the rites of just any culture are definitively transcribed, much less that they come to take on a life of their own as texts. If, as Aidan Nichols affirms, the paragon of Christian revelation is the *Word* of God,[91] it is not surprising that Christian liturgy has privileged *language* and countenanced its reification in and through liturgical texts. Thus Ricoeur can display keen insight into the cosmic symbols shared by Christianity and other religions while also insisting upon the unique manner in which, from the Old Testament onward, such symbolism is transformed by being assimilated to the proclamation of the word, reemerging as codetermined by its own "bound" character *and* by the scriptural narrative.[92] Any attempt, therefore, to interpret liturgical rites "in performance" must exercise caution lest it allow hierophany to usurp the due place of kerygma: Is it insignificant that the anaphora of the Divine Liturgy of St. John Chrysostom identifies its eucharistic action as *logikē latreia*, "rational worship"?[93]

In sum, it is not a matter of "either/or," but "both/and," in regard to the roles of text and performance in the interpretation of liturgy. Since the potential performances of a given rite are infinite, there will always be room for an analysis directed toward the specificity of a given instantiation of the tradition. This analysis, however, needs must be inscribed; ethnography, in other words, brings one full circle back to the imperative of hermeneutics. As Kelleher indicates, the collection of empirical data still leaves the ethnographer with the outstanding challenge of assuming "the role of mediator between the world of the liturgical assembly and that of the academy in an attempt to interpret the performance of the former to the latter." More acutely, as she later acknowledges, the ethnographer must confront the reality that "interpretation itself is a performance which includes among its central tasks self-appropriation on the part of the interpreter."[94]

Nicholas Lash concurs, arguing that *all* interpretation is performative, although the form of the performance depends on the kind of text interpreted. "The fundamental form of the Christian interpretation of scripture is the life, activity and organization of the believing community." He continues, "The poles of Christian interpretation are not, in the last analysis, written texts . . . but patterns of human action: what was said and done and suffered, then, by Jesus and his disciples, and what is said and done and suffered, now, by those who seek to share his obedience and his hope."[95] If all of Christian existence is in some sense a "performance" of the Gospel, an enacting of the text that solicits a corresponding labor of interpretation (providing the raison d'être for the various disciplines of theology), it does not thereby preclude attention to the biblical text qua text. Moral theology, for instance, involves attention not only to actual human behavior—to the performance of this or that discrete act—but to the moral "world" proposed by its textual resources. In a similar vein I would submit that the methodology of ritual studies, its fecundity notwithstanding, does not obviate a hermeneutical inquiry into the meaning of liturgy as given in its texts. And for this inquiry, there would appear to be no better contemporary guide than Paul Ricoeur.

The Topography of a Ricoeurian Itinerary

Bridget Nichols legitimately proclaims that "liturgical hermeneutics is responsible not only for finding an adequate way of approaching this unique form of discourse, but also for seeking an ever more precise means of discussing liturgical faith."[96] But this precision can surely only be achieved piecemeal by a response to specific questions. As Kelleher argues in a later article, method develops in tandem with the quest to explain that which is as yet unexplained. It is the nature of the object under investigation that contours the method to be used in any given exercise. She proposes that there are at least three areas that require attention in any sound liturgical theology, for "in accord with the social, symbolic and processual nature of liturgy, a particular method constructed for the purpose of objectifying the public horizon that is mediated in liturgical praxis will have to include questions about the assembly or ritual subject, the ritual symbols and the ritual process."[97] Although she expressly presents these criteria in terms of an ethnographic methodology more in keeping with the quantitative research of ritual studies than with the qualitative interrogations of hermeneutics, I think they prove useful in both spheres. Language and subjectivity are certainly twin concerns of Ricoeur, which come together in his considerations of the narrative operation—of which the ritual process is arguably a species. Hence our Ricoeurian itinerary will attend to an exploration of his work in these three interrelated areas, before concluding with an application to the *GBW*.

What will prove to be the unifying theme in our investigation? Philosopher David Kaplan explains that while Ricoeur's diffuse output is not easily categorized—such that even Ricoeur himself found it challenging to do so—there is nevertheless a "guiding thread" through the labyrinth: the notion of "the capable human being" (*l'homme capable*). In an eloquent passage worth quoting despite its inordinate length, Kaplan offers a remarkable summation of the Ricoeurian corpus, under the sign of *homo capax*:

> Unraveling the interrelated threads of the concept of capability has taken Ricoeur a lifetime. It is not difficult to see why; the concept of capability implies a web of related phenomena. It implies a notion of the will as embodied, free, and receptive. It implies an existential and material relation to the world, what Ricoeur once characterized as "the fault" (*la faute*). It implies a relation to language through which we relate to the world, initially described in terms of symbols, then texts, then narratives, then translation as successive models of the linguistic mediation of experience. Capability implies a relation to the unconscious and other structured systems, above all language and

systematically distorted communication. It implies a relation to the imagination that figures into action and language at the most fundamental condition of possible speech and action. It implies a relation to creative realms "as if" they could exist, including the realism of literature, poetry, and the divine. Capability implies a relation to the other with whom we live and without whom we would be unable even to understand ourselves. It implies moral relationships with others to whom we are accountable. Capability implies the imputatibility of actions undertaken and endured, as well as the quest for recognition of ourselves, other selves, and multiple forms of alterity. It implies a relation to memory, to history, and to forgetting, the interrelated concepts that attest equally to our human capacities as to our human vulnerabilities.[98]

In line with these implications, it is the question of how to construe the liturgical faculty of *l'homme capable*—how to discern in such a one the form of Schmemann's *homo adorans*—that will impel our reading and reflection upon Ricoeur. Conversely put, it is the question of how liturgy, as an instantiation of Ricoeur's axiom that "the symbol gives rise to thought," manifests *homo capax* as specifically *homo capax Dei* (the human person capable of God).

By following this line of inquiry, we implicitly acknowledge the famous query of Roman Catholic liturgist Romano Guardini, so instrumental in the twentieth-century Liturgical Movement: "Would it not be better to admit that man in this industrial and scientific age, with its new sociological structure, is no longer capable of a liturgical act?" Guardini's eminently pastoral concern revolves around a perception that radical changes in the twentieth century have compromised the intelligibility and viability of traditional forms of worship, eviscerating their meaningfulness for his contemporaries.[99] A strikingly similar question also animates Ricoeur's brief but poignant postface to *Taizé et l'Église de demain*.[100] Echoing the language of the former, Ricoeur asks whether the liturgy of Taizé, based as it is on the classical liturgical traditions of the Church, is not destined to suffer obsolescence together with them—cast aside as unnecessary in an industrial age; whether their rootedness in the agrarian and pastoral symbols of a bygone era does not necessitate their becoming a museum piece, a specimen of cultural exoticism deprived of relevance to the contemporary world.

Taking up his own admittedly grave challenge he ventures that liturgical symbolism, in its function as memorial, combats the forgetfulness of a technological generation expending itself in a utilitarian mode of being. Liturgy, that is, as also poetry (which it naturally embraces), offers a means to resist the loss of memory. Ricoeur thus invites "(post)modern man" to conclude a new "pact" between technology and poetry, to embrace progress but be founded poetically in the "archaic." He adds that in Christian liturgy the archaic is explicitly oriented to the eschatological: The gathering of the community through the symbolic tends toward its very sending forth unto effective action in the world. And he concludes by insisting that the liturgical symbol fulfills a role analogous to hermeneutics itself by enacting on the level of representation the theoretical passage navigated by the former, from a first to a second naïveté.[101]

Most intriguing, however, is Ricoeur's appreciation of the paradoxical role of liturgy in the (de)constitution of the self:

> I am grateful to the liturgy for delivering me out of my subjectivity, for offering me, not my words or gestures, but those of the community. I am happy with this objectification of my emotions; in entering into the ritual idiom, I am delivered from emotional effusion; I enter into a form that in turn forms me; by taking up in my own way the liturgical text I become text myself, in prayer and song. Indeed, by the liturgy, I am fundamentally divested of preoccupation with myself. . . . Behold the salutary disorientation that resituates the "I" amidst community, the individual amidst history and the human person amidst creation.[102]

For Ricoeur, liturgy thus opens a vista within which we can descry the salient features of *homo capax*. What remains in the following chapters is to explicate how. The next two chapters address the nature of ritual symbolism, especially the naming of God in liturgical language and the role of metaphor. Chapters 5 and 6 take up the questions of liturgical subjectivity and the problems attending to different kinds of truth claims, while penultimate chapter investigates the mnemonic operations deployed within the ritual process.

CHAPTER

3

MEANING IN/AND METAPHOR

Overview

The focus of this chapter and the next is the functioning of religious language and the role played therein by metaphor. The task is to consider the properties by which metaphor undertakes the "redescription of reality" with which Ricoeur credits it. To navigate this major current in his thought, we will proceed in three stages. In this chapter, we introduce the "linguistic turn" and then follow the course of Ricoeur's exegetical works to gain an appreciation of how his general theory of metaphoricity relates specifically to religious discourse: that is, the way in which the scriptural naming of God functions in a manner analogous to that of the metaphor. In Chapter 4, we next consider prominent attempts both at validating and discrediting Ricoeur's theory, in terms of their pertinence to liturgical theology.

In the conclusion of Chapter 4, I propose by way of synthesis that the metaphorical dialectic inhering between apophatic and kataphatic discourse—only marginally developed by Ricoeur—lies at the heart of Byzantine liturgical speech. This renders the idiom a "mixed" genre between the primary, pretheoretical discourse in which Ricoeur places biblical texts and the secondary, derivative genre to which he assigns theology as such. I argue that this idiom is also mixed because it incorporates a further dialectic beyond that of primary and secondary discourse—namely, that which obtains between the naming of God in the formulae of the liturgical text itself, and the recognition of him in the extralinguistic, sacramental phenomena to which the formulae advert. This triple line of inquiry will ultimately serve to orient our analysis of the unique way in which the *GBW* seeks to name (our experience of) God.

The Linguistic Turn

Our project of harnessing the work of Ricoeur in the service of liturgical theology needs to be situated in the context of a much broader intellectual trend: namely, the appropriation within philosophy and theology of what has been called the "linguistic turn." It has been suggested that this movement is as revolutionary as the "turn to the subject" initiated by Descartes and consolidated by Kant: By bringing into relief the primacy of language in the constitution of knowledge, it challenges the received view of it as a secondary, expressive phenomenon.[1] Thus, according to Roman Catholic theologian Michael Scanlon, "The most important lesson to be learned by the linguistic turn . . . [is] that language is primarily a vocal actualization of the tendency to see reality symbolically." The symbolic vision effected by language is taken here to be the "key to the specifically human," thus retrieving Aristotle's classic conception of the human person as a "speaking animal" (*to zoon logon echōn*).[2]

Presaging the seminal insight of contemporary liturgical theologians such as David Fagerberg regarding the distinction between *theologia prima* and *theologia secunda* (as discussed in the introduction), Scanlon asserts that the linguistic turn has brought into relief the difference between originary religious discourse and derivative theological discourse: "Narrative (with symbol and myth as its building blocks) is the primary language of religion and faith. The 'speech acts' of religion are worship, liturgy, and ritual, and here the speech is that of symbol and story. Theological discourse is secondary."[3] In sum, the distinction is between the language *of* faith and the language *about* it.

Since religious discourse as such emerges preeminently in liturgical action, it brings to light the essential intersubjectivity of language as well as its performativity—both salient concerns in contemporary philosophy. Scanlon notes in this respect that Aristotle already grasped the social dimension of language and the political implications of defining the human person as a "speaking animal"; therefore, the linguistic turn also entails a rehabilitation of the Aristotelian notion of *phronēsis*, "that practical knowledge that liberates people for responsible living in community." As we shall see, this category also plays a prominent role in Ricoeur's own thought. Scanlon concludes that all theology is bound henceforth to be both hermeneutical and praxiological: "It is difficult to overstate the import for theology of the contemporary linguistic turn. It is in no way a continuing chapter of the modern 'turn to the subject.' It is, rather, a 'horizon shift' of seminal significance for the future of theology. As a horizon shift, the linguistic turn is fundamentally sublative of previous antinomies, such as that between theory and praxis."[4]

While a Ricoeurian analysis of the intersubjectivity and performativity of liturgical language will occupy us subsequently, the present chapter delves into the attributes of liturgical speech in its role (in Scanlon's terms) as "symbol and story." In doing so, we take up one of the tasks that Zimmerman's methodology consciously "brackets": to "capitalize on the richness of the text's metaphoric prayer language."[5] Ricoeur views metaphor as exemplifying the fundamental creativity of language and serving as a bridge between symbol and narrative. Not only was an early monograph consecrated to the study of metaphor, but he has continually returned to the enigma of metaphoricity in his later works—such that one can consider it a Ricoeurian topos.[6]

Metaphoricity and Religious Experience

It must be emphasized that to consider the metaphorical aspects of language is decidedly *not* to depart from a practical concern for liturgy as enacted. A Ricoeurian understanding of metaphor substantiates Scanlon's claim that interpretation is essentially praxiological, since what is at stake is an imaginative construal of human action that results in such action's effective redeployment. Zimmerman likewise observes that of the three general methodologies adopted by contemporary approaches to language, the one represented by Ricoeur exhibits the greatest concern with the reference of speech.[7] She categorizes the trends within Anglo-American analytic philosophy as well as the work of such linguists as Noam Chomsky as being solely preoccupied with the *sense* of language—i.e., its internal operations as a system. Communications theorists, for their part, go a step further in their focus on linguistic *usage*; in this school she places the later writings of Ludwig Wittgenstein (1889–1951), and his heirs (e.g., J. L. Austin, J. Searle, and R. Jakobson) who in elaborating the notion of "language games" have clarified the modalities of performativity—i.e., the

relationship of language to its users. But it is the third group, broadly termed
"philosophers of language" (e.g., Husserl, Heidegger, and Ricoeur) who in
Zimmerman's estimation truly confront the enigma posed by language.
Such thinkers "are not content to say simply that language expresses human
experience. Rather, they wish to uncover the determinate relationship
between language and human experience and its ontological significance.
They seek to explain how language discloses being in new ways. For them,
language not only expresses human experience, but in fact constitutes a
creative redescription of reality."[8]

Ricoeur's own views on this matter are well articulated near the end of
Oneself as Another where, pondering the ontology connoted by linguistic
analysis, he issues a note of caution:

> Paradoxically, the linguistic turn, despite the referential twist of phil-
> osophical semantics, has often signified a refusal to "go outside" of
> language and a mistrust equal to that of French structuralism with
> respect to any extralinguistic order. It is even important to empha-
> size that the implicit axiom that "everything is language" has often
> led to a closed semanticism, incapable of accounting for human ac-
> tion as actually happening in the world, as though linguistic analy-
> sis condemned us to jumping from one language game to another,
> without thought ever being able to meet up with actual action.[9]

He proceeds to reiterate his commitment to the "ontological vehemence"
of all language, even those uses that *appear* nonreferential—for example,
metaphor and narrative fiction. Such uses display how meaning transpires
not so much in a realm of antecedent experience subsequently recalled by
language, but rather in the very interpretation of experience afforded by
ordinary languages; hermeneutics is in consequence an existential act. Zimmerman summarizes the outlook of Ricoeur, among others: "Interpretation of discourse is a process whereby meaning emerges as new possibilities
to be lived, with and through its potential redescription of reality. This process delivers an extralinguistic import that effects an ontological claim on
language-use and its relationship to human experience."[10]

From Text to Action

With this discussion we rejoin the debate addressed above concerning the
role of performance in liturgical hermeneutics. While it is clear that lit-

urgy as realized ritually manifests its "ontological vehemence" most efficaciously, it is surely the case that empirical study of actual celebrations cannot
exhaust the surplus of meaning borne by a liturgical text.[11] To adduce a
musical analogy: The study of a symphony can proceed deductively, through
attendance at performances or at least analysis of recordings of them. Yet
it may also inductively, through attention to the orchestral score itself; such
attention is neither devoid of awareness of the score's performative destiny
nor circumscribed by such concerts as have already taken place, but oriented toward discovering new dimensions of the musical "world" proposed
by the score.

In point of fact, Ricoeur adduces this very analogy on multiple occasions when discussing the way in which the text, distanciated from its
original context by the sheer fact of inscription, awaits performative reactivation on the part of the reader(s). Thus in "Naming God" he can de-
clare, "Writing, in its turn, is restored to living speech by means of the
various acts of discourse that reactualize the text. Reading and preaching
are such actualizations of writing into speech. A text, in this regard, is like
a musical score that requires execution."[12] And in *Interpretation Theory* he
elaborates thus:

> With writing, the verbal meaning of the text no longer coincides with
> the mental meaning of intention of the text. This intention is both
> fulfilled and abolished by the text, which is no longer the voice of
> someone present. The text is mute. An asymmetric relation obtains
> between text and reader, in which only one of the partners speaks
> for the two. The text is like a musical score and the reader like the
> orchestra conductor who obeys the instructions of the notation. Con-
> sequently, to understand is not merely to repeat the speech event in
> a similar event, it is to generate a new event beginning from the text
> in which the initial event has been objectified.[13]

To treat the phenomenon of metaphoricity in liturgical language, therefore, is to elucidate the process by which a "new event" is generated in a
given reading/performance, since the power of metaphor for innovation (in
which act the interpreter plays no small part) is what allows interpretation
to eschew mere repetition. While it is also certainly worthwhile to study
and transcribe instances of the text's reactivation (i.e., actual liturgical celebrations), such instances perforce refer back to the textual mediation
through which they are recognized to belong to a given tradition.

As we suggested above, it may well be that this feature of textuality (ubiquitous in liturgy due to the particular "scripturality" of Christianity) is what distinguishes it in principle from the phenomena conventionally considered in the field of ritual studies: Two celebrated examples would be the seminal treatment of the Balinese cockfight by anthropologist Clifford Geertz and the various case studies collected by Ronald Grimes in his well-known *Ritual Criticism*.[14] Where ritual studies stresses the primacy of ritual over myth/narrative and rightfully draws attention to the absence of linguistic mediation—written, if not oral—in given instances, liturgical theology must situate itself within a ritual matrix grounded in a tradition of inscription. Hence Ricoeur's declaration concerning the centrality of the Bible to Christian faith is also apposite to a hermeneutics of liturgy:

> What is presupposed is that faith, inasmuch as it is lived experience, is instructed—in the sense of being formed, clarified, and educated— within the network of texts that in each instance preaching brings back to living speech. This presupposition of the textuality of faith distinguishes biblical faith ("Bible" meaning book) from all others. In one sense, therefore, texts do precede life. I can name God in my faith because the texts preached to me have already named God.[15]

One might arguably even stretch Ricoeur's contention to affirm the *primacy* of the liturgical text over its celebration; if in the first instance the liturgy was orally transmitted, existent only as "living speech," its sedimentation through inscription has resulted in its becoming a similar "network" that actual celebration now restores to life. Liturgical texts in this sense do precede (liturgical) life; whatever the interplay between the descriptive and the prescriptive functions at their point of origin, the game is surely determined by the latter for those who live a tradition in the wake of its inscription. That is to say, the textuality of the liturgy, to the extent that it begs the question of its own status, ineluctably demands the labor of interpretation.[16]

A parallel may thus be drawn between Ricoeur's insistence on maintaining the dialectic between a reification of the text and a reification of spoken discourse: Accordingly, we may suggest that a study of liturgical performance needs to be held in tension with a hermeneutics of the liturgical script. Ricoeur helpfully observes that if it be true, as in Plato's *Phaedrus*, that something is lost when oral communication is committed to writing—that which "belongs to the voice, the facial expression, and the common situation of interlocutors in a face-to-face setting"—it is also true that the reconversion of writing into speech, while legitimately aspiring to a dialogical situation of communication, cannot pretend to identify the postscriptural experience with the prescriptural one, since the "scriptuary" step introduces an irreducible moment of mediation.[17]

"Naming God"

The intersection between the work of metaphor and that of religious discourse can be readily attained via the seventh and eighth of Ricoeur's Gifford Lectures, which were not published alongside the others in *Oneself as Another* due to their explicitly religious orientation.[18] These latter lectures will also prove germane to the effort undertaken in Chapter 5 to apply Ricoeur's philosophy of the self to liturgical subjectivity, given that they illustrate his novel treatment of selfhood in relation to the Bible. But since these hearken back to Ricoeur's earlier exegetical explorations of the way in which Scripture "names God," it is to the latter that we first must turn.

Ricoeur begins a principal exegetical essay, "Naming God," with an apologia: "Shall I tolerate the fact that thinking, which aims at what is universal and necessary, is linked in a contingent way to individual events and particular texts that report them? Yes, I shall assume this contingency, so scandalous for thinking, as one aspect of the presupposition attached to listening."[19] In other words, it does not suffice to treat the operations of language in abstract categories: An engagement with specific examples is required. Ricoeur sees the language of Scripture as a field ripe for the harvest of hermeneutical insights, as it were, wagering that laboring therein will furnish a richer theoretical comprehension than otherwise attainable. Faith as such is not accessible to hermeneutics: It represents both the opaque origin and the blurry limit of interpretation. Yet the linguistic mediations of faith *are* accessible, and it is in their confines that Ricoeur intends to carry out his investigation.

This investigation is impelled by the question of how best to categorize religious discourse as such. Ricoeur will "assume provisionally the assimilation of biblical [i.e., religious] texts to poetic texts" even as he distinguishes the poetic from other discourses (including "ordinary" quotidian discourse as well as scientific, historical and sociological forms). Anticipating criticism concerning the lack or unreality of *reference* in poetic discourse, he advances that such discourse does not celebrate only itself—despite appearances that, in the absence of an empirical correlate, it is "without any bearing on true knowledge of the world."[20] Conceding the criticism at first in order to then beg the question, Ricoeur contends as follows, in a passage worth quoting at length:

> In this sense, it is true that poetry is a suspension of the descriptive function. It does not add to our knowledge of objects. But this suspension is the wholly negative condition for the liberation of a more originary referential function, which may be called second-order only because discourse that has a descriptive function has usurped the first rank in daily life, assisted, in this respect, by science. Poetic discourse is also about the world, but not about the manipulable objects of our everyday environment. It refers to our many ways of belonging to the world before we oppose ourselves to things understood as "objects" that stand before a "subject." If we have become blind to these modalities of rootedness and belonging-to (*appartenance*) that precede the relation of a subject to objects, it is because we have, in an uncritical way, ratified a certain concept of truth, defined by adequation to real objects and submitted to a criterion of empirical verification and falsification. Poetic discourse precisely calls into question these uncritical concepts of adequation and verification. In so doing, it calls into question the reduction of the referential function to descriptive discourse and opens the field of a nondescriptive reference to the world.[21]

Of course, the claim that the descriptive function is most appropriately equated with scientific discourse has been contested in several quarters. It is important to grant the point, however, for the sake of argument; if anything, Ricoeur entrusts too *little* to poetic discourse rather than too much.[22]

If religious discourse is to be initially broached as a species of poetic discourse, as a form of language whose truth is to be termed "manifestation" rather than "adequation," what differentiates it from other such species? According to Ricoeur, it is the "naming of God" that "specifies the religious at the interior of the poetic."[23] (A later essay, "Philosophical Hermeneutics and Biblical Hermeneutics," will recapitulate his treatment of the problem: Despite the initial strategy to classify religious discourse as a species of *poetic* discourse, the ontological vehemence attaching to the naming of God causes an unexpected reversal, such as to afford religious discourse the prerogative of serving as the first principle or organon of all interpretation.)[24] Significantly, religious discourse is not to be confused with *theology*, whose recourse to speculative philosophical concepts disbars it from claiming the title "originary" after the manner of Scripture itself.[25] To listen to originary discourse is to bracket the "ontotheological" amalgamation of God and Being to which the theological tradition has historically borne witness—if not to disparage ontotheology as a valid project in its own right.

Here it bears mentioning that although Ricoeur sympathizes with the disdain felt by many modern theologians toward ontotheology, we see in his later work a steadfast refusal to condemn the intellectual labor that has struggled from the translation of the Septuagint onward to mediate between the Hellenic and Hebraic worlds of thought.[26] Indeed, he is uncertain that it would even have been possible to avoid this labor, given the exigencies of translation: "There is no innocent translation; I mean one that could escape the history of reception of our text, a history that itself is immediately a history of interpretation. To translate is already to interpret."[27] And he finds evidence up to the high Middle Ages of circumspect minds who maintained a dialectical approach to the ontotheological question, preserving in the midst of their analogical postulates the relativizing critique of the apophatic tradition. Hence he can admire the efforts of Aquinas and other Scholastics, even if he considers that another "event in thinking"— in which the ontotheological tradition will have to be unthought, as it were—may rightly be demanded by our contemporaries:

> [The Scholastics] held that Being could be spoken of in affirmative statements, at the horizon of an elevation to the highest point of the most sublime titles and attributes encountered along the road of not just rational speculation but also spiritual purification. These two ways, the apophatic and the analogical, mutually presupposed each other insofar as, on the one hand, what one negates is always something that one represents to oneself, even when it is a question of about the most sublime attributes of God, and, on the other hand, the elevation to the highest point of these titles and attributes by the way of eminence is equivalent to negating what we ordinarily affirm concerning such attributes.[28]

As we discover, this commendation of the dialectic of the kataphatic and apophatic favors the peculiarity of the "naming of God" as it characteristically occurs in Byzantine liturgy.

The "Polyphonicity" of Scripture

Ricoeur's concern with distinguishing theological discourse from the originary religious discourse displayed in the biblical texts does not derive
from a principled objection to the discipline of theology as such, to which
on several occasions he cedes due rights and responsibilities. Rather it expresses his sense that the self put in the position of "listener" must be di-
vested of the systematic integration to which theology is inclined (if not
necessarily bound), in order to confront the real dissonances articulated
by Scripture's "naming God."[29] For Ricoeur judges it an often overlooked
but immensely important fact that the forms of divine description are not
simple but multiple; discrete biblical genres name God in different ways
with the result that each genre produces a particular style of the confession of faith.

Ricoeur calls this phenomenon the "polyphonicity" of Scripture, and
he defends it against any attempt to reduce the music, as it were, to a monophony. Several "voices" emerge in his analysis—narrative is preponderant, with a naming of God in the third person as the primary agent of
history; prophecy speaks instead in the first person, doubling the ego of
the prophet with that of the divine "I"; hymns and laments address God
as the dialogue partner of prayer; Wisdom literature in turn also speaks of
God in the third person, but chiefly the inaugurator of an impersonal cosmic order rather than as one who interrupts the ordinary course of affairs
to intervene on behalf of his people:

> Thus God is named in diverse ways in narration that recounts the
> divine acts, prophecy that speaks in the divine name, prescription
> that designates God as the source of the imperative, wisdom that
> seeks God as the meaning of meaning, and the hymn that invokes
> God in the second person. . . . The word "God" . . . presupposes the
> entire context of narratives, prophecies, laws, wisdom writings,
> psalms, and so on. The referent "God" is thus intended by the con-
> vergence of all these partial discourses. It expresses the circulation of
> meaning among all the forms of discourse wherein God is named.[30]

In this perspective, the unity of Scripture appears as fundamentally canonical, in the sense that the disparate books are prima facie only coordinated in their variegation by having a recurring divine referent. At the risk
of sounding tautological, this means that although God is named differ-

ently by the biblical genres, it is nevertheless *God* who is named. Ricoeur deems it essential that the discrete means of naming God be brought into a "living dialectic" that will display their "interferences" with each other.[31] The provocation that ensues exemplifies the alterity of God himself, who cannot be circumscribed by any one mode of discourse but constantly escapes coherent determination.[32] Hence Ricoeur cites the contrast between the Old Testament narratives that found the identity of the people of Israel and the prophecies that jeopardize that very identity by proclaiming it vulnerable to the wrathful judgment of the "Day of the Lord": What is secured by one genre is menaced by another.

The scrambling that results from the juxtaposition of biblical genres inhibits the reader from forming a clear picture of who God is, and hence from being able to mat and frame such a picture; what is displayed therefore is a kind of definitive indefiniteness. As the referent of the different discourses of Scripture, God is also "the index of their incompleteness": the figure that escapes them all.[33] In consequence "God" becomes what Ricoeur terms a "limit-expression"—i.e., an expression that cannot be fully *thought* specifically because it dwells at the frontier of thinking. Limit-expressions simultaneously attract and resist the work of interpretation, revealing and concealing in dialectical fashion. Thus the naming of God inhibits a reification of the idea of God. Inasmuch as he gives himself he also withdraws, being at one and the same time *Deus revelatus* and *Deus absconditus*—the "revealed God" who is yet "hidden."

In this respect, the revelation of the Divine Name in Ex. 3:14 is seen by Ricoeur as quintessential. The pericope brings the paradoxical unnameability of God into focus in its very disclosure of a name that is, ultimately, not really a name. Rather than accomplishing an ontotheological "capping off" of other narratives, this passage is seen to refer the Name back to the narratives of the patriarchs—"He-Who-Is" is "the God of Abraham, Isaac and Jacob"—such that the *speculative* is subsumed by the *historical*. For its part, the New Testament offers an analogous "recession into infinity of the referent 'God,'"[34] in its naming of God under the ciphers of "the Kingdom of heaven" and "the Kingdom of God." This kingdom can only be signified by "parables, proverbs and paradoxes" whose cumulative connotations, according to Ricoeur, are as puzzling as the panoply of images of the divine in the Old Testament.

The metaphoricity of Jesus's parables also parallels the previous dialectic (i.e., that of Ex. 3:14), since it likewise displays both affirmation and negation: To the extent that "the Kingdom" is *like* that which is recounted in the parables, there is revelation; to the extent that it is only like unto it rather than being *identical*, a veil is drawn. As Ricoeur explains:

> Paradoxes and hyperboles dissuade hearers in some way from forming a coherent project of their lives and from making their existence into a continuous whole. . . . In the same way that the proverb (submitted to the law of paradox and hyperbole) only reorients by first disorienting, the parable (submitted to what I call the law of extravagance) makes the extraordinary break forth in the ordinary.[35]

By "law of extravagance" Ricoeur intends the element of the implausible in parables that confounds a facile interpretation of them; the tension between the implausibility of their plots and the everyday realism of their details compels the hearers to acknowledge the "Wholly Other":

> If the case of the parable is exemplary, it is because it combines a narrative structure, a metaphorical process, and a limit-expression. In this way, it constitutes a short summary of the naming of God. Through its narrative structure, it recalls the original rootedness of the language of faith in narratives. Through its metaphorical process, it makes manifest the poetic character of the language of faith as a whole. And finally, in joining metaphor and limit-expression, it furnishes the matrix for theological language inasmuch as this language conjoins analogy and negation in the way of eminence: "God is like . . . , God is not . . ."[36]

Now Ricoeur anticipates the Christological concern of those who might, on the one hand, be persuaded by his analysis of the Gospel genres but also, on the other, feel apprehension at its apparent displacement of the character of Jesus. Yet he refuses to assuage this concern by any move that will simply substitute, in Monophysite fashion, the naming of Christ for the naming of God.[37] Christ himself names God by praying to him as well as speaking about his kingdom, thereby complexifying the various namings of the Old Testament. But Christ is also associated with God in a unique way so as to place further pressure on the fragile consensus of those namings; the conflict is intensified to the degree that the limit-expression "God" is impelled to accept an equivalence with the Christ-figure. Ricoeur admits that it is equally difficult to write Christology from above and from below: Any effort must balance "under the form of the most extreme ten-

sion and conflict—God's determining the existence of Jesus and the naming of God by all the biblical texts."[38]

Our review of Ricoeur's exegetical work on the naming of God concludes with his momentous reversal (mentioned above) in the categoriza-
tion of religious discourse. We have seen that at a certain level he insists it
to be a species of poetic discourse, manifesting the characteristic traits of
such: a break with ordinary discourse because of the primacy of metaphor,
for example, and the opening up of a new world "constituted in the crucible of semantic innovation" that serves to inspire biblical readers, through
a new self-understanding, to become the sort of persons capable of inhab-
iting this world. Nevertheless, religious language transcends the poetic precisely because the naming of God is sui generis: It aims to refigure the
world by deploying a phalanx of *ultimate* concerns.[39]

Ricoeur submits an original account of how Scripture capitalizes on this
potential, arguing that biblical genres are established not at the level of concepts but rather that of the Kantian "schema": That is, they provide "models" for the Divine Name, "rules for producing figures of the divine" that
are not in fact principally figures of the divine itself, but rather figures of
God's presence in the midst of his people.[40] The import of this distinction
is that the biblical models are the source of the meaning of the name "God,"
long before ratiocination brings to the table ideas of a First Cause, for example, or Unmoved Mover. Hence Ricoeur can contend that the naming
of God in Scripture subverts any dominance philosophy might aspire to
exercise:

> The word "God" does not function as a philosophical concept,
> whether this be being either in the medieval or in the Heideggerian
> sense of being. Even if one is tempted to say—in the theological meta-
> language of all these pretheological languages—that "God" is the
> religious name for being, still the word "God" says more: it presup-
> poses the total context constituted by the whole space of gravitation
> of stories, prophecies, laws, hymns and so forth. To understand the
> word "God" is to follow the direction of the meaning of the word . . .
> its double power to gather all the significations that issue from the
> partial discourses and to open up a horizon that escapes from the clo-
> sure of discourse.[41]

In "opening up a horizon" beyond that of the Scripture itself, the naming of God exerts a corresponding force upon the reader, compelled as he

or she is to countenance a response to the enigma presented in the figures set forth.

Now such a thesis might well heighten the urgency of applying speculative thought to the biblical word. Ricoeur asserts that the scriptural figures of the divine naturally tend toward idolatry, due to their vivid anthropomorphisms; to function as models, therefore, they need to be set in a dialectical relationship with the ineffability represented by the Divine Name disclosed in Ex. 3:14. By dint of its incommensurability this name subverts the obvious meaning of the models, compelling the reader to "think more." Building on the thought of Ian T. Ramsey, Ricoeur also develops the category of limit-expressions—which he has already employed to designate the peculiar features of certain scriptural genres, e.g., the paradox and hyperbole in the Gospel parables—by recognizing the intervention of "qualifiers" that serve to complement and correct the models.[42]

Dan Stiver explains the partnership between models and qualifiers as conceived by Ramsey: "The application to religious language is that 'heavenly father' or 'kingdom of heaven' represent models that are given their metaphorical and disclosive impetus by a 'qualifier' from an 'odd' or very different realm. When we begin with 'father' and add 'heavenly,' we are alerted to the fact that language is being used in an unusual way and that a kind of reality is referred to that is likewise unusual."[43] While Ramsey's philosophy of models and qualifiers is similar to that of the apophatic tradition, the latter tends to emphasize, according to Stiver, the noncognitive but rather evocative character of religious language, whereas the former claims that a real, if oblique, disclosure obtains in and through it. For Ricoeur, models and qualifiers together expose the "mutation" of the poetic in the religious. The qualifiers, in the form of limit-expressions, intensify the naming of God and give rise to the negative way "at a higher degree of conceptuality" and also, to unpredictable applications in the realm of praxis.[44]

The One in the Many: Polyphonicity in Liturgical Discourse

We have seen in the treatment of "Naming God" above that Ricoeur places paramount value on recognizing the variety of forms of scriptural discourse, as so many ways of naming God. This variety in turn mirrors a range of possible applications in the world toward which the responding self may be directed. One such response, speculative thought, is brought to the limit in its encounter with the anthropomorphic appellations of the Bible. This situation is managed at one level by Scripture's own adducing of qualifying expressions into the naming of God; their cumulative effect is to further accentuate the elusiveness of "God." The later theological dialectic of the apophatic and kataphatic explicitly thematizes the very insufficiency of language with respect to the divine, a fact already implicit in the plurality of namings presented by the different biblical genres—a plurality Ricoeur names "polyphonicity." But how does all this concern liturgy?

Consider that Ricoeur vacillates between acknowledging what we might call the "specificity of liturgical language" (displayed in the appreciation of Taizé with which we concluded our introduction), while belying it by surprisingly minimalistic statements such as the following, made in the course of a 1994 interview: "I do not use liturgy at all in the sense of ritual but in the sense of the ritualization of the order of [biblical] reading."[45] Although positing a dialectic between the "cyclical time of reading" the Bible provided by the use of a lectionary and its fresh appropriation in preaching, Ricoeur appears to overlook the possibility that *other* texts used liturgically might affect this dialectic, or again that they might figure prominently in their own right within the ritual context: the possibility, in other words, that both liturgical and biblical genres might collaborate in producing a polyphonicity proper to the corporate doxological context. One might expect of Ricoeur, if not an appreciation of Byzantine hymnography, at least a due consideration of how Protestant hymns function with respect to the appropriation of Scripture.[46]

By contrast, Ricoeur does recognize such a link in his 1998 interpretation of the reception history of the Song of Songs. There he emphasizes the role of (re)use in regard to the surplus of meaning of a Biblical text: The citation of a given text in a new context, and especially its appropriation in liturgy, hymnody, and preaching, causes a new meaning to be born from the tryst of erstwhile strangers. Hence, "The restatement of the cited text in another situation for speaking produces a displacement, a transference . . . [which] stems from another epistemological category than the search for the true meaning, than an explication and the search for an adequation between this explication and the features that convey the obvious sense. We have to speak instead of a 'use' of the text or, if one prefers, of a re-use."[47] What ought to garner our attention here is Ricoeur's prescinding from the putatively original or authentic import of the text; he remains equally opposed to those who would reduce the Song of Songs to literal

erotica and to those who insist upon its allegorization, advocating rather
on behalf of the potential for the text to engender new meanings through
juxtaposition. Alluding to the mystagogy of St. Cyril of Jerusalem as well
as that of St. Ambrose, he marvels at how their baptismal mimesis re-
trieves the dramatic structure of the Song by its very transposition into a
new situation.

Importantly, Ricoeur is adamant that liturgical gestures require a verbal complement to be fulfilled:

> The liturgical gesture would remain mute without the aid of words
> from the Song of Songs, reinterpreted by the very gesture that
> seeks and finds its expression in these words. In this way, an ex-
> change is brought about between the rite and the poem. The rite
> opens the space of "sacramental mystery" to the poem, the poem gives
> the rite the rightness of an appropriate word. In this sense, it is not
> first the Song of Songs but rather the rite that one interprets in citing
> the Song of Songs. This latter is thus put in the position of an "in-
> terpretant" before being itself given over to interpretation. What is
> more, it is not just the rite that is interpreted by the words of the
> poem, but the faithful people themselves who recognize themselves
> in the gestures of the rite. Whence the place of exhortation in cate-
> chesis, the faithful being urged to put themselves in the place of the
> beloved so as to be able to speak the words of the Song of Songs.

Continuing his reflections, with respect to the creative role of hymnody
in recontextualizing Scripture, he adds:

> We can thus understand why the explicit or implicit quotations of
> the Song of Songs in hymns also find their final justification in the
> disposition of those who receive the text by quoting it. In truth, it is
> no longer a question of an explicit quotation, but rather of a genuine
> reuse, of a creation of new variations in those sung prayers that make
> up hymns. If we add that the hymn has not ceased to be a place of
> theological production . . . we also will recognize that the hymn is
> one of the privileged places where we can catch sight of the augmen-
> tation of meaning at work in certain forms of the reception of the
> biblical text.[48]

What impresses Ricoeur in both these instances, as in the phenomenon of preaching to which he more customarily refers, is the implication

of the "reader": The process is one in which he or she is addressed (and addresses others) in the second-person, releasing an ontological vehemence otherwise latent in the text.

Ricoeur concludes that given the intertextuality of the biblical canon, contemporary readings ought to feel at ease eclectically juxtaposing one text with another, confident in the new meaning issuing from their mutual reaction.[49] The displacement and transference that liturgy, hymnody, and preaching exemplify are already implicitly operative, after all, in the very combining of sundry texts between the same covers; there cannot but be polyphony we might say, given the presence of so many "voices" on the same stage.[50] What Ricoeur once termed the "ritualization of the order of reading," while certainly an integral aspect of liturgy, does not do justice to the complexity of the "augmentation of meaning" that actually occurs through the interaction of liturgical genres. As with the baptismal use of the Song of Songs, so also other texts—preeminently the Psalms—are in the course of the liturgy both heard as readings and uttered on the lips of worshippers as hymns, a reactivation of the text that in the case of the Psalms corresponds to its original use. Such reuse, moreover, incorporates the "creation of new variations" (the labor of "theological production") inasmuch as biblical texts are not simply rehearsed in toto but intercalated with hymnographic genres, woven into them and/or adopted as the paradigms according to which they are composed. Together with the act of preaching that Ricoeur so often credits with the task of restoring the biblical word to "living speech," hymnography does not simply lend orality to that word but truly speaks it anew.

In fact, in light of Ricoeur's twofold recognition of the role of utterance in liturgical discourse—rather than reading qua reading (although individual reading is performative in its own way)—and its assimilation of nonbiblical texts, we can discern a liturgical polyphonicity in which the genres of Scripture confront those not only of hymnography (troparia, stichera), but also greetings, blessings, exhortations and orations. Furthermore, to extend the musical analogy, this verbal polyphony is complemented by the "counterpoint" issuing from the architectural settings of liturgy as well as its images, objects, gestures, processions, and so forth. The symphony of liturgy thus resounds at both the textual and the aesthetic levels and between them; indeed, one might paraphrase Ricoeur to the effect that it is the orchestration of these levels, conducted according to rubrics, that specifies the liturgical at the interior of the religious.

Liturgy as "Language Event"

David Power, although not mentioned above in the context of those who have made Ricoeur's work the explicit burden of their own, has consistently endeavored to incorporate Ricoeurian insights into his liturgical theology. It is worth perusing his sketch of liturgy as a "language-event," since it will enliven our discussion of a liturgical "polyphonicity."[51] Power's "language-event" refers to the fact that liturgy, while not reducible to language, requires verbal articulation to be meaningful; it constitutes a particular kind of linguistic performance. There are in his estimation two key channels through which the resources of language issue forth within a postmodern theological context. The first he terms the "retrieval of the medieval" funded by "neoplatonic idealism"; although he does not cite examples, Power would appear to be referring to movements such as Radical Orthodoxy, whose valorization of medieval liturgy emerges most notably in Catherine Pickstock's apologia for the *usus antiquior* or Extraordinary Form of the Mass in the Roman Rite.[52]

The second course (to which Power himself adheres) is styled "the opening to the creative power of language." He explains his methodology as follows:

> The perception of sacrament as language-event seems an apt heuristic with which to engage the note of the discontinuous and the disruptive that marks our sensitivity to broken time. It allows us to see God's action in the past and in the present, without having to relate them by an unbroken sequence of events, and without having to look for some causative force outside language usage itself. A ritual or sacramental event relates to an event within time past through the capacities and power of language to carry it forward, and to allow it to enter afresh into lives, however they may have been disrupted and broken. By that same token, the heuristic of language event brings sacramental expression into the realm of the practical. Redescribing reality through remembrance of the Cross, sacrament points to the Christian praxis which goes with such remembrance. On this account, the heuristic of language event could also be called a heuristic of poesis and praxis. It is concerned with the forms and power of language, and at the same time with the paradigms of Christ-like action that are evoked through this language.[53]

Now there are many elements of this approach that resonate with the Ricoeurian hermeneutic of "naming God" adumbrated above. As in the literary approach of Ricoeur, Power wishes to bracket discussion of the primary denotation of liturgical speech and its extralinguistic field of reference—i.e., the chain of historical events to which it ostensibly refers. But he also follows Ricoeur in stressing the ontological vehemence of such speech, its capacity to refigure the lives of those who perform it. Thirdly, he sees language as funding through its mimetic resources a mediation of the experience of time; God can thus be encountered as a character in a plot that also includes us.[54] Further parallels can be also be drawn, particularly in regard to his treatment of sacrament-as-language-event as a "rupture."

Power employs the term *rupture* to describe the process by which the narrative deployed in liturgy comes to be challenged by dynamics from both within and without. There is external rupture resulting from the unbelief of culture at large, its blanket incredulity toward metanarratives, as well as from the existential crises suffered by participants who may well find the story they rehearse in worship to be inadequate to their experience. But is it fair to regard Christianity as a metanarrative after the fashion of the story of scientific progress, as told from the Enlightenment onwards? The author answers in the negative, pointing to the essential pluralism of the Christian story, its inclusion of "a number of related but nonetheless differing narratives." He contends that "looking back to the original Christ event as a language event one notes the plurality already present in the beginning, as well as the ways in which it is interrupted by other language forms that prohibit any excess of coherence and do not allow the system to leave the 'other' outside the pale of the community's story and values."[55] That is to say, the Gospel narrative is precluded from becoming the proprietary preserve of the Christian community in virtue of certain scriptural genres (e.g., the eschatological sayings and parables of Christ), whose subversive implications resist systematization. As Ricoeur also urges in this connection—and also with respect to the tension placed upon the founding narratives of the Old Testament by the weight of its prophetic literature—such texts destabilize the grounds of communal memory by calling the community itself into judgment.[56]

The Reconciliation of Metanarrative and Petits Récits

Power's emphasis on rupture further recalls Ricoeur's account of Scripture as polyphonic. As we have seen, Ricoeur finds in the Bible not a metanarrative but an array of *petits récits* whose mutual interference disrupt any projected coherence. The biblical genres generate friction between themselves and are thus subject to a *dynamic* coherence (effected by the elusive absence-in-presence of the naming of God) rather than to that of a static system[57]—despite the demonstrable network of typological correspondences to be found in Scripture, that "Great Code" most convincingly decrypted (in Ricoeur's estimation) by Northrop Frye.[58]

Interestingly, an early text of Ricoeur forthrightly argues for treating liturgy as the site par excellence where this dynamic coherence is generated, in the wake of the kind of rupture discerned by Power. Discussing the contemporary emergence of narrative theology, Ricoeur explains that while he looks unfavorably upon the notion of *Heilsgeschichte,* given its pretension to "hypostasize" a singular "Christian pattern," he still finds it pertinent as an expression of the way in which the biblical micronarratives invite the reader into a narrative "partnership." The stories of Scripture converge with his or her own circumstances and come to a "stage of reconciliation, when the story is reenacted in the liturgical celebration."[59] Similarly, he adds that if the typological use of biblical stories already distinguishes them from their mundane counterparts, it is through their liturgical use that they most truly come into their own: "The reenactment of the narratives in the cultic situation and their recounting through the psalms of praise, of lamentation, and of penitence complete the complex intertwining between narrative and nonnarrative modes of discourse. The whole range of modes can thus be seen as distributed between the two poles of storytelling and praising."[60]

Ricoeur rounds out his survey of the prospects of a specifically narrative theology, therefore, by suggesting the equiprimordiality of liturgy and narrative together with the sapiential genre; he muses that "narrative never existed without embryonic theological thinking, just as it never existed without its polar counterpart, praise. . . . We may therefore lay the stress either on the discontinuity between pure 'retelling' and theological thinking or on the continuity secured by the mediating sources, from the prescriptive to the hymnic."[61] In sum, he appears to be suggesting that liturgy serves to coordinate the "counterpoint," so to speak, of Scripture's polyphonicity.

Contrarily, Power clearly regards the originary pluralism attested by Ricoeur to be repercussive, impelling a diversity of historical interpretations and liturgical applications.[62] Power takes this as evidence of the general indeterminacy of metaphor understood as an "open sign"; inevitably, the metaphorical terms of the Bible catalyze myriad redescriptions of reality. Here he would seem to be implicitly pointing to the "semantic innovation" that Ricoeur places at the heart of metaphor. Such innovation manifests itself conspicuously (according to Power) in the liturgical context because the polyvalent narrative of Christ—with its concomitant interruptions— is there deployed exponentially. The range of interpretive possibilities are indicated by the actual plurality of extant liturgical traditions whose mutual irreducibility serves as an index of the surplus of meaning in the Christ-event. Citing the example of the commemoration of Christ's Baptism in different Rites, Power states, "In comparing such prayers, one would find both a plurality of prayer forms and a diversified interpretation of the same root metaphor for Christ's death or for the sacramental action, before which claims to meta-narrative would seem feeble."[63] In other words, where Ricoeur with a more facile understanding of liturgy privileges its capacity to *gather* together, Power draws attention to its propensity to *scatter* afresh, as it were, what it gathers.

We see in this connection an echo of the findings of liturgical history as illustrated in the work of the prolific Oriental liturgist Robert Taft. Presenting a defense for the formal recognition granted by the Catholic Church to the ancient Anaphora of Addai and Mari as used by the Assyrian Church of the East—in which the eucharistic *verba Domini* are conspicuously absent—Taft argues that the sacramental mystery of Christ's real presence is not the province of any one of the classical liturgies, much less of their derivative doctrinal systems.[64] Rather, there abides a hypogeal unity between all the ancient Rites, hidden as that may sometimes be by what emerges on the surface:

> I believe one can say there are irreducible local differences in the liturgical expression of what I would take to be the fully reconcilable teaching of both East and West on the Eucharist: that the gifts of bread and wine are sanctified via a prayer, the anaphora, which applies to the present gifts of bread and wine [that] Jesus handed on. How the individual anaphoras express this application has varied widely depending on local tradition, particular history, and the doctrinal concerns of time and place. In my view these differences cannot with any historical legitimacy be seen in dogmatic conflict with parallel but divergent expressions of the same basic realities in a different historico-ecclesial milieu.[65]

According to Taft, therefore, an intractable plurality of forms set forth an originally common (or at least complementary) experience. What remains undetermined here, however, as also in the analysis of Power, is the question of the criterology by which one may presume to arbitrate between a legitimate and illegitimate interpretation of the Christ-event. To what extent, that is, is not all "dogmatic conflict" potentially susceptible of a hermeneutic treatment—one that can frame it in terms of "parallel but divergent expressions of the same basic realities"?

This very point is raised in response to Power's paper, and has been made by numerous students of Ricoeur.[66] It is essentially the question of how the "poetic" cast of a text is related to its "truth" value. Essentially, it is a challenge that brings to light the problem of how best to construe metaphorical truth, whether it is proper to regard it in terms of "adequation," or instead, "manifestation." It is this challenge, then, that we will address in the next chapter.

4

AT THE INTERSECTION OF THE *VIA POSITIVA* AND THE *VIA NEGATIVA*

Overview

In this chapter we extend the preceding discussion of metaphor by focusing on the question of the kind of *truth* communicated in metaphorical utterance. Given the primacy of metaphor in liturgical speech, this question is of particular importance. Dialogue with several interlocutors will set up our concluding consideration of how Byzantine worship characteristically combines kataphatic and apophatic forms of discourse—resulting in a peculiar approach to naming (and experiencing) God.

Truth as "Manifestation"

In exploring the world of a poetic text, Ricoeur's colleague David Tracy suggests that one confronts a "forgotten notion of truth: truth as manifestation." Crediting Heidegger with its rediscovery and Gadamer and Ricoeur with its elaboration, Tracy contends that prior to the formulation of criteria of adequation or "correspondence," the encounter with a "classic" text, artifact, performance, or ritual generates a dialogical interaction between such an object's "power of disclosure and concealment" and the interpreting subject's "experience of recognition."[1] Truth emerges from this interaction as that which is first manifested, and only subsequently justified discursively:

> When interpreters claim to recognize any manifestation, they also implicitly claim a relative adequacy for that interpretation. Others

may or may not agree. At that point argument can enter anew. Arguments are by definition intersubjective and communal. As the demands of argument become explicit, the implicitly intersubjective nature of all truth as manifestation can also become an explicit claim to an argued consensus of warranted beliefs for a particular community of inquiry. Then models of truth as correspondence are acknowledged not as primary but as important, once understood as the consensual truth of warranted beliefs.[2]

I take Tracy to mean that there is an epistemological primacy to the experience of a phenomenon over against its reification, through conceptual abstraction, into a larger frame of reference. This very issue lies at the root of metaphor because (like poetic texts on a larger scale) it has conventionally had its alethic import placed in abeyance. Tracy may be taken as representative of a reaction against the radical cynicism toward figurative language promoted by logical positivism in the early twentieth century, a movement that held that "religious beliefs are not yet in the ballpark of truth and falsity or of being supported by evidence. In other words, they have not achieved the merit of being meaningful, albeit false; they are simply cognitive nonsense."[3]

As Dan Stiver explains, the tide eventually turned against the logical positivism of the so-called Vienna circle because its approach to verification and falsification began to be seen as facile and naïve by its own members. One result was that subsequent intellectual trends would favor metaphor as illustrating how language can mean in ways not strictly susceptible of empirical analysis. Ricoeur's work follows this development: As van den Hengel observes, "Of primary significance to Ricoeur's venture [has been] the growing awareness of the power of language to signify what could not be said, the capacity of language to bring us to the threshold of what cannot be said."[4] Metaphor is of seminal importance expressly because it solicits a manifestation of that which otherwise would remain latent. Poetic discourse unleashes, in Ricoeur's terms, the "power of metaphorical language, which says to us not, 'This is like that,' but 'This is that.' Only through the channel of poetry can one draw close to the kerygmatic language of the Bible, when the latter proclaims, in a metaphoric way: the Lord is my rock, my fortress . . . and so on."[5]

"At the Mercy of Metaphor"

To discuss the irreducibility of metaphor and further corroborate Ricoeur's theory, I would like to introduce a perhaps unexpected conversation partner. Like Ricoeur, C. S. Lewis (1898–1963) was preoccupied with the problem of the power of figurative language, although he treated the problem by recourse to literary criticism, theological apologetics, and fantasy literature rather than through philosophy.[6] In a key essay he distinguishes between objects to which we have nonmetaphorical access, and objects of thought that can only be predicated indirectly—metaphorically.[7] In the latter case, it is *impossible* to avoid the use of metaphor, if not to exchange a richer metaphorical discourse for a poorer. His argument is worth following as it will provide a foil for understanding the "metaphormania" of which Ricoeur is both disciple and master.[8]

Lewis contends that it is essential to distinguish two kinds of metaphor: What he calls "magistral" metaphors are those we employ to explain something that could well be explained otherwise, something that can be accessed independently and hence described in various ways; in contrast, "pupillary" metaphors are those that are necessary for the understanding of what they treat—those that serve as the unique mode of access to their object.[9] Pupillary metaphors involve a new form of seeing, by bringing into focus something hitherto obscure. Magistral ones are created rather for the express purpose of illustrating to another person something already perceived apart from the metaphor itself. This magistral use is possible "only because we have other methods of expressing the same idea. We have already our own way of expressing the thing: We could say it, or we suppose that we could say it, literally instead. This clear conception we owe to other sources—to our previous studies. We can adopt the new metaphor as a temporary tool that we dominate and by which we are not dominated ourselves, only because we have other tools in our box."[10]

The pupillary use of metaphor is activated instead in those instances where we have *no other means* to articulate the thing in question: "For all of us there are things which we cannot fully understand at all, but of which we can get a faint inkling by means of metaphor. And in such cases the relation between the thought and the metaphor is precisely the opposite of the relation that arises when it is we ourselves who understand and then invent the metaphors to help others. We are here entirely at the mercy of the metaphor."[11] Between these two extremes of metaphor (those by which we teach, and those by which we learn) lies the range of types that form ordinary discourse.[12] In discussing Ricoeur's view of metaphor Stiver affords a succinct restatement of Lewis's point:

> Metaphor has long been recognized as a literary device that enables us to depict well-known things in striking and focused ways; in other words, metaphor adorns what we already know in dashing new clothes. Philosophically speaking, what is important about metaphor is that it can do more than embellish; it can direct us to what we have never seen before. The primary reference is negated only to open up reference at another level, "another power of speaking the world." As Ricoeur puts it, metaphor possesses an "ontological vehemence" that leads us to redescribe reality.[13]

Lewis makes a further distinction, moreover, further accentuating the generativity of metaphoricity. He argues that as far as sensible objects go, it is evident that the words we use to refer to them are not determined by their etymology. A term can lose its original, perhaps metaphorical meaning but still be serviceable inasmuch as the object referred to is at hand. In the case of mental objects, however, the matter is more difficult: Since independence from a metaphor can only result from being able to know something otherwise, abstract thought—which depends upon language—is not readily dissociable from its idiom. When such a disassociation appears to occur, it is in effect to (perhaps unconsciously) exchange one metaphor for another, one set of symbols for another.

As a case in point, Lewis cites the metaphorical use of the word "soul": What it refers to, if not natural breath, is an enigma that can only be described by similarly metaphorical expressions. Where there is no literal apprehension we cannot but use metaphors.[14] But metaphor does offer a real, if limited vision of its object, according to Lewis; by keeping multiple metaphors in play, and remembering their metaphoricity, that which lies beyond our ken can yet be glimpsed. Rather than a quixotic quest for univocity, the prudent course is to become aware of the metaphoricity of one's own language and endeavor to create new metaphors—a productive task Lewis assigns the imagination.

As if foreshadowing the commendation of poetic discourse by Ricoeur, Lewis boldly asserts: "It will have escaped no one that in such a scale of writers the poets will take the highest place; and among the poets those who have at once the tenderest care for old words and the surest instinct for the creation of new metaphors."[15] And yet Lewis insists that he carefully distinguishes "truth" from "meaning"—and it is here we rejoin the question broached by Tracy in terms of "adequation" and "manifestation." Lewis insists: "We are not talking of truth, but of meaning: meaning which is the antecedent condition both of truth and falsehood, whose antithesis is not error but nonsense. I am a rationalist. For me, reason is the natural organ of truth: but imagination is the organ of meaning. Imagination, producing new metaphors or revivifying old, is not the cause of truth, but its condition." Nonetheless, he evocatively concludes "that such a view indirectly implies a kind of truth or rightness in the imagination itself."[16]

Truth vs. Meaning

We encounter here an eloquent statement of the problem: There is an inescapable dialectic between truth and meaning, as between adequation and manifestation, since what metaphor manifests through the imagination must still reckon with rational judgment (however this is construed!). Ricoeur in fact engages this very issue in his attempt to both relate and distinguish history and fiction, a topic we will treat in Chapter 7. Here we can simply cite an anecdote to which Ricoeur repeatedly returns in attempting to demonstrate the power-to-manifest of poetic discourse: He recalls that the storytellers of the Spanish island of Majorca traditionally began their tales with the paradoxical caveat "Aixo era y no era"—"it was and it was not."[17] For Ricoeur (like Lewis) insists upon the preeminence of poetic discourse precisely on the grounds that it restores an authentic belonging in the world. Recall Ricoeur's understanding of symbolism: The symbolic use of water, for example, is "bound" to a certain range of primordial meanings derived from the role of water in the cosmos.[18] Lewis similarly appeals to a kind of "psycho-physical parallelism" in the universe, on account of which our original metaphors (viz., symbols)—on the basis of which we make determinations of true and false—are themselves bearers of truth (e.g., "good" is inherently to be equated with "light"). It is because of the power of poetic discourse to manifest truth of some kind that the relation of *that truth* to truth taken as adequation becomes an issue.

In his writings on metaphor Ricoeur arrives at a similar verdict. Discussing the connection between first-order and second-order reference, with the latter (the kind of reference unlocked by metaphor) serving ultimately to ground the former (that which is intended by ordinary or univocal discourse), he elaborates:

> Poetic language is no less about reality than any other use of language. . . . [Metaphorical reference] is called second-order reference only with respect to the primacy of the reference of ordinary language. For, in another respect, it constitutes the primordial reference to the extent that it suggests, reveals, unconceals—or whatever you say—the deep structures of reality to which we are related as mortals who are born into this world and who dwell in it for a while.[19]

And Ricoeurian commentator David Pellauer concurs that the philosopher indeed situates manifestation at the basis of adequation as a function of his understanding of the truth of metaphor:

> Live metaphor suspends our ordinary way of referring to reality in favor of a second-order reference that redescribes reality. But this redescription is itself always another interpretation of the way things really are. There is a sense of truth at work here that is itself metaphorical. It operates as a kind of manifestation rather than as a simple relation of correspondence or coherence. As a heuristic fiction that can lead to new understanding, such metaphorical truth may even be said to be the ground for truth as correspondence or coherence.[20]

That metaphor serves to found truth, however, has proven to be one of Ricoeur's most controversial claims. We turn next to the charges that have been brought against Ricoeur in this regard.

The Limits of Metaphor

A trenchant critique of Ricoeur's view of metaphor has been set forth by Graham Ward in "Biblical Narrative and the Theology of Metonymy."[21] It would not be prudent to proceed without attempting to answer its momentous claims that, if correct, undermine the applicability of Ricoeur's work to the interpretation of liturgy. In short, Ward alleges that modern biblical reading has gone awry to the extent that it has accepted the view of metaphor promoted by those who have followed Ricoeur (e.g., David Tracy and Sallie McFague). Ward's intent is to show how metaphor must be counterbalanced by "metonymy."[22]

Given his view of metaphor, Ricoeur is guilty, according to Ward, of betraying the Bible's status as *revelation*. He has succumbed to a crypto-docetism by subordinating the historical, literal level of Scripture to one of existential disclosure, with the result that theological thinking becomes a form of "art-appreciation"—and the Bible, (merely) one more poetic text. By doing so Ricoeur allegedly relativizes what is in fact sui generis—namely, Christ and the biblical witness to him. Ward protests:

> The uniqueness of the Incarnation creates what Arthur Cohen, discussing the importance of the Holocaust, calls an historical rupture or caesura which leaves us without a language to define it. The corollary, then, of uniqueness is ineffability. The justification of Scripture being a sacred book must rest upon the fact it testifies, or claims to testify, to an event set apart from other events, an ineffable event. A narrative theology which views Christian historical narrative mediating or serving "as the occasion for the [disclosive] encounter," which views the authority of Scripture as "not something intrinsic to it as Scripture; its authority is in its role in the life of the Christian community," can only use the terms "revelation," "truth," or "Christian" metaphorically or inappropriately. The "truth" here is subjective experience that is only collectively defined as Christian because such individuals belong to "the Christian community." . . . Such a Christology has no ontological foundation independent of the reader's own. It is "revelation" only by misnomer.[23]

These are weighty charges, indeed; let us try to summarize them. Ward admonishes Ricoeur for (1) ignoring the uniqueness of the events attested in Scripture; (2) subverting the due authority of the Bible by making this authority a function of the believing community; and (3) subscribing to a perilously subjectivist notion of biblical "truth." These are complemented, in turn, by a further, compound charge: namely, that Ricoeur puts forward a vague and confusing idea of what constitutes poetic discourse, based on an erroneous estimation of the nature and role of metaphor.

History and Ineffability

While Ward's article appeared before Ricoeur's magisterial *Memory, History, Forgetting (MHF)*[24]—a tome expressly devoted to the issues arising from the singularity of historical events vis-à-vis their literary representation—it is nonetheless implausible that the latter did not have a sound appreciation for the uniqueness of the biblical witness. Already in 1982 he acknowledged the problem of historicity in Scripture: i.e., that there is a problem specifically because of the historical intentionality of the biblical text; it is irreducible to fiction. Criticizing the tendency of narrative theologians (such as the "Yale School" associated with Hans Frei) to bracket Scripture's claims to facticity, Ricoeur maintained that whatever may be gleaned from foraging among the immanent, literary qualities of the text—an activity to which he admittedly inclined—one cannot ultimately equate relevance and truth:

> But the practical use of the biblical stories is not a substitute for an inquiry into the relation between story and history. It is an indisputable trait of the basic stories of the Bible that they are history-like, with the exception of intended fictions such as parables and maybe some stories in the Old Testament, Jonah and others. . . . We are left, therefore, with a quandary: we can neither be content with a concept of story that would elude the dialectic of story and history nor use a concept of history that would not take into account this variable curve of relationships between story and history.[25]

In *MHF* Ricoeur will observe that the Holocaust does indeed precipitate a crisis of representation; but unlike Ward he argues that the very ineffability of such an event is what justifies, paradoxically, the role of historical fiction. To the extent that all representations are inadequate to what they "stand in" for, they are fictional. To mitigate the onset of forgetting there may even be warrant for them to *intensify* their use of fictive devices in order that the reader—otherwise ineluctably removed from the event concerned—may be at least brought to the threshold of appreciating what has in fact taken place. In other words, it is precisely because of the *uniqueness* of historical events that historiography recruits metaphoricity to its service, inasmuch as authentic historical description both *is* and *is not* the truth of what has occurred.

Ward's criticism would thus seem to lead into a cul-de-sac, for if the Incarnation were completely ineffable there could be no accounts of it, the Evangelists themselves presumably being bereft of appropriate language. But if ineffability does not altogether preclude description (and, in turn, inscription) then the resultant texts—whether treating of the Incarnation or the Shoah—ought to be duly subject to analyses in keeping with their genre. It is curious in this regard that Ward cites the example of Holocaust literature as analogous to the Bible on the basis of their common commitment to testify to "ineffable events" since he naturally does not wish to imply that such literature, purely on account of its dealing with "uniqueness," should be deemed equivalent to Scripture.

"The Sacred Text and the Community"

Ward's second criticism, that Ricoeur subordinates the authority of the Bible to the believing community, with an ensuing depreciation of the former's inspired status, is to a certain extent legitimate. Ricoeur's hermeneutical arc certainly requires a theory of inspiration to account for how the reader of the text is also inspired in the very act of appropriating the text—a theory that Ricoeur does not elaborate systematically. His stated views on this matter, moreover, are subtle and easily misunderstood. Because Ricoeur appreciates the historical process by which the Bible was produced and canonized, he is reluctant to speak of its authority apart from the community integral to this process. Indeed, he suggests that a critically edited text— to the extent that it is not the text of believers but of academics—may not merit the designation of "sacred text."[26]

Since the history of the biblical canon testifies to a gradual sifting of books in which some originally included were later excluded (and vice-versa), Ricoeur is wary of a reification of the Bible per se. It is the authority conferred upon the biblical anthology by the early Christian community— an authority, to be sure, that from the perspective of that community was warranted by the respective texts themselves—that has given us the Scriptures we know today. And these Scriptures have been further subject to the vicissitudes of a complicated reception history.[27] Ricoeur muses:

> It is a hermeneutical act to recognize oneself as founded by a text and to read this text as founding. There is a reciprocity between the reading and the existing self-recognition of the identity of the community. There is a kind of reciprocity between the community and the text. There comes to mind the distinction that Augustine makes in *De christiana doctrina* [sic] between *signum* and *res*: we are aware that the *signum* is not the *res*, and there is a history of possible critical approaches to the *signum*. I wonder whether this actually implies a certain distance between the text and its reality, what it is about.[28]

Thus the Bible's authority as intrinsically linked to the community that receives it; this is by no means to deprecate the Scriptures but simply to acknowledge that the corollary of any authority is a party that receives it as such.

Truth as Manifest in the Poetic Function

Finally, Ward contends that Ricoeur makes himself vulnerable to a subjectivist notion of truth. This is in fact a standard complaint against Ricoeur, but one that does not hold up under the evidence. As we have seen, Ricoeur undoubtedly affirms the possibility of truth considered as manifestation rather than adequation, but manifestation decidedly *not* reducible to "subjective experience." If there is a "disclosive encounter" it proceeds not from the predilections of the reader of a text but rather from the textual "world" whose haecceity imposes itself upon the reader.[29] The one who opens the Scriptures finds himself or herself in the position of a "summoned subject," the summons in question being—as Ricoeur's analyses of biblical polyphony are designed to demonstrate—coterminous with a given text's proper manner of naming God.

The most strident criticism laid out by Ward, however, concerns Ricoeur's allegedly vague and confusing idea of what constitutes poetic discourse, an idea Ward sees as based on an erroneous estimation of the nature and role of metaphor.[30] This criticism resumes at a deeper level those treated above since it is obvious that Ricoeur does place the operation of metaphor at the heart of biblical interpretation and equally, that he regards the language of the Scriptures as fundamentally poetic. Ward builds his case on the basis of Ricoeur's "Toward a Hermeneutic of the Idea of Revelation" with reference also to *The Rule of Metaphor*.[31] The three key postulates he identifies in these works are Ricoeur's distinction of biblical genres (explained above by reference to "Naming God"); his opposition of the referential function of poetic discourse to that of its "ordinary" and scientific counterparts; and his affirmation that poetic language restores participation in, through redescription of, reality. Ward submits that Ricoeur does not in fact base his theory of poetic discourse on specific texts; that he begs the question of what "ordinary" discourse is by subsuming all the genres of the Bible under the rubric of the poetic; and that the referentiality for which he advocates does not correspond to the objective reference of the text. We shall take up these contentions in turn.

As we have seen, Ricoeur does indeed treat specific poetic texts (if not especially in the context of *The Rule of Metaphor*). He consistently eschews theology in favor of a close reading of biblical excerpts, which he typically situates in terms of what contemporary exegetes have to say in their respect: *Thinking Biblically*, for example, is constructed (in collaboration with a prominent exegete) as an interpretation of a series of Old Testament texts. For its part, *Time and Narrative* includes in its second volume an extended treatment of three novels.[32] And already in the seventies Ricoeur's exegetical work on Christ's parables and sayings had been published as an extended article.[33]

In the second place, Ward asks if applying the designation "poetic" to the many genres of Scripture does not beg the question of what is *not* categorizable as such. But Ricoeur makes judicious distinctions: He does not say that the Bible simply *is* poetic discourse, but rather that the poetic function of language opens an avenue for approaching the term "revelation" both apart from and with respect to the Bible.[34] According to Ricoeur, its nonreligious sense proceeds from the way in which the poetic function "designates the emergence of another concept of truth than truth as adequation, regulated by the criteria of verification and falsification: a concept of truth as manifestation, in the sense of letting be what shows itself. What shows itself is each time the proposing of a world."[35] In other words, revelation in this sense refers to the potential of language to mean above and beyond the empirical categories espoused by, for instance, logical positivism.

The religious sense of revelation, although resonating with its nonreligious equivalent, is neither derived from it nor reducible to it.[36] This is so, not only because of its recurrent appeal to historicity (treated above) but cardinally because the naming of God has an ontological vehemence that places the Bible in a category all its own; as David Pellauer elucidates, the naming of God effects a kind of "limit-language" calling for "an intensity of discernment and commitment that exclude the ironic distance and skepticism that are still possible with regard to poetic language."[37] For Ricoeur, the very naming of God itself already constitutes a testimony to that ineffability that in Ward's estimation duly sets the Scripture apart.[38]

Furthermore, while Ward legitimately seeks precision with respect to the "ordinary function of discourse," which Ricoeur holds as "suspended" by the poetic function of language,[39] the latter actually does explicate his position: "Too often, we do not notice that we uncritically accept a certain concept of truth defined as adequation to real objects and as submitted to a criterion of empirical verification. That language in its poetic function abolishes the type of reference characteristic of such descriptive discourse . . . is not to be doubted."[40] Here as elsewhere Ricoeur is resisting the usurpation by logical positivism of the whole realm of linguistic meaning, and its corollary exiling of the poetic function of language to the domain of the aesthetic. It is unclear to me why Ward confuses this demarcation with an apology for poetry proper when Ricoeur states his purpose otherwise.[41] The poetic function of language is exercised whenever language, irrespective of genre, takes us across the frontier of the empirically verifiable into zones where it alone can guide. That is to say, ordinary discourse treats of objects immediately accessible to our senses that can be designated and/or manipulated. But poetic discourse speaks of phenomena that (in the vein of the argument made by C. S. Lewis above) cannot be described except metaphorically: by means of the application, through the organ of the productive imagination, of terms whose aptness is "invented"—an invention in which "finding" is tantamount to "making."[42] Thus any discourse that treats of God must be at some level poetic, by virtue of compelling a designation of that which cannot be named directly—i.e., that which is *not* a manipulable object. The articulation of the experience of evil, to which Ricoeur has also devoted much reflection, engages the service of metaphoricity in like manner.

In the third place, Ward pleads for a circumscription of the ambit of metaphor by adducing the notion of metonymy; in his estimation, metonymy allows for an objective reckoning with the "literal" reference of a text while not necessarily excluding a metaphorical complement to it. Ward seems to presume here that Ricoeur uses metaphor univocally. However, this is simply not the case, inasmuch as Ricoeur remains sensitive to the historiographical problem of the verisimilitude of (much of) Scripture.[43] Rather, as elaborated in *Time and Narrative*, Ricoeur proposes that the act of following history and narrative—and both genres are metaphorical in this respect—requires the heuristic of a "seeing-as" that is rooted in the work of the imagination, a "grasping together" of disparate elements through a kind of narrative intelligence in which an axial role is played by the reader's capacity to see the similar in the dissimilar: Through the mimetic processes by which narrative is constructed, historical and fictional alike, the reader comes to perceive the plot inhering in a given set of otherwise discrete events.[44] At issue is not metaphor *sensu strictissimo*, but metaphor taken as a paradigm for epistemology—which in no way excludes the role of metonymy as a literary device.

True, Ward recognizes that Ricoeur (and others after him, such as Nicholas Lash) views metaphor as the paradigm for text interpretation and not simply as one trope among many; what has not been appreciated, however, is that Ricoeur adopts this perspective not because he considers the biblical text to have no objective relation to the world and its history, to serve merely for an amorphous existential disclosure, but instead because he considers the dynamic of metaphor to be operative analogously at the level of the literary work and not only at the level of the sentence. As David Pellauer again clarifies, religious discourse places a tension on our vision of reality by referring not only to the world of the text—which reference includes what Ward calls the metonymic axis—but also to us, inasmuch as the limit-language expressed in the naming of God points to a figure that confronts us in the here and now: "Hence, there is a kind of double opening at work here that affects both poles of our subject-object model for organizing and interpreting our experience. On the object side, religious language points to the world of the text and beyond it to God. On the subject side, it points to our limit-experiences in and through this world. Religious language, in other words, represents an intensification of the metaphorical process that takes it to its limit, whether it be a matter of our limit-experiences or their wholly other limit-referent."[45] This "carrying over" (*metapherein*) of the world of the text into our world, of limit-*language* into our limit-*experience*, thus constitutes a metaphorical process par excellence.

Liturgy as a Form of Thought

Our final task in this part of the book, after having expounded Ricoeur's concept of the polyphonic "naming of God" in Scripture; advocated its significance for an understanding of liturgical language as metaphorical; and responded to views both favorable and critical of it, is to apply this concept in a general manner to the forms of discourse operative in the Byzantine Rite. This will prove a valuable preparation for our subsequent analysis of the *GBW*. My premise has been that liturgy manifests an analogous polyphony in its naming of God, resuming but also extending the genres treated by Ricoeur, to the extent that its interweaving of apophatic and kataphatic terminology allows for an incorporation of the speculative into the poetic—discourses that Ricoeur customarily regards as discrete.

At the end of our introduction we recalled the interview given by Ricoeur at Taizé, in which he posits liturgy to be a "language" and a "form of thought" distinct from that of theology. I suggested in turn that this admission implies the application to liturgy of a distinct mode of interpretation, a mode irreducible to the one proper to the biblical "form of thought"— an authentic, if "non-philosophical manner of thinking and being"—to which it is nonetheless related. To recap: This lack of equivalence derives not merely from the fact that liturgy makes use of nonverbal idioms (which liturgical language references especially, if not exclusively, through its rubrics) but from the very features of the forms of discourse themselves.[46] The liturgical would seem to qualify for inclusion in the set that Ricoeur terms "translation languages" in which the poetic and the conceptual meet. In an early, landmark essay in the journal of biblical criticism *Semeia*, he analyzes the features of such "languages": Beyond the impulse within Scripture to interpret the symbolic in terms of the speculative—already evident, for instance, in the Epistles' discursive interpretation of themes treated metaphorically in the Gospels—a "second intermediary step between 'figurative' and 'conceptual' discourse may be found in a variety of semiconceptual modes of discourse, typical of the didactic, apologetic, and dogmatic literature from which theology emerged, in conjunction with the Greek philosophies."[47] In this regard, he holds up Christology as exemplary, suggesting that already in the Wisdom literature of the Old Testament there are texts presaging its synthesis of different discourses. Ricoeur employs the term "translation language" because therein "the meaningful content is exploited as the basis of concepts and notions belonging to a train of thought distinct from the symbolic basis."[48]

Remarkably, Ricoeur does not treat liturgical language in this connection, despite it being a privileged environment for the epigenesis of the conceptual from the figurative. He is well aware that the act of canonizing the Scriptures provided an external impetus to the movement from originary forms of discourse to secondary, inasmuch as the tension introduced by having various genres confront one another begs the question of their compatibility, not to say complementarity.[49] But it is evident that liturgical traditions submit to a similar canonical process, whereby their multiple idioms are also fixed into a network. We are now in a position to consider the broader significance of this process. Given that Ricoeur places the genre of hymn as one of the eight forms of discourse identifiable in the Bible, we may ask how liturgy as a composite, hymnic form of discourse recapitulates on a doxological plane both the biblical and nonbiblical forms of discourse included in it, leading in consequence to a new, distinctive mode of naming God.[50]

Liturgy as Originary Discourse

Before pressing on, however, it is important to attend to the discrepancy that emerges from our claim that liturgical discourse is originary, and the remarks just made concerning its status as a translation language. How can it be both?[51] To the extent that liturgy operates as poetic discourse wherein multiple genres are subsumed under the metacategory of "hymn," it is undoubtedly the former; and yet, because it is a "form of thought" that synthesizes the originary discourse of Scripture with theological ruminations, it is also the latter. In this respect, Ricoeur's perspective sheds light on a tension in contemporary debate concerning the interrelationship of liturgy and theology. Certainly, despite—or perhaps because of—the currency given the ancient adage *lex orandi, lex credendi*, it is becoming de rigueur to challenge the status of liturgy as "primary theology."

Lutheran theologian Michael Aune, for instance, is adamant that this famous tag of Prosper of Aquitaine has outlived its usefulness and ought to be demoted or sent into "retirement."[52] But Aune's reading of the expression's origins appears to miss the paramount insight of hermeneutics— namely, that words and phrases take on a life of their own: There is such a thing as a *reception history*. As in the case of the term "orthodoxy," treated above, it is irrelevant whether (as Aune argues) Prosper himself did not originally intend his reference to the solemn intercessions of the Good Friday liturgy of fifth-century Rome to constitute a theological *point de départ*, favoring rather the cumulative teachings of the popes; as it happens, the adage in question has become a useful shorthand for expressing the intimate relationship between how one prays and what one believes. Schmemann, Kavanaugh, and Fagerberg—the theologians charged by Aune with the trespass of claiming that "liturgy is a 'source' for theology," and advancing such "to the status of a methodological principle"[53]—do not require Prosper for an accomplice. Ricoeur seems to make much the same point via the more oblique terminology of philosophy, in the famous concluding chapter of *The Symbolism of Evil*: "'The symbol gives rise to thought.' That sentence . . . says two things: the symbol gives; but what it gives is occasion for thought, something to think about."[54] We may say that liturgy inevitably constitutes a source for theology, to the extent that a genuine encounter with its symbolism will elicit reflection.[55]

We will return to Aune later on, when we explore Ricoeur's work on historiography. For the moment it suffices to note his unstable method of first chiding those theologians who would posit liturgy as a source, and subsequently invoking a disparate array of liturgical data in the service of the primacy of an abstract principle ("God's nearness and activity in Christian worship"). Aune is caught in a quandary, unable to locate what Ricoeur calls a "radical beginning."[56] The philosopher's comments on this issue help explain the equivocation besetting Aune's critique of the *lex orandi, lex credendi* principle:

> The beginning is not what one finds first; the point of departure must be reached, it must be won. Understanding of symbols can play a part in the movement toward the point of departure; for, if the beginning is to be reached, it is first necessary for thought to inhabit the fullness of language. . . . The illusion is not in looking for a point of departure, but in looking for it without presuppositions. There is no philosophy without presuppositions. A meditation on symbols starts from speech that has already taken place, and in which everything has already been said in some fashion; it wishes to be thought with its presuppositions.[57]

As far as theology is concerned, one cannot simply posit (as does Aune) that liturgical theology ought to respond to the contemporary fragmentation and relativism in the theological enterprise with a blithe invitation to "reconsider the concrete object of theology itself . . . the concrete character of revelation as the speech or discourse of the incarnate One, Jesus, about God," as if this furnishes a panacea for all hermeneutic woes.[58] To wit, if revelation is given as such only in the "concrete," this implies respecting the polyphonicity of the naming of God in that scriptural discourse to which Aune is presumably referring; and, in accord with the historical consciousness that forms one part of his recommended remedy, an appreciation of the polyphonicity that obtains in liturgical speech as well.[59] In other words, if theology is best understood in its originary, pre-Nicene sense of "speaking of God by speaking to God"—Aune's memorable term for it—then liturgical texts *are* indeed the place to seek "the beginning." It is in the particularity of such texts, as embodied in performance, that the naming of God in their respective traditions inheres, a naming that transmits the polyphonicity of Scripture but also transforms it, much as a fugue does to the melody announced by a prelude.

The Dialectic of the Kataphatic and the Apophatic

As we have seen, Ricoeur suggests that metaphor by its very nature points to the unsayable. Responding to a text of Karl Rahner, where the latter comments on Thomas Aquinas's view of the incomprehensibility of God, Ricoeur suggests that the "learned ignorance" (*docta ignorantia*) that Rahner counsels—a positive state of unknowing that is the corollary of a doctrine of revelation rather than its contrary—surfaces already in the ordinary experience of the creativity of language in its poetic function. There, our sense of mastery over the world is challenged by the discovery of a terra incognita.[60]

Contrary to that use of language that confirms the frontiers of our present knowledge, poetic use is unsettling, even dangerous, in its indication of a domain that lies beyond our reach. In metaphorical statements, "Language is raised to *ignorantia* to the extent that the horizon of the unexpressed, of the unsaid, is revealed as constitutive of the experience of language itself." Continuing, Ricoeur explains that metaphor presents in miniature the dialectic between the apophatic and kataphatic, between our inability to communicate the incommunicable, and our impulse to nevertheless attempt so to do: "*Ignorantia* resides in this restless oscillation between is and is not. But this *ignorantia* is *docta*, to the extent that it is not a capitulation of language but an untiring and everlasting struggle with the problematic of language—a struggle to bring language to the threshold of silence."[61] In lieu of a sort of mysticism that would prescind from linguistic mediation, Ricoeur recommends the arduous path of endeavoring to name God, despite the impossibility of adequately doing so.[62] This is a way of expressing, I think, his profound appreciation of human finitude as a benign feature of our existence with which we must make peace; freedom—in this case the freedom to truly name God—is achieved from within a recognition of our limitations, rather than from a denial of them. To "struggle with the problematic of language" is, in this sense, an act of humility.[63]

Now this struggle manifests itself conspicuously in the tendency of Byzantine liturgical discourse to interweave the way of affirmation with the way of negation. I would propose that this is in fact the most distinctive feature of such discourse: Byzantine texts arguably owe a great deal of their poetic force to the very intensity of verbal friction generated by prolixity both on the side of metaphors and of disclaimers.[64] The "work" of liturgy is thus displayed already on a linguistic level by the prevention of a ready synthesis; we are presented, that is, with texts that simultaneously pour forth in accolades and yet concede their very inadequacy. Equal resistance is shown to the view that God is utterly unknowable, as to its contrary, that our language (or understanding) is sufficient to its task. The treatment of the *GBW* in Chapter 8 will exemplify this process in regard to a specific rite; in what remains here, we will treat it in more general fashion.

With respect to the way of affirmation, we have seen that Ricoeur is interested in the contrast presented by how differently the various genres of Scripture name God.[65] The contrariety between these figures (e.g., judge, liberator, hero) holds forth a literary analogue to the doctrine of God's incomprehensibility that is "already presented by the mere clash of the opposed ways of speaking of God." In this vein Ricoeur asks, rhetorically:

> Is not this incomprehensibility presented to the extent that the name of God explodes the boundaries of each simple literary genre and keeps, so to speak, migrating from one kind of discourse to another? Not only the tension between different modes of discourse point toward the incomprehensibility of God, but the specific use of many of them does also. It has been shown by exegetes that the proverbs, the parables, and other saying of Jesus tend to become limit-expressions under the pressure of the paradoxes, hyperboles, and extravagance in narration. This too is *docta ignorantia*.[66]

In similar fashion, we can observe in a general way that the Byzantine idiom revels in paradoxical attributions, whose cumulative effect is to depict God in the style of a Picasso, so to speak, rather than that of a Michelangelo.

Here we can introduce Elizabeth Theokritoff's survey of the parameters within which Byzantine hymnography compasses biblical events: She argues the meaning of a given feast emerges in the play of intertextuality as it is made to ricochet from one typology to another. Just as for Ricoeur the figure of God recedes behind the plethora of its scriptural references, so the festal event (and concomitantly, its dramatis personae) "migrates" from one genre to another. Having indicated the breadth of allusions to be found in the hymnography for Theophany, for instance, Theokritoff observes:

When these and similar texts are interwoven with the Gospel accounts, it is not in the first instance a matter of interpreting one scriptural text by another. It is primarily a matter of understanding not the written word but the actions of the incarnate Word, different aspects and levels of which are signified in various ways by Gospels, Epistles, Old Testament events and prophecies. This then has the effect that the Gospel account is interpreted in the light of other scriptural texts.[67]

In other words, the hymnography provides a metaphorical lens through which to consider an object that in its pastness can never be given directly, nor even adequately represented by mere reportage; each allusion manifests—in Ricoeurian terms both discovers and invents—an "as if" that in turn both advances the *via positiva* and causes it to disappear, so to speak, around yet another corner.

The kataphatic therefore already implies the apophatic to the extent that its polyphonicity resists conceptual circumscription. If Ricoeur sees "the Kingdom of Heaven," for example, as the elusive referent of the New Testament, dodging capture on account of the intervention of the Gospel's limit-expressions, hymnography can analogously be regarded as camouflaging the very figure of Christ himself: Following this figure requires an imaginative bushwhacking, so to speak, through a typological thicket. As Theokritoff declares, "By presenting Christology in a pictorial way through images from the Old and New Testaments, the hymns intimate mysteries which cannot be contained in formulae."[68]

Alternatively, one could lay stress on the way that the network of correspondences established by hymnography *enhances* the intelligibility of the events inserted into it. We have spoken above about Ricoeur's appreciation for the work of Northrop Frye, who demonstrated the intersignifications obtaining within and between the biblical books themselves. This inner coherence of Scripture's field of reference, its "centripetal structure," opens a space for the responding self to be drawn into the world of the text:

> To the extent that one brackets the possible representation of real historical events, and therefore brackets the "centrifugal" movement of the text—a movement that prevails in argumentative language and still more in demonstrative language, which, in our culture, have covered over and suppressed metaphorical language—what is

important is neither the relation to nature, as in a book of cosmology, nor the relation to the actual unfolding of events, as in a book
of history, but the power of the biblical text to arouse, in the listener
and the reader, the desire to understand himself in terms of "the
Great Code."[69]

In this fashion Theokritoff can insist that the burden of hymnography
is to invite those who hear and take it on their lips to *participate* in the
mystery being celebrated. Rather than a mere exercise of the imagination,
it is a matter of existential import: "The texts also keep reminding us that
through sacramental experience, our Baptism and participation in the Eucharist, the scriptures are being fulfilled in us."[70]

For Ricoeur, however, there remains a liability in emphasizing the imaginative unity of the Bible: The richness of its polyphony must not be
muted lest it dampen the resonances possible for the responding self—a
theme we will examine in greater detail below. A similar peril perhaps confronts any attempt to compel the hymnography of the liturgy to circum-
navigate, as it were, the theological globe; one must recall in this respect
David Power's insistence on the fact of rupture *within* as well as between
liturgical traditions.[71]

The Via Negativa

The negative way emerges not only as a function of following the way of
affirmation, but is directly accessed by the apophatic terminology that in-
tersects the kataphatic along the poetic route of Byzantine hymnography.
But in contrast to the classic treatment of Pseudo-Dionysius, in which the
via negativa is the preferred angle of approach for moving from the foot-
hills of perception on to the mystic heights, liturgical texts tend to *begin* with
apophasis and continue on with kataphasis. Thus, for instance, the first of
three prolix prayers for the so-called "Kneeling Vespers" of Pentecost
Monday starts with God being acclaimed as at once "incorruptible, without beginning, invisible, incomprehensible, unsearchable, unchangeable,
unsurpassable, immeasurable"—ostensibly, the one about whom nothing
may be positively affirmed—and at one and same time, the one whose
historic wonders can and must be narrated and interpreted, and of whom
a corresponding cluster of particular actions ought to be requested and
expected.[72] This same pattern is rehearsed in the eucharistic prayer of the

Liturgy of St. John Chrysostom and in the *GBW*, where a paean to the *magnalia Dei* is prefaced by an apophatic appellation, excerpted from the Dionysian "On the Divine Names": "O Trinity, transcendent in essence, in goodness and in divinity, O Almighty, invisible and incomprehensible, who watch over all. . . . O Goodness of utter and unapproachable brilliance."[73]

We may observe that such a pattern recasts on a larger scale the relation of model and qualifier described above; an apophatic preface prevents— in both senses of the word—a facile comprehension of all that is subsequently posited of God. In this manner, liturgical discourse preserves what Ricoeur calls (in a Hegelian term) the "pain and work of the negative"; it serves as a kind of meta-"limit-expression" wherein multiple metaphors are multiply qualified, "maintain[ing] the incomprehensibility of God on the borderline between language and silence."[74] Moreover, according to Karl Rahner's interpretation of Thomas Aquinas (to which Ricoeur is responding in this connection), our *ignorantia* with respect to God is to be understood not privatively, but as a *positive* indication of the ineffability of our own nature.[75] For Rahner, the incomprehensibility of God expresses itself as an *excedere*, an excess; man must realize that his own self-realization involves a recognition of that which exceeds him, that this very thing (God) is his fulfillment. This word "excess," as we have observed, figures prominently also in Ricoeur's reflections as a descriptor for the surplus of any symbol. Liturgical symbols (including their language) can thus be seen as blazing a trail, by means of multiple but qualified namings of God, through the excess surrounding not only God but us as well. We too, being made in the image of God, are also veritable mysteries, never fully given even to ourselves.[76]

And it is also in light of the clash of opposed ways of speaking of God, of its juxtaposition of models and qualifiers, that liturgy can be regarded as truly theology, in the sense that Ricoeur gives the word. In his response to Rahner, Ricoeur suggests that theological discourse (as its own proper discourse) requires the kind of dialectical thinking that marks poetic speech generally, and religious discourse especially: the integration of the kataphatic and apophatic. Ricoeur lauds Thomas's solution to a perennial theological dilemma: "We could speak of God without any ambiguity if there were predicates common to him and to creatures. But this is not the case. Does that mean, then, that we can say nothing? Not at all; between sheer ambiguity and pure univocity, there is the analogical use of predicates."[77]

Ricoeur identifies analogy as the key to theology as a second-order discourse; it parallels the use of metaphors and models in poetic discourse, and the use of limit-expressions in religious discourse. It is clear, however, that liturgy is *also* theology, to the extent that it incorporates second-order reflection into the originary work of naming God that so fascinates Ricoeur.

Liturgy as (More Than) Metaphor

The crux of the last few chapters has been that Ricoeur's theory of figurative language, particularly its treatment of the naming of God, offers an incisive perspective on the operations of liturgical discourse. But metaphoricity is of course more than a linguistic phenomenon, not only in virtue of the deep intimacy between language and life,[78] but also on account of the way in which actions themselves can be viewed as metaphorical, to the extent that their combination—their being "spoken"—involves a seeing-as (in liturgy, a "touching-as," "hearing-as," "smelling-as," etc.), that results in a transformed "being-as." Following a Ricoeurian detour, we have reached the point of being able to endorse Mark Searle's bold assertion that the liturgical event as a whole has a metaphorical character.[79]

Searle calls for the kind of rehabilitation of metaphor recommended by Ricoeur, in order to recover the power of liturgical language and gesture. In Searle's estimation these have suffered from being assigned a merely ornamental or derivative status—the product of negligent epistemology: "We are starting from the supposition that the role of liturgical language is not simply to convey supernatural 'facts,' but to engage us in relationship; and that the actions of the liturgy are not undertaken for the purpose of getting a job done, so much as to constitute and express attitudes."[80]

Since the classical theory of metaphor as a superfluous trope has been rendered suspect, if not discredited altogether, Searle contends that a similar critique must be leveled at its liturgical counterpart—namely, the belief that the communications event of liturgy can be framed in terms of instrumental causality:

> The preoccupation with causality, rather than signification—the shift from seeing the sacraments as communications events to seeing them as causal operations—meant that the actual liturgical performance

was not taken seriously as a source of understanding. Instead the Thomistic axiom, *significando causant*, was effectively cut in two and the first half promptly forgotten as causality was discussed without reference to the meaning inherent in the liturgical structure as a whole. . . . In other words, the metaphor could be translated and, as the theologians showed in their commentaries, effectively dispensed with in favor of more conceptual statements.[81]

Searle instead advocates an appropriation of insights (current in the social sciences) that have challenged the positivism of received liturgical theology. Although not referring to Ricoeur, Searle arrives at a kindred understanding of the polyvalence of language.[82]

Searle further suggests that metaphoricity can be usefully applied to the ritual elements of liturgical celebration. Such elements, inasmuch as they involve regarding/effecting certain actions as if they were something other, conveying both "is" and "is not," constitute a further species of metaphor. Again, without quoting Ricoeur, Searle points to a similar process in describing what the former would call the "semantic impertinence" of ritual actions; such actions—which in Christian liturgy are often rooted in ordinary, quotidian practices such as washing and eating—are freighted with an import that defies measure. Thus Searle asserts, quoting P. Colin: "'It is the very solemnity of the liturgical gesture that prompts us to look for the fullness of its meaning beyond its immediate significance—and that is why it is important to maintain this solemnity.'"[83] That is to say, liturgical gestures carry what Ricoeur calls a "surplus of meaning" to the extent that they are charged with a meaning that exceeds the conventional or "literal." According to Searle, there is a marked tension in liturgical symbols as in metaphors, inasmuch as they risk on the one hand becoming too otherworldly, thereby losing the power to signify metaphorically in virtue of the attenuation of a primary, literal meaning; and, on the other hand, becoming purely mundane, being in inverse fashion thereby also rendered impotent.

One can claim that liturgical symbols taken as metaphors are a mode of naming God—a sort of genre that is superadded to the various genres of liturgical speech. Symbols share in the paradoxical process of manifesting that which eludes manifestation by laying out "figures" of theophany, even as the scriptural and liturgical genres present figures of God himself. We recall in this connection Ricoeur's claim that understanding oneself in front of the biblical text implies a breadth of application equal to the multidimensional character of its poetics, impinging on the cosmic, the ethical, and the political.[84] Given that the poetics of Scripture unfold liturgically in tandem with ritual action, we may venture to extend his hermeneutic accordingly, asking whether liturgy should be seen as effectively mediating the multiple dimensions disclosed in the naming of God?

Might we not well adapt Ricoeur's aversion to the notion of the Kantian schema, by positing that the liturgy serves as a sort of schema for producing figures of the cosmic, ethical, and political implications of authentic biblical understanding? Select examples from the Byzantine Rite might include the blessing of fruit on the Feast of the Transfiguration (cosmic); the collection of offerings for the poor (i.e., the blessing of bread, wheat, wine, and oil) at the vesperal rogation (*līte*) on festal days (ethical); and the Kiss of Peace in the Divine Liturgy (political). The necessity and value of these ritual actions are qualified by the "(biblical) canon within the (liturgical) canon," the counter-example of other liturgical traditions, and the iconoclastic critique of those outside the community, and yet they may yet serve as catalysts for transformation beyond the liturgical precinct. In this respect, liturgy could be seen to serve as a performance of the Gospel that mediates its realization in the "theater" of life itself.[85]

If the above claim holds good, then we must proceed to ask what sort of a *self* finds itself summoned to respond to such figures, biblical and/or liturgical. For Ricoeur has proposed that since the Bible is a polyphony lacking a singular center, one may query whether the self that responds to its call is not similarly "polycentric"; if liturgy is analogously polyphonic, as we have sought to demonstrate hitherto, then we ought to further probe the shape of liturgical subjectivity—an inquiry to which we proceed in the next chapters.[86]

PART

III

"TODAY YOU HAVE APPEARED TO THE WORLD"

CHAPTER

5

"THE SUMMONED SUBJECT"

Overview

In this chapter we trace the shape of liturgical subjectivity, employing the template provided by Ricoeur in his later works, especially *Oneself as Another* and *The Course of Recognition*. The focus here will be on the nature of human capability itself, as fulfilled within a liturgical context; having reflected in previous chapters on the polyphony of liturgical language and symbolism, we must now consider the kind of self that may respond to such "music." The subsequent chapters will afford the opportunity to examine the way in which the capable subject experiences the configuration of memory through the work of liturgy. The burden of our eighth and final chapter will be to integrate the preceding analyses in an application of Ricoeur's manifold hermeneutic to a select rite, the "Great Blessing of Water." It is perhaps worth reiterating at this juncture that this application with which we will conclude really does require the theoretical prolegomena constituting the better part of our labors. Ricoeur's thought has only begun to be appropriated by liturgists, and thus must have its theological properties further divined.

The Polyphonic Self

The last chapter concluded with the question of whether the self summoned to respond to the polyphonic naming of God in Scripture (and by extension in liturgy) is subject to a corresponding polycentricity. To recap:

Ricoeur's seminal observation is that "God is named differently in the narration, where he is designated as supreme Agent; in the code of prescriptions, where he is designated as source of the imperative; in the prophecy, where he is designated as divine I doubling the human I; in the wisdom, which searches for him as the meaning of the meaningful; and . . . in the hymn, which expresses in turn complaint and praise."[1] To this taxonomy of biblical genres, recapitulated in liturgical discourse, we added the genre of liturgical poetry, drawing attention to its restless oscillation between kataphatic acclamation of the *magnalia Dei* and apophatic avowal of the divine transcendence as well as the very insufficiency of doxological language.

Note that the kataphatic lens of such poetry is panoptic; as John Mc-Guckin underscores, the Byzantines inherited from Semitic Christianity the principle that Scripture should be interpreted by means of Scripture, with the resultant commentary ultimately becoming a distinct liturgical genre in itself—namely, the "midrashic hymn." In such a text "the central biblical narrative being considered is turned over and over again, like a man examining a rare jewel, from every related scriptural angle, so that in the end a veritable 'Persian carpet' of biblicisms emerges."[2] For its part, the apophatic lens of this poetry employs an array of devices intended to confute the ready comprehension of God's being and acting in the world: Qualifiers appended to common adjectives, the frequent use of paradoxical attributions, and the direct citation of terminology drawn from philosophically oriented discourse such as that of Pseudo-Dionysius, all contribute to thematizing the unknowability of God—itself already implicit in the kataphatic juxtaposition of competing imagery drawn from the Bible.

We also indicated further how a liturgical analogue to Ricoeur's notion of biblical polyphony emerges in the work of David Power. Here it is worth marshaling the pertinent insights of Russian literary theorist Mikhail Bakhtin (1895–1975).[3] For he too was taken with the notion of "polyphony," whose resonances he heard in the modern novel (particularly as crafted by Dostoevsky). Yet according to Anton Ugolnik, Bakhtin's "dialogism" was actually inspired by his trinitarian, Orthodox faith as experienced preeminently in the liturgy. There Bakhtin encountered not the "the single voice of 'God's proclamation,'" but rather "the multiple voices of a dialogic response"; this discovery parallels Bakhtin's distinction between the authorial bird's-eye view typical of classical literature, and the linguistic complexity of the novel.[4] As Ugolnik elsewhere explains:

> Bakhtin concentrates upon a plurality of voices among characters— each of them continually shaping and altering perception among the others. Meaning, then, is perpetually in a state of becoming, ever straining toward but never achieving full realization, neither within the text nor without. Nor is the text self-contained: the reader, taking the paradigm of the dialogue from the text, engages the work and in receiving meaning enacts it in further dialogue continuing the process.[5]

Bakhtin's liturgical sensibility pervades his dialogical hermeneutic, according to Ugolnik, because liturgy serves as the theater of "the divine dialogue that is the emblem of 'reciprocal definition'"[6]—the place where God vouchsafes to speak us into being, as it were, and we, each other.

On this view, liturgy constructs a transformative "plural persona" with respect to both its divine and human actants:

> The very purpose of liturgy is to celebrate and worship a pluralitive, or "Trinitarian" God. The emphasis upon Trinity is continual, and strong. The reciprocity of the three persons within Godhead is the element which fuses it into one. By the same order, the voices of Byzantine and Russian hymnography shift back and forth between first and third person. The contemplation upon God or upon a given saint causes one to break out, periodically, into the voice of the object of contemplation. Celebrants and worshippers may utter the voices of both saints and sinners, and utter the voice of God in response. Liturgy begets an internal discourse, then, which fractures the persona of those who celebrate it. It is vital to realize that liturgy does not, in this sense, have an "audience," but only actors or a *dramatis personae*. Liturgy begets a collective vision of the self.[7]

I think we see here *in nuce* the relation between the Ricoeurian themes of polyphonic naming and selfhood that this chapter will allow us to develop in greater detail. Where Power assisted us in grasping the pertinence of this relation per the liturgical naming of God, Ugolnik's interpretation of Bakhtin points us toward its ontological implications.[8] I trust that calling upon such admittedly sundry reinforcements (including the last chapter's overture to Lewis) has not compromised the cause at hand; I have sought only to follow the example of Ricoeur, who never fails to honor those from whom he learns.

Oneself as Another

To mine the rich vein of Ricoeur's reflections on selfhood, one can do no better than source *Oneself as Another* (henceforth *OAA*), which can boast of being his magnum opus not in terms of its relative size, but with respect to its thematic comprehensiveness.[9] Indeed, one may scarcely find threads of Ricoeur's thought that are not in some fashion interwoven into the fabric of this book. Charles Regan confidently proclaims it his "most elegantly written, clearly organized, and closely argued work."[10] Before quarrying there in earnest, however, it may be helpful to provide a conspectus and initial assessment of its pertinence to the present inquiry.

In the course of ten "studies" (a reworking of the better part of his 1986 Gifford Lectures), Ricoeur aspires to revisit, from multiple removes, the perennial and vexing problem of personal identity. The tripartite conceptual framework of the text includes a reflexive analysis of the term "self" in natural languages, as it operates both on the semantic and pragmatic planes; the polysemy of selfhood as manifest in its denotation both of that which is reidentifiable as the same (*idem*), and that which expresses identity in difference (*ipse*); and finally, the correlation of selfhood and the other-than-self, articulated at three levels: the lived body, the Other as another person, and the enigma of conscience.[11] As Regan observes: "The whole hermeneutic is led by the question, who: who speaks? who acts? who tells a story? and who is the subject of moral imputation?"[12] In terms of the schema of *OAA*, studies one and two are based on the philosophy of language; three and four, on that of action (i.e., Anglo-American or "analytic" philosophy); five and six focus on personal identity proper in terms of its relation to narrative; seven to nine treat the practical dialectic between the ethical and the moral, while the final study explores the ontology implied by the course of his studies.

John van den Hengel argues that the thrust of *OAA* is toward a contemporary rehabilitation of human subjectivity in the wake of its critique at the hands of Nietzsche. Although there can be no return to the erstwhile certainty of the Enlightenment, represented by the prestige and power accorded the cogito by Descartes, the Ricoeurian *via media* can restore to us a measure of epistemological confidence. As he explains: "The cultural crisis is not a crisis of methods but a crisis of the self-identity of the human. The ideological protagonists for Ricoeur in *Oneself as Another* are not the empiricists or the logical positivists but two traditions that in Ricoeur's terms either 'exalt' the subject too highly or 'humiliate' the subject to the point of its disappearance or death."[13] Ricoeur will avoid the foundationalism of the former tradition by keeping the subject as the destination he aspires to attain, rather than the place from which he begins his journey: "Subjectivity or the appropriation of the self lies not at the origin of the human venture, but it is an endless task of understanding accomplished only after painful critiques of the self."[14] Furthermore, the goal of this task according to van den Hengel is fundamentally practical; since the reflexive analyses lead, via a development of the notion of narrative identity, to specific modes of engagement in the ethical/moral realm, Ricoeur can be seen as revisiting the theme of human action already salient in his earliest writings.[15]

Van den Hengel is particularly intrigued by Ricoeur's critique of the tendency in Ordinary Language Philosophy (i.e., Speech-Act Theory) to make the use of the present tense the standard by which action is measured. Ricoeur's proposal is to shift the emphasis to promissives and commissives—i.e., statements that express intentionality in terms of "I have the intention to . . ." rather than in terms of "I do or have done something intentionally," or "I do something with the intention that . . ."; in the future orientation of promissives/commissives he finds an original way of construing the self that privileges its capacity for action:

> With language the self projects itself into the future, committing the self to a future action in accordance with a word given in the present. Since this action is still future, it is not observable, it is not yet an event. In the present it is a speech-event, a word to be kept. In this expression of intentionality the focus falls fully upon the agent, the "Who?" of action. Since the commissive or promissive projects the self of the agent into an open future, the self emerges here in a context of action whereby, through the kept word (*la parole tenue*), the self attests to itself as a project and not as a possession. It is this projected self that is the touchstone of Ricoeur's reflections on the human self. In a similar manner, this projected action or initiative must be considered the paradigm of human action.[16]

The treatment of action in *OAA* thus serves as a roundabout approach—in Ricoeurian vocabulary, a "detour"—allowing the author to compass the question of the self from a different elevation, a hitherto remote vantage point. Van den Hengel considers the terrain surveyed to be demarcated by borders common to practical theology. These include the primacy of praxis over theory, the role of the human subject as bearer of responsibility for action and the importance of narrative, and hence temporal, considerations.[17]

It should be evident already from this synopsis that *OAA* has much to offer to liturgical theology, directed as the latter is to that "performance" of identity that for van den Hengel constitutes the distinctiveness of Ricoeur's nonsubstantialist ontology.[18] Ricoeur finds this ontology in the "fragility of the kept word"—surely voiced with all tremulousness in the hall of liturgical remembrance and promise. It is there also that we find an effective consciousness of the historical, to the extent that liturgy situates its agents between past and future, in an eschatological "today." Hence van den Hengel can affirm:

> Ricoeur's refined approach to the human self can greatly help to deepen our understanding of the self shaped by the faithful word, the kept word, of God. The self that emerges in the hearing of God's word is the self of faith, or, as Ricoeur has observed a number of times, the self of hope, the self that is given and configured in the promise of God's fidelity. . . . The self which emerges in the worship of God in the liturgy of the Church is a "*sujet convoqué,*" a self configured by a prophetic vocation. This self is not an isolated self but a self responding to a call within a community, or, to put it in other terms, a self "*coram Deo*" in the obedience of faith.[19]

Given this assurance, let us proceed to consider the liturgical significance of several theses that emerge in *OAA*. In what follows, I would like to draw attention to the following themes: (1) the way in which selfhood is narratively mediated; (2) the various modalities of passivity identified by Ricoeur: one's body, encounter with the Other, and the witness of one's conscience; and (3) the notion of attestation. We shall examine each of these in turn.

Narrative Identity

Ricoeur has long advanced the view that it is in and through narrative that we negotiate the tension between our awareness of ourselves as both remaining who we have always been and, simultaneously, of ever becoming more and other than we were before.[20] Narrative manages (without resolving) the aporias between these aspects of personhood by showing how they are a function of our existence in time; narrative offers a means—indeed, for Ricoeur, the integral means—of understanding how personal identity actually coheres. This is so because changes of fortune in the course of a narrative confront a given character with the challenge of responding to new situations and committing to new possibilities. As a result, such a character "becomes other without losing personal identity, that is, it becomes itself without in some manner remaining the same."[21] It is therefore appropriate to hold up narrative as a mirror of life itself, to admit that we grasp the multiplicity of reality in and through representing it narratively: Only by arranging the elements and sequencing the episodes of experience into a "personal history"—an act corresponding to the "synthesis of the heterogeneous" by which narrative is composed—does human being, being incontrovertibly temporal, make any sense.[22]

Consequently, it is axiomatic for the identity of the self to be perceived amidst continuity and change, between what Ricoeur in *OAA* terms identity qua "sameness" (*idem*), and qua "selfhood" (*ipse*). The former bespeaks identity as that which perdures, recognizing itself in its very permanence through time; the latter, as that which corresponds to the self as agent and patient of vicissitudes, in function of which it may pass through radical transformation. The helix formed by these two identities spins at the core of the nonsubstantialist ontology concluding *OAA*, an ontology predicated not on being-as-actuality but being-as-potentiality. Ricoeur presents the notions of *idem*-identity and *ipse*-identity in tandem with those of "character" and "commitment." Character is equivalent to "the set of lasting dispositions by which a person is recognized" while commitment denotes the fidelity of a person to a word spoken—i.e., to his or her self-regulation in the intersubjective realm of language.[23] Character has its own history and produces its own plot, the impulse of "habit" precipitating a "set of acquired identifications."[24] Ricoeur asserts further that "the identity of a person or a community is made up of these identifications with values, norms, ideals, models, and heroes, in which the person or community recognizes itself. Recognizing oneself in contributes to recognizing oneself by."[25] In other words, through force of repetition our actions result in the acquisition of dispositions that propel but also delimit the habits themselves.

Commitment is open-ended, by contrast, since the exigencies of keeping one's word (e.g., fulfilling a promise) may involve the dramatic modification of one's habits—a "losing one's life in order to find it," as it were. Ricoeur terms this trait "self-constancy" and sees in it a phenomenon that "cannot be inscribed, as character was, within the dimension of something in general but solely within the dimension of 'who?'"[26] That is to say, we cannot capture the interpersonal dynamism of commitment in the same terms as the stasis of character: What character deposits, as it were, commitment may erode. Van den Hengel summarizes:

> The self develops in a process, on the one hand, of actions that have "sedimented" themselves in what Ricoeur calls the human character. Here the self displays a consistency, a constancy, a substantive identity, which endures as something that can be identified again and again as being the same. On the other hand, he or she also undertakes actions which are innovative or initiatives. The human person is not only a settled self. At the level of ipseity the self's authenticity consists in remaining truthful to the self by keeping a given word. The self is determined by actions which we have described above as commissives and promissives.[27]

According to Ricoeur, then, selfhood is subject to an essential indeterminacy. An apt analogy might reasonably be drawn with the Heisenberg's uncertainty principle: In certain pairs of properties, such as position and momentum, an increased precision with regard to the apprehension of one involves a decreased precision with regard to the other. So too with respect to selfhood: The self as both *idem* and *ipse* can be postulated, but not simultaneously measured.

How may we apply the foregoing speculations to our liturgical concerns? Van den Hengel ventures that practical theology in the wake of *OAA* ought to be grounded in a new kind of ontotheology, not based on a classical substantialism but instead on activity and passivity, phenomena disclosed by a narrative interpretation of human subjectivity. Such an ontotheology redux "would seek to understand the substructure of human and Christian living as action. It is in relation to this, what Ricoeur calls prefiguration of action, that the Judaeo-Christian textual and living resources can be introduced in order that the Christian project can be realized. Its main thrust will be performance (not only ethics)."[28]

In such a light liturgy attains paramount importance as the sine qua non act of genuine Christian identity. In and through the performance of liturgical narrative the selfhood of its agents develops in respect of their capacity for activity and passivity.[29] The mediation of narrativity is exercised liturgically not only in the actual stories proclaimed but also in the narrative circuit of the ritual ensemble, where symbolism boomerangs, as it were, giving rise to thought that returns again to it. While Ricoeur describes literature in general as a kind of laboratory wherein a person may experiment with discrete existential possibilities ("imaginative variations" on life), liturgy actually *embodies* narrative, arguably conveying thereby a qualitatively different ontological vehemence than the act of reading. As Nicholas Lash eloquently remarks, the liturgy epitomizes the performativity inherent in all genuine interpretation of the scriptural narrative: "Here, that interpretative performance in which all our life consists—all our suffering and care, compassion, celebration, struggle and obedience—is dramatically distilled, focused, concentrated, rendered explicit. In this context, the principal forms of discourse are 'practical' [i.e., illocutionary]: in praise, confession, petition, they seek to enact the meanings which they embody."[30]

"The Self in the Mirror of the Scriptures"—and the Liturgy

The application outlined above is brought into relief when we probe the connection between the two Gifford Lectures omitted from *OAA* and the series as a whole. Ricoeur declares this connection be located at the level of "the ontology of action" and explains: "Setting up a self through the mediation of the Scriptures and the application to oneself of the multiple figures of naming God happens at the level of our most fundamental capacity for action. It is the *homo capax*, capable man, who is interpellated and restored."[31] We shall reserve our discussion of the last lecture for later; since the penultimate illustrates how "the entirely original configuration of the biblical scriptures can refigure the self," let us for the moment seek to grasp the liturgical implications of this process.[32] As mentioned above, Ricoeur observes that the Scriptures *can* be interpreted in terms of the inner coherence of their field of reference, their "centripetal structure"—a feature he finds common to all great poetic texts—but only by detracting from the fecund diversity of the actual biblical genres.[33] Seeming to anticipate criticism of a reductio ad absurdum, in which the contents of Scripture would become an arbitrary miscellany, he stakes a kind of middle ground between, on the one hand, endless fragmentation according to genre and, on the other, typological homogenization. This is accomplished by dividing the text according to the traditional Jewish triad of Law, Prophets, and Writings, and effort yields the prospect of a corollary, threefold experience of selfhood.

Beginning with the Law, Ricoeur observes that it is actually subdivided into legislation and story, genres that interpenetrate inasmuch as the narrative of the *giving* the Law receives its value from the social necessity of apodictically establishing the *origins* of the Law: "Thus it can be said that the Law is a word or speech with regard to the origin of the call, the convocation, the injunction, but Scripture or writing inasmuch as the legislator has absented himself."[34] But the security established by the narrative tradition, its assurance to Israel of being the "Chosen People," finds itself unexpectedly shaken in the subsequent prophetic tradition. In Ricoeur's view prophecy represents fragility: Not only does the prophetic word intimate a historical distance and spiritual departure from that of the founding time and place, but it frequently announces itself as the harbinger of judgment and even destruction.

Finally the genre wisdom appears, at a certain altitude above both the Law and the Prophets, providing a somewhat atemporal perspective on the great questions of life and death, "articulating the singularity of Israel together with the universality of cultures."[35] Having established that God is named differently in the three genres of the Tanakh (thereby revisiting the discussion in "Naming God" treated above in Chapter 3) Ricoeur pronounces upon the kind of responding self these genres solicit. His conclusion? "The triad of the call—Torah, Prophets, Wisdom—is answered, on the side of the self, by the triadic rhythm of a grounded identity, a fragmented identity, and an identity at once singularized and universalized." The corporate self secured by the Law, subsequently threatened by the Prophets, is ultimately taken out of itself, as it were, by Wisdom literature— "The Torah is addressed to a people, Wisdom to each individual."[36]

I think that this pattern allows us to stencil the shape of selfhood envisioned by the genres of the liturgy. While postponing a discussion of the specific form it assumes in the *GBW* to Chapter 8, we may here draw the following parallels, based on the considerations with which we concluded the foregoing chapters. There we discerned a dialectic between the apophatic and kataphatic in the liturgical hymns and prayers, one that amplifies the polyphony of biblical genres resounding throughout the rite. Firstly, the self addressed by the liturgy may certainly be termed at one level a grounded identity. As we shall see in more detail below with respect to the liturgical experience of otherness, the self in worship is one that the Byzantine liturgy addresses with exhortations such as "Peace be with all!"; "The blessing of the Lord be upon you"; and perhaps most poignantly, in the context of the Eucharist: "The servant of God [name] receives the most precious, most pure, body and blood of our Lord and God and Saviour Jesus Christ, for the forgiveness of sins and for life everlasting. Amen."

Such utterances surely communicate the assurance of belonging to a chosen people, especially as this latter is accompanied by an elemental action, an enactment of Ricoeur's "surplus of meaning" if ever there were.[37] Here identity is built upon the terra firma of an event itself, not merely a textual record of an event. Nevertheless, the liturgy is also replete with the sort of critique Ricoeur associates with prophetic literature, corroding the very presumption it elsewhere strains to galvanize. Such "fragmentation" of liturgical subjectivity reaches its apogee in the Lenten hymnography, but resounds throughout the year as well.[38] The following texts are representative:

Woe is me for provoking the wrath of my merciful God and Lord.
O Christ, how often I have promised to repent and been found a senseless liar.
For I have soiled the garment in which I was first baptized, and I have also
    disregarded the covenants I had made with You. . . .

What answer shall you give at the day of judgment, O my wretched soul?
Who shall draw you out of the eternal fire and all the other torments?
Only yourself, by rousing the pity of the compassionate Lord, by forsaking
    your lawless habits, and living in a way that is acceptable to God;
By shedding tears each day for your endless faults committed in thought,
    word, and deed;
And by beseeching Christ to grant you complete forgiveness of all your sins.

O Christ, do not let the compelling habit of sin prevail over me;
Do not let the demon that is battling with me gain possession of me or bear
    me down under his will.
Save me from his mastery and reign with me, making me wholly Yours, O
    Lover of Mankind.
Grant that I may live according to Your will, O Word, and to have rest in
    You alone,
And to find the means of repentance, salvation, and mercy.[39]

Note the themes of being subject to judgment and punishment on account of forces within (the sin of the hymnographer), but also without
(diabolical intervention). Here one meets a self subject to dissolution,
holding on to an eschatological hope: It is not a saved soul but one that
may be such.[40] The consoling assurance given in the Eucharist (as reflected
in the formula cited above) is thus almost withheld—as something yet-
to-be-given. Importantly, the fragmented identity represented by this
contrast also obtains on a level of action, but in a converse motion to that
of the grounded identity offered in the Eucharist; the liturgical tradition
countenances not simply narratives of exclusion but also corresponding
practices by which a self may be deprived of Holy Communion, on account of its own or another's determination of its fault. In such an instance what is sung is also enacted—the hope for salvation acquires a
corporeal "vehemence" extirpated only by fasting, penance, or (in certain
cases) a dramatic alteration of lifestyle.

Finally, I would suggest that the liturgical analogue to Ricoeur's "identity at once singularized and universalized" (biblically engendered by the
wisdom genre) is to be found in the very oscillation of kataphatic and apophatic terminology to which we referred in Chapter 4. The insertion of
philosophical terminology into the liturgical idiom has the effect—as
Ricoeur puts it with respect to the inclusion of Near Eastern mythological
motifs in the Old Testament—of "another Logos . . . com[ing] between the
believers and the living Word of their God."[41] The singular identity affirmed
in the ebullient acclamation, "We have seen the true light. We have received
the heavenly Spirit. We have found the true faith. We worship the undivided Trinity for having saved us," is thus compelled to confront the universality of the quest for the transcendent, whom the liturgy itself
acknowledges to be utterly other.[42]

We can also perhaps descry this aspect of identity also in the practical
field when we consider that Byzantine ritual draws freely from the font of
what Ricoeur calls "bound" symbolism: It too is destined to exploit the
"renewing power of the sacred cosmos and the sacredness of vital nature"
since "only the incarnation of the ancient symbolism ceaselessly reinter-
preted gives [the] word something to say, not only to our understanding
and will but also to our imagination and our heart."[43] Thus while the
narrative invoked by the liturgy is unified to a particular ritual configuration, the individual elements of this configuration are also susceptible
of serving a quite different narrative: The cult of a typical Hindu temple,

for example, employing as it does iconography, chant, incense, processions and prostrations, sacred foods, and even blessed water, surely evinces the kind of originary experience ubiquitously deployed by "bound symbolism" and exploited by metaphor.[44]

The "Embodied Self"

As we have seen, Ricoeur adopts the lens of narrative to examine the operations by which identity obtains as *selfhood* rather than *sameness*. Now *ipse*-identity can be seen as perforated with the experience of passivity, since its characters are both agents and the patients or sufferers of the actions of others. In *OAA* three forms of passivity conspire to betray the presence of alterity in oneself, the first being one's awareness of oneself as a "lived body," which we have already broached in our endeavor to follow into the practical field the itinerary of the self responsive to the polyphony of liturgical discourse. Let us now examine the features of corporeality more closely.

It is clear that contemporary philosophy and theology have both undergone a "turn to the body," as a dimension or extension of the turn to language referred to above.[45] According to Dan Stiver, this widespread emphasis on embodiment has served as an effective challenge to the hegemony of what he calls a Cartesian "dualistic intellectualism." It has been impelled by discoveries in the social sciences pertaining to the role of physiological processes in the act of learning, for example, as well as to the importance of unconscious thought and the degrees to which it is subject to physical well-being or lack thereof.[46] But in theology a similar emphasis has resulted rather from biblical studies' disenchantment with classical Hellenistic anthropology in favor of the allegedly more integrated and holistic Hebraic approach to personhood. Alternatively, Scott Holland argues that ritual studies has been the key agent provocateur, reminding theology and hermeneutics alike that narrative is corporeally rehearsed: "Every story, every text, happens somewhere and in somebody as well as sometime."[47]

In any event, Ricoeur appears to have anticipated this trend in his early philosophy of the will, developed in terms of the relationship between the "voluntary" and the "involuntary." As Stiver explains:

[Ricoeur] pointed out how tied to our decision making are bodily givens such as temperament, emotions, needs, and habits. . . . The embodied and embedded nature of the self undergirds the entire hermeneutical project because it suggests that we ourselves are not transparent texts, whose meaning is to be read off univocally. We are more like a rich poetic text, full of allusions and depth. It is not just that others must interpret us, but we must interpret ourselves.

The upshot of this is that selfhood "is a task and not a given. We cannot start from scratch, from pure mind or thought, or from a blank slate. We start too late—consciously that is. This approach is therefore a frontal assault on the modern and even premodern project that often assumed the clarity of the mind apart from the body, reason apart from emotions, and a conscious self apart from the unconscious."[48] Thus in the first instance, in the very immediacy of our own bodies, there is already an experience of alterity.

Now in one sense Ricoeur is merely recalling us to a former not-quite-forgotten way of doing things. The ascetical writings of the Fathers of the Church, for instance, offer abundant witness to the machinations with which our bodies threaten our selfhood. Usually, this involves a chastening of the body in the vein of the dominical admonishment, "Watch and pray that you may not enter into temptation. The spirit indeed is willing, but the flesh is weak" (Matt. 26:41),[49] or the Pauline lament concerning the maneuvers of a personified "sin" wreaking havoc throughout the corporeal domain.[50] We certainly find in this patristic context a "wounded cogito," humbled by its inability to master itself and dependent in consequence on the divine Other for its vindication and sustenance. It is a hermeneutic self that struggles to interpret dreams and visions; to discriminate between motives and causes; to configure its life to the narrative paradigm of Christomorphism, of "putting on Christ." As George Maloney observes with regard to Evagrius of Pontus (345–99), the ultimate aim of the ascetic life is "the ordering of the deep-seated emotions that brings about a state of interior wholeness and becoming one's true self. . . . [T]he human personality, the ego, resists the emergence of the natural self, which would, by human nature being according to the image and likeness of God himself, be exclusively involved in the contemplation of God but instead is taken up with the demands of the false self in its striving for self-gratification."[51]

Yet the patristic legacy depicted by Maloney has been obscured by the Enlightenment "exaltation of the cogito," what Fergus Kerr terms the "self-conscious and self-reliant, self-transparent and all-responsible individual which Descartes and Kant between them imposed upon modern philosophy."[52] This independent and autonomous self has explained away the phantasms that menace the world of the Fathers, whose wiles render the acquisition of authentic selfhood so arduous and interminable a process. Ironically, it is the very plenipotentiary status of such a discarnate self that has recently been called back into dispute—with Ricoeur as one of the key prosecutors. A first essay into the "absolutely irreducible signification of one's own body" occurs in the second study of *OAA*: A dissection of "identifying reference" leads the author to consider the actualization of language in the event of interlocution *between* speaking subjects. It is not language that means so much as speaking subjects who, "employing the resources of the sense and the reference of the statement in order to exchange their experiences in a situation of interlocution [are] put on stage by the discourse in act and, with the utterers in flesh and blood, their experience of the world, their irreplaceable perspective on the world."[53] Here Ricoeur points to the way that our corporeality inexorably delimits the conditions of selfhood.

We thus find ourselves restrained by the specificity of our speech acts; circumscribing the meaning of our statements is the fact of their having to be uttered in a *hic et nunc* that necessarily conditions them in a unique way; statements are subject to "anchoring," tied to "a unique center of perspective on the world."[54] Ricoeur concludes that the embodied self is thus a conundrum, a mixed phenomenon: "As one body among others, it constitutes a fragment of the experience of the world; as mine, it shares the status of the 'I' understood as the limiting reference point of the world. . . . [T]he body is at once a fact belonging to the world and the organ of a subject that does not belong to the objects of which it speaks."[55]

Here one may well ask whether it is not significant that the Fathers of the Church devote so much time and energy to mystagogy, to teaching the faith on the basis of their congregation's prior experience of it. Consider, for example, the representative exhortation of St. Cyril of Jerusalem (313–86) to his neophytes:

> For some time now, true and beloved children of the Church, I have desired to discourse to you on these spiritual and celestial mysteries. But I well knew that visual testimony is more trustworthy than mere hearsay, and therefore I awaited this chance of finding you more amenable to my words, so that out of your personal experience I could lead you into the brighter and more fragrant meadow of Paradise on

earth. The moment is especially auspicious, since you became receptive to the more heavenly mysteries when you were accounted worthy of divine and vitalising baptism. It remains therefore to lay before you a feast of more perfect instruction; so let me give you careful schooling in this so that you may know the true significance of what happened to you on the evening of your baptism.[56]

It is perhaps indicative of the philosophical acuity of patristic and medieval theologians—their awareness of the corporeal "anchoring" of the liturgical subject—that they indulge in the much-maligned allegorical interpretation of the liturgy. As Paul Bradshaw wryly remarks, regarding the hermeneutical mutations to which liturgical history bears witness: "It is probably inevitable, in spite of all that liturgists may do to resist it, that the desires of popular spirituality will always tend to draw liturgical practice toward a more pictorial representation of the mysteries of the faith."[57] Otherwise put, is it not the case that "all narratives must pass through the body—the hermeneutics of gesture"?[58]

The "Interpersonal Self"

Concerning that aspect of selfhood revealed in the reciprocity of language, Ricoeur could well have uttered those famous lines of John Donne (1573–1631):

No man is an island entire of itself; every man is a piece of the continent, a part of the main; if a clod be washed away by the sea, Europe is the less, as well as if a promontory were, as well as any manner of thy friends or of thine own were; any man's death diminishes me, because I am involved in mankind.[59]

Our linguistic self-expression is at once the most and the least idiosyncratic functions of personal identity: the most, because of the freedom to literally "speak *our* mind," which flows from our individual appropriation of language; the least, because of the inexorable limitations attaching to language as a rule-bound and rigid structure imposed on us apart from our consent. Stiver clarifies:

The turn to language in the first place is already recognition that the meaning of the self lies in part outside the self. Language is a public phenomenon in which we express ourselves, refer to ourselves, and have others refer to us. We swim in language as fish swim in the sea, but we are not the sea. Language is in a sense given to us; it does not arise from us personally. . . . [L]anguage is both a part of the larger tradition or horizon that is given to us before we are self-aware and the background with which we approach anything. In this sense, as Gadamer and Heidegger would say, language speaks us.[60]

Whether to speak *to* ourselves and to others, or to speak *about* ourselves and others—such acts are explicit indications of selfhood, for we know ourselves as the persons represented in and through language. As detailed above, Ricoeur points to the sense of obligation attaching to the giving of a promise, the imperative to act in accordance with one's word inasmuch as such a word is in a certain sense a veritable extension of oneself: "Keeping one's promise . . . does indeed appear to stand as a challenge to time, a denial of change: even if my desire were to change, even if I were to change my opinion or my inclination, 'I will hold firm.' . . . The properly ethical justification of the promise suffices of itself, a justification which can be derived from the obligation to safeguard the institution of language and to respond to the trust that the other places in my faithfulness."[61]

Liturgy is of course shot through with this kind of performative language, language that accomplishes something rather than—or at least in addition to—describing something. There is for instance the significant if overlooked assumption of the first person plural by those who participate in a celebration: The self is clearly decentered in its identification with a collective persona, a "we" that places the worshipper in relation with others both present and absent (e.g., the dead or those absent in body but present to the memory of the community) and with the Other addressed as God, not to say the constellation of other "Others," such as Mary, the angels and the saints. To paraphrase 1 Cor 10:17, we might say that "we who are many, are one body, for we all share in the one story." The character trait common to the variety of people who show up for a liturgy is arguably the common willingness to allow themselves to be interpreted by the story that will be communally enacted presently. And the choice to refrain from engagement in the liturgy is itself a narrative choice, establishing a different trajectory whose outcome (no less than that of the fully conscious, actively participating worshipper) cannot be anticipated. Neither course of (in)action can be fully scouted. As Ricoeur queries, "When I interpret myself in terms of a life story, am I all three [i.e., 'author, narrator and character'] at once . . . ? Narrator and character, perhaps, but of a life of which, unlike the creatures of fiction, I am not the author but at most . . . the coauthor." After all, "in our experience the life history of each of us is caught up in the histories of others. . . . Can one then still speak of the narrative unity of life?"[62] The answer, for Ricoeur, seems to be that one can indeed, but only from within an interpersonal perspective.

We therefore depend on reciprocity. Take the dialogical structure of liturgy, with its formal requirement for the clergy and people to collaborate in the act of blessing, inter alia: The priest requires the assent of the people's "Amen" for the ratification of the blessing offered. Or again, in the *Sursum Corda* dialogue introducing the eucharistic prayer in all the classical Rites, neither role may be assumed by the other; rather, clergy and congregation must together animate the conversation that will generate their common identity as the laity, the "people of God." Each self requires the confirmation of another for its own fulfillment; each requires (to use Ricoeur's term) another's "solicitude."

Ricoeur suggests that the very act of presenting oneself to another, of being available (*disponible*) by saying "Here I am!," is already a movement toward that responsibility or commitment through which we come to know ourselves—even as we abandon ourselves to the potential transformations ensuing upon such a commitment.[63] The portentousness of this act comes to light in the various figures of the "summoned self" Ricoeur traces in the biblical record.[64] If we examine in turn the analogues of "Here I am!" articulated by the liturgy, we find a fragile web of personhood stretched between them. For the liturgical "we" boasts a herculean measure of confidence in (and commitment to) God, the exigencies of which are not readily sustained by the individual self upon its exit from the sacred precinct. Indeed, it is not uncommon for those who have entered most intensively into the life of the liturgy to find themselves undergoing a "dark night of the soul" wherein the question "Who am I?" is aggravated to the point of being an apophatic "crucible of [the] nothingness of identity."[65]

The self is therefore dispossessed by the liturgy even as it is possessed, for it is brought to the point of ever beginning again. The liturgical self is a suspended self, subsistent not only on the mercy of God but on the supplications of all those present who implore said mercy. What Ricoeur sees in the "puzzling cases" of literary fiction that expose the "tormenting question 'Who am I?,'" surely also shows itself in the diffidence of the liturgical subject:

"Who am I, so inconstant, that notwithstanding you count on me?" The gap between the question which engulfs the narrative imagination and the answer of the subject who has been made responsible by the expectation of the other becomes the secret break at the very heart of commitment. This secret break is what makes the modesty of self-constancy differ from the Stoic pride of rigid self-consistency. . . . What is suggested . . . by the narrative imagination is a dialectic of ownership and of dispossession, of care and of carefreeness, of self-affirmation and of self-effacement.[66]

In the context of the Eucharist, for instance, this dialectic translates into the soul-searching interrogation: "Who am I, that I may dare to be counted 'worthy to partake with a pure conscience of Your awesome and heavenly Mysteries'?"; or "Who am I, that I may do so 'not for judgment or condemnation but for the healing of soul and body'?" The response is the temerity expressed with equal force by the rite itself, adjacent to the phrases just mentioned: "The holy Things for the holy!" cries the priest before communion in the Byzantine Rite, as in others of Eastern provenance.[67] The liturgy allows us to testify to ourselves and to others that we have indeed been made worthy—that mercy has been outpoured, grace bestowed. It is to this experience of truth as *testimony* that we will turn momentarily.

The Liturgical Subject: Divine or Human?

Before doing so, however, it is worth perusing Joyce Ann Zimmerman's sketch of the pertinence of *OAA* to liturgical subjectivity, which in its own way may be designated a "puzzling case" with respect to personal identity. Citing the criteria by which liturgy is defined in the teaching of the Catholic magisterium—a public action, carried out by a unified body, differentiated in ministry, with the full, conscious, active participation of all the faithful—she argues that Ricoeur's probative concern with the question of "Who?" invites application to the issue of who, exactly, ought to be deemed the subject of liturgical action. She insists that notwithstanding common opinion, the answer is far from obvious; is it Christ, for example, or the priest, or the assembly? For liturgical texts evince a multiplicity of subjects (through indicators of identifying reference); that is, not only are different actants identified in the rubrics (priest, deacon, people, etc.) but, as we saw above in Ugolnik's treatment of Bakhtin, this form of discourse readily mixes and matches pronouns.

The actants of the rite are placed now in the role of supplicant—itself divisible into instances of first person plural and singular (with the latter divisible again into instances where one's own soul is implied, and those where one expresses the words of another)—now that of narrator, or indeed God himself. In consequence, Zimmerman wonders how a liturgical service may still be comprehended as a unitary action: "I propose the following thesis: the liturgical assembly can be understood to be the subject of liturgy if we take 'liturgical assembly' as a single referent with two predicates (God and liturgical ministers). This thesis sets two tasks before us: to account for all the actants uncovered by the indicators and to show how these indicators are differing predicates for the one referent, the liturgical assembly."[68]

For Zimmerman there is thus one, single subject of liturgy, one "liturgical person" who constitutes, in the terminology of P. F. Strawson (1919–2006) as cited in *OAA*, a "basic particular." She continues her outline of this intriguing concept as follows: "Liturgy obviously unfolds as an action of various interlocutors, even though the speaker(s) and one(s) spoken to may change as the ritual progresses. But there is an interconnectedness (subjectivity) that suggests none of the interlocutors acts independently of the others. The 'I' of liturgy, then, can be assimilated to both God and the liturgical ministers at the same time."[69] Inasmuch as the power to act liturgically resides in the assembly as a whole—i.e., as a corporate subject, its ministers are simply a predicate without independent standing. Zimmerman quotes Vatican II's *Lumen Gentium* to the effect that because the Church subsists not only as the People *of* God but also as the People *in* God, one can duly regard liturgy as an action attributable at once to God and to human beings. Consequently, this action becomes the fundamental locus of identifying reference in the Church; the liturgical assembly is not simply a gathering of people to do something extraneous but the means whereby what the Church *is*, is divulged: "The most concrete expression of Church comes from the most basic of its actions: interconnectedness (intersubjectivity) with one another and God in the act of worship. Any other notion of church (for example, as institution) derives meaning only from this fundamental identity."[70]

It seems to me that Zimmerman has pointed us in the right direction, but that the course needs to be altered somewhat to attain its desired end.

By analogy with the Trinity, one might posit a singularity of being with multiple personal predicates: God is Father, Son, and Holy Spirit. But to advance that the "I" of the liturgical subject (represented by the assembly) is predicable simpliciter of God and the liturgical ministers seems potentially problematic.[71] For it appears to court a pantheism in virtue of which God becomes immanent to the liturgical action without remaining also transcendent to it. In point of fact, for all its alternation of dramatis personae, the liturgy presumes an orientation toward an unrepresentable beyond.

The most powerful semiotic marker of this "beyond" is arguably the physical *orientation* by which the worshipping community intentionally turns to face not itself, but out onto the eastern horizon. "The East" serves to symbolize the bestowal and withdrawal of divine presence that, for his part, Ricoeur locates in Exodus 3:14's concession of a name that is in fact, not a name. Orientation functions, I would say, as a kind of corporeal correlate to the apophatic language by which the liturgy represents sublimity of God: That to which the assembly looks in facing east is, paradoxically, an eschatological reality only visible to the mind's eye. One must accordingly exempt God from being the agent of liturgy in this sense; he is rather the one before whose presence-in-absence, so to speak, the action of the rite is carried out. To stretch the theatrical metaphor: If multiple persons are predicable of the dramatic subject we know as "the cast," there is yet an audience elsewhere—even if invisible in the darkness beyond the light of the stage—to which such persons "face" (following the Greek etymology of persona [*prôsopon*]).

And yet Zimmerman's position does attempt to do justice to the doctrine that the liturgy is truly, in another sense, the work of God himself. The Byzantine Rite, after all, begins with the diaconal exhortation: "It is time for the Lord to act."[72] In this respect, a trinitarian theology becomes imperative; it is by attributing agency to Christ specifically, rather than God generically, that we may follow Zimmerman's lead in positing divine and human predicates for the subject constituted by the liturgical assembly. It befits the ecclesiological emphasis of the author as well, inasmuch as the Church is traditionally said to be the Body of Christ and its liturgy, therefore, the joint work of the whole Christ, Body and Head.[73] Moreover, it follows upon the semiosis of orientation just mentioned, since Byzantine liturgical rubrics also indicate that the assembly should be turned inward at times (for greetings, blessings, biblical readings, the distribution of Communion, etc.), thereby treating itself, one might say, as "another."

Alterity within the Life of the Trinity

May we dare to go even further, transferring Ricoeur's description of the experience of passivity to the "narrative identity" of the Trinity itself, as depicted by the liturgy? We keep good company in indulging in such speculation, for Ricoeurian commentator David Klemm insists that the philosopher would have us treat not an abstract idea of God but rather the actual figure traced by the Scriptures—the imprint of divine agency: "For Ricoeur, these biblical texts represent the concrete existence, the linguistic embodiment of the idea of God. In other words, 'the God-referent' of biblical texts appears (exists) in and through the texts themselves such that the 'I' can respond to the God-referent of biblical texts precisely in the concrete act of understanding and interpreting the texts themselves."[74] Let us then try to trace a liturgical parallel to Klemm's draft, formulated as a variation upon Ricoeur's "biblical thinking."

How do we construe such an idea of God in the biblical text? Following a template derived from the anthropology of Ricoeur's *Fallible Man*, Klemm constructs his model of divine being as the confluence of three principles: universal essence, particular embodiment, and absolute individuality. He avers that "only this idea of God can account for the infinity and eternity of God along with the concrete appearance of God."[75] Remaining within the sphere of *OAA*, however, I intend to frame the divine protagonist active in liturgy along the lines of Ricoeur's nonsubstantialist ontology. Since he argues, according to van den Hengel, that "we cannot think of agency as a power without taking account of the other or of suffering action (passion)," how might our thought of God as liturgical agent require a concomitant consideration of divine passivity?[76]

We recall van den Hengel's resumé of the threefold experience of passivity informing Ricoeur's ontology: (1) the otherness of one's own body that mediates between one's self and the world; (2) the otherness of the other than self, neither another "I" (as in Husserl), nor a totally other (as in Lévinas), but the self of reciprocity or dialogue ("I know the other to be another self in the ethical response that the other enjoins on me. In this sense, the self is responsibility to and by the other"); and (3) the otherness subsisting in one's conscience, an irreducible testimony of the self to itself. Might we in consequence, adhering equally to this schema as to the classical trinitarian datum, propose the following analogues: (1) that the incarnate, ascended Christ fulfills a corporeal mediation between the divine selfhood and the world; (2) that the Church in turn embodies the other than self—to whom God extends, on the Orthodox understanding, the reciprocity not merely of dialogue, but of divinization; and (3) that the Holy Spirit abides as the ineffable voice of divine conscience, that "primary power through which the self attests to itself"?[77]

Sacramental Presence as a "Limit-Experience"

Prior to appraising how liturgy exhibits this paradigm, it bears repeating that the frequent use of apophatic appellations would undoubtedly appear to favor a nonsubstantialist ontology: God cannot per se be known as a being. And yet the *magnalia Dei*, the mighty acts of God, can indeed be attested and acclaimed. Indeed, the supplications of the liturgy's manifold litanies bespeak the divine action as potency and not simply actuality, articulating an expectation that he will *continue* to act in keeping with the "history" of his character. Taking up Ricoeur's modes of passivity in sequence, we can observe first that the Eucharist brings into relief the corporeal mediation of divine selfhood vis-à-vis the world. Not, of course, that sacramental presence (as an enigma meriting the designation "limit-experience") can be assimilated without remainder to Ricoeur's "lived body." As Klemm admits, "In strict conceptual terms, limit experiences are impossible experiences; they cannot be conceived because they arise outside the limits of thought. But, religiously speaking, limit-experiences are necessary experiences; they give actual content and power to the meanings of biblical [viz., liturgical] texts."[78] He describes limit-experiences as being essentially the experience of eternity in time, of the resolution of dialectics that remain theoretically aporetic. By definition, one can never adequately think limit-experiences, though they can nevertheless be attested by recourse to limit-expressions.[79]

In Louis-Marie Chauvet's estimation, the traditional Western account of sacramental presence (i.e., the Latin Christian doctrine of transubstantiation) must actually be repudiated as a "philosophical monstrosity"—terminology borrowed from Ricoeur's analysis of original sin. *Presence* cannot be thought of substantively, he argues, but only in a narrative framework of remembrance and expectation. Or, we might add, of *action* and *potency*—i.e., of what divine agency has accomplished and promised henceforth to fulfill. The distension of the Eucharist between the double parousia "reminds us that, from the point of view of ancient tradition, of which liturgy continues to let us hear the echo, the category of 'memory' is far more important than the one of 'presence,' and that, from the properly Christian point of view, the second asks to be understood starting from the first."[80]

Chauvet's narrative account of the Eucharist further insists upon the fact that the body of Christ is only given as presence for others, that is, for the sake of *communion*. Sacramental presence is thus a phenomenon enacted and suffered; the body of Christ is given to be broken and received. Surprisingly, the author even sees the Latin Rite's reification of the Eucharist (through the twin practices of reservation and adoration) as imploding the static ontology it might at first be thought to imply. This is so, because the very incongruity between the particularity and givenness of the Eucharist and the one of whom it is said to be the body preserves its liminality as the "symbolic expression of this 'always greater' or rather of this 'always more other' which the apophatic tradition has attempted to express on the theoretical level by affecting its affirmations on God by a negative petitioner of supra-eminence."[81] As we shall demonstrate in our final chapter, Chauvet's insight here has ramifications also for how one may appreciate the kind of sacramentality to which the *GBW* attests.

Dialogue and Divine Solicitude

Secondly, if the Eucharist may be plausibly categorized in terms of a Ricoeurian understanding of the body, as an initial sign of the alterity within divine selfhood, the fact that as per Chauvet it is offered to us in *dialogue* connotes the solicitude by which Ricoeur marks alterity's second remove. For the one given in the Eucharist is not only acclaimed as the Word, after all, but is encountered as a partner in the liturgical conversation: One who speaks, and is spoken to. And this conversation is itself predicated on that of the Scriptures, as the witness to the communication of the divine self with the world.

In the inscription of dialogue in the Scriptures, as restored to "living speech" in liturgy, we find exemplified that passivity of the self that Ricoeur insists is ubiquitous on the linguistic plane, inasmuch as "every participant [in the speech situation] is affected by the speech addressed to him or her." He explains:

> The self-designation of the agent of action appear[s] to be inseparable
> from the ascription by another, who designates me in the accusative

as the author of my actions. In this exchange between ascription in the second person and self-designation, one can say that the reflexive recovery of this being-affected by the ascription pronounced by others is intertwined with the intimate ascription of action to oneself.[82]

Is not an intuition of this ontological significance of language represented by the esteem with which Orthodox theology regards the Virgin Mary, as the one whose fiat in some sense *affected* God by *effecting* the Incarnation?[83] Or to return to Ricoeur's cherished Exodus pericope: To what extent may one say that the revelation of the Name illustrates the divine agency suffering itself to be questioned—compelled to designate itself by the address of another?

To apply this to liturgy, it is as though the very condescension by which God deigns to speak with humanity—upon which possibility liturgy as prayer, as communication with God, is predicated—affects all parties concerned. And we may go further, resuming Ugolnik's treatment of Bakhtin above, where he stressed the fragmentation of personae in liturgical speech, on which account self-designation by the worshippers frequently involves ascription to themselves of the very words of God.[84] Just as in the Eucharist the body of Christ suffers assimilation to the bodies of others, so too the words of God are transferred to another. To the objection that the fluidity of self-designation symptomatic of liturgical speech is a purely rhetorical phenomenon without ontological contours, we may rejoin Ricoeur's assertion that through the imaginative variations on ascription afforded by fiction—in this instance, poetic/religious discourse—the self returns to the practical field transformed: "It thus appears that the affection of the self by the other than self finds in fiction a privileged milieu for thought experiments that cannot be eclipsed by the 'real' relations of interlocution and interaction. Quite the opposite, the reception of works of fiction contributes to the imaginary and symbolic constitution of the actual exchanges of words and actions. Being-affected in the fictive mode is therefore incorporated into the self's being-affected in the 'real' mode."[85]

The Holy Spirit as the "Conscience" of God?

Finally, with regard to Ricoeur's third mode of passivity—that of conscience—we mused whether it would be appropriate to view divine selfhood as patient to such an analogue in the other of the Holy Spirit. That is, can we view the Holy Spirit as in some sense the conscience of God? Briefly, we may note that such a relation suits Ricoeur's description of conscience as on the one hand irreducible, and on the other, as something that manifests itself in and through the otherness of others. It is displayed obliquely, that is, as an attestation to the self elicited by the experience of another.[86] Do we perhaps meet something similar in the frequency with which the Spirit is said to bear witness? It is even given for humanity to prompt the Spirit in its intercession with God—fulfilling the dual roles Ricoeur assigns the conscience of attestation and injunction—and thereby inserting a moment of reflection, we might say, into the divine agency: "Likewise the Spirit helps us in our weakness. For we do not know what to pray for as we ought, but the Spirit himself intercedes for us with groanings too deep for words. And he who searches hearts knows what is the mind of the Spirit, because the Spirit intercedes for the saints according to the will of God" (Rom 8:26–27).

It would be hazardous to continue much further along this vector of speculation, whose purpose has only been to indicate a potential application of Ricoeur's thought to the matter of liturgical subjectivity. As St. Gregory of Nazianzus's caveat has it: "Not to everyone, my friends, does it belong to philosophize about God; not to everyone; the Subject is not so cheap and low."[87] Yet perhaps it has not been an altogether inappropriate excursus, insofar as the liturgical naming of God (and imputation of agency to him) does beg the question of divine selfhood. If the specificity of religious discourse is to be discerned in the ontological vehemence of its naming of God, the question surely arises as to the identity of the one in whose image, according to the biblical testimony, humanity is made. It is to this notion of testimony or attestation, as a mode of truth, that we now turn.

CHAPTER

6

TRUTH AS ATTESTATION

Overview

As has by now become evident, Ricoeur approaches questions of selfhood via the "long route" of symbols, metaphors, and narratives. There is no a priori grasping of truth—although there is an intuitive guess in its regard—but only the arduous path of the imaginative exploration of, and eventual ontological validation of, possible worlds.[1] This dual sense of description of a world of meaning and subscription to it in the form of a corresponding way of life is conveyed by the notion of truth as "attestation." In the first part of this chapter, therefore, we further probe *Oneself as Another* (*OAA*) in order to understand the dynamics of attestation and in turn discern how they express themselves within the liturgical context. In the second part, we attend to the related phenomenon of recognition, as this is systematically examined in Ricoeur's *The Course of Recognition*.

The Long Route

Dan Stiver explains that for Ricoeur, "symbols are lacking apart from some affirmation that concretizes them. In other words, apart from a witness, someone to embody the symbols and something about which the witness testifies, symbols lack 'historic density.'"[2] It is thus only through attestation, rather than through a process of argumentation capable of establishing its own veracity, that certain claims to truth subsist. This is, I think, an elaboration of what is at one level a matter of common sense: Whereas one's reasoning in a syllogism may be in order, the premises on which it is based cannot themselves be established syllogistically. Hence Ricoeur affirms the following:

> To my mind, attestation defines the sort of certainty that hermeneutics may claim, not only with respect to the epistemic exaltation of the cogito in Descartes, but also with respect to its humiliation in Nietzsche and his successors. Attestation may appear to require less than one and more than the other. . . . Attestation presents itself first, in fact, as a kind of belief. But it is not a doxic belief, in the sense in which *doxa* (belief) has less standing than *episteme* (science, or better, knowledge). Whereas doxic belief is implied in the grammar of "I believe-that," attestation belongs to the grammar of "I believe-in." It thus links up with testimony, as the etymology reminds us, inasmuch as it is in the speech of the one giving testimony that one believes.[3]

What is germane here with respect to liturgy is that while the primary meaning of *doxa* is *opinion*—i.e., knowledge that is less than secure—it has a secondary connotation of knowledge held in common by others regarding oneself—i.e., one's reputation or glory, as explicated in our discussion of Pelikan's commentary on the matter in Chapter 1. I would therefore broach the possibility that the doxological knowledge afforded by liturgy constitutes just that kind of truth eligible for the designation "attestation," given its adoption of the "the grammar of 'I believe-in.'" For the Nicene Creed—recited in the Eucharist of all the classical Rites— invites one to express belief "in one God, the Father Almighty . . . in one Lord Jesus Christ . . . in the Holy Spirit, the Giver of Life . . . [and] in one, holy, catholic and apostolic Church," a belief warranted by the testimony of the saints whose very lives have borne the burden of its consequences.

The "Truthful Mode"

According to van den Hengel, Ricoeur is attempting in *OAA* a reinterpretation of Aristotle's modes of being ("being-true" and "being-false") with attestation falling under the sign of the former and "suspicion," of the latter. Concurring with the correspondence just mentioned between attestation and the testimony furnished in and by the Creed, van den Hengel expounds: "Against the deconstructionists Ricoeur maintains that, despite the lack of an absolute guarantee of truth, there is a confidence—an unverifiable confidence—in the self, in what the self says, and in what the self believes it can do. The self, in other words, exists as a belief, as a 'fiance,' as an assurance of truthfulness. Ricoeur calls it a '*mode aléthique*,' a truthful mode, which expresses not so much 'I believe that . . .' but, as in the credal formula, 'I believe in . . .'"[4]

Further light is shed on the operations of this "truthful mode" in the ruminations of Jean Ladrière concerning the peculiar relationship between the illocutionary force of the credal affirmation "I believe" and the truth value of the propositions to which it is directed. Truth in credal context is thus in one sense recognized (as evidence that imposes itself on the believer) while in another sense being *constituted* by the very fact of being professed:

> The evidence which intervenes here is a kind of visibility accessible only to the act of faith, as connoting at the same time an intervention of our faculty of understanding and an intervention of the will, which brings into this complex act that moment of decision by virtue of which, precisely, what was at first sight the simple presentation of a possibility becomes the self-manifestation of a reality.[5]

In other words, the person enunciating the Creed is both describing and subscribing—processes inseparable if not indistinguishable—because an authentic description of the credal data cannot but involve a corollary subscription, after the fashion of St. Thomas's acclamation to the risen Christ: "My Lord and my God!" (John 20:28).

The epistemological quandary to which Ladrière draws our attention is effectively the following: While propositions can be said to be true if and when they correspond to facts, the latter are ever subject to interpretation—reality does not divide without remainder into language. One is reminded of Nietzsche's famous aphorism that "Against that positivism which stops before phenomena, saying, 'there are only *facts*,' I should say: no, it is precisely facts that do not exist, only *interpretations*."[6] This is mirrored in the following assessment of Jewish theologian David Novak: "At the ontological level, both philosophy and theology are universal inasmuch as they both make assertions about the entire cosmos. Both are also particular inasmuch as they both stem from the constructions of cosmic reality by particular cultures, cultures that locate their origins in revelation given to them. Each, then, is universal in principle, but particular in fact."[7]

Ladrière continues by arguing that because the propositions of the Creed are not of the empirical order and hence cannot be referred to by a demonstrative gesture, the one confessing the Creed contributes to the meaning of the propositions by the interpretation he or she gives them, determining in consequence the respective function of the notion of truth:

> Thus the truth which is recognized is, so to speak, an active truth, which transforms the existential condition of the speaker who proclaims it. As what is described in the very process of that transformation, it can be said that the meaning, in this context, is its own actualization, the becoming of its truth, and that its truth is its fulfillment: it is in the measure in which the meaning of what is proclaimed becomes effectively active in the life of faith that it receives its truth.[8]

One realizes immediately that such a way of casting the matter augurs the plague of relativism, not to say nihilism. The obvious rejoinder is to ask whether it then reduces the act of faith into a beneficent delusion—from which the better part of humanity suffers in its adhesion to multitudinous, contradictory religious propositions. And yet it is not readily apparent how one might serve a logical, if not moral, riposte to Ladrière: Surely he is correct in insisting that empirical verifiability cannot suffice for matters that by their very nature abide either wholly on another level, or straddle the divide between the perceptible and the imperceptible.

We are apparently thrown back upon the "fact" of manifestation and the truth it conjures through the workings of the imagination. As Ladrière has it, truth in religious matters ultimately, inexorably links up with testimony: "In the last analysis, the ultimate criterion of truth, in general, must be an experience in which what is said is recognized as expressing adequately something that is manifest. The last foundation of truth is a manifestation."[9] That is, even if faith *originates* in an event, it must still be mediated to the present via the testimony of others, a testimony that must exert an appeal and exercise an attraction upon those it would persuade. Nonetheless, as Ladrière skillfully shows (in a manner reminiscent of the inversion performed by Ricoeur in "Philosophical Hermeneutics and Biblical Hermeneutics"),[10] the specificity of the Christian testimony offers what we might call a sort of shock therapy to those laid low by the malaise of hermeneutical melancholy. Because Christ uniquely calls himself "the truth," he is disclosed as the foundation of all other truth claims; his testimony is not to an extrinsic reality but rather to himself. Our use of such terms as "truth" and "word," therefore, rather than serving as the basis for an analogy in which Christ is taken as "Truth" and "Word," finds itself unexpectedly bollixed. *Our* use instead is discovered to be a participation in *his* reality: He constitutes the referent of our analogies.

Does such a contention amount to fideism? Is one left without room for autonomous rational inquiry? Ladrière will not go so far, acknowledging only the primacy of the discourse of faith with which second-order discourse must reckon as best as it can. The latter cannot get a foothold above the former, as it were, but must move along pari passu. Its claims are subject to perennial contestation and revision inasmuch as "a categorical scheme is never the ultimate truth." Here the author quotes the Whiteheadean dictum, "Every philosophy, in its turn, will be deposed,"[11] but one might also aptly cite C. S. Lewis's remonstration: "We have no abiding city even in philosophy: all passes, except the Word."[12] However feasible in principle it might be to abstract and systematize the object of faith, it is never disclosed in its actuality save in the first-order testimony of/to revelation—a testimony that always already compels a corresponding existential stance.[13] And it is the power of this stance to sustain the self, its attestation to what van den Hengel calls the "unverifiable confidence . . . in what the self says, and in what the self believes it can do," that renders it so formidable.

Attestation

We shall return to this theme in our treatment below of the self's recognition of its own capacities. But here it is appropriate to single out the intimate relation between "attestation" and the testimony offered by the figure of the martyr, which Ricoeur evaluates in his most important work on testimony prior to *OAA*, "The Hermeneutics of Testimony": "This engagement, this risk assumed by the witness, reflects on testimony itself which, in turn, signifies something other than a simple narration of things seen. Testimony is also the engagement of a pure heart and an engagement to the death."[14] Testimony at its limit both includes and surpasses narrative, because the martyr gives a self-effacing witness by his or her death to the "narration of things seen."[15] Still, this witness is itself subsequently transmitted preeminently through narrative inscription: We typically adjudicate a martyr's testimony—if not ourselves occupying the place of first-hand witnesses—by rehearsing it through our own narratives about him or her.

Now Ricoeur portrays testimony as marked by irreducibility: Although we can and must contest any narrative set forth with universal intent, we cannot for all that get behind it or render it univocal. To the contrary, it must be confronted (and perhaps challenged) in all its particularity. This resumes the issue of biblical polyphony treated in Chapter 3, since examples of testimony such as biblical prophecy acquire gravitas in respect of their claim to proceed from a divine initiative. There it is primarily God who bears witness, the prophet in turn appropriating the divine testimony by doubling its first-person ascription.

Like the narratives of the martyrs, the narrative(s) of the liturgy invites a judgment for or against the authenticity and validity of its claims. As with the narratives of biblical prophecy, the stakes are high—the liturgy purports to be fundamentally the action of God himself. And we ourselves give witness by acceding (or not) to the divine testimony. Stiver astutely observes that Ricoeur, in endeavoring to explain this kind of phenomenon, never simply explains *away*: "[He] takes great care not to reduce that which is beyond the self, preeminently God, to a possession of the self. In this sense, he does not shy away at all from saying that when God is encountered, the encounter is mediated by the imagination, but this does not mean that the meaning of God is the imagination—or even that texts about God are produced solely by the imagination."[16] Similarly, there is no guarantee that the liturgical celebration by which we attest to the divine witness is not duplicitous; it is only proved genuine by a life steadfast in its appropriation of the truth to which it ritually subscribes. At stake is a wager contingent upon an eschatological outcome.

Attestation and "Objective Knowledge"

Finally, it is worth commenting on the occasional apparition of what Stiver deems a passé, modernist Zeitgeist, haunting the threshold between the potential subjectivity of attestation (expressed in the grammar of "I believe-that") and the putatively objective knowledge of the sciences. Postmodernity, for Stiver, is marked by a firm protestation that science itself is not an edifice supported by what Ricoeur calls "self-founding knowledge," but rather by the scaffolding of particular prejudices whose validity is *itself* hermeneutical.

We encountered a similar phantom in Chapter 3, in the course of our rumination on the facticity of metaphorical reference; there Ricoeur posited a sharp contrast between first- and second-order discourse, the former being in his parlance an index to the actual world of manipulable things treated by scientific inquiry and the latter, to the nonostensive, but nonetheless real, realm of our ownmost possibilities.[17] Stiver thus alleges:

> Ricoeur seems to appeal to what we might call a pre-Kuhnian understanding of science (in honor of Thomas Kuhn's hermeneutical turn in the 1960s, seeing the sciences as interpretive and shaped by history and context much like the humanities). Kuhn has been followed in large part by contemporary philosophy of science. . . . [This argues that] science is situated in history, is constructed, involves the imagination along with metaphorical models, is socially embedded, and is affected by power and ideology.[18]

Nevertheless, this "blind spot" actually serves only to augment the value of Ricoeur's estimation of attestation, as again with respect to metaphor. Testimony, which may be validated but not verified in an absolute sense, is now accorded jurisdiction throughout the domain of knowledge. While holding a quasi-empirical stake on experience—van den Hengel notes such truth is not, in Ricoeur's judgment, psychological but rather epistemological[19]—it is yet vulnerable to critique, and in the end must be substantiated by action: "Attestation is not totally clear, always faces the restriction of suspicion, and allows for the expansion of a surplus of meaning. It never escapes the conflict of interpretation but is a risk, backed by one's life, looking forward to vindication in hope."[20]

The Role of Recognition

To review our itinerary thus far: Ricoeur argues for a notion of a corporally situated self, narratively mediated, intrinsically communitarian, validating its authenticity through claims to truth that it is prepared to actualize through suffering. It is a self that confesses, to paraphrase the famous dictum of St. Anselm of Canterbury (1033–1109), "Spero ut intelligam"—"I hope, in order to understand."[21] My own position has been that the shape of this personal identity is deeply congruent with that which is presupposed by, and proposed within, the liturgical gestalt.

In the remainder of this chapter I would like to canvass Ricoeur's inquiry into the phenomenon of recognition, since it serves as a central node for the interface of his determinations concerning selfhood and attestation, whence they can be effectively channeled toward a liturgical application. He describes his course, starting from a discovery of the rich polysemy of the verb "to recognize" (especially the contrast between its active and passive forms), as "the passage from recognition-identification, where the thinking subject claims to master meaning, to mutual recognition, where the subject places him- or herself under the tutelage of a relationship of reciprocity, in passing through self-recognition in the variety of capacities that modulate one's ability to act, one's 'agency.'"[22]

Curiously, a backward reading of *The Course of Recognition* (one beginning with mutual recognition) is encouraged by Ricoeur himself in the conclusion to the work, where he seeks to reintegrate his analyses of recognition back into a general discussion of alterity. "In a word, the figures of alterity are innumerable on the plane of mutual recognition," he writes, although he has chosen to privilege the manner in which the "struggle for recognition"—the fact of "social competition" between people compelled to justify their standing within the "plurality of cities or worlds" they inhabit—can end in a truce through the reconciliation promoted by occasions of "shared generosity."[23]

Liturgical Recognition: Gift and Sacrifice

We catch a glimpse of the liturgical horizon onto which Ricoeur's thoughts grant passage when he calls attention to two interrelated occurrences that exemplify shared generosity: "states of peace" and "gift exchanges." Of the first he asserts, "The thesis I want to argue for can be summed up as follows: The alternative to the idea of struggle in the process of mutual recognition is to be sought in peaceful experiences of mutual recognition, based on symbolic mediations as exempt from the juridical as from the commercial order of exchange."[24] In Western culture, Ricoeur continues, the supreme state of peace is that connoted by the biblically and theologically contoured term "agape," expressing as this does the mystery of the gift.[25] It is in the state of peace generated in and through the "paradox of the gift and the gift in return" that one can discern within the "struggle" for mutual recognition an inherently benevolent motivation.

Now in the Christian tradition, liturgy arguably qualifies as the consummation of this peace-inducing ceremonial gift exchange. The principal service in all the classical Rites of the Church is of course the Eucharist, the great "thanksgiving" featuring a threefold exchange: Bread and wine, produced from the fruits of the divine munificence in creation, are themselves presented in sacrifice to God from whom they are pneumatically received back again as a means of sharing in the divine life. Intriguingly, Ricoeur's contemporary Jean-Luc Marion has carefully elaborated upon the philosophical significance of the Eucharist, understood alternately in terms of "gift" and of "sacrifice"—complementing Ricoeur's more inchoate insights in this regard. Cristina Gschwandtner notes that for Marion, theology, "as speaking (*logos*) about God (*theos*), must proceed from God and be grounded in the Eucharist, which functions as the locus for the hermeneutics of the divine Word (which ultimately refers to Christ). In the Eucharist, we are enabled to cross from 'sign' (word) to the referent (the Word himself). The Eucharist is a gift of God's love and not merely the imagination of the assembled community."[26]

According to Marion, sacrifice becomes the corollary of an authentic gift. Concretizing Ricoeur's approach to metaphor as that which promotes a "seeing-as" unto a "being-as," Marion's argument is that sacrifice "enables the gift to appear again as such, because it no longer lays claim to the gift or attempts to possess it. The sacrifice allows us to 'see' differently. It makes possible the response to the given in which the gift (and ultimately even the giver) is able to appear."[27] In this connection it is important to remember that the Eucharist, while the sacrifice and gift par excellence, also serves in the Byzantine tradition as the exemplar for a myriad of other liturgical services—other "sacrifices" or "gifts"—that redeploy its fundamental dynamic of *blessing*. We shall of course have more to say below concerning phenomenon of blessing.

Given that Ricoeur appears to view the struggle for recognition as preceding the mutual recognition induced by the exchange of gifts, we should pause to respond Martin Blanchard's complaint—namely, that Ricoeur falls into the "commonplace error of situating the hermeneutical understanding of interacting selves before the communicative moment."[28] As evidence, he cites Ricoeur's decision to treat the theme of "the capable human being" prior to that of "making space for the other." What I retain from Blanchard is that there does seem to be no particular reason why the ceremonial exchange of gifts must be perceived as a truce, a momentary pause within the battle, as it were, rather than as an *originary* state.

Indeed, according to David Bentley Hart, the biblical vision is distinguished precisely by a primordial gratuitousness, displayed in the act of creation and fulfilled in a disposition of welcome: "an openness before glory, a willingness to orient one's will toward the light of being, and to receive the world as a gift, in response to which the most fully 'adequate' discourse of truth is worship, prayer, and rejoicing."[29] In other words, if the state of peace linked by Ricoeur with the economy of the gift may, sociologically speaking, not infrequently be purchased only at the price of conflict, there are surely figures of mutuality in which struggle has not played such a role. If the extravagant hospitality offered to a stranger in many traditional cultures is an eloquent witness in this respect, so too is that hospitality extended by liturgy in extension of the divine welcome. For there the exchange of gifts constitutes a normative rather than exceptional event. Not that mutual recognition can be *guaranteed* by liturgical action, as if its very gratuitousness could be controlled, but rather that in liturgy (as in hospitality) mutuality is a presupposition rather than a conclusion. In entering a liturgical assembly, for example, one is ipso facto addressed as a member of a community—greeted, exhorted, and blessed by means of second-person pronouns, and invited to add one's own voice to the assembly's responses enunciated in the first person. Liturgical action presents itself phenomenologically, in the words of Ricoeur, as belonging to that form of "non-commercial reciprocity marked by what is without price."[30]

Moreover, because Orthodox tradition holds the liturgy to be in fact the very work of God himself, acting in and through those who celebrate, there is additional reason to associate it with Ricoeur's invocation of agape as the paradigmatic of gift exchange—a figure he says is better spoken of as "a response to a call coming from the generosity of the first gift."[31] As in the Johannine admission, "We love because he first loved us" (1 John 4:19), so also the work of the liturgy is, from a theological perspective, pure *gift*— the gift of being enabled to efficaciously integrate one's *own* giving into the divine self-donation.[32] Hence the patristic notion of *perichoresis*, that ineffably mutual interweaving dance of love that is said to bespeak, paradoxically, the unspeakable inner life of the Trinity.[33]

Liturgical attestation thus leads to a kind of self-recognition—as what Ricoeur elsewhere calls "summoned subject." But the summons in question surpasses that discussed by Ricoeur in his treatment of the biblical/ hagiographical figures representative of such a subject.[34] In liturgy the subject-in-community is summoned not on the plane of the Old Testament prophet, mandated to communicate a divine message; nor that of the New Testament disciple, called to the *imitatio Christi*; nor yet that of St. Augustine, inspired to hearken to the voice of the "inner teacher." Instead, the summons is one shared by all of the cosmos and more, by the unseen host of angels and saints, a doxological summons to "not conceal God's benevolence." Such a call resounds continuously throughout the book of Psalms and, as we shall see below, is deployed in full force throughout the *GBW.*

Asymmetry in the Course of Liturgical Recognition

To conclude this chapter, I would like to enter into Ricoeur's discussion of the asymmetry abiding at the heart of recognition. He is quick to caution that his privileged occasion, the exchange of gifts, belies an essential asymmetry between its protagonists—one that must not be forgotten, lest the paradox of the gift be reduced to an economy of quid pro quo in which the personhood of giver and receiver alike is effaced. That is to say, there is a uniqueness in every exchange of gifts that is inscrutable, insofar as the moment itself is unrepeatable, sui generis, resistant to insertion into a system. In Ricoeur's words, "Forgetting this asymmetry, thanks to the success of analyses of mutual recognition, would constitute the ultimate misrecognition at the very heart of actual experiences of recognition." He continues:

> Admitting the threat that lies in forgetting this dissymmetry first calls attention to the irreplaceable character of each of the partners in the exchange. The one is not the other. We exchange gifts but not places. The second benefit of this admission is that it protects mutuality against the pitfalls of a fusional union, whether in love, friendship, or fraternity on a communal or cosmopolitan scale. A just distance is maintained at the heart of mutuality, a just distance that integrates respect into intimacy.[35]

Now the temptation to forget such an asymmetry is poignantly countered in a liturgical context by the very absence, as it were, of the Other with whom the exchange of gifts (and hence mutual recognition) is supposed to occur. For of course the face, tasked by Lévinas with revealing the otherness of the Other, cannot be beheld.[36] Instead, all that is unveiled, as with Moses on Mt. Sinai, is the *shekinah* or glory of the Lord—and this from behind. And such glory, altogether gratuitous and sublime—a "limit-experience," as we advanced above—may only be accessed (if not experienced in person) through the testimony of another. Proof of life, we may say, concerning the existence of the absent Other is granted only in the words and actions of the rite, which factor in the legacy of the Scriptures while exceeding it. Excess horizontally, as it were, by the inclusion of other literary genres (hymns, litanies, prayers, blessings, etc.) proper to the liturgical tradition, but also vertically, by the conversion of all of the textual traces into a ritual medium addressed to the whole person.

As for the integration of respect into intimacy, if it is perhaps a condition with which the mystic may dispense in the rapture of ecstasy, it nonetheless finds ample ratification within the liturgy. For the articulation of distance in the liturgical idiom is, paradoxically, the precondition for any expression of intimacy. That is to say, it is in the very naming of God as radically Other that a space opens up for a metaphorical approach. Recall in this connection our discussion in Chapter 4 of the dialectic between the apophatic and kataphatic that is typical of Byzantine hymnography. There we discovered that Byzantine liturgical discourse revels in the frequent invocation of paradoxical attributions, juxtaposing florid embellishments of episodes either laconically recounted in the Bible or excerpted from extrabiblical literature, with a speculative "naming" of God not easily reconcilable to the way of affirmation.

Here we may add that the liturgical subject encounters scandal not only in the naming of God, but in the manner in which space and time are impossibly collapsed in the liturgy, with past being recognized as present: The events celebrated are described as occurring in the "today" (*sémeron*) of the service. This applies analogously on a spatial plane, with the river, lake, or seaside before which the congregation gathers (in the *GBW*) becoming in virtue of the prototypical Jordan River a fluid *axis mundi*. In this connection, the operation of recognition-identification is brought to the brink, in a subjective movement paralleling the objective dialectic of kataphasis and apophasis promoted by the rite. As mutual recognition within the liturgy involves the striving for mutuality with the invisible; and self-attestation calls for a recognition of capacities ordinarily felt to be mute if not absent; so with regard to the very faculties of sense as these apprehend time, space, and matter, the course of liturgical recognition is ultimately one that runs inexorably toward the Ricoeurian "limit-experience."

Concerning the possibility of misrecognition, Ricoeur speaks of the need to come to terms with "the fallibility of the credit given to the appearance of what is perceived, which Merleau-Ponty called a kind of faith or primordial opinion."[37] Given the polysemy of *doxa* (explained above) can one perhaps identify this phenomenological "faith" as subterraneously joined to what we might call a doxological risk? Ricoeur asserts that the course of recognition involves the risk that one will *misrecognize* something, thereby misrecognize oneself and others and hence experience "self-deception." Recognition thus remains a humble enterprise, unable to attain to a totalizing perspective free of doubt. To combat the "threat of failure," the "fear of error," Ricoeur counsels an "acceptance of a kind of companionship with misunderstanding, which goes with the ambiguities of an incomplete, open-ended life world."[38] He indicates subsequently the manner in which the very power to act that enables self-recognition labors under the shadow of incapacity, limitations, and liabilities. Speech suffers from being found inadequate to the task of articulating experience; memory, from forgetfulness; promising, from perjury.

For a theology of the liturgy, however, such a conclusion is felicitous, for it preserves a space for what the Christian tradition has called *grace*. One only and ever employs, for example, the blessed matter of the *GBW* in faith, at the risk of taking it for something it is not, with the "fear of being mistaken" ready at the door. Liturgy fosters the acceptance of an "open-ended life world" because it lays forth the world as always more than we can grasp. There is no mastery of the meaning of the Eucharist, or of any sacrament or sacramental such as holy water, but only an aporia, traversed in the wager of a Ricoeurian surplus of meaning—itself only validated in respect of the "narrative unity of a life." The wager is, in sum, that by following the course of the liturgy, one will ultimately come to a place of mutual recognition with the One who, in the words of the *GBW*, "while remaining boundless, without beginning, and beyond all words, deigned to come down upon earth, to assume the likeness of a servant, and to become like man."[39]

Up until now we have examined the various dimensions of liturgical subjectivity, after having treated, in the first part of the book, the question of liturgical language. To complete our hermeneutical toolbox we turn next to a consideration of the multifaceted way in which liturgical memory functions. With that in hand, we will be positioned to finally attempt a Ricoeurian interpretation of the rite to which have hitherto only been able to refer in passing.

CHAPTER

7

LITURGICAL TIME, NARRATIVE, MEMORY, AND HISTORY

Overview

In this chapter I propose a Ricoeurian approach to the mnemonic operations animating the ritual process—implicit though they may be. Specifically, through an investigation of several key sections of his magisterial antepenultimate work, *Memory, History, Forgetting* (henceforth, *MHF*), we will come to apprehend the complexity of the liturgical act construed as a quintessential form of "remembering." In order to bring into relief certain elements of *MHF* that will prove germane to our intended liturgical application, we will first enter into a recent debate concerning the role of history (and historiography) in liturgical theology: The resolution of this debate (or lack thereof) would appear to have wide-ranging hermeneutical repercussions.[1]

"Lex Orandi, Lex Credendi"?

In a two-part article in *Worship* (introduced summarily in Chapter 4), Michael Aune argues that the contributions of a particular generation of scholarly luminaries—namely, Schmemann, Aidan Kavanaugh, David Fagerberg, and Gordon Lathrop—have reached their term, leaving the task of propounding an authentic liturgical theology to be taken up afresh by a new cohort employing a different methodology. The essence of Aune's argument is that "a new generation is about to unfold that will take seriously the fruits of historical research [and] be more explicitly theological as well."[2] The

150

meaning of the latter part of this challenge, according to the author, is the "recovering [of] a deepened awareness of the divine initiative in the church's worship," while that of the former is taken to be straightforward. But is it indeed? Is the recommendation that a discipline be "more historical . . . in its content and character" as unequivocal as it at first appears?

MHF demonstrates why Ricoeur would likely demur. Where Aune steps lightly from the positing of historical fact to an understanding of its contemporary pertinence, Ricoeur perceives a perilous leap over a precipitous hermeneutical crevasse. The gap in the surface evinces, in turn, a deeper fault line running between the mnemonic and historiographical operations, which Ricoeur exposes in *MHF* through successive phenomenological, epistemological, and ontological analyses. The result is to disrupt the conceptual stability of such theories as would move too quickly from the "since" or "because" of the assumed past to the "therefore" of the present. As we shall see, the irony of Aune's call for greater scholarly attention to be paid to "recent historical research" is that it ignores recent research into the very *nature* of the historical, including that conducted in the present volume by Ricoeur.

It is my suspicion that we need the sort of interrogation carried out by Ricoeur in order to chasten the hubris of a facile historicism, which is the opposite of what Taft calls the "great contemporary illusions . . . that one can construct a liturgical theology without a profound knowledge of the liturgical tradition"[3]: The contrary illusion here is that one can attain a total grasp of history, upon which one may subsequently presume to critique a tradition from *above* rather than from *within*. No doubt Aune is prudent to ask of the next generation of liturgical scholars a "rethinking of how we regard the liturgy-theology relationship"[4]—of the meaning of the *lex orandi, lex credendi* topos. We shall see if *MHF* may not offer some of the requisite tools.

MHF is surely Ricoeur's densest and most complex work and that which solicits the greatest amount of propaedeutic reading in both classical and recent philosophical literature.[5] As Michael Johnson opines, "Ricoeur tracks the traces of memory into the labyrinths of the human mind and the archive of human history. In the end, however, he is in pursuit of an enigma that eludes capture. If the reader sometimes may feel frustrated in the attempt to pin down the ultimate import of Ricoeur's reflections in their full range, then perhaps that is the nature of the case."[6] For our purposes, I would like to provide a cursory analysis of several of *MHF*'s themes, reflecting in turn upon their potential implications for the "rethinking" called for by Aune. The triadic structure of *MHF* lends itself well to being treated in like manner, and I will thus proceed to explore the text in terms of its successive phenomenological, epistemological, and hermeneutical-ontological moments.

Phenomenology: The Dialectics of Memory

In the first chapter of *MHF*, Ricoeur sets forth a taxonomy for the phenomenon of memory, drawing upon the categories posited by Aristotle and Plato. His ordering proceeds in pairs of opposites. Thus the functioning of memory is differentiated between its passive mode, as something suffered (*mnēmē*), and its active mode, as the effort of recollection (*anamnēsis*); memories themselves may be fictive, a representation (*eīdolon*) of a phantasma, or correspond to the reality (*tupos*) of which they are a faithful image (*eikōn*). Ricoeur's investigation of such texts as the *Sophist, Phaedrus*, and *Theaetetus* serves to probe the conventional notion of memory as *replacing* what is now absent. The problems addressed include the following: In what sense does a representation participate in the reality of its other? How does that which is gone continue to exist in memory? How is that which is past recovered after being lost?

Memory is further distinguished by Ricoeur into the power at work in the act of remembering (*la mémoire*) and the object of the act (*le souvenir*). And we can note the further bifurcation of *la mémoire* into the notions of "habit-memory" and "recall-memory": The former designates memories that have been incorporated into our present such that we are not conscious of their origin in the past, e.g., techniques that are retained on a subconscious level and displayed in our actions; the latter, the distinct events that become lodged in our memory—and that remain available to be summoned up by the imagination as representations—through the impression they make upon us. All the pairs of opposites presented by Ricoeur help place in view the multifariousness of the phenomenon of memory latent in ordinary, pre-reflective experience.

Reflexivity vs. Worldliness

I would like to privilege the final set of polarities introduced by Ricoeur in his phenomenological sketch of memory. He observes that memory oscillates between the poles of "reflexivity" and "worldliness," resulting in a subtle dialectic between our interior witness to the past and the inscription of the past in the world. Thus "one does not simply remember oneself, seeing, experiencing, learning; rather one recalls the situations in the world in which one has seen, experienced, learned. These situations imply one's own body and the bodies of others, lived space, and, finally, the horizon of the world and worlds, within which something has occurred."[7] This physical dimension of mnemonic data can be expressed by the category of "corporeal memory": This refers to the capacity for the body to archive its experiences for subsequent evocation or recollection by "secondary memory," in which process they may become narrativized and move along the spectrum from the worldly to the reflexive pole.

The exercise of corporeal memory is vividly manifest, according to Ricoeur, in our memory of *places*; an experience is contiguous with its environment to the extent that the former impresses itself upon us in the particularity of the latter: "it is not by chance that we say of what occurred that it took place."[8] In other words, we remember events by reference to location, which becomes in consequence a species of "inscription" wherein the record of the past is attested—"whereas memories transmitted only along the oral path fly away as do the words themselves."[9] Ricoeur explicitly connects the memory of places to the enactment of ritual commemorations, civic and religious, but does not develop the trajectory further at this point, beyond voicing a series of questions concerning the "nature of the space and of the time in which these festive figures of memory unfold."[10] Ricoeur thus demonstrates once again his awareness of the full rotation implied in the linguistic turn—namely, a corollary turn to the body itself. Already in *OAA*'s thematizing of the "lived body," Ricoeur showed himself conversant with the philosophical trend displayed, for example, in Lakoff and Johnson's *Philosophy in the Flesh*.[11]

Holy Memories, Holy Places

As an illustration of how Ricoeur's development of "corporeal memory" in *MHF* is relevant to our current enterprise, let us consider the way in which memory (re)attached to place through liturgical commemoration in the fourth-century historicizing of Jerusalem's holy places. Robert Taft suggests that it was only natural for "pilgrims to go where Jesus did or said this or that, preferably on the anniversary of the event." On the other hand, he acknowledges that the realism characteristic of the hermeneutical style of the Antiochian tradition played its part; this is brought into relief by its contrast with the "dehistoricizing, spiritualizing propensity in heortology [i.e., theology of the liturgical year]" of the Alexandrian tradition.[12]

If indeed the establishment of the holy places was a normal development, it was nevertheless controversial. Brouria Bitton-Ashkelony argues that while pilgrimage was very common in late antiquity, it was often regarded with ambivalence; moreover, pilgrimage to the Holy Land per se, rather than to local sites hallowed by their respective Church's saints, evoked a particularly mixed reaction from theologians and church leaders. At issue was the merit of "earthly sacred journeying to encounter the divine versus interior journeying to an inner space": the extent to which, we may say, spiritual anamnesis benefitted for its mnemonic efficacy from a spatial correlate.[13]

Now as Taft notes above, the kind of commemorations to which the late-fourth-century Spanish nun Egeria testifies expressed a devotional interest in both days and places.[14] Again, if the establishment of the holy places was to be expected, it is remarkable that it appears to have taken a long time—almost four centuries—to obtain, and even then in the face of criticism. Of course, Jerusalem was to a certain extent inaccessible, due to the destruction suffered in the wake of the first Jewish-Roman war in A.D. 70 and the city's conversion into Aelia Capitolina.[15] Yet Bethlehem, Bethany, Nazareth and a host of other sites that were to become enduring shrines might well have hosted an incipient sacralization; as is clear from Bitton-Ashkelony's discussion of the pilgrimage experience of St. Gregory of Nyssa, the eventual rise in popularity of Jerusalem, the place of Christ's death, readily embraced also those locales associated with his earthly life.[16] Read in light of Taft's assertion that the early Christians "were intensely concerned to establish the exact chronology of Jesus' death," one is struck by the contrast between the nascent preoccupation with a temporal orientation toward the Passion, and the apparent delay in the development of a similar concern for its *localization*.[17] It begs the question of whether Ricoeur is correct in his hypothesis that the insertion of memory into calendrical time occurs in parallel to its spatial sedimentation.

In any event, "the articulation of phenomenological space and time onto cosmological space and time" is ultimately, for Ricoeur, a function of the existential need to resist the encroachment of forgetfulness.[18] Was it the fear of amnesia then that led the Church of the fourth century to exploit its imperial status by focusing the commemoration of specific events in the life of Christ on locations that seemingly had hitherto been regarded, as it were, as neither here nor there? The prescience that tradition accords St. Helen in respect of her erection of the Church of the Holy Sepulchre/Anastasis is displayed in the popularity enjoyed—and interconfessional rivalry suffered—by this alleged place of Christ's burial/resurrection down through the centuries and into our own day. Whether or not the miracles verifying its identity, as recounted in the hagiography of St. Helen, "actually" occurred is a moot point: The belief of the Orthodox in its authenticity is perennially rejuvenated, to their satisfaction if not necessarily to others', by the well-documented miracle of the "holy fire" at the celebration of Pascha on the Julian calendar.[19] This phenomenon dramatically illustrates what Ricoeur calls the insertion of commemoration within the context of worldliness. That is, the Anastasis exhibits the conversion of a memory into a place that, on account of the very continuity of liturgical commemoration, is then experienced as a *proof* of the veracity of the event originally memorialized.

And yet the value of the fixation of this holy place par excellence does not ultimately mitigate the consequences of the "strong dehistoricizing of the Pasch (and of all liturgy, for that matter)," which, as Taft remarks above, marks the Alexandrian tradition. This tradition's "decided attenuation of the importance of Salvation History as history," wherein "the salvific event becomes a type, a symbol of an interior, spiritual reality," is actually reproduced by the inscription of the commemoration of the Anastasis in the liturgical hymnography of the Byzantine Rite.[20] The third "Anatolian" sticheron of Tone 1, originally composed to be sung in the resurrectional vigil at the Anastasis, and now sung every eighth week at Saturday evening Vespers in Byzantine-Rite churches, declares: "as we stand unworthily before Your life-bearing grave, we offer a hymn of praise to your ineffable tenderness of heart."[21] Such is the Ricoeurian "surplus of meaning" in this sort of poetic text that there can be no warrant for contesting those who would now see the text as referring to the *altar* of the church in which the rite is celebrated—the altar being classically understood as a *symbol* of the tomb of Christ. The tomb itself as an actual, putatively historical location, has been poetically spiritualized anew, in a rediffusion of that meaning erstwhile concentrated in the specificity of a site of memory—a site from which the memory/meaning of the Resurrection had nevertheless originally become independent. In other words, the theological significance of the (empty) tomb has been handed down in liturgical prayer through an "invented" correspondence to the shrine at the Anastasis, as if memory could not obtain apart from a physical reference point.[22]

Many other examples of this kind of ritual occurrence in the Byzantine Rite could be adduced, most obviously the hymnography composed to commemorate the universal exaltation of the True Cross (Sept. 14); or the many stanzas celebrating myrrh-streaming relics or tombs, or wonder-working icons; or services that present those at prayer as inhabitants of a given city or as congregants in a given church building (e.g., the office for St. Demetrius, Oct. 26). The process by which certain propers for the liturgical services became widely adopted in the Byzantine Rite, outside of the context in which they were written, does not seem to have in the least been hindered, therefore, by their ostensive reference to unique data; in Ricoeurian terms, the "world in front of the text" has not depended upon the "world behind [it]." Have such references even been noticed, much less troubled anyone, over the course of liturgical history? Given how adept Byzantine Christians have proven at elaborating spiritual interpretations for even the most utilitarian of liturgical actions and items, as the genre of liturgical commentaries bears witness, one would not be surprised at a negative reply. And the typological interpretation of the Scriptures characteristic of the patristic period would seem to favor the constant redeployment of meaning even within specifically ecclesiastical compositions.

The Ars Memoriae and Liturgical Paideia

Chapter 2 of *MHF* offers a "pragmatic" approach to the phenomenon of memory intended to complement the "cognitive" approach taken in the first chapter. As we saw above, this approach was already anticipated in the first chapter. Here Ricoeur's interest lies in the way in which memory "exercises" itself in the "search" to remember; in anamnesis, the cognitive and pragmatic overlap, for although the culmination of the process is mental recognition, the process itself is characterized by practical effort. This very combination of cognitive and pragmatic operations (termed by Ricoeur *la remémoration*) is exhibited in the techniques of memorization (*ars memoriae*): These enable a mastery of skills such that someone is not required to constantly relearn the requisites of a given action.

Memorization is a form of habit-memory, except that the habits concerned are acquired intentionally rather than through simple repetition.

The vulnerability of memory, however, as that which can be *manipulated* through memorization, casts a shadow of equivocation over its reliability. Ricoeur thus devotes much of this chapter to an exploration of the notion of the abuse of memory, thereby laying the groundwork for his later reflections on the credibility of testimony—itself the basis of claims to historical truth: "The ultimate stakes of the investigation that follows concern the fate of the desire for faithfulness that we have seen linked to the intention of memory as the guardian of the depth of time and of temporal distance. In what way, with respect to these stakes, are the vicissitudes of the exercise of memory likely to affect memory's ambition to be truthful?"[23]

Paideia

What is germane here for liturgical theology is the notion of paideia—including but not limited to the notion of education—which Ricoeur presents as the transmission by ancients to the next generation of the founding works of their common culture. Societies benefit when paideia operates effectively: "For each generation, the learning process . . . can dispense with the exhausting effort to reacquire everything each time all over again."[24] Ricoeur cites the memorization of the catechism as a model of this operation, alongside that of the acquisition of language, as well as the preservation of art forms like dance and music whose savoir-faire, while passing through a manner of textual inscription, is only fulfilled in corporeal enactment. Such arts "require of their practitioners a laborious training of the memory, based upon a stubborn and patient repetition, until an execution, at once faithful and innovative, is obtained, one in which the prior labor is forgotten under the appearance of a happy improvisation."[25]

Curiously, Ricoeur does not consider in this connection his earlier reference to civic and religious rituals. Such rites depend, of course, upon a proper functioning of tradition, an accurate handing over from one generation to the next of the ritual patrimony. Although they may well be textually anchored, rites are by nature fundamentally performative, a species of those actions executed on the basis of a structured work, such as a libretto or score. One can speak of learning the "language" of a liturgy, but this metaphor does not bring into relief those aspects of worship that correspond rather to corporeal memory—i.e., its choreographic, musical, and dramatic aspects, all of which invite the application of a specific paideia.

That there is a reciprocity in liturgical paideia, however—a ritualization of memory inherent in the very memorization of ritual—is poignantly
displayed in an anecdote drawn from the life of Walter Ciszek, S.J. Jailed
by the Soviets from 1941–61 on the charge of being a Vatican spy, this priest
was a testament to the vitality of an *ars memoriae*. During his five-year im-
prisonment in Moscow, he suffered extensive, excruciating periods of soli-
tary confinement. His autobiography recounts how he maintained
psychological stability through a purely mental performance of the Eucharist.[26] Even after being transferred to a prison camp, when he was once
again able to enjoy the company of other human beings, Ciszek found that
both he and others would risk whatever was necessary for the sake of the
Divine Liturgy, with only the barest essentials to orient their memory:

> We said Mass in drafty storage shacks, or huddled in mud and slush
> in the corner of a building site foundation of an underground. The
> intensity of devotion of both priests and prisoners made up for every-
> thing; there were no altars, candles, bells, flowers, music, snow-
> white linens, stained glass or the warmth that even the simplest
> parish church could offer. . . . The realization of what was happen-
> ing on the board, box or stone used in place of an altar penetrated
> deep into the soul.[27]

Such was the power of this experience, according to Ciszek, that despite
their constant malnutrition and hunger, the prisoners would observe the
then-standard eucharistic fast from midnight onwards (even to the end
of the following day), if only to be able to receive Holy Communion.

The dialectic between interiorization and exteriorization evident in
the above episodes relates in turn to the question of the link between the
liturgical action and its inscription. One notices, for example, an indication of the primacy of memorization. A rite that has been internalized,
requiring little or no aid of texts, would seem to possess perforce a greater
degree of intimacy and intensity—to occasion a more "full, conscious
and active" participation.[28] If the *quid* of prayer is stored in memory,
either as representations to be recalled or skills to be exercised on the basis
of habit-memory, is it not thereby uniquely integrated into the very identity of the worshipper? This in turn invites consideration of the degree to
which the memory of the Church (upon which liturgy as a form of anamnesis draws) is conserved through *texts*, versus the degree to which it subsists rather in a *performative* tradition in which texts function as aids

to that "integrated memory . . . always actual, a living tie to the eternal present."[29]

Collective Memory and Personal Identity

The question of how much memory must be exteriorized to be perpetuated, and the mode of this exteriorization, impinges not only on the dialectic operative in the liturgy between the oral and the written, but also on that which obtains between *lex orandi* and *lex credendi*. To illustrate this point, we may defer to that cynosure of twentieth-century Orthodox theology, Vladimir Lossky (1903–58). In a well-known essay on Mariology, he explains that, in principle, the Orthodox Church (in contrast here to the Catholic Church) does not discourse about the Mother of God at length, in terms of a formal *lex credendi*—i.e., by promulgating doctrines through councils; it holds as definitive only the teaching of the Fourth Ecumenical Council (held at Ephesus in 431) that Mary is to be called "Theotokos." Lossky writes:

> [Dogma and devotion] are inseparable in the consciousness of the Church . . . the Christological dogma of the [Theotokos] taken *in abstracto*, apart from the vital connection between it and the devotion paid by the Church to the Mother of God, would not be enough to justify the unique position, above all created beings, assigned to the Queen of Heaven, to whom the Orthodox liturgy ascribes "the glory which is appropriate to God" [*he Theoprepes doxa*]. It is therefore impossible to separate dogmatic data, in the strict sense, from the data of the Church's cultus, in a theological exposition of the doctrine about the Mother of God. Here dogma should throw light on devotion, bringing it into contact with the fundamental truths of our faith; whereas devotion should enrich dogma with the Church's living experience.[30]

He proceeds to equate the Church's tradition with the "holy memory" of those who hear and keep the revealed word. This memory is a criterion of identity, a source of the *selfhood* of the Church; it is memory that justifies the Church's commemoration of Mary after a fashion that Lossky admits to not be evidently warranted by Scripture (understood as the documentary basis of Christian theology). Ricoeur sheds further light on this issue in discussing the polemical shade to remembering: A given memory has the potential to protect those by whom it is recalled, "in the confrontation with others, felt to be a threat."[31] Memory is fragile: Susceptible to ideology, it is always on the cusp of being manipulated one way or another, and in turn forming or deforming identity. Certainly the rhetorical antagonists of Lossky include those Christians who reject the veneration of Mary outright; such people are thereby rejecting the Tradition of the Church and violating her memory. What is perhaps more surprising is that Lossky remains equally troubled by those who seek to establish Mariology *elsewhere* than in the inner sanctum of communal, liturgical memory—that is to say, in the external arena of authoritatively posited doctrine.

Proceeding even further, Lossky asserts not only that Marian devotion is the legitimate expression of Holy Tradition, but that Mary's own life serves as the paradigm of anamnesis: "'But Mary kept all these things pondering them in her heart' (Luke 2:19, 51). She who gave birth to God in the flesh kept in her memory all the testimonies to the divinity of her Son. We could say that we have here a personification of the Church's Tradition before the Church was."[32] At this point, we stand far removed from Aune's suspicion that liturgy founds belief, with which we began this chapter. While he does well to critique a cavalier use of *lex orandi, lex credendi*, innocent of the complexities attendant upon the historical dialectic between praying and believing, he continually approaches the matter from the *outside*. That is, perhaps he treats Schmemann's synchronic recourse to the liturgy—shared by those who follow after him—as insufficiently historical, because Aune himself does not share in that same history; what for the one is the *subjective* memory of the Church, for the other is an *objective* datum. Approaching a tradition as an archive rather than as an element of one's own personal and communal identity may of course yield a wealth of insights; this is why, after all, documentary history is written. But such cannot presume to replace the qualitatively different, existential engagement with the past that is memory: the past as lived from *within*. According to Ricoeur, the former actually depends in great measure upon the latter.

Ricoeur concludes Part 1 of *MHF* with a reflection on the work of French philosopher and sociologist Maurice Halbwachs (1877–1945). The point that I wish to retain here (intersecting as it does with the arguments of Lossky) is the idea that memory is fundamentally tied to community: "to remember, we need others."[33] We do not exercise memory alone, that is, but rather by situating ourselves within a social and spatial context; from childhood (argues Halbwachs) our memories are bound up with other people and places, and this grants epistemological primacy to an external chain of references over internal recollection. Ricoeur proposes in addition a mediating function, assumed by one's close relations, between the larger social reality of other people and the individual ego.[34]

Epistemology: Testimony vs. Schematization

Part 2 of *MHF* is devoted to an examination of historiography, as submitted to three distinct but not necessarily successive phases: the documentary, the explanatory, and the representative. The leitmotif is culled from the myth of the origin of writing in Plato's *Phaedrus*: The phenomenon of inscription, inasmuch as it is operates as an "antidote" to the frailty of memory, doubles as a poison inasmuch as it contaminates memory's originary trustworthiness with an element of doubt. The need for writing suggests the *unreliability* of memory, engendering in Ricoeur's estimation an opposition between the mnemonic and the historiographical.

Now Ricoeur sees the act of interpretation as characterizing all three phases of historiography, contrary to a more conventional but facile view that would regard historians as simply offering their interpretations of facts. The documentary phase begins with the phenomenon of archives: These transcribe the irreducible core of history—testimony—which is typically expressed in the phrase "I was there." Testimony in the first instance refers to a lived time and space that have not yet been schematized by scientific discourse. It adheres to the unique self-designation of the witness, deriving its validity from "the reality of the past thing and the presence of the narrator at the place of its occurrence." This self-designation is marked in turn by a "triple deictic . . . the first-person singular, the past tense of the verb, and the mention of there in relation to here."[35]

Schematization follows testimony, through geography and cartography with respect to space, and historiography with respect to time. In being assimilated to the categories of these disciplines, however, what was experienced as visceral becomes virtual, causing memory to lose immediacy and suffer reification. Ricoeur goes on to suggest that this process involves a structuring on the spatial plane akin to the narrativization employed on the temporal plane. Thus memory is transformed into history both through chronological operations, which the latter shares with fiction, as well as through the physical orientation effected by reference to inhabited space,

itself determined in respect of architectural construction. Ricoeur's essential point, presaged in the first part of *MHF*, is that "narrated time" and
"constructed space" parallel one another: "To the dialectic of lived space,
geometrical space, and inhabited space corresponds a similar dialectic of
lived time, cosmic time, and historical time. To the critical moment of localization within the order of space corresponds that of dating within the
order of time."[36] We shall see in Chapter 8 that this dialectic is operative
in the respective way that the *GBW* establishes the place of its celebration
as "the Jordan," and its time as the moment of Christ's Baptism.

The Crisis of Testimony: Experiences "At the Limits"

Ricoeur is preoccupied throughout *MHF* with the question of experiences
"at the limits," of which the Holocaust/Shoah serves as the cause célèbre.
Such experiences foment a "crisis of testimony," defying ready transcription
from lived memory to historical record, because they beg the possibility of
an appropriate and accurate mode of representation. One might quote in
this connection the proverb that "truth is stranger than fiction." For Ricoeur,
the Shoah exceeds "the ordinary, limited capacities for reception" of those
who would seek to make sense of it. The "shared comprehension" between
the members of a society "built on the basis of a sense of human resem-
blance at the level of situations, feelings, thoughts, and actions," is con-
futed in the face of "an inhumanity with no common measure with the
experience of the average person."[37] Testimony in this context encounters a
crisis because it demands by its very nature to be received by another; to
witness to *something* is to witness to *someone*. Ricoeur sees here a reverse of
the dilemma faced centuries earlier by Lorenzo Valla (1407–57), the Renaissance humanist who proved the fraudulence of the Donation of Constantine. Where Valla struggled against an excess of credulity, seeking to
insinuate in his audience a healthy dose of doubt, the one who would recount the Shoah must overcome "incredulity and the will to forget" on
the part of his contemporaries.

It seems to me that one is not far, in appreciating the strictures imposed
upon those who would textually compass the scope of the Holocaust, from
grasping the main problem of liturgical hermeneutics—namely, how one
may appropriate the marvelous events commemorated by liturgy that—
whether it be the Theophany celebrated by the *GBW* or the resurrection
from the dead of a man who is God—do not correspond to the ordinary

experience of those who celebrate a liturgical rite. Do not "incredulity and the will to forget" threaten the memory of the *magnalia Dei* that Christian worship attempts to preserve through a manifold deployment of poetic and aesthetic resources? This deployment is surely vulnerable to what Ricoeur (following Saul Friedlander), in reference again to the Holocaust, calls an "exhaustion in our culture of the available forms of representation for giving readability and visibility to the event," while simultaneously responding to "a request, a demand to be spoken of, represented, arising from the very heart of the event."[38] Does not this dichotomy impel the very mutation and multiplication of forms of worship to which liturgical history bears witness, while also occasioning the atavism within this same history of iconoclastic (and fundamentalist) movements—as well as the perennial presence of mystical currents eschewing corporate prayer altogether in favor of silence and solitude?

Historiographical Representation and the Imagination

There is thus a potent creative element at work in historiography. One cannot avoid the use of the imagination in construing history, since to interpret the past is to emulate the process by which people ever interpret the present. Unlike the natural sciences that focus (in principle) on such phenomena as are reiterable and homogeneous, history takes as its object particulars, which only fit together on the basis of the narrative templates composed by a historian. Hence Ricoeur can muse:

> Does the historian . . . not mime in a creative way the interpretive gesture by which those who make history attempt to understand themselves and their world? This hypothesis is particularly plausible for a pragmatic conception of historiography that tries not to separate representations from the practices by which social agents set up the social bond and include multiple identities within it. If so, there would indeed be a mimetic relation between the operation of representing as the moment of doing history, and the represented object as the moment of making history.[39]

Following Louis Mink (1921–83) while drawing on his previous work in *Time and Narrative*, Ricoeur argues that historical explanation involves a synthetic, configuring act of emplotment. Yet the process by which disparate events are collected into a meaningful whole remains ambivalent, since to a certain degree the singularity of each event is leveled by its coordination with the others included in the plot: "If the event is a fragment of a narrative, it depends on the outcome of the narrative, and there is no underlying, basic event that escapes narrativization."[40] This is because inscription is ever already a mediation between the "as it actually happened" and our perception of it. Representation involves an evocation of an absent past through substitution; the substituted object tends in turn to efface the prototype and ultimately replace it. Inasmuch as historical representations function as verbal images of the past, they paradoxically obscure that which they purport to illumine.[41]

The problem emerges clearly in the perennial conflict between different versions of what is ostensibly the same event; there is no way to purge an event of its narrative context such that it can be accessed free of interpretation. History can nonetheless be distinguished from fiction, but not by any aspect immanent to the text itself; rather, it is the *intentionality* of the work—in the case of the former, its "claim to truth," in the latter "the voluntary suspension of disbelief"—which is decisive. Common sense tells us that these two intentions are discrete, but since the means by which each is fulfilled are common, the specter of dissimulation can never be put to rest completely. It forever inhabits the philosophy of history. Indeed, "it would be futile to seek a direct tie between the narrative form and the events as they actually occurred; the tie can only be indirect by way of explanation and, short of this, by way of the documentary phase, which refers back in turn to testimony and the trust placed in the word of another."[42]

We perhaps find in this sober conclusion an insight as to how liturgy recounts sacral history. Is it possible—and if so, is it necessarily desirable—to go *around* the narrative form of a religiously charged event, as conveyed by its liturgical representation? Is such a representation not worthy of honor as representing the communal testimony to the past—that is, to the present significance of that past? To the skepticism of Hayden White (1928–), who sees history as inexorably suffering an ideological subterfuge, Ricoeur contrasts the work of Carlo Ginzburg (1939–), characterized by a plea on behalf of the merit of testimony as that which intends "historical reality." Prior to the work of inscription by which a historian schematizes the past, there is the irreducible immediacy of the lived experience, preserved in memory and existentially warranted. And such lived experience brings into relief the role of the community: "It is the citizen as much as the historian who is summoned by the event. And he is summoned at the level of his participation in collective memory before which the historian is called upon to give an account."[43] This summons is particularly acute in the case of those dramatic events that Ricoeur terms "at the limits." Inasmuch as the events commemorated by the liturgy can be considered also as "limit-experiences," it would seem that the ritual process that serves for the preservation of the Church's collective memory must similarly constitute, in some sense, a final court of appeal.

Ontology: "The Historicization of Human Experience"

Before returning to the debate in liturgical theology with which we began this chapter, we must give summary treatment also to Part 3 of *MHF*, where Ricoeur ferrets out the existential implications of his historiographical inquiry. He contends: "On the side of ontology, hermeneutics assigns itself the task of exploring the presuppositions that can be termed existential . . . in the sense that they structure the characteristic manner of existing, of being in the world, of that being that each of us is. They concern in the first place the insurmountable historical condition of that being."[44]

History vs. Histories

The first presupposition to be unpacked is that of the verisimilitude generated by the very concept of history as a "metacategory" that is indivisible. The term "history" is ambivalent for Ricoeur, since it designates both "the collective singular comprising a series of events and the ensemble of discourses pronounced regarding this collective singular."[45] By contrast, Ricoeur notes the growing awareness already in the nineteenth century of the irreducible pluralism of human experiential data, and the corollary impossibility of obtaining a neutral vantage point from which one could write a cosmopolitan history without belonging to (and thus being formed by) the history of a particular community.[46] (We recall here David Power's emphasis in Chapter 3 on the siren call of metanarrative, and the resistance offered to it by an awareness of narrative rupture.) To be sure, such skepticism did not in and of itself fragment the received unitary vision of human history, since even according to Christian *Heilsgeschichte* (salvation history)—as formulated by German theologians from the eighteenth century on—the future is held to contain the fulfillment of the past and the present. Nonetheless, the seeds of an ideological pluralism grew up in

the twentieth century into an all out historical relativism or "historicization of human experience." The philosophical consequence of this is that
one is seemingly left with nowhere to stand:

> The idea of a plurality of viewpoints, once stripped of any overview,
> is proposed as the antidogmatic view par excellence. But the ques-
> tion then arises whether the thesis affirming the relativity of every
> assertion does not self-destruct through self-reference. . . . One can
> wonder if the idea of truth, but also the ideas of the good and the
> just, can be radically historicized without disappearing. The rela-
> tivity resulting from the temporalization of history can nourish
> for a while the charge of ideology addressed by a protagonist to an
> adversary—in the form of the peremptory question, "Where are you
> speaking from?"—but it finally turns against the one making it and
> becomes internalized as a paralyzing suspicion.[47]

One theological response to such a Weltanschauung is to prescind from
historicization by reasserting the ultimately transcendent character of Tradition. Orthodox theologian Andrew Louth (1944–), for instance, queries
whether the "development of doctrine" is a "valid category for Orthodox
theology." Given the standard equivalence drawn by Orthodoxy between
"correct doctrine" and "correct worship" referred to above, it is not surprising that he comes around to evaluating such "development" according to
liturgical criteria. The essay begins with a brief genealogy of historicization
that synchronizes with that of Ricoeur; the former's burden, however, is to
demonstrate that Orthodoxy does not share in this intellectual pedigree,
located as it historically has been outside "the West." While the Orthodox
Church has learned from the Western experience, and even offered creative reinterpretations of certain movements—such as the Slavophiles' co-
opting of the Romantic ideal of "organic life" in their theology of *sobernost*
(togetherness)—it has generally rejected "a sense of critical distance" vis-à-
vis the past. And this is so, Louth explains, because for Orthodoxy the
past (viz. the Fathers of the Church) is the font from which we must
drink: "We do not stand over against the Fathers; we come to them to learn
from them."[48] The presumption ought to be, in fact, that we will never
know as much as or more than the Fathers, given the paucity of our sources.

But when asking rhetorically how one is to know *who* is a "Holy Father,"
Louth comes to the crux of his argument: "The Fathers are our Fathers,
because we are their children. Behind this assertion lies faith in the Holy

Spirit's guiding of the Church through the tradition of the Fathers and the Councils. . . . The Holy Spirit is manifest through his residing with us— it is in the community of the Church, in the sacramental community, that the Spirit is revealed."[49] Since this is so, he continues, we should look to the manifest continuity of the Church's liturgical tradition as that which gives direction to the theological enterprise.[50] And in doing so we may well employ historical methods. "Historical theology is, if you like, a way of refreshing, or revitalizing, the memory of the Church."[51] Such a memory, a "living memory," is the burden of the last part of *MHF* that we will examine.

The Living Memory

In the second chapter of Part 3, Ricoeur clarifies how one is to avoid the "paralyzing suspicion" that the historicization of memory casts over the philosophy of history. The way to sail in safety past the Charybdis of historical relativism and the Scylla of ideological fundamentalism is to keep both perils within one's peripheral vision:

> To be sure, in the conditions of retrospection common to memory and to history the conflict remains undecidable. But we know why this is so, once the relation of the past to the present of the historian is set against the backdrop of the great dialectic that mixes resolute anticipation, the repetition of the past, and present concern. Framed in this way, the history of memory and the historicization of memory can confront one another in an open dialectic that preserves them from the passage to the limit, from that hubris, that would result from, on the one hand, history's claim to reduce memory to the level of one of its objects, and on the other hand, the claim of the collective memory to subjugate history by means of the abuses of memory that [commemorations] . . . can turn into.[52]

Memory and history are thus symbiotic; the life of history is nourished by memory, which history in turn conditions by a subtle process in which description becomes prescription. Memory is ineluctably reshaped by the "cultural forms" of thematization and inscription that it spawns. Drawing again on Halbwachs, Ricoeur observes that it is through an initiation process that one is tutored in a "collective memory"—the public narrative of a given community.[53]

For our purposes, what is most pertinent is Ricoeur's discussion of the book *Zakhor* by Yosef Hayim Yerushalmi. This text "provid[es] access to a universal problem through the exception constituted by the singularity of Jewish existence."[54] The problem, as we have seen, is the resistance of memory to the pretensions of history. Ricoeur cites Halbwachs's insight that the beginning of history is in a certain sense contingent upon the end of tradition: The distanciation of the historian alters memory, "consolidates it, corrects it, displaces it, contests it, interrupts it, destroys it." The reason why the Jewish people stands out is that, at least until the Enlightenment, it preserved a "memory charged with meaning but not with historiographical meaning."[55] Important here is the fact that the Jewish memory was written—i.e., it is not a case of oral tradition opposed to inscription; rather, the practice of historiography, of the "writing of history," simply did not imply the critical distance and detachment that is often associated with the term. The whole Jewish people understood itself to be "summoned" to not forget God and his dealings with their fathers.

Moreover, this peculiar vocation to remember was not regarded as an obligation to merely preserve a chronicle of events—and this, for Ricoeur, is the Hebraic, distinctive vis-à-vis the Greek, notion of history—but to protect the *meaning* of the past. Where historiography in the critical sense of the word is regnant, meaning may well be absent, since secular history fails to do justice to the Jewish conviction concerning divine providence, that is, to their perception of the continuing role of God as a protagonist in the affairs of the world. Ricoeur explains: "The vertical relation between the living eternity of the divine plan and the temporal vicissitudes of the chosen people, which was the very principle of the biblical and Talmudic meaning of history, cedes its place to a horizontal relation of causal connections and validations by history of all the strong convictions of the tradition. More than others, pious Jews resent the 'burden of history.'"[56]

I think that this "burden of history" clearly weighs upon the shoulders of the Church as well, at least in the persons of her liturgists. Maxwell E. Johnson's appraisal of the condition of *Liturgiewissenschaft* in the twenty-first century brings this into relief. In contrast to Vatican II's confident distinction "between what the Council Fathers saw as 'unchanging' and 'divinely instituted' and, therefore, 'irreformable' in liturgy," and what was susceptible to being altered, Johnson doubts whether such categories can hold up under scholarly scrutiny. Contemporary research indeed challenges the idea that there is or ever has been a normativity in the worship of the

Church that could be attributed to divine authority, and therefore seen as irreducible to historicization. Hence Johnson contends, "When someone like Geoffrey Wainwright states that 'rather than present experience being allowed to hold sway over the inherited tradition' . . . I want to ask immediately, 'which inherited tradition and from what church in that "tradition.""'[57]

Treating in succession the thought of Gordon Lathrop, James White, and Paul Bradshaw, Johnson explores the models offered by each for simultaneously attending responsibly to historical criticism *and* preserving a viable liturgical theology for the praying Church. Without examining in detail each model, we can summarize as follows: For Lathrop, it is the historic *ordo* observed in the classical, first-millennial rites that is determinative for the present; for White, it is a given assembly's own experience of authenticity and efficacy in their worship, idiosyncrasy being part of what he considers the kaleidoscope of both the historical and contemporary practice of liturgy; and for Bradshaw, it is somewhere in between Lathrop and White—a conscientiously historical orientation that remains attuned to the polysemy of all rites, given their pastoral *Sitz im Leben*. Johnson ultimately resists the notion that liturgists should be reduced to the work of cataloguing the past, avoiding judgment of the present and recommendations for the future. All is *not* relative in the liturgical tradition and thus one must take up the theological task of prescription, since "what appears to be at stake is the very identity and liturgical self-expression of classic orthodox Christianity itself."[58]

History and/or Tradition?

With Johnson's verdict, we rejoin Ricoeur's aforementioned concern at the potential suppression of the true, good, and just at the hands of historicization, and Yerushalmi's apprehension over its eclipse of the originary memory of the divine presence. Let us revisit in this connection the essay of Aune with which we began the chapter. To recap: We observed that Aune criticizes Schmemann for privileging the received liturgical tradition of the Church (i.e., the Byzantine Rite) as a source for theology; this is taken by the former to involve a disregard for history.[59] Aune then calls to account the work of Fagerberg for adducing the patristic genre of liturgical commentaries in his argumentation on behalf of the liturgical tradition as *theologia prima*.[60] And shortly thereafter, he criticizes Lathrop for the exact opposite: deducing the subsistence of a universal *ordo* within the various liturgical traditions of the Church, and deriving from it a liturgical theology.[61]

Aune is effectively caught in the very historiographical knot that Ricoeur's *MHF* attempts meticulously to untangle. Keen, on the one hand, to preserve the claim to truth of liturgiology, and disturbed by a focus in the contemporary study of liturgy "on what we think liturgy means rather than on historical evidence," Aune seeks to give pride of place to what "we know" on the basis of the most recently ripened "fruits of historical research."[62] But fearful, on the other hand, of a perceived trend toward the detheologizing of the study of liturgy, its co-optation by a focus on human agency, he insists upon a hermeneutical stance that would have as its sine qua non a preeminent regard for the prevenient action of God in the liturgy.[63] As we will see in the next chapter, the *GBW* illustrates this tension between the traditional interpretation of a rite, and the interpretation proposed by a critical history: The question it frames is that of who, exactly, is addressed by the prayers of the rite, and who, in consequence, is the author of its action. If not a matter of displacing divine agency for human, it yet concerns the representation of the Trinity, the revelation of whom is paramount among the received meanings of the rite.

PART

IV

"THE VOICE OF THE LORD CRIES OUT UPON THE WATERS"

8

MANIFESTATION AND PROCLAMATION

Overview

In this chapter we will finally endeavor to apply the insights acquired from our reading of Ricoeur to the interpretation of a particular liturgical rite—namely, the Byzantine tradition's "Great Blessing of Water" (*GBW*) to which we have hitherto referred only obliquely. Following a brief description of the service, I provide a historical overview of its development. Then I offer an analysis according to the threefold schema proposed in Parts II and III above, treating in turn the rite's metaphors and symbols, its models of subjectivity and, finally, its dynamics of mnemonic transformation.

Before proceeding any further, it will be worthwhile to outline the shape of the service as reflected in the *textus receptus*.[1] The rite begins in the church, at the end of Vespers on the eve of the feast of Theophany, or of Matins (or Divine Liturgy) on the day, with the clergy and servers processing out from the altar (with cross, bells, incense, and torches) into the nave itself (when the blessing is celebrated indoors). Alternatively, exiting the church proper, and followed by the congregation, they continue on to a nearby body of water, to the singing of the opening hymns.[2] When the blessing is celebrated in the church, the community gathers rather around the font or vessel containing the water to be blessed.[3] After the font and church (or open body of water), and the people have been censed, the readings begin. There are three from Isaiah (35:1–10; 53:1–13; 12:3–6), followed by a brief Psalm response (26:1 [LXX]) and an Epistle (1 Cor. 10:1–4). Next the Alleluia is sung (intercalated with Ps. 28:3 [LXX]) and the Markan baptismal Gospel

(1:9–11) is proclaimed with the usual solemnity. Thereafter come the general intercessions segueing into the great prayers over the water. These concluded, the theme songs of the feast are sung while a cross is immersed three times into the water. Finally, the people are sprinkled with the holy water and approach to partake of it, also taking some into their own containers for domestic use throughout the rest of the year.[4] Such use includes consumption and the blessing of family members, in keeping with the identity of the Christian home as a "domestic church." This identity is reinforced when, in the weeks following Theophany, the priest of the parish conducts a visitation of all his parishioners, at which time he solemnly blesses their homes with Theophany water. As mentioned above, "Theophany water" is conserved in the precincts of the church as well, for use in the manifold blessings of persons, objects, and places.

Historical Evolution of the "Great Blessing of Water"

Having spoken at length in the last chapter concerning the importance of the dialectic between the critical history of an event and its interpretation, it behooves me to refer to Nicholas Denysenko's definitive historical-critical study of the *GBW*.[5] What follows here is a resumé of the salient findings of his research. Since the oldest extant Byzantine liturgical manuscript, Codex Barberini 336 (reflecting the cathedral usage of Constantinople),[6] dates only from the second half of the eighth century, Denysenko concedes the prehistory of the rite to be obscure. To mitigate the lack of explicit liturgical evidence, however, he adduces the witness of several church fathers and of select saints' vitae, among other discrete sources. The import of these texts is that from at least the fourth century, if not earlier, Christians commemorated the Baptism of Christ by blessing water and reserving it for domestic consumption and sprinkling. A key witness in this respect is St. John Chrysostom (c. 349–407) whose "Homily on the Baptism of Christ" testifies to the practice: Water was kept for the remainder of the year or longer, even up to three years, during which period it allegedly retained its purity and freshness. Epiphanius of Salamis (c. 310/320–403) corroborates the account of Chrysostom. The sources clearly exhibit a faith in the miraculous and beneficent properties of such water, accruing from the liturgically mediated sanctification of the Jordan by Christ.

The history of the actual *GBW* rite proper is arranged into three stages through recourse to more than two dozen euchologies (sacramentaries) and typika (customaries) representing the breadth of the relevant Eastern (Byzantine, West Syrian, Armenian, Coptic) liturgical traditions. In Stage One (eighth to tenth centuries), the majority of the ritual components are variable across the sources, with only the four principal, presidential prayers achieving stability in all.[7] Readings, for example, vary in number, content, and position in the rite, as do hymnography and gesture. Important to our reflections below is the fact that the early texts show the rite to have been celebrated at a courtyard fountain or other contained water source, whereas its prehistory favors live water—a dialectic that will abide in the rite down to the present day.

Stage Two (eleventh to thirteenth centuries) is marked by the influence of the Constantinopolitan Studite and Palestinian Sabaitic monastic traditions, displayed in the proliferation of hymnography at the opening of the service, for instance, and a tendency toward detailed rubrical specifications. For their part, the readings remain in a state of flux with respect to number and content, but are now consistently found near the beginning of the service (rather than at the end, as in the first stage). Since it does not appear in the monastic typika that dominate this stage, the received prologue to the "Great Are You" prayer is posited to be of cathedral provenance. Finally, a salient gesture, rare in the sources of Stage One, comes now to be widespread: the plunging of the Cross into the blessed waters to the singing of a festal hymn.

In Stage Three (fourteenth to sixteenth centuries), several additions and enrichments obtain, including the reappearance of elements from the first stage absent in the second—illustrative in Denysenko's view of Taft's "law of the paradox of the periphery." According to this "law," churches on the margins of a given territory—in the Byzantine Rite, *Magna Graecia* would be exemplary—retain older usages despite their respective liturgical center undergoing development.[8] From the perspective of this stage, Denysenko can affirm the office to be "most likely a collection of materials created by anonymous authors and collated into a cohesive whole," despite the occasional attribution of certain elements to prominent churchmen, notably St. Basil (329/330–79) and St. Germanus of Constantinople (634–733/740).[9] He concludes:

> Collectively, the three stages constitute a snapshot into the life of a liturgical rite that continues to develop. The Byzantine blessing of waters has multiple variants particular to local communities in Stage

One, and even though certain elements become prevalent in most Euchologia by Stage Two, the ritual is not settled by Stage Three, but appears to represent a continued attempt to sort out the order for the celebration. The only certain conclusion is that the core prayers of the rite are stable, while accompanying components like hymnody, gestures and their accompanying texts, and secondary prayers tend to vary from one source to the next.[10]

Among the three prayers that remain stable throughout the entire history of the *GBW*, as charted by Denysenko ("Lord Jesus Christ," "Great Are You," and "Incline Your Ear"), he identifies the second as the longest and most important, consequently singling it out for an in-depth analysis. Deriving from a prayer presumably originating in the rite of Baptism, with which it overlaps to a large degree, "Great Are You" can be seen (following the pioneering work of Miguel Arranz) to exhibit the classic, tripartite structure of anaphoras (eucharistic prayers) deriving from the Antiochene tradition. Although the customary initial dialogue (i.e., the *Sursum Corda*) of such is completely missing, and the *Sanctus* ostensibly so, there is nonetheless a clear movement from doxology to anamnesis to epiclesis; moreover, the angelic worship to which the eucharistic *Sanctus* bears explicit witness is invoked obliquely in the "Great Are You" prayer, which also employs apophatic terminology—another integral feature of the Antiochene liturgical idiom. In Denysenko's estimation, the prayer thematically encapsulates the significance of the rite as a whole:

Five themes from the "Great are You" prayer set the stage for greater elaboration of the theology of the blessing of waters on Epiphany. First, the prayer is highly Christological, as it addresses Christ and employs language that draws upon the anamnesis of the Epiphany feast as its main source. Second, the image of angelic worship is evoked to emphasize worship of Christ, who is the initiator of divine activity in the liturgical assembly, and the assembly joins the angels in glorifying him. Third, the prayer also has a Trinitarian motif, referring to divine work as an act of the Holy Trinity, with each person of the Trinity acting in a particular way revealed by the story of the feast. Fourth, creation is also a prominent theme . . . as creation participates in the divine activity, and is also illuminated. Fifth, the prayer refers to the Baptism of Christians, as it frequently interprets the gifts granted to the participants through baptismal motifs.[11]

The coherence implied in this thematic synthesis discloses Denysenko's conviction that there is a consistent theology in the *GBW*, notwithstanding a certain plurivocity deriving from its composite authorship. Incidentally, I would suggest here that Ricoeur's dialectic between selfhood as *idem* and as *ipse* (elaborated in our discussion of *OAA* in Chapter 5) may also be helpful in understanding the "identity" of a liturgical office such as the *GBW*. For, despite claiming a thematic coherence for the rite, Denysenko acknowledges that its *formal* unity derives rather from editors compiling and rearranging elements to suit the practical exigencies of actual celebration. Is not the service's identity then to be found in its potentiality for action/passion? The *GBW*'s history, that is, witnesses a diversity of recensions and, hence, exhibits only a modicum of *idem* identity; nevertheless, there is *ipse* identity in the potentiality/actuality of communities blessing water—and being blessed by it.

We will have occasion to return to Denysenko's work in the course of our discussion below. The present resumé may be drawn to a close by rehearsing the theological claim advanced by the author for the importance of the rite. It is said to be an effective recapitulation of Baptism, a reminder and renewal for its participants of a sacramental event they may have forgotten, and whose commission they may have neglected. He muses that virtually the same graces may be sought of both Baptism and the *GBW*, an affirmation of the erstwhile practice of administering Baptism during the celebration of Theophany.[12] In this vein, he also proposes that a sharp differentiation between sacraments and sacramentals, characteristic of Western (and scholastically influenced Orthodox) systematic theology, is both artificial and counterproductive: "My analysis of the blessing of waters on Epiphany suggests that an encounter with God and the reception of sanctification are not limited to a prescribed number of sacraments, but can occur in a variety of liturgical celebrations. This warrants a spirit of openness in defining sacramentality and suggests the importance of recovering a patristic understanding of what constitutes a sacramental event."[13] Of course, there are many contemporary (Western) theologians who would wholeheartedly agree.[14]

"We Do Not Conceal Your Benevolence": Naming God in the *GBW*

With Denysenko as a dialogue partner, we can proceed in our hermeneutical analysis of the *GBW*. Recall that in Chapter 3 we explored Ricoeur's approach to the naming of God in Scripture and its corollary use of metaphor, teasing out its general implications for liturgical theology. Let us now attend to the specificity of the world opened up by the *GBW*, treating, in turn, its Christological orientation; the spectrum of "namings" displayed in the rite's various genres; and the implicit theodicy expressed by its construal of evil.

"You Are Our God"

The most conspicuous feature of the naming of God in the *GBW* is its preponderantly Christological orientation—comparatively rare in the Byzantine liturgical corpus, as Denysenko rightly observes.[15] He speculates that such an orientation actually serves to challenge the normative (Chalcedonian) conception of liturgical prayer as properly addressed to the Father, through the Son, in the Holy Spirit.[16] Particularly unusual is the form of epiclesis by which *Christ*—rather than the Father—is supplicated to send the Spirit: "For the Byzantine tradition, the possibility that an entire liturgical rite addresses prayer to Christ, and invokes Christ to send the Holy Spirit, suggests a liturgical theology that challenges this monarchical priority of Trinitarian theology."[17] Denysenko later acknowledges there to be ambiguity in regard to the addressee of the rite's core prayer ("Great Are You"), which has alternatively been taken to invoke the Father—the result, in his estimation, of a collusion between the composite authorship of the rite and said "monarchical priority."

Here Ricoeur's understanding of polyphony would seem apropos. For if on the one hand the *GBW*'s diverse contents indicate it to have been a living euchological text, with several authors contributing to its final contents, this diversity has nevertheless been susceptible to homogenization, given the strictures of Orthodox trinitarian and sacramental theology. For his part, Denysenko counsels a renewed appreciation for the peculiar Christological orientation of the rite, judging that it issues a constructive challenge to the received understanding; in place of an a priori, univocal description of the operations of liturgical prayer, therefore, he advocates the value of the alternative framework permitted by the text's equivocity. We shall explore this framework further below, when discussing the modes of subjectivity licensed by the *GBW*. Here it suffices to submit that such equivocity serves to exemplify Ricoeur's "surplus of meaning." That is, where historical-critical inquiry rightly endeavors to reconstruct the original form(s) of the rite, a hermeneutical consideration duly listens for the polyphony voiced in the received text, thereby vindicating its potential enrichment of the communication in question.

This polyphony is in fact more momentous than it might at first appear, for the Christological interpretation entails a metaphorical "seeing as" by which the divine initiative acclaimed in the rite's Old Testament allusions is assimilated to Christ, that is, by which the "God" referent becomes predicable of Jesus, in precisely the fashion that Ricoeur ironically disavows: "I will not hesitate to say that I resist with all my strength the displacement of the accent from God to Jesus Christ, which would be the equivalent of substituting one naming for another."[18] Denysenko explains that such allusions, which he terms "anamnetic doxologies," do not mention the Father and are thus indeterminate, being ascribable to the agency of either the Father or the Son. On the Christological reading, favored by the position of the doxologies in the *GBW*, the Son may be efficaciously supplicated to sanctify the water because he is taken to be the self-same God "who in the days of Noë drowned sin through the water of the flood. . . . [W]ho through Moses freed the Hebrew race from the slavery of Pharaoh through the sea. . . . [W]ho split open the rock in the desert, and waters rushed out and torrents flooded down, and [who] satisfied your thirsty people. . . . [W]ho through Elias turned Israel from the error of Baal." These doxologies thus serve to allow Christ to be credited with the typological water-related miracles of the Old Testament.

Now such a discrepancy may be accepted by granting the intimate association of the person of Christ with that of the Father, such that the agency of the latter may be seen as predicable in some sense of the former; this is indeed how Denysenko concludes the matter:

> The blessing of waters offers a paradigm of divine activity performed by the entire Holy Trinity, with Christ as the initiator and author whose presence blesses the waters by the descent of the Holy Spirit. This paradigm modifies the notion common to East and West that all liturgical prayer addresses the Father, as the prayer of this celebration consistently addresses Christ. This does not entail the absence of the Father from the Trinitarian economy operating in the blessing of the waters. The Trinitarian model based on the monarchy of the Father is not overturned by the implications of this liturgy, as the Father's role as the source of being is not compromised.[19]

Thus the admittedly unusual Christological focus of the *GBW* is for Denysenko not ultimately out of step with the classical trinitarian teaching
of the Eastern Church, in which the three persons of the Trinity are said
to have a common will and a common energy or power of operation. And
yet, Byzantine Christology has been accused of being crypto-Monophysite,
with its promotion of the deity of Christ unwittingly obscuring the full
stature of his humanity.[20] It seems to me that this tendency naturally invites also a blurring of the distinction between his person and that of the
Father. Regarding such an interpretative trajectory, Jaroslav Pelikan observes (citing Tertullian) that already by the turn of the third century the
Christian faithful would resist overdistinction in the nature of God and
his acts toward the world, preferring to err on the side of glorifying Christ
in excess—to "clai[m] the titles 'God' and 'Lord' for Christ without
qualification"—rather than risk denying him rightful glory, or worse, jeop-
ardizing his divinity.[21]

In this respect, the extant *GBW* serendipitously exploits the continuity
between the Old and New Testaments established by the tandem use of
the term "Lord" (*kyrios*) in the Septuagint's reference to Yahweh, and the
New Testament's designation of Christ. By calling Christ "kyrios," that is,
all the divine attributes and actions associated with that title in the Old
Testament accrue to him; not only is he seen to be one with the God of
Israel, but the God of Israel is now seen to be one with him—indeed, in a
preincarnate form, to *be* him. The language of Scripture would thus seem
to have conspired with the determinations of dogmatic theology, as expressed in the decrees of the early ecumenical councils, to "Christify" the
Old Testament, providing approbation for ambiguity of the kind Denysenko discerns in the received version of the "Great Are You" prayer—
although, as mentioned above, he considers this ambiguity to actually
result from a situation of multiple authorship. Of course, it is debatable
whether or not one is dealing here with a hermeneutical *felix culpa*.

"Sing to the Name of the Lord"

Set within this broader dialectic between (in Ricoeur's terms) the "poem
of God" and the "poem of Christ," how do the respective genres of the
GBW cause the naming of God to "migrate"? The processional hymn of
the *GBW* melds a phrase from Psalm 28:3 (LXX) with a gloss on Isaiah
11:2, immediately establishing a narrative setting: "The voice of the Lord

upon the waters cries out, saying, 'Come all of you, receive the Spirit of wisdom, the Spirit of understanding, the Spirit of the fear of God, of Christ who has appeared.'" This opening text offers an interesting variation upon the primacy Ricoeur accords to narrative as indicative of "God's imprint [being] in history before being in speech. Speech comes second inasmuch as it confesses the trace of God in the event."[22] For, whereas biblical narrative recounts the operations of divine agency in the past, the hymn in question acclaims it as occurring in the present: The voice of the Lord *is* calling out.

Ricoeur does acknowledge this phenomenon to an extent, in his consideration of the "time" of the hymn—which, given his biblical frame of reference, he terms the "time of the psalms"—as that which envelops all other modes of temporality: "This time is that of today and everyday. . . . It is the privilege of worship to reactualize salvation, to reiterate the creation, to remember the exodus and the entry into the promised land, to renew the proclamation of the law, and to repeat the promises."[23] Note, however, that he regards the psalms as celebrating, by means of the vivid present tense, past events; the past is called to mind via the use of the present.

In our liturgical hymn, by contrast, what is described does not correspond to a particular biblical event; there is no instance in Scripture of God calling out over the waters, "Come all of you." Instead, one is faced with the prospect of either a gnomic affirmation—namely, that water categorically carries the resonance of the divine voice—or more plausibly, the claim that in the moment of the liturgy the specific waters before which the congregation is gathered themselves bear witness to said exhortation on God's part. In the latter case, a metaphorical injunction is once again imposed: The worshippers are beckoned to a "seeing-as," or better, a "hearing-as," in which the sound of water is taken to convey the words actually uttered by the cantors, if not indeed by the worshippers themselves. Implicitly commended here, in my opinion, is what we have called "truth as manifestation." If one does take the statement as constative (i.e., *not* as one whose illocutionary force is to constitute the very thing articulated, which would be tantamount to considering the voice of God to speak merely in *our own* performing of the liturgical text "over" the respective font or body of water), then the worshippers are invited to verily encounter the "waters" as disclosing a word that, paradoxically, cannot be articulated save by the ancillary work of language.

Ricoeur captures this concept deftly:

> A symbolism is operative only if its structure is interpreted. . . . And in this sense, any functioning of a symbolism requires a minimal hermeneutics. Yet this linguistic articulation does not suppress but rather presupposes what I have called the adherence of the symbolism that seems to me to characterize the sacred universe. . . . The sacredness of nature shows itself in symbolically saying itself. And the showing founds the saying, not vice versa. Its sacrality is immediate or it does not exist.[24]

We shall return to this below, in considering the "bound" symbolism of water. We shall also remand until later a discussion of the second and third stichera sung at the beginning of the rite. In the present connection, I wish simply to evince how the service starts by adverting to truth as manifestation, to a "showing" that founds a corollary "saying."

After the opening hymns come three readings from Isaiah. The liturgical setting of these readings conditions the import of their naming of God, since the eschatological "world in front of the text" would appear to be realized in an immediate, albeit partial way, by the rite itself. When the text declares, for example, that "[God] himself will come down and save us . . . there will be a spring of water for the thirsty land," the respective divine condescension might be readily equated to the grand narrative of the Incarnation whose protagonist, in his conversation with the Samaritan woman, identified himself as the source of the living water that would forever quench thirst (John 4:14). And yet this is still to circle within what Ricoeur calls the centripetal movement of the biblical text; aside from the fruitful intertextuality reaped by such a messianic interpretation of the Isaian prophecy, the more obvious and fecund reference is to the tangible water about to be blessed. The Great Litany will evoke a synthesis, indeed, of these two approaches, by its own allusion to, and sacramental extension of, the Gospel pericope just mentioned: "For this water to become water springing up to eternal life, let us pray to the Lord."

Strikingly absent from all three readings from Isaiah is any hint of the threat that Ricoeur often associates with the prophetic genre. Recall that in the penultimate Gifford Lecture, he presented prophecy as occasioning a "fragmented identity."[25] Nevertheless, Ricoeur is also well aware of the transition within the genre from, we may say, critique to conviction: Passing through the denunciations of an Amos, Scripture inexorably courses

toward the consolations of an Isaiah, credited by Ricoeur for his "eschatology [which] liberates a potential of hope, beyond the closure of the
established [i.e., narrative] tradition."[26] Now if we follow the Ricoeurian
account of the influence exercised upon this tradition by prophecy, i.e., that
its temporal dialectic casts the founding narrative as incomplete—"the
promise contained in the tradition itself now appears as not saturated by
prior accomplishments"—we gain a new perspective on the baptismal narrative already announced in the opening hymns of the *GBW*. Inasmuch as
one may designate this narrative as the liturgical analogue of the Torah to
which Ricoeur's discussion of biblical time refers, its orbit within the "grav-
itational space" of the succeeding prophecies of Isaiah causes it to similarly acquire a new temporal meaning: That is, whereas the narrative
presents the Baptism of Christ as a *completed* action, the prophetic readings float the possibility that it is in some sense unfinished, yet to be fulfilled in a future event inaugurated truly, if not definitively, by the rite to
unfold. Ricoeur asserts that "the past"—in this instance, the singular event
of Christ's Baptism—"is not simply exhausted . . . rather, it leaves behind
a storehouse of inexhaustible potentialities. But it requires prophecy and
its eschatology to open this initial surplus of meaning that, so to speak,
lies dreaming in the traditional narrative."[27] One may perhaps draw a connection here to Schmemann's own *liturgical* eschatology, which Frøyshov
characterizes thus: "For Schmemann, the Kingdom is inaugurated and yet
to come, though it is clear that this is the same reality which manifests
itself at each instant. Instead of the 'already *but not* yet' [of conventional
eschatology], Schmemann seems to say 'already *and* now *and* yet.'"[28]

For it is surely apparent that the surplus of meaning borne by the baptismal narrative requires for its harvest an extraordinary interpretative labor;
after all, no dominical injunction, like those to baptize or celebrate the
Eucharist, sanctions the *GBW*, nor does any other New Testament text even
countenance such a rite. One may, therefore, be forgiven for presuming
Christ's Baptism to have reached fulfillment in his Passion and, by extension, the sacrament of Baptism by which humanity is made to share therein.
Only in the light of the prophetic text interpreted synchronically in the
context of the liturgy does one glimpse the ritual world *in front of* the Gospel text, even as it is given to the rite's opening hymn to deploy the virtuality of the cosmic symbolism conveyed by the creature of water. Not only
are the prophecies harbingers, moreover, of the narrative's potential, but
they function to ground the scaffolding of action undergirding a liturgical

hermeneutic. For does not the entire rite ostensibly qualify as a perlocutionary effect of the third reading?

> Thus says the Lord: Draw out water with gladness from the wells of
> salvation. And you will say in that day, Sing to the Lord and cry out
> his name. Proclaim among the Nations his glorious deeds, remind
> them that his name has been exalted. Sing to the name of the Lord,
> for he has done great things. Proclaim these in all the earth. Exult
> and be glad, you that dwell in Sion, because the Holy One of Israel
> has been exalted in the midst of her? (Isaiah 12:3–6)

Is it not here in the *GBW* itself that the Lord is vividly hailed in song; that
he is offered praise and thanksgiving for his great deeds; that the Holy One
is experienced in the midst of the faithful who will "draw out water with
gladness," as the litany prescribes, "for every suitable purpose"? Interestingly, this third reading from Isaiah is the first to receive any historical
documentation, as far as the *GBW* is concerned, in the compilation of fifth-
through eighth-century Jerusalemite liturgical material known as the
Georgian lectionary.[29]

Moving on, we observe that the Epistle serves willingly to enshrine the
typological method, as if to literally defend the liceity of applying the preceding lections to the actions soon to follow. Fortuitously, Ricoeur actually happens to argue that the kind of "creative repetition" dominating
restorationist prophecies like Isaiah presages the use of typology exemplified in this text: "The early church will turn this procedure [i.e., 'creative
repetition'] into a hermeneutic and find in it the basic structures of its typological reading of the Old Testament. This development authorizes us
to speak . . . of an interpretation of the New in terms of the Old already at
work in the Old Testament."[30] Our text sees St. Paul describing the Children
of Israel as "baptized" into Moses, as having imbibed "the same spiritual
drink" as the Corinthians themselves: "For they drank from the spiritual
rock that followed them. Now the rock was Christ" (1 Corinthians 10:4).
The person of Christ is thus projected back upon the sacred history of the
Hebrews, such that they are portrayed as having sojourned with the
trinitarian God without having known him as such. Not only does this
text, therefore, endorse a typological correspondence between the thirst-
quenching of old and that with which the rite will conclude, but it anticipates the ascription to Christ of other Old Testament water-related
miracles that the "Great Are You" prayer will condone, as related above.

At this juncture it is also important to draw attention to the brief psalm response (*prokeimenon*) preceding the Epistle. Identical to that sung in the baptismal liturgy, a sacrament known from ancient times as "enlightenment" (*photismos*), its appropriateness follows from the Septuagint version of the text: "The Lord is my enlightenment and my Saviour. Whom shall I fear? The Lord is the defender of my life, of whom shall I be afraid?" (Psalm 26:1 [LXX]). Notice here that in addition to rendering "enlightenment" for the Hebrew "light," the Septuagint also differs in its choice of "saviour" over "salvation," and "defender" over "stronghold," illustrating an observable tendency in the Septuagint Psalter toward personal rather than impersonal appellations for God—despite its otherwise rigorously literal translation style.[31] We recall that for Ricoeur, a Psalm text like this is a capital instance of the kerygmatic language of the Bible, appreciable in its recourse to metaphor only by comparison to the poetic language to which it is akin.[32] And yet, one wonders whether this tendency betrays a certain discomfort with metaphor, the insertion perhaps of "another Logos" (the philosophical scruples of a nascent ontotheology?) into the "seeing as" produced by the sacred word.[33]

Such a dialectic in the naming of God would actually seem to obtain throughout the *GBW* in the space between its respective treatment of light and of water: In Denysenko's assessment of the rite's historical variants, light (as mentioned above) was counted a theme as persistent as water. In the Great Litany, for example, amid a series of petitions for exceptional graces to be bestowed on, in, and through the water to be blessed, stands out a request for the "enlightenment of knowledge and true religion through the visitation of the Holy Spirit"—the naming of God being thereby projected onto spheres as ethereal as epistemology and ethics, and as tactile as the ritual consumption, indeed, "communion" of water.[34] This symbolic contrast between the immateriality of light and the materiality of water will recur elsewhere in the service, notably in the festal kontakion and the concluding idiomelon.[35] It shall also prove significant in our evaluation of the soteriology of the *GBW* below.

The Psalm verses sung at the Alleluia following the Epistle likewise invite a metaphorical "seeing-as," the first ("The voice of the Lord is upon the waters") repeating the reference of the rite's opening hymn to its aquatic setting; the second ("The God of glory thundered upon the waters"), functioning by dint of its past tense as a narrative preface to the baptismal account about to be proclaimed. The sway in the biblical text's tenses reiterates the temporal oscillation already introduced at the beginning of the service in the third of the opening hymns: "As a man, Christ King, you came to the river, and in your goodness you hasten to accept the baptism of a servant at the hands of the Forerunner." Next we have the Gospel, the laconic, Markan account of Christ's Baptism.[36] Perhaps the most salient aspect of the text is its obvious brevity, particularly arresting given the amplitude of the gloss inscribed upon it by the liturgy. We will attend to its interpretation momentarily, in our discussion below of the soteriology embraced by the *GBW*, and return to it again in our historiographical determinations near the end of the chapter.

We must finally recover, in this present analysis of the naming of God by the rite, the potent dialectic of apophasis and kataphasis treated at length in Chapter 4. The epic prologue to the central prayer of the *GBW*, "Great Are You," commences with an address to the "Trinity beyond all being, beyond all goodness, beyond all godhead, all-powerful, all-vigilant, invisible, incomprehensible; Creator of the spiritual beings and rational natures, innate goodness, unapproachable Light that enlightens everyone coming into the world." The first three phrases, taken verbatim from the opening lines of *The Mystical Theology* of Pseudo-Dionysius[37]—a treatise consecrated to a kind of theological "work of the negative"—intone a note of *docta ignorantia* that reverberates like an ostinato under the ensuing paean to the acts wrought by God in history. That is to say, with the rite already having spoken in rhapsodic terms (through the preceding hymns, readings, and prayers) of God as *revealed*, the prologue contrastingly disclaims any pretension to a mastery of meaning. Again, if the multiple namings in the preceding genres already caused a certain "migration" of God's name, in their rapid juxtaposition of multiple figures, the present prayer explicitly thematizes the unknowability of God, speculatively qualifying such figures as metaphorical.

And yet the metaphors are not, to use C. S. Lewis's terms, "magistral," but rather "pupillary"; the insertion of apophatic terminology does not reduce that of the kataphatic, but makes it mean more, serving as a qualifier that pushes us not outside of metaphorical speech but deeper into it. For as Gorazd Kocijančič neatly puts it:

> The main philosophical characteristic of ecclesiastical apophaticism is the knowledge that the real apophasis (i.e., the real negation of our words and thoughts because of the otherness of the Other, the real

openness for the mystery) is only that one which does not prescribe [what] should "be" and what "not." . . . [The] apophaticism of the Church, contrary to the (post)atheistic thematisation of mystery, thus demands in the name of philosophical reasoning not only apophasis, the negation of everything which could be said and thought about Mystery, but also the negation of negation . . . i.e., the possibility of cataphasis as the free self-communication of Mystery.[38]

This recalls Ricoeur's insistence that the labor of language, its struggling through metaphor toward silence, is a duty that must not be abdicated by a preemptive mystical retreat.

In this sense, the audacity of the prayer, first asseverating the divine transcendence, and immediately thereafter bubbling forth in acclamations to God's immanence in Christ, exhibits how the prolixity of the kataphatic is not the contrary of the terseness of the apophatic, but its necessary consequence and complement. Admitting that "no word is adequate to sing the praise of [God's] wonders," we must nevertheless defy limitations in stammering forth, lest these wonders not be known at all. The paradox is particularly acute given the fact that the apophatic terminology is employed not only in the first lines of the prologue, addressed to the Trinity as a singular, ineffable entity, but also in the subsequent naming of Christ as him who "being God uncircumscribed, without beginning and inexpressible, came upon earth, taking the form of a servant." As with the assimilation of the naming of Christ to the naming of God in the Old Testament, discussed above, there is here an extravagance of ascription—a Ricoeurian "reorientation by disorientation," to which we will return below.

"Crushing the Heads of the Dragons on the Waters"

We turn now to the central prayer of the *GBW*, "Great Are You." This text confesses Christ to be the agent of creation, the artisan of the cosmos, to whom it—along with the spiritual powers of heaven—ought to render obeisance. Having descended to earth in the "compassion of [his] mercy," he "sanctified the streams of Jordan by sending down from heaven [his] All-Holy Spirit and [he] smashed the heads of the dragons that lurked there."[39] In this line of the prayer, we encounter a surprising, seemingly incoherent and misplaced allusion to Psalm 73:12–15 (LXX) wherein God is depicted—in imagery borrowed from Near Eastern mythology—as having established the world by vanquishing a preternatural sea-monster. I would propose, however, that this allusion is actually the unexpected *key* to the soteriology of the rite. Why? Consider that the *GBW,* prima facie, lacks any reference to the Paschal Mystery; conspicuous by its *absence* is any indication of the Passion or the Resurrection. Only the gesture of plunging the Cross into the waters at the conclusion of the service is connotative in this respect.[40] Does the *GBW* promote what Kevin Vanhoozer calls a "pristine soteriological model," before which the "myth of penal substitution" ought to recede?[41]

The matter is profoundly dialectical, inviting an application of Ricoeur's determinations concerning the naming of evil, which according to van den Hengel serves as one of the "twin goads" to his lifework—alongside the naming of God.[42] Now Ricoeur argues that evil, if approached speculatively, leads to an aporia: It cannot be thought in rational terms *adequate* to our experience. Indeed, it is an enigma that calls into question reason's very requirement of logical coherence—i.e., that propositions be submitted to the rules of noncontradiction and systematic totalization.[43] Part of the challenge is that we seem unable to avoid placing phenomena as heterogeneous as sin, suffering, and death within the common category of evil.[44] The genre of theodicy aspires to just such a comprehensive taxonomy and has historically had a prolific career: There is no dearth of speculative discourse on evil.[45] Nevertheless, Ricoeur regards its successes as pyrrhic; genuine gain is afforded rather by those less ambitious genres preceding theodicy—in particular, myth (which narrates evil, typically in terms of a given cosmology); wisdom (which reflects on how and why evil affects me personally); and gnosis (which dualistically posits its necessity— thereby appreciating the sheer magnitude of evil—if also renouncing upon its contestation).

Such genres compel us to think more, by thinking *differently*. Ricoeur singles out wisdom as being particularly productive in this regard—"one of the possible paths by which thought, action, and feeling may venture forth together"[46]—but we meet another, I think, in the myth of evil sustained by the liturgy. For although the doctrine of God proffered by the *GBW* is perforated by speculative thought (as displayed by the rite's apophatic un/naming of him), the rite's treatment of evil does appear to abide on the purely mythical level. True, something of an exception may obtain in the priest's apology, embedded within the prologue to "Great Are You." Recognizing his sinfulness, he makes the following request: "May my supplication for the people here present be acceptable, so that my offenses may not prevent the Holy Spirit from being present here; but permit me now without condemnation to cry out to you." For the most part, however, evil is located in the extrinsic power of dragons: a cosmic, rather than moral, etiology.[47]

But how does myth actually amplify thought? Ricoeur explains: "The realm of myth . . . is a vast field of experimentation, or even of playing with hypotheses in the most varied and the most fantastic forms. . . . The counterpart of this tremendous contribution of mythical thought to speculation on evil is that one is ceaselessly brought back to the question of origin: From whence comes evil?"[48] By its narrative of Christ conquering the dragons, accordingly, the liturgy can be seen to prevent us in our thinking about evil, and this in both senses of the word: It "goes before" us, expressing our sense of evil being somehow, mysteriously, always and already there; but it also "obstructs" our attempts at discursive circumscription.[49] But is this not rather to reduce the scope for thinking through evil, than broaden it? To justify our contention, we must integrate Ricoeur's pertinent exegetical inquiry on the first chapter of Genesis.[50]

By way of introduction, however, let us recall that for Orthodox theology, as represented by Schmemann, the blessing of the waters constitutes a type of spiritual cosmogony:

> The waters of creation, darkened and polluted by the fall, which had become the very symbol of death and demonic oppression, now revealed as the waters of Jordan, as the beginning of recreation and salvation. The Holy Spirit, the Giver of Life, who 'moved on the face of the waters' in the beginning, descends again on them; and they— and through them the world—are revealed to be that which they were meant and created to be: the life of man as communion with God. The time of salvation begins again.[51]

Schmemann's lyricism belies a dichotomy exposed by Ricoeur's text: the commingling in the Old Testament of two contrary models of creation. The earlier model, adopted from Near Eastern mythology and cited in Psalm 73:13–14 (LXX), consists in the divine conquest over the dragon (Leviathan, Rahab).[52] The later, distinctively Hebraic model, is that of a divine wind hovering over the waters with an ensuing *"Fiat lux!"* In short, there is scriptural warrant for seeing creation as preeminently the result of *deeds*, but also for favoring the role of *words*—with this latter process incorporating, without effacing, the former: "Genesis 1 is continuous with Psalms 89 and 74. And so understood, the thought process at work in such a creation narrative consists in linking the archaic form of the myth, foreign to the faith of Israel, to the history of salvation specific to the Hebraic theological world."[53]

Noteworthy here is the fact that the pagan model involves not only action, but conflict, while the Hebraic seems to infer a *gratuitousness* in creation. I would like to propose that the *GBW* preserves this tension in a dialectic between the symbolism of water and that of light, introduced above. Water and light, respectively, can be taken as representing the two creations by deed (act proper) and word (speech-act). How so? On the one hand, the rite emphasizes Christ's victory over the dragons at the consummation of his Baptism, the event whose salvific repercussions are felt in the sanctification of the waters transmitted to participants in and by the *GBW*. On the other hand, there is a definite soteriological theme of light and the disclosure of a concomitant knowledge, proclaimed, inter alia, in the kontakion: "Today you have appeared to the inhabited world; and your light, O Lord, has been marked upon us; who with knowledge sing your praise. You have come, you have appeared, the unapproachable Light."[54]

The rite thus exhibits its salvation/creation drama as a rehearsal of Genesis, but one that distends the *action* element in the biblical text; where Scripture combines a hovering over the abyss with a speaking into the void, the *GBW* revivifies (and co-opts) the ancient motif of God engaging as a warrior in the battle against primordial, preternatural foes.[55] The sequence of the narrative flows from the Spirit descending upon the Son (reflected, respectively, in the Gospel itself and the litany's petition, "For us to be enlightened with the enlightenment of knowledge and true religion through the visitation of the Holy Spirit, let us pray to the Lord"); through the epiclesis of the Spirit upon the water; to the reenactment of Christ's marine combat in the plunging of the Cross. Similarly, the "Lord Jesus Christ" prayer passes effortlessly from rational illumination to sacramental sprinkling,[56] a movement anticipated also in the very identification of Baptism as enlightenment, to which the prokeimenon alludes.[57]

Arguably, the soteriology of the rite *does* therefore herald the Paschal Mystery, but in a mythical idiom resistant to conversion into some other. The Jordan River, in virtue of its putative lurking leviathans, serves unto a "seeing-as" of the ultimately unrepresentable mystery of evil; the *GBW* shows the waters of death, the monster of sin, and the chaos of the Fall—

all to recede before the ineffable "being-as" engendered by Christ on the Cross. As Pope Benedict XVI suggests, the Baptism of Christ is rightly to be grasped as an anticipation of the Passion and his reemergence, of the Resurrection; his Baptism is the interpretative key to his death and vice-versa:[58]

> The Eastern Church has further developed and deepened this under-standing of Jesus' Baptism in her liturgy and in her theology of icons. She sees a deep connection between the content of the feast of Epiphany . . . and Easter. She sees Jesus' remark to John that "it is fitting for us to fulfill all righteousness" (Mk. 3:15) as the anticipa-tion of his prayer to the Father in Gethsemane: "My Father . . . not as I will, as thou wilt" (Mt. 26:39).[59]

The icon of Theophany, he explains, further illustrates the connection to Pascha inasmuch as the baptismal pool is customarily made to resemble a watery cave, corresponding in the iconographical canon to Hades.[60]

In sum, the liturgy demonstrably promotes the kind of "broken dialec-tic" commended by Ricoeur; evil is annihilated by Christ, if still found to be resurgent in us—as the celebrant's prayer of apology in the *GBW* sug-gestively admits—insinuating itself into our own intentions and actions. Evil, in the *GBW*, is not simply the *privatio boni* of St. Augustine but an *active* principle, set in confrontation with the figure of Christ. And as Ricoeur asserts: "This 'christological turn' given to the problem of evil is one of the paradigmatic ways of thinking more about evil by thinking dif-ferently."[61] Moreover, such "thinking more" is not, as we shall see further below, a mere matter of cogitation. Van den Hengel, for instance, argues as follows:

> The "issue" of the myths is to be found in the promise of an ending to the "reign" of evil. Hence, the good is pronounced, proclaimed, as more originary than evil. . . . In other words, fault or evil is para-doxically at the same time a crucial experience of the sacred. Evil is experienced as a threat to the bond with the sacred. The myths of evil do not reveal the heart of darkness except through an even stron-ger hope of an end to evil and suffering.[62]

In this vein, I would contend that the *GBW* entails at least in principle a program of *acting* against the evil whose inexorable defeat has been litur-gically vouchsafed.

"The Nature of Waters Is Made Holy"

We have indicated that Ricoeur distinguishes symbols based on their capacity to be "bound" to an array of meanings primordially disclosed upon
the cosmos itself, if nonetheless rendered articulate by language. That is to
say, he understands symbolic operation to yield a meaning congruent with
a definite *quid* inherent in the symbol, inchoate though such may be. According to Ricoeur, therefore, things do not mean whatever we wish them
to—although they submit to our wishes, as it were, to the extent they are
able. He situates this dialectic between the poles of "manifestation" and
"proclamation": The former term denotes the Eliadean assertion of nature's
essentially hierophanic character; the latter, the complementary movement
of linguistic interpretation that reflects upon natural hierophany and subjects it to symbolism proper—that is, of being "thrown together" with significations of one sort or another. Thus, "Symbols come to language only
to the extent that the elements of the world themselves become transparent, that is, when they allow the transcendent to appear through them. This
'bound' character of symbolism—its adherence—makes all the difference
between a symbol and a metaphor. A metaphor is a free invention of discourse, whereas a symbol is bound to the configurations of the cosmos."[63]

Convenient for our present inquiry is Ricoeur's concentration upon the
symbolism of water. Water is seen to exemplify the drama of the cosmos,
its "principal function [being] to evoke the universal source of potentialities from whereon existence emerges as both real and experienced. Through
this power of water . . . nature speaks of the depth from which its order
has emerged and toward which chaos it may always regress."[64] Now this
"power of water" is not simply a function of its awesome ubiquity in nature, of what we might call the "far side" of its linguistic symbolization;
rather, the persona water acquires in our narratives gains gravitas from the
actual use of water in manageable forms in religious ritual. On the "near
side" of the symbol there is thus a renewed contact, albeit structured and
controlled, with that which originally gave rise to the symbol. Ricoeur observes that "the element becomes once again immediately meaningful"
through "rituals of immersion, emersion, ablution, libation, baptism, and
so on."[65] Manifestation is thus combined with proclamation: "Water sym-
bolizes something virtual or potential, but we are the ones who speak of
virtuality and potentiality, yet it is the epiphanies of water itself that 'bind'
this discourse about virtuality, potentiality, the unformed, chaos."[66] In fact,

not only does water inspire a flood of particular symbols, mediated by narratives and rites, but the sum of its symbolic "life" is greater than the parts, such that the water-ness invites a hermeneutical response: "We may also say that the innumerable particular revelations related to water form a system capable of integrating them and that this structuring and totalizing character, which the word 'symbolism' itself suggests, brings into play a labor of language."[67]

Now this hypothesis is well substantiated by the Byzantine liturgical tradition, in which the blessing of water serves as the necessary condition of most other blessings.[68] Holy water is the medium whereby persons and objects are blessed, such that the attendant rites find their *fons et origo*, literally, in the "system" condensed within the *GBW*.[69] Water readily lends itself to establishing a "system," as we can see in the network of blessings promised by this service. And as Ricoeur observes, if "any functioning of a symbolism requires a minimal hermeneutics,"[70] it is also the case that once interpreted, a symbolism such as that of water seems capable of effectively functioning on its own: The various blessings in which holy water is used, for instance, do not themselves rehearse the symbolism of the latter but simply assume and invoke it. Explication is given in the blessing of water itself and elsewhere only *indirectly* secured.

We can recall in this connection the conclusion of Chapter 4, in which we discussed Mark Searle's notion of liturgy as metaphor. Searle argued that liturgical metaphors become dead when the metaphorical tension between the "is" and "is not" is effaced either by an insufficient or an excessive stylization of the symbol in question. The metaphoricity of bread as the body of Christ, for example, requires both that the eucharistic bread be *real* bread, but also that it be handled and spoken of in such a way as to disclose its liturgical status as other than (or more than) "normal" food. Liturgy must strike a balance, that is, between grounding its symbols in common human experience and effectively deploying them as vehicles of that which *transcends* such experience.[71] Lamenting the historical eclipse of axial liturgical symbols, Searle muses: "Paradoxically, the very reverence which their disclosure-potential inspired has resulted in the collapsing of the tension upon which their communicative effectiveness depended. . . . Only when there is enough water to allow baptism to recover its original contact with drowning and death will its claim to be the sacrament of life grip us as something more than a tired cliché."[72] Searle's insights challenge the facility with which we might accept Ricoeur's consideration of the operation of a symbolism such as that of water. Indeed, I think *GBW* dramatically illustrates the difficulty of preserving an equilibrium between the worldly and the otherworldly—between the "boundedness" of a symbol and its thematization for and by us.

Consider on the one hand how Searle's "attenuation of sacramental signs" (by which they "lose their metaphorical potential to point beyond themselves"[73]) would appear to be occasioned by the prescription that on the eve of Theophany the entire *GBW* be conducted around an ordinary, manipulable container of water, *inside* the church building. Thus domesticated, this water is nevertheless made to bear the full weight of cosmic imagery unfurled by the ritual script, readily appreciable in an uncircumscribed outdoor setting where the sun, moon, trees *et alia* are visible, and the vastness of nature can impress itself unfettered. Since the water to be blessed is to be taken as the Jordan River, does an indoor celebration perhaps mute the symbolism of water—drowning and death, for Searle, potentiality and chaos, for Ricoeur—and with it, the raft of metaphors with which it is laden? Certainly, in such a context, jumping or diving into the blessed water—a cherished custom in many places—is impossible.

On the other hand, if such an indoor celebration appears resistant to Ricoeur's account of the prefiguration of the symbolism of water—and in turn to this symbolism's configuration in the *GBW* by means of a panoply of paradisal prophecies and numinous invocations—it is yet perfectly suited to the refiguration countenanced by the rite: that the blessed water will serve for a "cleansing of souls and bodies for all those who draw from it with faith and who partake of it." Why? People naturally do not drink salt water, and yet it is customary in many locales to celebrate the *GBW* oceanside. Similarly, even where fresh water is concerned, it is frequently not potable—and the ephemerality of river water, for instance, begs the very question of distinguishing the blessed water as such. In fact, outdoor celebrations of the *GBW* not infrequently *also* involve a simultaneous blessing of a portable container of water, erected adjacent to the natural body of water where the service takes place.

I think we can regard this discrepancy as indicative of the aporia between the moments of Ricoeur's narrative arc. If he is correct with respect to his estimation of the natural symbolism of water, that it is already "bound" to an array of significations in virtue of its properties and role within the cosmos, one wonders to what extent this primordial symbolism is susceptible of metaphorical mutation. I would even venture to suggest that the blessing of water is analogous to the (ontotheological) giving/ withdrawing of the Name in that topos of Ricoeurian exegesis, Exodus 3:14; for at one level the holy water is given, mastered by its very circumscription in the font: The blessing is *here*, as opposed to *there*. At another level, as the blessing of an outdoor body of water makes evident, the same blessing can be viewed as incorrigibly elusive. Where, after all, is the blessed water of a river that has been blessed? It is gone—but with the blessing or without? Does one return to a blessed place upon leaving and returning to such a river, or does the blessing depart with me, inasmuch as it is ordered to my own outlook, my "representation" (to use the language of Owen Barfield mentioned above)?

"Let Us Therefore Draw Water with Gladness"

The foregoing consideration encapsulates what I would call the liturgical dialectic of the cosmic and the domestic. Just as God himself, according to Ricoeur, recedes behind the plethora of figures by which he is depicted in Scripture, compelling an implicit movement toward the threshold of unknowability—which the apophaticism of speculative discourse will render explicit—so the sacramental "metaphor" of holy water "names" the divine presence in a polyphonic manner such that it is both *localized* and *diffuse*. The self-same blessing, given subsequently or simultaneously to both a reified quantity and an undefinable mass of water, appears to challenge the very intelligibility of sacramental presence. If the blessing is *here*, how can it be *there*? If *everywhere*, how is it not then in a sense *nowhere*, or at least superfluous? If the purport of blessing is said rather to consist in a species of Bultmannian existential decision, rather than in an objective transformation of the world, one faces the same critique Ricoeur addresses to those who would, in that vein, demythologize the Scriptures. To accept the facticity of the Incarnation and balk at sacramental realism is surely to swallow the proverbial camel while straining at the gnat.

But here we must also be mindful of David Power's argument that the sacramental imagination of Christianity originally distinguished itself, vis-à-vis its pagan counterparts, by an unexpected restraint. Power claims that what is original in Christianity is the surprising transition from the cosmic to the domestic. In the faith of those following in the footsteps of the humble, kenotic Christ, Power finds justification for an instinctive aversion to grandiose, cosmogonic rites:

There is a ritual distinctiveness in Christian sacrament that puts the focus on domestic rites, not on festive or cosmic ones, however much these are appropriated or respected. It is this which gives the particular sense of being in time that is proper to the memorial of Christ. There is ritual transfer from sacrifice, rites of passage, cosmic rites, indeed from the whole language of cosmic identity, to the loaf and the cup, to the tub of water, to the jar of oil, shared in daily living.[74]

Is a service such as the *GBW* then to be viewed as a metastasis from the healthy quotidianness of Christian practice? In its naturalistic orientation, its "mythical projection, offering the vision of a well ordered universe where all falls under divine providence and plan,"[75] does it not displace the *petit récit* of the Gospel in favor of another grand narrative? One may respond that a dialectical sacramentology may need to allow for the cosmic alongside the domestic, respecting thereby the divinity of Christ as well as his humanity, his twofold identity as Pantocrator and Suffering Servant. Only thus would it correspond to the veritable challenge of a genuine Christology—in Ricoeur's estimation, one that duly adheres to the imperative to link the naming of God in the Old Testament to the proclamation of Christ in the New.

"Your Light, O Lord, Has Been Marked Upon Us": Personal Identity in the *GBW*

We argued in Chapter 3 that despite a common criticism of hermeneutics—namely, that it does not do justice to the performative dimension brought into relief by ritual studies—Ricoeur's later thought makes ample room for both narrative and ritual, and indeed, for interweaving them. Ronald Grimes was cited as an exemplar of the ritual studies school, which generally takes exception to a text-based approach to phenomena.[76] As we discovered in Chapter 5, however, Ricoeur's *OAA* evades this species of criticism by construing the primary object of hermeneutics as the human person—i.e., the self whose interpretation requires a detour through pragmatics as well as semantics. This route arrives at the development of practices that in turn serve as targets for our aiming at a "good life." If Ricoeur does not here elaborate the role of ritual per se, his focus on the role of action both in the prefiguring of narrative (for example, his discussion of the "constitutive rules" by which practices are recognized) and in its refiguring, or ethical appropriation, encourages a narrative-ritual integration.

A liturgical approach to the question of selfhood highlights the complementarity between story and service: The narrative configured in the *GBW* finds its ritual fulfillment in the practices of the domestic context, as the Great Litany anticipates: "For this water to become a gift of sanctification, a deliverance from sins, for healing of soul and body and for every suitable purpose, let us pray to the Lord. For those who draw from it and take from it for the sanctification of their homes, let us pray to the Lord." The contradistinction between narrative and ritual posited by Grimes only obtains if one maintains an a priori separation between the two, a separation that, if not untenable, is certainly unnecessary. The *GBW* presents rather their interdependence, not least because the form and content of the rite are to a great extent common to the rite of Baptism, which refers simultaneously to both a singular sacramental act and (by force of metonymy) to the totality of Christian faith taken as a baptismal vocation.

One relives, or better, recapitulates his or her Baptism in the course of the *GBW*: by first hearing the prophetic narrative in which the self is encountered as a "summoned self"; by assisting in the configuration of the hoped-for Theophany through the exercise of the productive imagination in tandem with one's corporeal participation in the rite; by performing a response to this call in ritually consuming the blessed water; and finally, by transforming one's daily existence through a continuous appropriation of the wager concluded in the rite—namely, that in seeking God's blessing in the sacramental mode in which it has been vouchsafed, one will continue to receive its refigurative power.

The Summoned Subject of the GBW: Psalmist or Thaumaturge?

Now in Chapter 5 we only explored the general features of a liturgical analogue to Ricoeur's notion of the "summoned subject," a figure he elaborated through recourse to biblical and hagiographical figures. We found there that the liturgy presented the self as *capax Dei*, able to recognize itself as susceptible to a doxological vocation to bless God. How then does this obtain in the *GBW*? The rite issues a particular kind of summons, inviting the congregants to process outside to a natural body of water before which they are to remember Christ's baptism (and all the great works of God that, according to the *GBW*, are fulfilled by that event) and bind themselves to the diffusion, through the medium of the blessed water, of the meaning communicated in the Theophany feast.

The liturgical idiom revels in exploiting for this purpose what Ricoeur calls "the support and renewing power of the sacred cosmos"; it is in being placed before the grandeur of the natural world that the panegyric enjoined by the following prayer speaks, as Ricoeur writes, "not only to our understanding and will but also to our imagination and our heart; in short, to the whole human being."[77] Consider the following excerpt from the *GBW*:

> All the spiritual Powers tremble before you. The sun sings your praise, the moon glorifies you, the stars entreat you, the light obeys you, the deeps tremble before you, the springs are your servants. You stretched out the heavens on the waters; you walled in the sea with sand; you poured out the air for breathing. Angelic Powers minister to you. The choirs of the Archangels worship you. The many-eyed Cherubim and the six-winged Seraphim as they stand and fly around you hide their faces in fear of your unapproachable glory.

The doxological summons issued here corresponds best, I think, to the biblical figure who witnesses an *epiphany*. While an epiphany is frequently unanticipated by the party concerned, occurring as an unpredicted "I-Thou" encounter (e.g., Moses's experience at the Burning Bush), there are also instances of another sort. In Elijah's confrontation with the prophets of Baal on Mt. Carmel (1 Kings 18), for instance, the protagonist ritualizes in anticipation of an epiphany, calling the people to sacrifice in order that God may be made known. Indeed, the "anamnetic doxologies" following the "Great Are You" prayer put forward this very incident as a prototype of what is transpiring in the rite at hand ("And give to [this water] the grace of redemption . . . [For] You are our God, who through Elias turned Israel from the error of Baal").

In like manner, there emerges in the fourth of the opening hymns a New Testament analogue to the summoned self represented in the figure of Elijah: "At the voice of the one crying in the desert, 'Prepare the way of the Lord', you came, Lord, having taken the form of a servant, asking for Baptism, though you did not know sin. . . . The Forerunner trembled and cried out, saying, 'How will the lamp enlighten the Light? The servant place his hand on the Master? Saviour, who take away the sin of the world, make me and the waters holy.'" The Forerunner is here enjoined by Christ to allow the epiphany that the liturgical action will in fact disclose at his hands to take place—personal unworthiness and lack of comprehension notwithstanding. Participants in the *GBW* appear in turn to reiterate this summons by inviting Christ to be baptized anew, as it were, in the waters before which they are gathered. The subject modeled on St. John the Baptist—according to Christ, the Elijah who was to come (Matt. 11:14)—is one who evangelizes by exhorting all to draw near and behold the mystery, but one who also addresses the divine persons—the actual agents of the manifestation to be wrought in the rite.[78]

The summoned self of the *GBW* is thus caught up in the Ricoeurian dialectic between proclamation and manifestation described above, and that we explored earlier in the chapter under the soteriological signs of word and deed, light and water. For the anamnesis of Christ's Baptism is expressed both in a doxological summons to proclaim the narrative as well as a kind of sacramental throwing down of the gauntlet: a charge to manifest the narrative in practices that, in van den Hengel's words, "reorient human action in response to the excess, disproportion or extravagance of the Naming of God."[79] If the memory is textual—i.e., enshrined in the account of the Baptism given in the Gospel and recited in the course of the Great Blessing—the *remembering* is ritual, both in terms of the aural/oral character of the encounter with the textually inscribed memory, as well as in repercussions of the rite beyond the moment of its transpiring.

Ricoeur argues, with respect to the figure of the inner teacher elaborated by Augustine, that it is grafted onto what philosophy has recognized as the natural faculty of the human person: "Through the conscience, the self bears witness to its ownmost power of being before measuring and in order to measure the inadequation of its action to its most profound being. In this sense, we can note the neutral character of the phenomenon of conscience as regards its religious interpretation."[80] Conscience is already serviceable in its own right, that is, but fortified by the scriptural figures welded onto it. Similarly, might we propose that conscience also bears witness to an inchoate aptitude for gratitude? That it constitutes a stem, so to speak, which liturgy supports like a trellis? That the religious response budding forth in Ricoeur's obedient "I hear" ("where the superiority of the call—by which we mean its position as Most High—is recognized, avowed, confessed") is thus strengthened to respond to a doxological calling and to develop a sacramental capability?[81]

The Self as Another

Denysenko proposes that the *GBW* underwrites an alternative view of the trinitarian economy, one that takes the body's dialogue with Christ as head as the point of departure. Christ as mediator implies two dialogues, he explains, following Boris Bobrinskoy: one with the Father, and another with the Church; the Church, on this view, ought to enjoy "the freedom . . . to ask Christ to initiate divine activity."[82] We can develop the implications of this claim further by asking if Christ's identity is not thereby seen to be constituted by a kind of Ricoeurian solicitude for the other. For it is in the naming of him by the Father, and the showing effected by the descent of the Spirit, that he is *recognized* as Christ. As Denysenko observes: "The Father bears witness to the manifestation of Jesus as the Christ and Son through his baptism in the Jordan, while the Holy Spirit confirms the authenticity of the revelation by revealing Jesus' true identity."[83] Analogously, in the intracorporeal dialogue of Christ and the Church, is there not a sense in which we too are only recognized, revealed in our true identity, in virtue of our being named and shown by the liturgy to be *in* Christ? Dare we go so far as to suggest that Christ also fully knows *himself*, in virtue of our solicitude?

Hence Denysenko's assessment of the unique Christological orientation of the *GBW*—he is "the author, initiator and chief celebrant of the liturgical event"—appears to dovetail with Ricoeur's determinations concerning selfhood, for we recall from Chapter 5 that the self knows alterity both in its experience of others and that of its own body, as well as in its interior colloquy with conscience. The liturgical subject then, adapting Zimmerman's account of its dual predication, can be regarded as experiencing in the *GBW* the opportunity to encounter God both as *self* and as *another*: In the measure that the assembly speaks to *God* in Christ, it speaks to one who can never be but altogether Other; in the measure that it speaks to God in *Christ*, however, it speaks to one connatural with itself—a dialogue (as Denysenko has it) of the body with the head.[84] And yet even in this dialogue there is the aporia of alterity, since the body suffers under the threat of a distension, so to speak, from its head; the priest must pray—with no assurance being given either way—for his sins to not impede the coming of the Holy Spirit: namely, the power of life sustaining the body and head as one organism.[85]

This threat also parallels the moment of Ricoeur's "fragmented identity" to the extent that it affects the union of the assembly with Christ and its corollary capacity for addressing God. What the baptismal narrative secures, in its account of the victory of Christ over the evil represented by the dragons in the water, suffers a definite—if subtle—rebuke in the admission of interior forces that cannot be so readily or permanently vanquished. *Passivity* accompanies the very recognition by the liturgical subject of its power, in Christ, over extrinsic evil, betraying the subject's concomitant vulnerability to an intrinsic evil that may divide it even from itself, splitting head from body. In turn, the identity that passes through the waters is universalized to the extent that the fullness of blessings is made available to it, albeit in hope; and yet it is simultaneously singularized by the arduous task of realizing the potential of said blessings. Like the blessed water itself, the ontology of the liturgical subject of the *GBW* obtains not in the *state* of being blessed, but rather in a continual *dynamic* of blessing corresponding to Ricoeur's *ipse* identity. This identity is constituted by a faithful keeping of the ritual word, an on-going refiguration of the world by using the blessed water "for cleansing of souls and bodies, for healing of passions, for sanctification of homes, for every suitable purpose."

"Today Things on High Keep Festival with Those Below": Remembrance of Time and Place in the *GBW*

In the last part of this chapter we will examine the process of mnemonic transformation triggered by the *GBW*. But by way of background, it may be helpful to first set forth in brief a general theory of how blessings "work"— informed, of course, by the thought of Ricoeur as developed hitherto—and thereafter to zone in on the specific operations evident in our service.

"Speaking Well" and/or "Sanctifying"?

As was suggested in Chapter 1, blessings can be seen as demonstrating our essentially liturgical vocation, succinctly expressed in Schmemann's classic definition of the human person as *homo adorans*:

> But the unique position of man in the universe that he alone is to *bless* God for the food and the life he receives from Him. He alone is to respond to God's blessing with his blessing. The significant fact about the life in the Garden is that man is to *name* things. . . . To name a thing is to manifest the meaning and value God gave it, to know it as coming from God and to know its place and function within the cosmos created by God.[86]

Our priestly capacity for "stand[ing] in the center of the world and unif[ying] it in [the] act of blessing God, of both receiving the world from

God and offering it to God"[87] was impaired by the Fall but restored through the Incarnation. Humanity's privileges and prerogatives have in consequence been reclaimed, legitimating in turn the commerce of blessings transacted in the sacramental economy. But in what exactly does "blessing" consist?

Orthodox liturgist Elena Velkovska contends that the eucharistic blessing, the anaphora, "is the paradigm and model of every blessing."[88] This assertion is confirmed, as we saw above, by Denysenko's historical analysis of the *GBW*, arguably the most significant of Byzantine blessings and the most integrated into the Church Year; it is also structured like an anaphora, with an epiclesis employing language akin to that found in the eucharistic epiclesis.[89] Alongside the use of the Greek term *eulogein* to denote blessing, Velkovska notes the frequency of the term *hagiazein* (to sanctify). These are to a great degree interchangeable, as Denysenko again concurs, although according to Velkovska the former term is preponderant in the blessing of persons. She concludes that in contemporary Eastern Christianity, as a result of the frequent use of unintelligible sacral idioms combined with an inordinate emphasis on sacerdotal mediation, "the meaning of the blessing is in fact twisted into a kind of magico-ritual consecration."[90] This observation seems particularly ironic given that one of the short, alternate prayers in common use (for blessing water outside of the *GBW*) petitions that through the blessed water the faithful will obtain "freedom from superstition"![91]

There is something of a dialectic at work in this ambivalence, I would venture, corresponding to Ricoeur's "manifestation" and "proclamation." For on the one hand, to bless (*eulogein*) is literally to proclaim, to "speak well" of something/someone: a hermeneutical act, as Schmemann indicates in his association of blessing with *naming*. On the other hand, to sanctify (*hagiazein*) is more than verbal, implying a ritual transformation or at least a consecration or setting apart. Now while *eulogein* has a primarily oral connotation, the standard equivalent in English (to bless) appears conversely to connote *action*. For the Anglo-Saxon root of the English is *bledsian* (or *bloedsian*), that is, "to redden with blood."[92] If we allow etymology to serve for "thinking more"—as Ricoeur is wont to do—then we find ourselves brought back to the treatment of evil above, specifically, the role of conflict in Christ's own sanctification of the waters. The battle with the dragons rehearsed there is only intelligible (as Pope Benedict XVI proposed) in terms of the Passion in which Christ will have his *own* blood shed—

rather than that of his aquatic foes. The English term "blessing," then, felicitously connotes the role of sacrifice portended in the *GBW*: It is only by the Cross reddened with blood, we may say, that the waters and we ourselves can be either "spoken well of" or "made holy."[93] Indeed, should we further indulge in word-play, and place the root of "to bless" in conjunction with that positive state of mind and body denoted by blood-redness in the word *sanguine* (cheerfully confident; optimistic), we find confirmed that integral consequence of blessing as envisaged by the *GBW*: *health* of body and soul.

Toward a "Narrative Unity of Life"

Let us see whether Ricoeur's treatment of narrative identity can help us more fully relate the dual roles of speaking and acting connoted by blessing. Now Reiner Kaczynski observes that "through the sanctifying action of blessings, material things, both those that are natural and those that are the product of human work, are interpreted for human beings in their connection with the saving event of creation and redemption."[94] This interpretation, however, is yet a process mediated by a *text*. Hence Ricoeur's "narrative arc" commends itself: For its part, a *prefiguration* of blessing appears to obtain in the natural appreciation of material things that prompts their original presentation for blessing. We only bless that which is *already*, in some sense, spoken of as good. Cultures the world over, after all, express gratitude for the yield of the earth and its skillful transformation through human ingenuity—a gratitude displayed preeminently in the rich traditions of hospitality expressed in what Margaret Visser calls the "rituals of dinner."[95]

The liturgy in turn invites a *configuration* of this quasi-sacramental behavior: The *mythos* of a blessing subsumes the activity associated with the object, event, or person at hand into a theological plot. The imaginative variation upon life conjured by the rite's metaphorical "seeing-as" discloses a new way of being-in-the-world, those participating being challenged to see said object, event, or person as if it were now—in consequence of the blessing—*changed* in some respect. The "ontological vehemence" of this process arises inasmuch as the challenge is issued not simply to the imagination but to the senses and to the will; one is charged to *act* in accordance with the "seeing-as." The quality of the consequent response constitutes, in turn, the moment of *refiguration*. In sum, one cannot have access to the blessing otherwise than in and through the blessing itself. It retains an irreducibility, a hermeneutic uniqueness proper to the existential implication of each participant in it. Blessings do not differ in this respect from the general gamut of events that may be highly significant in the life of a given person, being similar in their operation to other customs or ceremonies or, for instance, participation in artistic performances or athletic pursuits of whatever kind.

What may be distinctive, however, is the manner in which blessings contribute profoundly to what Ricoeur, following Alisdair MacIntyre, calls the "narrative unity of a life." If it is true, as Ricoeur claims, that life is in fact narrated and only thus lived, then blessings may be seen to provide a privileged moment of narrative mediation wherein the life of Christ with its "soteriological vehemence," so to speak, is retold in our own "acting and doing"—wherein our own life is rendered poetic, a human mimesis of the divine praxis.[96] In the evocative tag of Pope St. Leo the Great, "What Christ did visibly during his earthly ministry has now passed over into sacrament,"[97] we find a basis for considering blessings, inasmuch as they approximate the sacraments, a form of sacramental narrative. Writ large, the narrative so reprised includes the doings of the pre-Incarnate Logos in the Old Testament, duly celebrated in the *GBW*.

If "our Redeemer's visible presence" is taken to comprise his self-implication in the ordinary affairs of those whom he encountered, it becomes understandable that the liturgical tradition should provide blessings for all manner of daily needs. Christ's blessing of particular events, objects, or persons, is less significant than the fact that he lived an incarnate *life*. Moreover, if "what has not been assumed, has not been redeemed,"[98] as St. Gregory of Nazianzus writes (summarizing a common patristic notion), then the Church's manifold blessings actually testify to a belief that in Christ, God has redeemed the full ambit of human "being-in-the-world." The Church honors this conviction by endeavoring to bless all that is possibly "blessable," an enterprise that remains ongoing and open-ended—as the blessings for modern objects like cars and airplanes makes clear. Hence Anscar Chupungo can state: "There is hardly any proper use of material things that cannot be directed toward sanctification and the praise of God."[99]

But such is the narrative shape of experience that our "proper use of material things" seems to require an emplotted reference, a paradigmatic episode in accordance with which our present scenario can be configured. If the Incarnation, taken as a metanarrative, can be seen as the necessary and sufficient dogmatic cause for blessings, the liturgy still tends to refract it through the kind of *petits récits* discussed by Power, specific episodes in the life of Christ deemed to presage whatever blessing is to be conducted. In their absence, the liturgy mines the Old Testament and even apocryphal literature for suitable precedents, its claim to a divine disclosure here and now being legitimated by a sort of narrative casuistry.[100]

As we saw in Chapter 7, however, this is potentially problematic to the extent that the narrative referent of a given rite may be historically dubious. Inasmuch as Christianity is ostensibly obligated to take historicity seriously—in the spirit of the Pauline admonition, "And if Christ has not been raised, your faith is futile and you are still in your sins" (1 Cor. 15:17)—the following question arises: In what regard ought one to hold narratives (such as those drawn from apocryphal sources) whose historicity does not seem to be worth the wager of the Resurrection itself? Do they occasion a second naïveté, the imperative to recover meaning merely from the text/rite, rather than from the event at stake? Ought their narrative reference to be omitted as a possible "abuse" of memory and only the doxological component retained? After all, the tradition knows prayers that exhibit only a modicum of narrative concern, privileging the world "in front of" the text rather than that which lies behind it.[101] If so, do we rightly subject such prayers to contemporary historiographical consensus, or do we rather defer to the Yerushalmi-esque "living memory" of generations of worshippers whose history can only be known from within?

For, on the one hand, it is possible that to treat as veracious, events that one actually only regards as parables at best, subtly undermines the necessary—if somewhat fluid—distinction between fiction (representing what Ricoeur terms "the conditions of possibility") and history ("the conditions of actuality"). Indeed, a blatant indifference to this distinction would perhaps constitute grounds for deeming a given blessing aberrant. Such a blessing would arguably be one that compromised the Christian story at large by promoting episodes or ideas not in keeping with the drift of the plot, as it were: one that thwarted the fundamental configuration of this plot, threatening the reference points necessary for its own narrative coherence as also for the "narrative unity" of a Christian life responsive to it. On the other hand, Ricoeur has enabled us to see, in light of his understanding of metaphor (and its role in narrative), that there is *never* an unmediated access to the events of the past, and that in certain instances the very incredulity that might naturally arise in response to a singularity of a given event almost *requires* a flouting of historiographical modesty.

The "Poetics of Love"

Where, then, does the narrative configuration of the *GBW* stand in this respect? For there is in fact an extravagance in its emplotment, bearing an affinity with Christ's parables, as understood by Ricoeur. Hyperbolic language is employed not only with respect to the water being blessed, but also in regard to the meaning of the episode upon which the ritual action is based, effecting a Ricoeurian "reorientation by disorientation." Both the celebration of the service and its perpetuation in the subsequent use of the blessed water are made to bear an almost insupportable weight of eschatological scandal. The limits of sight are transgressed by the boldness of faith in its expectation of a divine munificence—a superabundance in keeping with the "economy of the gift." For such a common part of nature is here made to convey the significance of an utterly singular event, known not externally through the "history-like" record of the Gospels, so much as through the schematization of memory effected by (participation in) the rite.

The *GBW* requests, for instance, that God "give to [this water] the grace of redemption and the blessing of Jordan [and] make it a source of incorruption, a gift of sanctification, a deliverance from sins, an averting of diseases, unapproachable by hostile powers, filled with angelic strength." Hearing these petitions one might well wonder why water so blessed is not even more assiduously employed by the faithful than it already is; why indeed, after some sixteen centuries of celebration, the inordinate benefits of assisting at this rite have not proven themselves to all and sundry. In other words, one might well be forgiven for requesting some *evidence* for the singular qualities attributed to the blessed water.

I would contend that the answer to this question—or rather, the response to this suspicion—is to recognize the mystery represented by the *GBW* as intelligible only in terms of what Ricoeur calls the "poetics of love." As he explains: "The discourse of love is initially a discourse of praise, where in praising, one rejoices over the view of one object set above all the other objects of one's concern." In this discourse "key words undergo amplifications of meaning, unexpected assimilations, hitherto unseen interconnections, which cannot be reduced to a single meaning."[102] Thus, the act of blessing, taken as an act of love, an incarnate discourse by the Word who became flesh, ought by rights to be irreducible to empirical proofs, or to the evacuation of meaning contained in a univocal explanation of its import. In a similar vein, let us submit the following: We cannot *understand* the rite in the literal sense of "standing under" it, analyzing it from a remove; we can nevertheless *comprehend* it—i.e., "take [it] with" ourselves, carrying it forward into our lives.

To be sure, the rite itself does advance a kind of narrative "proof": a rehearsal of the historic *magnalia Dei* that allegedly justify the present liturgical action. But these divine deeds remain subject to the criterion of attestation by which, as we heard Jean Ladrière explain in Chapter 6, the one receiving the testimony to them becomes himself implicated therein. In this sense, the Baptism of Christ does not abide on a plane distinct from the multitude of other events said to occur in the "today" of Byzantine-Rite celebrations. Having already occurred, such events do not recede into the horizon but follow rather the inverse perspective associated with iconography: They move toward us, confuting the normativity of our conventional distinction between then and now, there and here. Hence the *GBW*'s uninterrupted account of the creation of the world and of the theophanies of the Old Testament alongside Christ's kenotic *exitus* from the Father forth into the world: There is no background, as it were, but only a foreground.

And yet it is still the Baptism of Christ in the Jordan that towers high in salvific significance:

> The Jordan turned back . . . seeing him drowning the death from disobedience, the goad of error and the bond of Hell in Jordan and granting the Baptism of salvation to the world. . . . For you could not bear, Master, in the compassion of your mercy to watch the human race being tyrannised by the devil, but you came and saved us. You sanctified the streams of Jordan by sending down from heaven your All-holy Spirit and you smashed the heads of the dragons that lurked there.

The rhetoric exhibited here surely illustrates that property of love that according to Ricoeur tends to extol one thing over all others: The Baptism of Christ becomes in the *GBW* the divine chef d'oeuvre, serving as a metonym for the Paschal Mystery—and all that *it* means. And yet, as the saying goes, "love is blind": The myopia besetting the soteriological vision of the rite makes it dependent on the guidance of another narrative that cannot itself be circumscribed within the celebration, any more than its protagonist can be kept within the bounds of description. Paradoxically, it is as if the *GBW* points to its own contingency in the very attempt to attach all possible meanings to itself.

But is the liturgical labor therefore in vain? Of course not, since it is altogether too easy to fail in transmitting to future generations the "unbelievable" truth of the past—in this instance, the genuine import of Christ's Baptism. Ironically then, as suggested above, literary transgression of the historical genre through fictive devices may actually be necessary here (as elsewhere) in order to render due justice to the history in question, that is, "to realize our debt to the past." As Richard Kearney comments, in regard to Ricoeur's reflections on the matter: "[Narrative has] the responsibility to refigure certain events of deep ethical intensity that conventional historiography might be tempted to overlook in favour of a so-called objective explanation of things. . . . The refigurative act of standing for the past provides us with a 'figure' to experience and think about, to both feel and reflect upon."[103]

If we compare the brevity of the Markan account of the Baptism of the Lord, taken here as the equivalent of the "objective explanation of things," with the rhetoric of the *GBW*, we find the liturgy attempting to fulfill a debt, striving to communicate to all generations the depths of the mystery—hidden beneath the waters, as it were—of an event that the Gospel treats in a rather straightforward way. Thus the *GBW* can aspire, on the one hand, to be equal to the event it treats: "We acknowledge your grace, we proclaim your mercy, we do not conceal your benevolence"; and yet, on the other hand, the rite admits its utter failure to do so: "No tongue is adequate to sing the praises of your wonders." This paradoxical confession flows from a sense of the event as a limit-experience. Ricoeur's approach to the Holocaust appears applicable also, mutatis mutandis, to our concern here. As van den Hengel summarizes:

> Limit-events and limit-experiences force us toward the outer edges of, or even beyond, language. It is no wonder, therefore, that, as a limit-event, the Shoah [viz. the baptism of Christ] tests the capacity of representation. What the figurative forms must achieve is what representation cannot achieve: to make a singular claim of truth. No realist novel, no naturalist history is up to it. It requires the idea of the exemplarity of the singular. . . . What is at work here, according to Ricoeur, is a moral singularity of an absolutely incomparable event.[104]

When van den Hengel speaks of us being forced beyond language, one thinks of the way in which the *GBW* by its very nature directs the participants forward, by its exhortation to refigure their lives through the manifold use of the blessed water; the only way to honor the past is by the effort to put one's testimony into practice.

Yet one may ask: Is the simulacrum enthroned by such representation not a kind of usurper? After all, we must remember Kearney's caveat: "The deployment of novelistic techniques by historians to place some past event or personage vividly before the reader's mind . . . [serves as] a way of making things visible as if they were present. The danger is, of course, that the figural 'as if' might collapse into a literal belief, so that we would no longer merely 'see as' but make the mistake of believing we are actually seeing."[105] Indeed, this is the crux of the matter. For it must be admitted that liturgy in this respect increases the transgression. The "hallucination of presence" is the very spell the rite endeavors to cast.[106] By its pneumatic invocations (e.g., "Therefore, O King, lover of mankind, be present now too through the visitation of your Holy Spirit, and sanctify this water"), it seeks to push the imagination to its limit—over the cliff, we might say. Whereas Kearney posits narrative's "double responsibility: to the past as *present*, and to the past as *past*,"[107] the realized eschatology of the liturgy begs the question of whether this is the proverbial "distinction without a difference."

The Transfiguration of Time and Space

Consider in this connection the effacement of temporal distance perpetuated by the use of "today," ubiquitous in Byzantine liturgical texts and recurring no less than twenty-two times in the received form of the *GBW*. By this adverb an event of the past is announced as present to the assembly in and through its own celebration. The Baptism of Christ—an episode in the personal history of one transcending the limits of time and space—is selected for anamnesis; in and through the ritual calling to mind, the worshippers are (through the efficacy of the Holy Spirit) purportedly made contemporaries of that which they "remember." This mnemonic operation, epitomized in the diaconal address commencing the Byzantine Eucharist (referred to above: "It is time for the Lord to act"), implies the possibility of an authentic encounter in the present with those things historically accomplished by Christ.[108] Hence Taft contends, "Liturgical feasts, therefore, have the same purpose as the Gospel: to present this new reality [i.e., the life in Christ] in '*anamnesis*,' memorial, as a continual sign to us not of a past history, but of the present reality of our lives in him. As St. Paul says in 2 Cor 6:2: 'Behold *now* is the acceptable time; behold *now is* the day of salvation.'"[109]

We can elucidate Taft's contention by noting how liturgical feasts revolve around a certain inversion of both the idiom of testimony and the operations by which it is schematized (as discussed in Chapter 7). For the testimony given in such celebrations, exemplified in their festal hymnography, exhibits peculiar deictics: the use of the first-person plural (together with the present tense of the verb) and an emphasis on "here" versus "there"—or rather, a rhetorical assimilation of "there" to "here" (and "then" to "now"). Thus the following can be sung: "In the preceding feast we saw Thee as a child, while in the present we behold Thee full-grown. . . . For today the time of the feast is at hand for us: the choir of saints assembles with us and angels join with men in keeping festival. . . . Today the waters of the Jordan are transformed into healing by the coming of the Lord."[110] Actually, as observed above in our treatment of the *GBW*'s naming of God, the verb tenses of Byzantine hymnography typically oscillate between past and present, promoting a contraction of the temporal distance between the liturgical "testimony" and the referent it indicates.

The schematization of place also plays a critical role in the revivification of an "I was there." We can chart in the *GBW* a centrifugal dynamic by which "geometrical space" becomes "lived" by being ritually inhabited. The procession from the church to a given body of water spatializes the festal narrative of Christ going forth to Baptism; the blessing of the water renders it a physical metaphor for the Jordan River, whose currents proceed to "flow" into the homes of the faithful. By being employed for blessing in the domestic milieu, the Theophany water functions both to further integrate lived space into the sacral topography, spreading outward from the body of water blessed, and to incorporate lived time into the narrative of salvation. Finally, the place where the rite occurs, converted through the blessing into an object (namely, "holy water") acquires ontological "density" to the extent that this object is sprinkled or drunk as sacramental, experienced as mediating prayer for the welfare of oneself and others.

One sees in the dynamics of the *GBW*, therefore, an utter reversal of Ricoeur's "transition from living memory to the 'extrinsic' positing of historical knowledge," as it ordinarily obtains in the historiographical movement from testimony to document.[111] The liturgy is ordered rather to what we might call (to coin a neologism) an "abscription"—a movement *away* from writing—of the witness conserved in the liturgical archives. What is remarkable, though perhaps no more so than other instances in Christian heortology, is the way in which such a rich and complex web of liturgical practice and religious devotion can hang upon such a thin Scriptural thread—namely, the laconic account of the Baptism of the Lord in the Gospels. Or to change the metaphor: The *GBW* rests not on terra firma, but floats upon a trust in the veracity of the evangelists' testimony. To paraphrase 1 Cor. 15:17: "And if Christ has not been baptized, your faith is futile."

CONCLUSION

I nspired by Ricoeur's well-known aphorism "The symbol gives rise to thought," this book has engaged the symbolic manifold of the Byzantine Rite, and specifically its Theophany "Great Blessing of Water," by means of Ricoeur's own hermeneutical philosophy. It has sought to make a contribution to Orthodox liturgical theology, inspired by the legacy of Schmemann, through whom I first discovered the power of a Weltanschauung grounded in the worship of the Church. While respecting Schmemann, I have sought to go "beyond" him by questioning, at various removes, what it means to "seek in the liturgy the vision implied in its own ordo."[1] I have brought into relief the extent of theological and philosophical conversations underway with respect to the Ricoeurian corpus, endeavoring to introduce the Byzantine liturgy as an "interlocutor." Hopefully, the reader has found the effort worthwhile, and will concur that Ricoeur's thought, as well as the Orthodox liturgical tradition, have both deployed a "surplus of meaning" by being interpreted in light of each other.

Part I entertained the question "Why Ricoeur?" by reflecting on the imperative for liturgical theology to engage with contemporary philosophy; by examining and evaluating the use of Ricoeur by liturgists working out of the Western tradition (Joyce Ann Zimmerman and Bridget Nichols); by considering the larger debate that such use has occasioned, especially vis-à-vis the methodology of ritual studies; and finally, by listening to what Ricoeurian scholars and Ricoeur himself have had to say in regard to the potential of liturgy to serve as a site of hermeneutical inquiry. I concluded that a liturgical hermeneutic informed by Ricoeur would profit from a triple

213

thematic orientation, encompassing ritual symbolism, as represented preeminently in the metaphorical cast of its linguistic idiom; ritual selfhood, the form of subjectivity presumed and produced by the liturgical
context; and ritual transformation, taken as a shorthand for liturgy's deployment of specific mnemonic operations.

In Part II we investigated Ricoeur's treatment of the polyphonic "naming" of God as illustrative of the metaphoricity of poetic discourse, subsequently developing a liturgical analogue to it through reference especially
to C. S. Lewis, David Power, and Graham Ward. This discussion high-
lighted the distinctiveness of liturgical naming as an idiom inclusive of
models and qualifiers, of kataphasis and apophasis. I concluded that the
subjectivity countenanced by the liturgical naming of God merited designation as a form of Ricoeur's "summoned self," one manifesting a corresponding polyphony.

Ricoeur's understanding of subjectivity and its application to a liturgical context were the burden of the first section of Part III. To mine the
rich vein of his reflections, we delved into his celebrated *Oneself as Another*,
guided in our explorations by the hand of John van den Hengel. His assessment of the import of this work for practical theology at large informed
a canvassing of its themes and concepts for insight into the features of liturgical selfhood. We were also aided in this task by considering further
the work of Joyce Ann Zimmerman. What emerged was a corroboration
of Ricoeur's threefold account of otherness—namely, that of the lived body,
other persons, and the testimony of conscience. The latter was considered
with respect to the liturgical actants, both human and divine. This led to
a reflection on the notion of truth as attestation, and in turn, to its connection to recognition; I concluded that liturgy attests to the self's portentous recognition of itself as *capax Dei*, "summoned" to a doxological
vocation.

The latter section of Part III involved a probing of Ricoeur's compendi-
ous *Memory, History, Forgetting*, in order to uncover the dynamics endemic
to liturgy as a form of embodied remembering. We situated our exploration within a current debate among liturgical theologians, concerning the
vital question of how critical historiography impinges upon the communally sanctioned, theological interpretation of the past, a question brought
into relief by liturgy's recourse to fictional devices in the commemoration
of salvation history. Adapting Ricoeur's apologia for the "limit-experience"
represented by the Shoah, I argued that the miraculous events celebrated

in liturgy exhibit an analogous, if obverse, singularity: The transmission of their truth, paradoxically, depends upon the service rendered by the productive imagination.

Finally, in Part IV, we drew upon the multiple tools in our Ricoeurian tool-kit to unpack the Byzantine-Rite "Great Blessing of Water" in dialogue with Nicholas Denysenko's historical-critical analysis of the service. In attending to its naming of God, we found striking examples of polyphonicity: in the ambiguity of divine addressee, whether God the Father or Christ; in the combination of apophatic and kataphatic discourse; and in the soteriological dialectics presented by the *GBW*'s contrasting narratives of (re)creation, with their respective testimony to the roles of rational word and conflictual deed and their invocation of the differentiated symbolism of light and water. Subsequently, in our ruminations on the form of subjectivity engendered by the rite, we found a unique "summoned self" constituted by the call to bless, an action discovered to have both verbal and sacrificial connotations. Such a call, we ventured, could exploit our natural faculty for gratitude, after the manner in which, for Ricoeur, conscience is galvanized by fusion with a range of biblical/hagiographical figures. Thirdly, we plotted the narrative arc extending through blessings in general, and attempted to follow the particular trajectory coordinated by the temporal configuration and spatial schematization of the *GBW*. In sum, I have sought to demonstrate how the diverse resources offered by Ricoeur can assist in responding to at least *some* of the challenges faced by liturgical theology in our day. If this book serves to engender further reflection on Orthodox Christianity and contemporary thought, it will have achieved its purpose.

I am fully conscious that there is much that remains *undone* in the present work; favoring Ricoeur has required passing over other crucial figures in contemporary thought, whose contributions have been (and hopefully will continue to be) exploited in enriching the scope of liturgical theology. I think particularly of the kind of groundbreaking research done by Orthodox philosopher Terence Cuneo in his recent *Ritualized Faith: Essays on the Philosophy of Liturgy*—a highly original, even eclectic analysis of Byzantine-Rite worship, covering themes as varied as liturgical singing, icons and the nature of forgiveness. (Happily, he also has much to say about Schmemann!)[2] Of course, I am also well aware that the literature on Ricoeur continues to burgeon—even as this book has been in production. There are not only many important texts of Ricoeur that I have had to put aside to keep my volume to a manageable length, but I have hardly done justice to the multifarious applications of his oeuvre represented by the vibrant international community of scholars known as the "Society for Ricoeur Studies,"[3] and their on-line journal, *Études Ricoeuriennes/Ricoeur Studies*.[4] There is indeed much territory to explore; nonetheless, as a winsome Korean proverb has it, "Starting is half"!

It is striking that Ricoeur uses the metaphor of travel to describe the work of interpretation, presenting his hermeneutical philosophy as a "long route" through the landscape of symbols, an indirect, narrative itinerary to the hidden reaches of personal identity, ultimately seen to be otherwise inaccessible. This metaphor corresponds to the élan of the *GBW*, in which the procession of clergy and faithful set forth from the relative safety and security of the church proper toward the wilds of the water, where they will seek the God at once known and unknown. Their *exitus* images the perennial human quest for Theophany, itself an apt characterization for the journey theology must make out of the precincts of its natural home, into the turbulence of the philosophical stream, there to cast forth the Cross of Christ and witness him conquering the dragons that lay therein.

Appendix: "Service of the Great Blessing of the Waters"

From "The Menaia," Archimandrite Ephrem Lash

After the Prayer behind the Ambo, we go out to the Font, the Priest going ahead with lights and incense, and we chant the following Idiomels in Tone 8, during which the Church and people are censed. (By Sophronios, Patriarch of Jerusalem).

The voice of the Lord upon the waters cries out, saying, 'Come all of you, receive the Spirit of wisdom, the Spirit of understanding, the Spirit of the fear of God, of Christ who has appeared'. (x3)

Today the nature of the waters is made holy, and Jordan is parted and holds back the flow of its waters as it sees the Master washing himself. (x2)

As man, Christ King, you came to the river, and in your goodness you hasten to accept the baptism of a servant at the hands of the Forerunner, on account of our sins, O Lover of mankind. (x2)

Glory. Both now. Same Tone.

At the voice of the one crying in the desert, 'Prepare the way of the Lord', you came, Lord, having taken the form of a servant, asking for Baptism, though you did not know sin. The waters saw you and were afraid. The Forerunner trembled and cried out, saying, 'How will the lamp enlighten the Light? The servant place his hand on the

Master? Saviour, who take away the sin of the world, make me and the waters holy.'

And immediately the Readings. The Reading is from the Prophecy of Isaias. [35, 1–10]

Thus says the Lord: Thirsty desert rejoice, let the desert exult and flower like a lily. And the deserts of Jordan will flower and be overgrown and exult. And the glory of Lebanon has been given to it and the honour of Carmel. And my people will see the glory of the Lord and the majesty of God. Be strong, enfeebled hands and palsied knees. Give comfort and say to the faint-hearted. Be strong and do not fear. See, our God is giving judgement and will give it. He himself will come and save us.

Then the eyes of the blind will be opened and the ears of the deaf will hear. Then the lame will leap like a deer and the tongue of stammerers will speak clearly, because water has broken out in the desert and a channel in a thirsty land. And the waterless land will become pools and there will be a spring of water for the thirsty land. There will be joy of birds there, folds for flocks and reed beds and pools. And there will be a pure way there, and it will be called a holy way, and no one unclean may pass along it. There will be no unclean way there. But the scattered will walk upon it and not go astray. There will be no lion there, nor will any evil wild beasts go up on it or be found there. But the redeemed and gathered by the Lord will walk on it. And they will return and come to Sion with joy and exultation, and everlasting joy will be upon their head. And on their head praise and exultation and joy will possess them. Pain, grief and sighing have fled away.

The Reading is from the Prophecy of Isaias. [55, 1–13]

Thus says the Lord: You that thirst, go for water. And as many of you as have no money, make your way and buy. And eat and drink wine and fat without money and price. Why do you spend money on what is not food, and toil for what does not satisfy? Hear me, and eat what is good, and your soul will delight in good things. Give heed with your ears and follow in my ways. Listen to me and your soul will live among good things. And I will make an eternal Covenant with you, the sure mercies of David. See, I have given him as a testimony among the Nations, a ruler and commander among the Nations. See, Nations who do not know you will call upon you, and peoples who are not acquainted with you will take refuge with you, for the sake of the Lord your God and the Holy One of Israel, because he has glorified you. Seek the Lord, and when you find him, call upon him. But when he comes near you, let the impious abandon his ways and a lawless man his plans. And return to the Lord and you will find mercy, and cry out, for he will abundantly forgive your sins.

For my plans are not like your plans, nor are my ways like your ways, says the Lord. But as far as heaven is from earth, so far is my way from your ways and your thoughts from my mind. For as rain or snow comes down from heaven and does not return until it has saturated the earth and it brings forth and sprouts and gives seed to the sower and bread for food, so will my word be. Whatever comes out of my mouth will not return to me empty, until everything that I wished has been fulfilled. And I will make my ways and my commands prosper. You will go out with gladness and be taught with joy. For the mountains and hills will leap up, welcoming you with joy, and all the trees of the field will clap with their branches. And instead of brambles cypress will come up, and instead of nettles myrtle will come up. And there shall be for the Lord a name and an everlasting sign, and it will not fail.

The Reading is from the Prophecy of Isaias. [12, 3–6]

Thus says the Lord: Draw out water with gladness from the wells of salvation. And you will say in that day, Sing to the Lord and cry out his name. Proclaim among the Nations his glorious deeds, remind them that his name has been exalted. Sing to the name of the Lord, for he has done great things. Proclaim these in all the earth. Exult and be glad, you that dwell in Sion, because the Holy One of Israel has been exalted in the midst of her.

Then the Prokeimenon in Tone 3. [Psalm 26]

The Lord is my enlightenment and my Saviour. Whom shall I fear? Verse: The Lord is the defender of my life. Of whom shall I be afraid?

The Reading is from the First Epistle of Paul to the Corinthians. [10, 1–4]

Brethren, I do not want you to be ignorant of how our Fathers were all under the cloud and all passed through the sea. And they were all baptised into Moses in the cloud and in the sea. And they all ate the same spiritual food. And they all drank the same spiritual drink. For they drank from the spiritual rock that followed them. Now the rock was Christ.

Alleluia. Tone 4. [Psalm 28, 3]

Verse 1: The voice of the Lord is upon the waters.
Verse 2: The God of glory thundered upon the waters.

The Reading is from the holy Gospel according to Mark. [1, 9–11]

At that time, Jesus came from Nazareth in Galilee and was baptised by John in the Jordan. And immediately as he was coming up from the water, he saw the heavens being parted and the Spirit like a dove coming down upon him. And there was a voice from heaven, You are my beloved Son, in whom I am well pleased.

And the Deacon at once begins the Litany of Peace. While this is being said by the Deacon, the Priest says the prayer Lord Jesus Christ . . . quietly. [If there is no Deacon, the Priest reads this prayer during the reading of the Prophecies]

Deacon: In peace, let us pray to the Lord.

People: Lord, have mercy. And so after each petition.

Deacon: For the peace from on high and for the salvation of our souls, let us pray to the Lord.

For the peace of the whole world, for the welfare of the holy Churches of God, and for the union of all, let us pray to the Lord.

For this holy house, and for those who enter it with faith, reverence and the fear of God, let us pray to the Lord.

[For all devout and Orthodox Christians, let us pray to the Lord.]

For our Archbishop N., for the honoured order of presbyters, for the diaconate in Christ, for all the clergy and the people, let us pray to the Lord.

For [our Sovereign Lady, Queen Elizabeth, the Royal Family, her Government, and] all in authority, let us pray to the Lord.

For this city [Or this holy monastery], for every [monastery] city, town and village, and for the faithful who dwell in them, let us pray to the Lord.

For favourable weather, an abundance of the fruits of the earth, and temperate seasons, let us pray to the Lord.

For those who travel by land, air or water, for the sick, the suffering, for those in captivity, and for their safety and salvation, let us pray to the Lord.

For this water to be sanctified by the power and operation and visitation of the Holy Spirit, let us pray to the Lord.

For there to come down upon these waters the cleansing operation of the Trinity beyond all being, let us pray to the Lord.

For there to be given them the grace of redemption, the blessing of Jordan, let us pray to the Lord.

For us to be enlightened with the enlightenment of knowledge and true religion through the visitation of the Holy Spirit, let us pray to the Lord.

For this water to become a gift of sanctification, a deliverance from sins, for healing of soul and body and for every suitable purpose, let us pray to the Lord.

For this water to become water springing up to eternal life, let us pray to the Lord.

For this water to be shown to be an averting of every assault of visible and invisible enemies, let us pray to the Lord.

For those who draw from it and take from it for the sanctification of their homes, let us pray to the Lord.

For it to be for cleansing of souls and bodies for all those who draw from it with faith and who partake of it, let us pray to the Lord.

For us to be counted worthy to be filled with sanctification through communion of these waters by the invisible manifestation of the Holy Spirit, let us pray to the Lord.

For the Lord God to hear the voice of supplication of us sinners and have mercy on us, let us pray to the Lord.

For our deliverance from all affliction, wrath, danger and constraint, let us pray to the Lord.

Help us, save us, have mercy on us, and keep us, O God, by your grace.

Commemorating our all-holy, pure, most blessed and glorious Lady, Mother of God and Ever-Virgin Mary, with all the Saints, let us entrust ourselves and one another and our whole life to Christ our God.

The Priest reads the following prayer in a low voice.

Lord Jesus Christ, only-begotten Son, who are in the bosom of the Father, true God, source of life and immortality, Light from Light, who came into the world to enlighten it, flood our mind with light by your Holy Spirit and accept us as we bring you praise and thanksgiving for your wondrous mighty works from every age, and for your saving dispensation in these last times. By it you clothe yourself in our weak and beggared matter and coming down to the measure of our servitude, King of all, you accepted also to be baptised in the Jordan by the hand of a servant, so that, having sanctified the nature of the waters, you, the sinless one, might make a way for our rebirth through water and Spirit and re-establish us in our original freedom.

As we celebrate the memory of this divine Mystery, we entreat you, Master, lover of mankind: Sprinkle on us, your unworthy servants, cleansing water, in accordance with your divine promise, the gift of your compassion, that the request of us sinners over this water may become acceptable by your goodness and that through it your blessing to be granted to us and to all your faithful people, to the glory of your holy, venerated Name. For to you belong all glory, honour and worship, with your Father who is without beginning, with you all-holy, good and life-giving Spirit, now and forever, and to the ages of ages. Amen.

And having said the Amen to himself, when the Deacon has finished the Litany, the Priest begins this Prayer in a loud voice [the first part only on day of the Feast itself]

[A Composition of Patriarch Sophronios of Jerusalem].

Trinity beyond all being, beyond all goodness, beyond all godhead, all-powerful, all-vigilant, invisible, incomprehensible; Creator of the spiritual beings and rational natures, innate goodness, unapproachable Light that enlightens everyone coming into the world, shine also in me your unworthy servant. Enlighten the eyes of my mind that I may dare to sing the praise of your measureless benevolence and power. May my supplication for the people here present be acceptable, so that my offences may not prevent the Holy Spirit from being present here; but permit me now without condemnation to cry out to you and say, Master, lover of mankind, beyond all goodness, Almighty, eternal King. We glorify you, the Creator and Fashioner of the universe. We glorify you, only-begotten Son of God, without father from your Mother, without mother from your Father. For in the preceding feast we saw you as a babe, but in the present one we see you full and perfect man, our God, made manifest as perfect God from perfect God.

For today the moment of the feast is here for us and the choir of saints assembles here with us, and Angels keep festival with mortals. Today the grace of the Holy Spirit in the form of a dove dwelt upon the waters. Today the Sun that never sets has dawned and the world is made radiant with the light of the Lord. Today the Moon with its radiant beams sheds light on the world. Today the stars formed of light make the inhabited world lovely with the brightness of their splendour. Today the clouds rain down from heaven the shower of justice for mankind. Today the Uncreated by his own will accepts the laying on of hands by his own creature. Today the Prophet and Forerunner draws near, but stands by with fear seeing God's condescension towards us. Today the streams of Jordan are changed into healing by the presence of the Lord. Today all creation is watered by mystical streams. Today the failings of mankind are being washed away by the waters of Jordan. Today Paradise is opened for mortals and the Sun of justice shines down on us. Today the bitter water as once for Moses' people is changed to sweetness by the presence of the Lord. Today we have been delivered from the ancient grief, and saved as the new Israel. Today we have been redeemed from darkness and are filled with radiance by the light of the knowledge of God. Today the gloomy fog of the world is cleansed by the manifestation of our God. Today all creation shines with light from on high. Today error has been destroyed and the coming of the Master makes for us a way of salvation. Today things on high keep festival with those below, and those below commune with those on high. Today the sacred and triumphant festal assembly of the Orthodox exults. Today the Master hastens towards baptism, that he may lead humanity to the heights. Today the One who does not bow bows down to his own servant, that he may free us from servitude. Today we have purchased the Kingdom of heaven, for the Kingdom of the Lord will have no end. Today earth and sea share the joy of the world, and the world has been filled with gladness.

The waters saw you, O God, the waters saw you and were afraid. The Jordan turned back when it saw the fire of the godhead descending in bodily form and entering it. The Jordan turned back as it contemplated the Holy Spirit in the form of a dove, descending and flying about you. The Jordan turned back as it saw the Invisible made visible, the Creator made flesh, the Master in the form of a servant. The Jordan turned back and the mountains leapt as they saw God in the flesh, and the clouds uttered their voice, marvelling at what had come to pass, seeing Light from Light, true God from true God, the Master's festival today in Jordan; seeing him drowning the death from disobedience, the goad of error and the bond of Hell in Jordan and granting the Baptism of salvation to the world. Therefore I too, a sinner and your unworthy servant, recount the greatness of your wonders and, seized with fear, in compunction cry out to you:

After completing this, he says in a more powerful voice,

Great are you, O Lord, and wonderful your works, and no word is adequate to sing the praise of your wonders (x3). [People: Glory to you, Lord, glory to you!]

For by your own will you brought the universe from non-existence into being, you hold creation together by your might, and by your providence you direct the world. You composed creation from four elements; with four seasons you crowned the circle of the year. All the spiritual Powers tremble before you. The sun sings your praise, the moon glorifies you, the stars entreat you, the light obeys you, the deeps tremble before you, the springs are your servants. You stretched out the heavens on the waters; you walled in the sea with sand; you poured out the air for breathing. Angelic Powers minister to you. The choirs of the Archangels worship you. The many-eyed Cherubim and the six-winged Seraphim as they stand and fly around you hide their faces in fear of your unapproachable glory. For you, being God uncircumscribed, without beginning and inexpressible, came upon earth, taking the form of a servant, being found in the likeness of mortals. For you could not bear, Master, in the compassion of your mercy to watch the human race being tyrannised by the devil, but you came and saved us. We acknowledge your grace, we proclaim your mercy, we do not conceal your benevolence. You freed the generations of our race. You sanctified a virgin womb by your birth. All creation sang your praise when you appeared. For you are our God who appeared on earth and lived among mortals. You sanctified the streams of Jordan by sending down from heaven your All-holy Spirit and you smashed the heads of the dragons that lurked there.

Therefore, O King, lover of mankind, be present now too through the visitation of your Holy Spirit, and sanctify this water. (x3)

And give to it the grace of redemption and the blessing of Jordan. Make it a source of incorruption, a gift of sanctification, a deliverance from sins, an averting of diseases, unapproachable by hostile powers, filled with angelic strength. That all who draw from it and partake of it may have it for cleansing of souls and bodies, for healing of passions, for sanctification of homes, for every suitable purpose. For you are our God, who through water and Spirit renewed our nature made old by sin. You are our God, who in the days of Noë drowned sin through the water of the flood. You are our God, who through Moses freed the Hebrew race from the slavery of Pharao through the sea. You are our God who split open the rock in the desert, and waters rushed out and torrents flooded down, and you satisfied your thirsty people. You are our God, who through Elias turned Israel from the error of Baal.

And now, Master, do you yourself sanctify this water by your Holy Spirit. (x3)

Give to all who partake of it sanctification, blessing, cleansing, health.

And save, Lord, our faithful Rulers [our Sovereign Lady Queen Elisabeth]. (x3) [The triple form of this petition is a relic of the imperial liturgy of Agia Sophia in Constantinople before 1453.]

And guard them [her] under your protection in peace. Subdue beneath their [her] feet every foe and enemy. Grant them [her] all their [her] requests that are for salvation and eternal life.

Remember, Lord, our Archbishop N., the whole order of Presbyters, the Diaconate in Christ, every rank of the clergy, the people here present and our brethren who with good reason are absent, and have mercy on us in accordance with your great mercy. So that through elements and through Angels and through mortals and through things visible and through things unseen, your all-holy name may be glorified with the Father and the Holy Spirit, now and for ever, and to the ages of ages.

> PEOPLE: Amen.
> PRIEST: Peace to all.
> PEOPLE: And to your spirit.
> DEACON: Let us bow our heads to the Lord.
> PEOPLE: To you, O Lord.
> And the Priest says the Prayer in a low voice,

Incline your ear and hear us, Lord, who accepted to be baptised in Jordan and to sanctify the waters, and bless us all, who signify our calling as servants by the bending of our necks. And count us worthy to be filled with your sanctification through the partaking and sprinkling of this water. And let it be for us, Lord, for healing of soul and body.

Aloud

> For you are the sanctification of our souls and bodies, and to you we give glory, thanksgiving and worship, with your Father who is without beginning, and your All-holy, good and life-giving Spirit, now and for ever, and to the ages of ages.

People: Amen.

And the Priest immediately, blessing the waters in the figure of the Cross, immerses the precious Cross, plunging it upright into the water and lifting it out again, chanting the following Troparion in Tone 1. The Priest once and the Choirs once each.

> As you were baptised in the Jordan, Lord, the worship of the Trinity was made manifest, for the voice of the Father bore witness to you, naming you the Beloved Son; and the Spirit, in the form of a dove, confirmed the sureness of the word. Christ God, who appeared and enlightened the world, glory to you.

[Both the typikon of the Monastery of Dionysiou and that of the Church of Cyprus prescribe that the Kontakion be sung after the singing of the Apolytikion.

> Kontakion. Tone 4. Model Melody.

> Today you have appeared to the inhabited world; and your light, O Lord, has been marked upon us; who with knowledge sing your praise. You have come, you have appeared, the unapproachable Light.

When the feast falls on a Monday and the first blessing takes place on Sunday, then the Kontakion of the Forefeast is sung.

> Kontakion. Tone 4. Today you have appeared.

> Today the Lord has come to the streams of Jordan, and cries aloud to John: Do not be afraid to baptise me; for I have come to save Adam the First-formed.]

And he sprinkles all the People with the water. They drink from the water.

> As we enter the Church we chant the following Idiomel in Tone 6.

Let us the faithful praise the greatness of God's dispensation concerning us. For in our transgression he, alone clean and undefiled, becoming man, is cleansed in Jordan, sanctifying me and the waters, and crushing the heads of the dragons on the waters. Let us therefore draw water with gladness, brethren. For the grace of the Spirit is being given invisibly to those who draw with faith by Christ, God and the Saviour of our souls.

Then Blessed be the name of the Lord as usual and then the Psalm [33], I will bless the Lord at all times. And the broken fragments [Antidoron] are distributed.

Then the full Dismissal.

ACKNOWLEDGMENTS

I am extremely humbled by the support I have received from several people, who believed enough in the value of this work to encourage—and not infrequently goad—me to complete it. In the first place, I owe the profoundest debt of gratitude to my *Doktorvater*, the Very Rev. Dr. Peter Galadza, who has proven to be a mentor in so many ways; he is an exemplary scholar and a devoted priest, in addition to being a model husband and father. From the day I unexpectedly met him (on which he set aside his tasks in order to have coffee with me and respond—over the subsequent hours!—to my many theological questions) to the present, when we now have the privilege of together inaugurating a new phase of the life of the Sheptytsky Institute of Eastern Christian Studies in the University of St. Michael's College, Fr. Peter has been for me one of whom I can quote Isaac Newton's dictum: "If I have seen further, it is by standing on the shoulders of giants."

Secondly, I would not have completed the research on which this book is based without the assistance of my grandfather Richard Lebrun, Rector Emeritus of St. Paul's College, and Professor Emeritus of History at the University of Manitoba. Beyond seeking me out and welcoming me into the Lebrun family—the maternal birth family I discovered as an adult— he accompanied me throughout the course of my PhD studies, continually spurring me on. His careful reading and constructive criticism of my dissertation improved it immensely, preparing the soil for the maturing of the monograph that has occurred since.

Harold Visser served as unofficial copy editor for the dissertation, attending to the form of the work with rigorous attention, animated by a peculiarly Dutch sense of practicality and efficiency. He saved me from myself, as it were; and on other fronts he has ever proven to fulfill Prov. 27:17 in my regard: "Iron sharpeneth iron; so a man sharpeneth the countenance of his friend."

More recently, I have been assisted in preparing this book for publication by Louise St. Germain, a former graduate student who has been an indefatigable aide-de-camp, reading and rereading each chapter; suggesting additions and revisions; checking citations and references; and even proposing various designs for the book's cover. To put it all too succinctly (and thus risk belying her contribution): This book would not be in your hands, had it not passed through hers.

As a first-time author, I extend my especial appreciation to the editors of the series to which this book belongs, Telly Papanikolaou and George Demacopoulos, who saw the potential in my work and have patiently guided the process by which it has come to light. I could not have hoped to be part of a finer series than "Orthodox Christianity and Contemporary Thought"—a title which perfectly captures my own aspirations as a theologian. Others at Fordham University Press who have collaborated on this project, and graciously borne with me, include Edward Batchelder, Eric Newman, and, of course, Will Cerbone and Fredric Nachbaur. May the Lord recompense you for labors on my behalf!

Together with Fr. Peter, the community of the Sheptysky Institute, especially those who have prayed with me over the years in our former Chapel of Ss. Joachim and Anna at Saint Paul University and at the parish of St. John the Baptist in Ottawa—and, indeed braved the outdoor celebration of the Great Blessing of Water amidst our often foreboding Ontario winters—have taught me everything I know about the "icon of Christian reality" that we call liturgy. They are too many to name, but know who they are: of them, my brothers and sisters, I can eagerly confess with the Psalmist, "I was glad when they said unto me, 'Let us go up to the house of the Lord'" (Ps. 121[122]:1).

My colleagues in the Liturgical Hermeneutics Seminar of the North American Academy of Liturgy have generously allowed me to present portions of my research over the past several years, and helped me in better understanding the thought of Ricoeur and, more broadly, the spectrum of theoretical approaches to worship. I have learned so much from them, and am blessed to have been numbered among them.

Last but not least, I wish to thank Fr. Andrew Louth, who consented at the eleventh hour to read my manuscript and write a foreword to it; he did not need the burden, and I did not deserve the compliment. I have revered Louth's work from the early days of my doctoral work, when I was introduced to his masterful *Discerning the Mystery: An Essay on the Nature of Theology* (Oxford: Clarendon Press, 1983). To have his approbation at this stage has been a spur to press on in my scholarly "epektasis."

June 27, 2017
Feast of the New Martyrs of Ukraine

Notes

Introduction

1. Alexander Schmemann, "Russian Theology: 1920–1972. An Introductory Survey," *St. Vladimir's Theological Quarterly* 16, no. 4 (1972): 178, cited in Pantelis Kalaitzidis, "From the 'Return to the Fathers' to the Need for a Modern Orthodox Theology," *St. Vladimir's Theological Quarterly* 54, no. 1 (2010): 14.

2. Kalaitzidis, "From the 'Return to the Fathers,'" 6n4. Kalaitzidis is here describing the ethos of Metropolitan of Pergamon John Zizioulas, who he says "has tried to articulate a creative version of the 'neo-patristic synthesis' which is open to contemporary philosophical thought and to the dialogue between East and West." See John Zizioulas, *Being as Communion* (Crestwood, N.Y.: St. Vladimir's Seminary Press, 1985).

3. Robert F. Taft speaks appreciatively of the "Schmemann phenomenon," noting that the churchman "was a main protagonist of this growth [i.e., of liturgical theology] not only for Orthodoxy but for all Christians who can be said to have a liturgy" ("The Liturgical Enterprise Twenty-Five Years after Alexander Schmemann [1921–1983]: The Man and His Heritage," *St. Vladimir's Theological Quarterly* 53, no. 2–3 [2009]: 159–60).

4. Michael Plekon, "The Russian Religious Revival and Its Theological Legacy," in *The Cambridge Companion to Orthodox Christian Theology*, ed. Mary B. Cunningham and Elizabeth Theokritoff (Cambridge: Cambridge University Press, 2008), 208.

5. Plekon, "The Russian Religious Revival," 208. Peter Galadza, a Ukrainian Greco-Catholic liturgist deeply influenced by Schmemann, makes the following apologia for an interdisciplinary approach to liturgical theology:

To facilitate the process of enabling the rite to enflesh and communicate
more directly the realities of *koinonia, diakonia, metanoia*, etc., Byzantine
Christian liturgists must research not only the theology and history of
liturgy, but also the human sciences in their relation to liturgy. Anthropology, ritual studies, semiotics, psychology, sociology, economic analysis, and
communication theory—to mention only a few—must be brought into
comprehensive dialogue with Byzantine liturgiology because . . . this
dialogue with the human sciences conforms to the patristic mind. The
Cappadocians, for example, became specialists in Greek rhetoric in order,
inter alia, to facilitate a reception of the gospel among educated Hellenes. The
lack of an appropriation of the human sciences is among the stumbling
blocks to comprehensive liturgical analysis and renewal among Eastern
Christians. And unless one accepts a deforming divorce between nature and
grace, one will have to admit that these disciplines also relate to the *lex orandi*
and *lex credendi*, most basically because they relate to the *vita ecclesiae*, which
is where these *leges* are rooted to begin with. ("Schmemann between
Fagerberg and Reality: Towards an Agenda for Byzantine Christian Pastoral
Liturgy," *Bollettino Della Badia Greca Di Grottaferrata* 4 [2007]: 24–25)

6. In a similar vein, Jacob D. Myers has proposed that phenomenology, especially the interpretation of Husserl and Heidegger found in Ricoeur's fellow continental philosopher and countryman Jean-Luc Marion, has the potential to
extend the trajectory of Schmemann's thought in new ways, while remaining
faithful to his essential vision:

It is clear that Schmemann is concerned not merely with the *lex orandi* but
rather with how the *lex orandi* expresses (or ought to express) the church's
lex credendi. Thus, two aspects of liturgical theology are objects of consideration: the phenomena of liturgical expression and that which is conveyed or
intended through the phenomena. Therefore, in addition to the move
toward a more historical engagement with liturgical rubrics in their
contextual particularities, I am suggesting that we need a more robust
analytic by which we may investigate the *lex credendi* in the *lex orandi*.
Phenomenology provides just such an analytic. ("Toward an Erotic
Liturgical Theology: Schmemann in Conversation with Contemporary
Philosophy," *Worship* 87, no. 5 [September 2013]: 400)

7. As Christina Gschwandtner observes:

Ricoeur was always eager to fuel conversation and attempt translation and
mediation between extremes and to pay attention to the value and truths in
a great variety of apparently antagonistic positions and thinkers. Although
religion (or specifically Christianity) is certainly not the central focus of his

writing or teaching and he usually rigorously separates his more religious reflections from his other philosophical work, an interest in and concern with religion are visible at every stage of his philosophical journey. This extends from his early writings on myth and fallenness, over his reflections on biblical hermeneutics and a Christian concept of history, to his final writings on justice, faithfulness, and forgiveness. (*Postmodern Apologetics? Arguments for God in Contemporary Philosophy* [New York: Fordham University Press, 2013], 85)

8. In remembering his friendship with Mircea Eliade, the Romanian Orthodox master of *Religionswissenschaft,* Ricoeur displays a keen sensitivity to the merit of an approach that begins with the ritual embodiment of meaning. Despite his ambivalence concerning Eliade's actual accomplishments, Ricoeur applauds his methodological a priori: "The liturgical sense of Orthodoxy nevertheless allowed him to affirm that before doctrine comes belief, before belief the rite, before the rite the liturgy." (Paul Ricoeur, *Critique and Conviction: Conversations with François Azouvi and Marc de Launay,* trans. Kathleen Blamey [New York: Columbia University Press, 1998], 32)

9. Available on-line: http://www.taize.fr/en_article102.html (last updated May 25, 2005).

10. Van den Hengel posits the relevance of Ricoeur to theology taken as an enterprise conducted "under the sign of the dialectic of the Same and the Other." He esteems Ricoeur's recognition, on the one hand, of the importance of the *via negativa* in the vein that this has been developed by various twentieth-century theorists, preeminently Emmanuel Lévinas; on the other hand, van den Hengel appreciates Ricoeur's insistence on the preservation of an ontology or realism in discourse about God, inasmuch as the metaphorical language of Scripture opens up a vista that truly "let[s] see the Same in the Other or the Other in the Same" (John van den Hengel, "From Text to Action in Theology," in *Memory, Narrativity, Self and the Challenge to Think God,* ed. Maureen Junker-Kenny and Peter Kenny [Münster: Lit Verlag, 2004], 124, 127). Briefly put, whereas Lévinas begins with the concept of God and ends with a chimerical "*Dire sans dit,* a Name without theology," Ricoeur begins with a reflection on the polyphonic naming of him in biblical language and discovers therein an authentic and actual revelation of the divine.

11. Van den Hengel, "From Text to Action," 132–33. In other words, as van den Hengel concludes, "a practical theology will have to explore further what Ricoeur has identified as the hyper-ethical acts that flow from the Gospel. It might encourage us to return perhaps to the acts that the Church originally identified as her response to the Gospel: *kerygma, koinonia, leitourgia* and *diakonia*: the acts of proclamation, communion, giving praise and service as hyper-ethical acts."

12. David W. Fagerberg, *Theologia Prima: What Is Liturgical Theology?* (Chicago: Hillenbrand Books, 2004), ix. The felicitous terms of *theologia prima* and *theologia secunda* have gained considerable coinage in liturgico-theological literature, principally because of the work of Fagerberg. He himself credits Schmemann as his mentor, as well as Aidan Kavanaugh and Robert Taft.

13. John van den Hengel, "Jesus between Fiction and History," in *Meanings in Texts and Actions: Questioning Paul Ricoeur*, ed. David E. Klemm and William Schweiker (Charlottesville: University Press of Virginia, 1993), 147–48. The text is oriented toward the world in front of it, through the mediation of the believing community—revealing as much about the first generation of Christians, as about Christ. For van den Hengel, there is nothing insidious in this claim: It simply points to the way in which historiography proves meaningful, i.e., by incorporating our own response to the action of the past. The genesis of history, indeed, lies in our narrative preunderstanding, as the faculty enabling our collection of disparate events into a coherent whole; if historical-critical research can adumbrate the contours of the events that inspired the Gospels, it is nonetheless the Gospel text that offers the "historical Jesus," i.e., that "makes the life, death, and resurrection of Jesus intelligible and followable" In response to van den Hengel's Ricoeurian reading of the Gospel genre, we might perhaps think of the Gospels as presenting a textual equivalent of the Möbius strip: there is only one side to the protagonist of the Gospels, one surface upon which to encounter the "Jesus of history" ever already known as the "Christ of faith."

14. Van den Hengel, "Jesus Between Fiction and History," 149. He concludes: "Finally, at the level of appropriation I would agree with a more recent text of Ricoeur where he proposes liturgy as the most adequate setting for the reading of the scripture text. Liturgy includes not only the proclamation of the Word in preaching but the refiguration of the death and resurrection of Jesus in a ritual reenactment as well. The configuration of the life, death and resurrection in the Gospel text finds its fullest appropriation in its liturgical remembering."

15. As Andrew Louth observes: "'Liturgical theology' is a relatively new concept and it is, I think, pretty well universally agreed that the very notion of 'liturgical theology' is closely associated with the name of Fr. Alexander Schmemann: liturgical theology, that is, as opposed to liturgiology—the study of liturgical rites (usually actually liturgical texts) over the ages—or the theology of liturgy, or of worship. Liturgical theology is theology that springs from the liturgy." (*Modern Orthodox Thinkers: From the "Philokalia" to the Present* [Downers Grove, Ill.: IVP Academic, 2015], 194).

16. The feast of Theophany/Epiphany is celebrated on January 6 on both the Julian and Gregorian calendars, though since the Julian calendar is currently offset by 13 days from the Gregorian calendar that is also the standard civil calen-

dar, January 6 on the Julian calendar falls on January 19 of the civil/Gregorian calendar.

17. Nicholas Lash, *Theology on the Way to Emmaus* (London: SCM Press, 1986), 32–33.

18. I use the term "Eastern Orthodox tradition" advisedly. As a Ukrainian Greco-Catholic, I am not canonically Orthodox—that is, according to the reckoning of the member Churches of the Eastern Orthodox communion. My perspective, however, is that of one who prays in the Byzantine tradition, and seeks to be faithful to the theological, liturgical, spiritual, and canonical patrimony of both my particular Eastern Church, and that of the Eastern Christianity as a whole, inclusive as this latter term is of not only the Eastern Orthodox Churches, but also the Oriental Orthodox Churches, the (Assyrian) Church of the East, as well as the twenty-three sui juris Eastern Catholic Churches. For the most up-to-date overview of Eastern Christianity, see Ronald Roberson, *The Eastern Christian Churches: A Brief Survey*, 7th ed. (Rome: Edizioni "Orientalia Christiana," 2008). For a more cursory treatment, with a special focus on the common role played by liturgy in the different Eastern Christian traditions, see my "Orthodox Tradition," in *Encyclopedia of Christianity in the United States*, vol. 4: N-S, ed. George Thomas Kurian and Mark A. Lamport (London: Rowman & Littlefield, 2016), 1711–18

19. Paul Ricoeur, *The Course of Recognition*, trans. David Pellauer (Cambridge, Mass.: Harvard University Press, 2006).

20. Ricoeur is surely alluding to the thought of Pseudo-Dionysius when he speaks of the "half-philosophical, half-theological speculation on the divine names," opining that "the critique of the names that are unsuitable for God is at once the philosophical injected into the religious, but also a sort of asceticism internal to the religious that seeks to rid itself of what is unworthy of God" (Ricoeur, *Critique and Conviction*, 164). See Pseudo-Dionysius, *The Complete Works*, The Classics of Western Spirituality, ed. Paul Rorem, trans. Colm Luibheid (New York: Paulist Press, 1987).

1. "After Schmemann": Introducing Ricoeur into the Conversation

1. "We start with God, not as knowing him, but as standing before a mystery that is, and will remain, beyond our understanding. . . . Our worship is a response to an unfathomable mystery. . . . This sense of theology as rooted in experience, and yet the idea that this experience is beyond us, so that we are constantly pushed back to repent, to turn again to God: this seems to me absolutely central to the Orthodox experience of theology, of coming to know God" (Andrew Louth, *Introducing Eastern Orthodox Theology* [Downers Grove, Ill.: IVP Academic, 2013], 1, 7).

2. Boris Bobrinskoy credits Schmemann with "demonstrat[ing] in his *Intro-duction to Liturgical Theology* that one may truly speak of liturgical theology, thus introducing a new concept into scholarship" ("God in Trinity," in *The Cambridge Companion to Orthodox Christian Theology*, ed. Mary B. Cunningham and Eliza-beth Theokritoff [Cambridge: Cambridge University Press, 2008], 51). In this text, which has now become a classic in the field, Schmemann limns a tripartite pro-cess. First, the concepts and categories that are capable of articulating liturgical experiences must be identified. Second, these must be connected with those that are operative in the other domains of theology. Third, the data of liturgical expe-rience must be reconstituted as a whole, as a similar "rule of prayer" that deter-mines the Church's "rule of faith." Schmemann declares his method to have two modes, historical analysis and theological synthesis, which seem to occur simul-taneously in his actual reflection, despite his description of them as successive scholarly moments. The leitmotif of the work as a whole is the history and signifi-cance of the typikon as an arbiter of the Orthodox Church's *lex orandi*. See *Intro-duction to Liturgical Theology*, trans. Asheleigh E. Moorhouse (Bangor, Maine: Faith Press, 1970).

3. Peter Galadza, "Twentieth-Century and Contemporary Orthodox Sacra-mental Theology," in *Oxford Handbook of Sacramental Theology*, ed. Hans Boers-man and Matthew Levering (Oxford: Oxford University Press, 2016), 443.

4. These hermeneutics are in turn associated with three periods of liturgical history: the Judaeo-Christian, Constantinian, and monastic, which correspond, furthermore, to three locales or contexts. The first is the Church herself, under-stood in her original purity and integrity; the second, the *oikos* or "Christian Empire"; and the third, the "desert," which in company with the Empire "ob-scured the reality of the Church" and caused an "eclipse of ecclesiological con-sciousness" (*Introduction to Liturgical Theology*, 166). Schmemann unpacks the loaded titles of his three hermeneutical models in the course of his study, com-paring the worship of the primitive Church with its precedents in Judaism, its competition in the Greco-Roman mystery religions and its cultural counterparts in civic ceremonial, and tracing the course of its assimilation of various elements, practices and patterns of thought from these sources. He also attends to the dia-lectic between the monastic and secular (cathedral) traditions in Byzantine litur-gical history, their conflicts, reciprocal influence, and eventual merging.

5. The following description of Hegel's philosophy seems to approximate Schmemann's approach to his own Orthodox tradition: "He gives a picture of all nature and history as a progressive unfolding and realization of an inner *telos* of which our knowledge in various academic and scientific disciplines, our social and political institutions, and our own human self-realization are all a part. He even includes periods of apparent decline as part of an inevitable progress. Every re-versal makes a contribution to an even greater realization of that *telos* inherent in

reality itself" (Diogenes Allen and Eric O. Springsted, *Philosophy for Understanding Theology*. 2nd ed. [Louisville, Ky.: Westminster John Knox Press, 2007], 174).

6. *Introduction to Liturgical Theology*, 155–56. He especially esteems Middle Byzantium for having negotiated the tensions within the tradition, reserving highest praise for its elaboration of the typikon: "It is impossible to deny that in the overall design of the Ordo, in its essential and eternal logic, it was, is and always will be the Ordo of the *Church's* worship, a living and vital revelation of her doctrine about herself, of her own self-understanding and self-definition" (*Introduction to Liturgical Theology*, 166).

7. Alexander Schmemann, "Symbols and Symbolism in the Byzantine Liturgy: Liturgical Symbols and Their Theological Interpretation," in *Liturgy and Tradition: Theological Reflections of Alexander Schmemann*, ed. Thomas J. Fisch (Crestwood, N.Y.: St. Vladimir's Seminary Press, 1990), 119.

8. Schmemann, "Symbols and Symbolism," 115–16, 117 (emphasis mine).

9. Andrew Louth contends as follows: "The heart of what Schmemann thought liturgical theology to be can be put . . . in terms of *eschatology*—eschatology, not as concerned with what lies beyond death, but rather with the presence of the ultimate, the end, communion with God, in this life: what is sometimes called 'realized eschatology'" (*Modern Orthodox Thinkers: From the* Philokalia *to the Present* [Downers Grove, Ill.: IVP Academic, 2015], 205).

10. Vladimir Lossky, *In the Image and Likeness of God* (Crestwood, N.Y.: St. Vladimir's Seminary Press, 1974), 152.

11. W. Jardine Grisbrooke, *Liturgy and Tradition: Theological Reflections of Alexander Schmemann*, in *Liturgy and Tradition*, ed. Thomas J. Fisch (Crestwood, N.Y.: St. Vladimir's Seminary Press, 1990), 40.

12. Translation mine. Stig Simeon Frøyshov, "Symbole et symbolisme liturgiques chez Alexandre Schmemann," in *La joie du royaume. Actes du colloque international "L'héritage du Père Alexandre Schmemann" (Paris 11–14 décembre 2008)*, ed. André Lossky, Cyrille Sollogoub, and Daniel Struv (Paris: YMCA Press, 2012), 179n96. The ancient commentators, indeed, were often much more nuanced in their understanding than Schmemann gives them credit for, in their ability to appreciate the polysemy of the rites they sought to interpret. For example, Jeremias II, in his *Reply to the Augsburg Confession* (1576), could at one and the same time appreciate the received mysteriological interpretation of the Divine Liturgy, i.e., what Schmemann calls its "illustrative symbolism," as well as what I term its "existential thrust." See my "Orthodox Sacramental Theology: Sixteenth–Nineteenth Centuries," in *Oxford Handbook of Sacramental Theology*, ed. Hans Boersman and Matthew Levering (Oxford: Oxford University Press, 2016), 330–33.

13. It seems to me that this hermeneutical discrepancy is reflective of a methodological dichotomy within Schmemann's own thought: On the one hand, he

is duly concerned for the restoration of the pristine, clarion liturgical theory and practice of the early Church, latent if unrecognized in the Ordo; on the other, he recognizes the need to preserve a usable history, an appreciation of Tradition that can perceive therein positive theological development and not merely liturgical disintegration—lest he cut off the branch upon which he is sitting, as it were. Given that in the history of the Church, reforming impulses have not infrequently led to iconoclastic agendas of one sort or another, one can appreciate that Schmemann might sensibly intend to avoid casting excessive aspersions on Holy Tradition. Yet his critical acumen cannot resist identifying those liturgical perspectives and paradigms that have, in his estimation, wandered far from home. Peter Galadza makes the following probative observation in regard to Schmemann's commitment to liturgical reform, which I find to be pertinent, mutatis mutandis, to our present concern: "I suspect that the conflicting roles of prominent churchman on the one hand, and prophetic scholar on the other, help explain Schmemann's 'completion anxiety' in the area of liturgical renewal. Certainly his recently published Journals provide a sense of how often the coupling of these two roles proved burdensome" (Peter Galadza, "Schmemann between Fagerberg and Reality: Towards an Agenda for Byzantine Christian Pastoral Liturgy," *Bollettino Della Badia Greca Di Grottaferrata* 4 [2007], 19). Did the need to serve as official spokesman for the tradition prove similarly burdensome to Schmemann when he found himself disposed to radical critique of it?

14. The title of one of Ricoeur's early and influential collections of essays. Paul Ricoeur, *The Conflict of Interpretations: Essays in Hermeneutics*, New ed., ed. Don Ihde (Evanston, Ill.: Northwestern University Press, 2007).

15. Anton Ugolnik, "An Orthodox Hermeneutic in the West," *St. Vladimir's Theological Quarterly* 27, no. 2 (1983): 96.

16. Schmemann, "Symbols and Symbolism," 121.

17. Ironically, the two sources upon which Schmemann bases his challenge to the received wisdom of his own Orthodox tradition are of Western provenance: Robert F. Taft, *The Great Entrance: A History of the Transfer of Gifts and Other Pre-Anaphoral Rites of the Liturgy of St. John Chrysostom* (Rome: Orientalia Christiana Periodica, 1975) and René Bornert, *Les Commentaires Byzantins de la Divine Liturgie Du VIIe Au XVe Siècle* (Paris: Archives de l'Orient Chrétien, 1966).

18. Hugh Wybrew observes that in the time of Chrysostom, for example, the Divine Liturgy began with an "uninterpreted" entrance of clergy and faithful: The first words spoken were simply "Peace be with you," after which the readings began. *The Orthodox Liturgy: The Development of the Eucharistic Liturgy in the Byzantine Rite* (Crestwood, N.Y.: St. Vladimir's Seminary Press, 1989), 50.

19. Schmemann, "Symbols and Symbolism," 127.

20. Peter Galadza perceptively comments on this omission:

Whether anyone likes it or not (and Schmemann does not), as it stands today, the Byzantine Eucharist begins with a semiotic of descent and revelation: the sanctuary is frequently partially revealed, a deacon emerges to cense the nave and then lead it in prayer, and the gospel is eventually brought . . . into the midst of the assembly for its veneration by the faithful. . . . No one committed to theologizing from the actual rite, as opposed to "abstract, purely intellectual schemata" should be allowed to ignore this. . . . The fact that for centuries in the past the Byzantine Eucharist began with a real entrance of the clergy and faithful into the church does not mean that one should be allowed to theologize on the basis of this "archeology." Schmemann should have either insisted on the restoration of this practice or . . . interpret what is actually happening. There are few things in liturgical theology more frustrating than being exhorted to experience the significance of something that is actually not happening—especially when it need not be happening for the worship to be sound. But almost all twenty-two pages of the chapter "Sacrament of the Entrance" are devoted to precisely this kind of reflection. ("Schmemann between Fagerberg and Reality," 16–17).

21. Schmemann, "Symbols and Symbolism," 119.

22. Alexander Schmemann, "Liturgical Theology, Theology of Liturgy, and Liturgical Reform," in *Liturgy and Tradition: Theological Reflections of Alexander Schmemann*, ed. Thomas J. Fisch (Crestwood, N.Y.: St. Vladimir's Seminary Press, 1990), 42.

23. Regarding the "exegetical optimism" of the Reformers, Alister McGrath writes as follows: "Luther appears to suggest that the ordinary pious Christian believer is perfectly capable of reading Scripture and making perfect sense of what he finds within its pages. A similar position is defended by Zwingli. . . . 'The Word of God, as soon as it shines upon an individual's understanding, illuminates it in such a way that he understands it'" (*Reformation Thought: An Introduction*, 2nd ed. [Oxford: Blackwell Publishers, 1993], 152). Regarding the *Quadriga*, see *Reformation Thought: An Introduction*, 147–48.

24. Peter Galadza, "Schmemann between Fagerberg and Reality," 19.

25. For instance, Schmemann declares that there is a "eucharistic crisis in the Church . . . consist[ing] in a lack of connection and cohesion between what is accomplished in the Eucharist and how it is perceived, understood and lived. To a certain degree this crisis has always existed in the Church. . . . With time, however, this crisis has become chronic" (*The Eucharist: Sacrament of the Kingdom* [Crestwood, N.Y.: St. Vladimir's Seminary Press, 1987], 9).

26. Paul Ricoeur, *The Symbolism of Evil*, trans. Emerson Buchanan (Boston: Beacon Press, 1967), 348–49.

27. Ricoeur develops this idea in several places. See especially *The Rule of Metaphor: Multi-Disciplinary Studies of the Creation of Meaning in Language*, trans. Robert Czerny, Kathleen McLaughlin, and John Costello (Toronto: University of Toronto Press, 1977), and *Interpretation Theory: Discourse and the Surplus of Meaning* (Fort Worth, Tex: Texas Christian University Press, 1976).

28. "Ontological vehemence," for Ricoeur, refers to his "conviction that—even in the uses of language that appear to be the least referential, as is the case with metaphor and narrative fiction—language expresses being, even if this ontological aim is as though postponed, deferred by the prior denial of the literal referentiality of ordinary language" (*Oneself as Another*, trans. Kathleen Blamey [Chicago: University of Chicago Press, 1992], 301).

29. The "fusion of horizons" (*Horizontverschmelzung*) is discussed in several places in Gadamer's magnum opus, *Truth and Method* (New York: Seabury Press, 1975).

30. Ricoeur, *Interpretation Theory*, 64.

31. Robert F. Taft, *The Byzantine Rite: A Short History*, American Essays in Liturgy Series (Collegeville, Minn.: Liturgical Press, 1992), 18. The term *Erscheinungsbild* is that of Hans Joachim Schultz, coined in the German original of his influential study *Byzantine Liturgy: Symbolic Structure and Faith Expression*, trans. Matthew J. O'Connell (New York: Pueblo Publishing Company, 1986).

32. David Tracy, *Plurality and Ambiguity: Hermeneutics, Religion, Hope* (Chicago: University of Chicago Press, 1994), 28.

33. Paul Ricoeur, *The Course of Recognition*, trans. David Pellauer (Cambridge, Mass.: Harvard University Press, 2006), 250.

34. Ricoeur, *The Course of Recognition*, 254. As van den Hengel clarifies, in a piece on Ricoeur's *Oneself as Another* also apposite to the present consideration: "[Ricoeur] insists that the speaker of a language and the agent of action both make a commitment to the real that takes them beyond themselves. In a constative proposition a speaker affirms, 'This is so.' Similarly, in a promissive proposition an agent commits, 'This I will do.' This is the 'ontological vehemence' of the speaker or agent. The speaker and the agent make an affirmation not only about reality and about the world of action but also about a mode of existence of the self. This mode of existence of the self Ricoeur names 'attestation'" ("Can There Be a Science of Human Action?" in *Ricoeur as Another: The Ethics of Subjectivity*, ed. Richard A. Cohen and James L. Marsh [Albany: State University of New York, 2002], 87).

35. A cursory presentation of the evolution of Byzantine mystagogy can be found in Taft, *The Byzantine Rite*, 37–38, 45–48. A helpful comparison of the different schemas proposed by commentators working out of the Antiochene tradition can be found in Wybrew, *The Orthodox Liturgy*, 182–83.

36. Per *Mystagogia* 13–15 *PG* 91.692A–693C, as cited in Alan J. Hauser and Duane F. Watson, *A History of Biblical Interpretation, Vol. 2: The Medieval through the Reformation Periods* (Grand Rapids, Mich.: Eerdmans, 2009), 182.

37. Regarding the nature of promising, Ricoeur writes as follows: "Imputability, assumed by the agent, makes him or her responsible. . . . Promising is possible on this basis. Human subjects commit themselves by their word and say that they will do tomorrow what they say today. The promise limits the unpredictability of the future, at the risk of betrayal. The subject must keep his or her promise—or break it. He or she thereby engages the promise of the promise, that of keeping one's word, or being faithful" (*Philosophical Anthropology: Writings and Lectures, Volume 3*, ed. Johann Michel and Jérôme Porée, trans. David Pellauer [Cambridge: Polity Press, 2016], 292).

38. Alexander Schmemann, *For the Life of the World* (Crestwood, N.Y.: St. Vladimir's Seminary Press, 2002), 15.

39. Paul Ricoeur, *Figuring the Sacred: Religion, Narrative and Imagination*, ed. Mark I. Wallace, trans. David Pellauer (Minneapolis, Minn.: Augsburg Fortress Press, 1995), 262.

40. Ricoeur, *Figuring the Sacred*, 262.

41. Joris Geldhof contends that,

> as it stands, liturgical theologians do not attach great weight to a philosophical underpinning of their theoretical endeavors. When reading them, one sometimes has the impression that liturgy and tradition are all-encompassing, but one only has to know a little bit of hermeneutics to understand that such appeals necessarily require nuance, interpretation, and critique. . . . Liturgical theology can and needs to be substantially supported by philosophical theorizing. This does not imply that liturgical theology should betray itself or that it needs philosophy because the liturgy is somehow insufficient. The philosophical import I suggest is not meant to fill a gap but to assist in a more convincing and encompassing way the work of clarification and understanding inherent in any theology. ("Liturgy as Theological Norm: Getting Acquainted with 'Liturgical Theology,'" *Neue Zeitschrift für systematische Theologie und Religionsphilosophie* 52, no. 2 [2010]: 174–75)

42. See Max Charlesworth, *Philosophy and Religion: From Plato to Postmodernism* (Oxford: Oneworld Publications, 2002), 6–9.

43. Charlesworth, *Philosophy and Religion*, 68.

44. Aidan Nichols, *The Shape of Catholic Theology* (Collegeville, Minn.: Liturgical Press, 1991), 51. Nichols is undoubtedly one of the foremost Western interpreters of Eastern Christian church history and theology. See, for instance, *Rome and the Eastern Churches: A Study in Schism* (San Francisco: Ignatius Press, 1992); *Light from the East: Authors and Themes in Orthodox Theology* (London: Sheed & Ward Limited, 1999); and *Theology in the Russian Diaspora: Church, Fathers, Eucharist in Nikolai Afanas'ev (1893–1966)* (Cambridge: Cambridge University Press, 2008).

45. Aidan Nichols, *The Shape of Catholic Theology*, 49.

46. For example: John van den Hengel, *The Home of Meaning* (Lanham, Md.: University Press of America, 1982); Mario Valdés, ed., *A Ricoeur Reader: Reflection and Imagination* (Toronto: University of Toronto Press, 1991); Richard Kearney, *On Paul Ricoeur: The Owl of Minerva* (Burlington, Vt.: Ashgate, 2004); and David M. Kaplan, ed., *Reading Ricoeur* (Albany: State University of New York Press, 2008).

47. Aidan Nichols, *The Shape of Catholic Theology*, 54. The Dominican himself does not go this far, understandably cleaving to the Angelic Doctor as the unsurpassed master of the *philosophia perennis*. Joyce Ann Zimmerman, however, hitherto the principal liturgist to have engaged Ricoeur, asserts that an advantage of his hermeneutical theory is the provision it makes for the inclusion of different methods within the "explanatory moment" of the interpretive process. Zimmerman finds in Ricoeur a comprehensive heuristic for the contemporary study of liturgy, one informed by a spectrum of disciplines, contending that he has enabled her to provide "the most complete philosophical framework for a viable liturgical hermeneutics that can capitalize on both critical and post-critical methods" (*Liturgy and Hermeneutics* [Collegeville, Minn.: Liturgical Press, 1999], 98–99). She explains: "Drawing heavily on his textual hermeneutics, I have also profited hermeneutically from his works on symbolism, metaphor, narrative, imagination, action theory, and return to the subject, to name a few. In each case, nevertheless, I have always been careful to place the particular aspect of his theory with which I might be working within his larger philosophical framework" (*Liturgy and Hermeneutics*, 99).

48. Dan R. Stiver, *Theology after Ricoeur: New Directions in Hermeneutical Theology* (Louisville, Ky.: Westminster John Knox Press, 2001), 248.

49. Stiver, *Theology after Ricoeur*, 238.

50. Hans Urs von Balthasar, *Cosmic Liturgy*, trans. Brian E. Daley (San Francisco: Ignatius Press, 2003).

51. von Balthasar, *Cosmic Liturgy*, 57.

52. von Balthasar, *Cosmic Liturgy*, 56.

53. von Balthasar, *Cosmic Liturgy*, 61–62.

54. Leonard Lawlor, *Imagination and Chance: The Difference between the Thought of Ricoeur and Derrida* (Albany: State University of New York Press, 1992), 3, 5.

55. von Balthasar, *Cosmic Liturgy*, 55.

56. Incidentally, one can add that on an autobiographical level a further parallel between the two thinkers comes to light; both suffered suspicion, hostility, and exile on account of their views, albeit to different degrees, manifesting thereby an unwillingness to embrace compromise for the sake of political expediency: in the case of Maximus, the reconciliation of the Churches with the Empire, in

Ricoeur, the securing of his reputation and professional status in the French academy.

57. See, for example, Christos Yannaras, *On the Absence and Unknowability of God: Heidegger and the Areopagite* (London: Continuum, 2005); *Postmodern Metaphysics* (Brookline, Mass.: Holy Cross Press, 2004) and *Freedom of Morality* (Crestwood, N.Y.: St. Vladimir's Seminary Press, 1984). For Zizioulas, the classic work is *Being as Communion* (Crestwood, N.Y.: St. Vladimir's Seminary Press, 1985).

58. Rowan Williams, "Eastern Orthodox Theology," in *The Modern Theologians: An Introduction to Christian Theology since 1918*, ed. David Ford and Rachel Muers (Malden, Mass.: Blackwell Publishing, 2005), 587. For an Orthodox engagement with Gadamer, see Andrew Louth, *Discerning the Mystery: An Essay on the Nature of Theology* (Oxford: Clarendon Press, 1983).

59. More significant than Kireevsky is the figure of Vladimir Soloviev, since the story of twentieth-century Orthodox theology, according to the author, is that of the ambivalent reactions to Soloviev's legacy: on the one hand, of those who felt comfortable with his philosophical idealism, such as Sergei Bulgakov; on the other, of those committed rather to a patristic retrieval of the particularity of historic Orthodoxy, such as Georges Florovsky (Williams, "Eastern Orthodox Theology," 573).

60. Williams, "Eastern Orthodox Theology," 587.

61. David Bentley Hart, *The Beauty of the Infinite: The Aesthetics of Christian Truth* (Grand Rapids, Mich.: Eerdmans, 2003).

62. John A. McGuckin, review of *The Beauty of the Infinite: The Aesthetics of Christian Truth*, by David Bentley Hart, *Scottish Journal of Theology* 60, no. 1 (2007): 93.

63. David Bentley Hart, "Response from David Bentley Hart to McGuckin and Murphy," *Scottish Journal of Theology* 60, no. 1 (2007): 96–97.

64. Hart appears to be quite appreciative of Ricoeur's contributions, not least the latter's thorough investigation of metaphor: see *Beauty of the Infinite*, 303–4, as well as 8–9, 379.

65. Ugolnik, "An Orthodox Hermeneutic," 93–94.

66. Regarding the role of Bible study, Ugolnik writes: "Private reading of the Bible is analogous to private devotion; it is profoundly important, yet supplementary to the proper arena, the communal and liturgical environment which we understand as the central context for our encounter with the Word" ("An Orthodox Hermeneutic," 109). Part of what makes this contention problematic, however, is that the Byzantine liturgical tradition does not provide for a communal encounter with a great many texts of the Bible, as they are not prescribed in the lectionary. Only a small portion of the Old Testament, for example, is read throughout the course of the liturgical cycle. Robert Taft has argued that one of

the distinctive features of the Byzantine Rite is precisely its historical tendency to supplement liturgical hymnography for the reading of Scripture—even where the original purpose of the latter was to serve as a gloss upon the former. Not only at the Eucharist—which no longer has any reading whatsoever from the Old Testament, save for the select use of psalmody (itself greatly pared back in respect of former practice)—but in the other offices as well, the liturgical reading of Scripture has suffered attrition, and this not only in practice, but also in the prescriptions of the typikon, the manual that prescribes the order for Orthodox worship. See Robert F. Taft, *Beyond East and West: Problems in Liturgical Understanding* (Rome: Pontifical Oriental Institute, 1997), 175–76.

67. Ugolnik, "An Orthodox Hermeneutic," 107.

68. Jaroslav Pelikan, *Credo: Historical and Theological Guide to Creeds and Confessions of Faith in the Christian Tradition* (New Haven: Yale University Press, 2003), 407–8.

69. For a summary see John Anthony McGuckin, *Standing in God's Holy Fire: The Byzantine Tradition* (Maryknoll, N.Y.: Orbis Books, 2001), 131–33.

70. Pelikan, *Credo*, 405.

71. Pelikan, *Credo*, 406.

72. Pelikan, *Credo*, 412. Apposite to this connection is the challenge of a hermeneutics of the *sung* word. Given that classical liturgy in both East and West was sung in its entirety, and remains so in the Eastern Churches today, how is it possible to interpret the words of a rite apart from their embodiment in song? Naomi Cummings has broached this inquiry in a remarkable book (*The Sonic Self: Musical Subjectivity and Signification* [Bloomington: Indiana University Press, 2000]), but it is not at all evident how the semiotics of music she undertakes there, on the basis of the thought of Charles Sanders Peirce, can in turn be extended to a liturgical hermeneutics, given the myriad musical traditions represented even within the Byzantine tradition, and the distinct fusion of text and melody that constitutes *sacred* song. Hermeneutics necessarily returns to the interpretation of texts, even where it is recognized that the phenomenon under consideration is only ever grasped in a fragmentary way by the liturgical text. See also Maeve Louise Heaney, *Music as Theology: What Music Says about the Word* (Eugene, Ore.: Pickwick Publications, 2012). A similar challenge faces the interpretation of dramatic works, of course, inasmuch as both liturgy and such works presume an enactment of their respective "scripts." It is beyond the scope of the present study both to explore the musical dimensions of the liturgical rite under consideration and to entertain an inquiry into the potential of Ricoeur's thought in regard to the relationship between hermeneutics and music. Nonetheless, it would seem to be a fruitful avenue for further research, especially as Peirce is referenced occasionally in Ricoeur's oeuvre.

73. "Augustine's dramatic setting creates a powerful hermeneutical paradigm. This confessional model underlies the encounter with the text. Certain axioms of interpretation emerge through the model: the encounter is with a written text (*lege*); its motivation is personal, private need (Augustine's tears); it occurs in isolation (Augustine's withdrawal into solitude); and the encounter's subject is a 'theological persona,' a first person singular respondent who constitutes the 'interpreting self'" (Ugolnik, "An Orthodox Hermeneutic," 97). It must be said that this reading of Augustine's conversion is myopic—the arc of the narrative that spans the *Confessions* includes many moments in which relationships prove Augustine's saving grace: the patient mentoring of Ambrose in Book VI; Book VIII's account of St. Antony's conversion inciting a chain reaction leading to Victorinus's embracing of the Faith; and, of course, Augustine's experience in Book IX of mystic rapture on the beach in Ostia—not, as one might expect, alone, but in the company of his mother, with whose love he had struggled from the beginning, and in whom he finds a figure of the embrace of the Church. See Kim Paffenroth and Robert P. Kennedy, eds., *A Reader's Companion to Augustine's* Confessions (Louiseville, Ky.: Westminster John Knox Press, 2003).

74. Ricoeur, *Interpretation Theory*, 32.

75. Ugolnik, "An Orthodox Hermeneutic," 110.

76. Ugolnik writes:

> The West sees Orthodoxy strictly in terms of Western methodology, with its continual retrospective quest for the authentic text, the historical context, the Moment of Encounter. Paul Ricoeur described this process as a "dialectic of distanciation." An encounter with tradition in this context becomes centered on the historical transmission of a heritage. . . . But it is time for the West to take Orthodoxy on its own intellectual terms. In acknowledging Orthodox preservation of its past in doctrines and rites, Western scholarship pays Orthodoxy the compliment of perceiving some dimension of its Tradition, at least, as being authentic. But in confining the usefulness of that Tradition to history, Western methodology utterly fails to see the real value Orthodoxy places in Tradition. As history, tradition is subject to the critical faculty. As a charismatic principle, however, Tradition demands no "distanciation." Orthodoxy exercises its hermeneutic when together, as a community of believers; the Church celebrates a common assent. In liturgy Orthodoxy recovers the "first certainty" in a state akin to what Ricoeur calls "the second naïveté." Confident of its history, not only of the Moment of Encounter but also of all past Moments which brought us to this, the Orthodox mind perceives its Tradition chrismatically, forever in contemporaneity. ("Tradition as Freedom from the Past: Eastern Orthodoxy and the Western Mind," *Journal of Ecumenical Studies* 21, no. 2 [Spring 1984]: 283)

77. André LaCoque and Paul Ricoeur, *Thinking Biblically: Exegetical and Hermeneutical Studies*, David Pelllauer (Chicago: University of Chicago Press, 1998), xiii.

78. LaCoque and Ricoeur, *Thinking Biblically*, 279.

79. Ugolnik, "An Orthodox Hermeneutic," 114.

80. Paul Ricoeur, *Critique and Conviction: Conversations with François Azouvi and Marc de Launay*, trans. Kathleen Blamey (New York: Columbia University Press, 1998), 145.

81. One must remember that the Byzantine Rite, while fairly uniform today, was only finally standardized as a result of the publication of printed editions of Byzantine liturgical books in Venice in the sixteenth century (for a succinct history, see Taft, *The Byzantine Rite*). This standardization marked the nadir of local Orthodox traditions; the whole Byzantine East that had erstwhile proudly had a variety of usages came to be almost entirely dominated by a single ritual recension—arguably a veritable triumph of the written word. To be sure, this uniformity has come to be cherished by Orthodoxy as an expression of its unity, although it has not gone unchallenged, as the notorious schism of the Old Believers bears witness. On a practical level, deacons must interpret the rubrics of the typikon, cantors, and the various books from which the hymnography to be sung is taken. Schmemann indicates something of the diversity of interpretation that can occur even with a uniform *textus receptus* in his dual indictment of "liturgical 'rigorists,' i.e., those who stress long services, compliance with rubrics and the typikon, and liturgical 'liberals,' always ready and anxious to shorten, adapt, and adjust" (*For the Life of the World*, 133). If one keeps in kind Ricoeur's explanation of the polyphonicity of Scripture (discussed below, in Chapter 3), that each distinct genre in the Bible is nonetheless affected by the intertextuality of being juxtaposed to others, one can see how the omission or shortening of a given liturgical text certainly has an effect upon the interpretation given to those to which it is otherwise juxtaposed.

82. Ugolnik, "An Orthodox Hermeneutic," 99.

83. Ricoeur, *The Symbolism of Evil*, 349.

2. Western Perspectives

1. Only three major monographs have brought a liturgical agenda to bear upon Ricoeur's thought. None of these volumes, published in 1988, 1993, and 1996, respectively, had the opportunity to take into consideration the final works of the philosopher. Each has, however, made a significant contribution to the task at hand, and warrants examination. It is principally from these three works that the state of the question emerges; in light of them, we will better be able to appreciate where an original contribution may yet be made—and where an Eastern

Christian perspective may bring new things to light. A review of the other pertinent sources will follow forthwith. See Joyce Ann Zimmerman, *Liturgy as a Language of Faith: A Liturgical Methodology in the Mode of Paul Ricoeur's Textual Hermeneutics* (Lanham, Md.: University Press of America, 1988), and subsequently, Joyce Ann Zimmerman, *Liturgy as Living Faith: A Liturgical Spirituality* (Scranton, Pa.: University of Scranton Press, 1993). See also Bridget Nichols, *Liturgical Hermeneutics: Interpreting Liturgical Rites in Performance* (Frankfurt: Peter Lang, 1996).

2. As Zimmerman duly expounds elsewhere:

> Today, as never before we have methodological tools at hand that permit us to delve deeper and ask other questions. Until recently scholarship and pastoral approaches have consistently "asserted" and "described" the relationship of Jesus Christ's redeeming actions and our participation in it. . . . As soon as we ask the "why" question, we have stretched the limits of the traditional historical-critical methods and push ourselves to take advantage of the methodological tools of the post-critical methods. Far from merely an academic endeavor, moving into this new methodological direction offers us fresh insight into how we might existentially grasp our own participation in the paschal mystery. ("Paschal Mystery—Whose Mystery? A Post-Critical Methodological Reinterpretation," in *Primary Sources of Liturgical Theology: A Reader*, ed. Dwight W. Vogel [Collegeville, Minn.: Liturgical Press, 2000], 303)

3. Zimmerman argues that a distinction must be maintained between Ricoeur's philosophical hermeneutics as a framework out of which a given study might be carried out, and the use of a particular heuristic tool applicable to a specific text (review of *Christian Hermeneutics: Paul Ricoeur and the Refiguring of Theology*, by James Fodor, *International Philosophical Quarterly* 38 [1998]: 87). She views this distinction between theory and method as critical to ensuring the preservation of Ricoeur's dialectical, indirect approach to ontology, which remains open-ended, oscillating between poles of interpretation rather than collating them. Within the basic dialectic of participation-distanciation-appropriation, there remain almost limitless possibilities. Hence her critique of Fodor's assessment of Ricoeur's project:

> What Fodor portrays as problematic—"Ricoeur also attempts to incorporate the emphases and contributions of literary and philosophical analyses which are, in character, fundamentally anti-referential"—is exactly the point of Ricoeur's dialectical method: the ontological moment is located in the moments of participation and appropriation; the moment of distanciation is epistemological and admits of any number of possible methods, even

"anti-referential" ones. This is an important distinction for actually applying Ricoeur's hermeneutics to real texts (which Ricoeur rarely does, as Fodor rightly points out): exegesis of texts requires an analytic moment, and Ricoeur allows for any number of methods to be used. Different texts (e.g., biblical text or liturgical text) may best be interpreted by very different analytical tools (including semiotics, structuralism, etc.) without sacrificing reference because of the dialectic between sense and reference (or, if you will, between configuration and refiguration, or between epistemology and ontology). (Review of *Christian Hermeneutics*, by James Fodor, 87–88).

4. Hence Zimmerman's thesis: "Ricoeur's hermeneutics is known as a textual or methodical hermeneutics whereby he is able to address the question of text and the relation of written texts to human cultural existence. Ricoeur's textual hermeneutics suggests a framework in which a written text, in our case a liturgical text, can be studied analytically without relinquishing 'understanding' which Ricoeur sees as a mode of human existence. Thus his hermeneutic allows the placing of a textual analytic within a framework of a hermeneutics of understanding" (Zimmerman, *Liturgy as a Language*, xiii). Chapter 3 elaborates Ricoeur's overarching method, adumbrated above according to the axial terms participation, distanciation and appropriation. For Ricoeur, one brings to a text a "guess" as to its meaning, based upon one's experience of life, one's sharing in the common lot of man from which any text originates. This guess has to be validated critically, however, in the moment of distanciation, by unpacking the composition, genre and style of a text and thereby coming to appreciate what it is in and of itself; the knowledge gained through this validation must then be reintegrated by a reader, in terms of a corresponding transformation of the antecedent self-understanding, with all the risks that this process entails. Thus Zimmerman asks, "Is not the purpose of a liturgical text in a worshipping community to present possibilities for self-understanding to the community? Further, is it not the challenge to let go of the ego that is brought to the celebration (one side of the text) in order that, through the text's celebration, a new self might emerge (the other side of the text)?" (Zimmerman, *Liturgy as a Language*, 90).

5. Zimmerman, *Liturgy as a Language*, xi.

6. Zimmerman explains that while Ricoeur invites the use of synchronic methods of analysis, such as mentioned above, in the explanatory moment, he has not been wont to engage in them himself. Her response is to integrate one such method, the communication theory of Roman Jakobson, into her methodology, not least because it is a method approved by Ricoeur, if not exercised by him. The scope of her study, in turn, is limited and defined by this choice: its foci are two aspects of liturgical language, action and communication, and not any others (e.g., intention, poetics, etc.). Such exploration of other aspects she reserves

to others, asserting that if indeed her methodology is sound, it will prove able to facilitate the application of other analytics to the explanatory moment of interpretation of other texts.

7. Zimmerman, *Liturgy as a Language*, 47.

8. J. L Austin, *How to Do Things with Words: The William James Lectures Delivered at Harvard University in 1955* (Oxford: Clarendon Press, 1963).

9. Zimmerman, *Liturgy as a Language*, 69.

10. Mark Searle, "*Fons Vitae*: A Case Study in the Use of Liturgy as a Theological Source," in *Fountain of Life*, ed. Gerard Austin (Washington, DC: Pastoral Press, 1991), 217–42. Searle treats post–Vatican II form of the rite that is, it must be noted, considerably different from that found in the *Benedictionale* of the Extraordinary Form. This latter form, in the richness of its metaphorical language and ritual gestures, bears a greater affinity to the blessing of water in the Byzantine tradition.

11. Zimmerman, *Liturgy as a Language*, 186–87.

12. Michael B. Aune, review of *Liturgy as a Language of Faith: A Liturgical Methodology in the Mode of Paul Ricoeur's Textual Hermeneutics*, by Joyce Ann Zimmerman, *Journal of the American Academy of Religion* 58, no. 4 (Winter 1990): 734–35.

13. Paul Ricoeur, *Oneself as Another*, trans. Kathleen Blamey (Chicago: University of Chicago Press, 1992).

14. Joyce Ann Zimmerman, "Liturgical Assembly: Who Is the Subject of Liturgy?" *Liturgical Ministry* 3 (Spring 1994): 41–51.

15. The author proceeds to conduct a reading of the Lucan narrative of the Last Supper, seeking to uncover therein the form of the Paschal Mystery. Her structural analysis brings to light two dynamics: the "not yet" and the "already": The Paschal Mystery is to be understood as a phenomenon situated between two kingdoms, a dialectic in the truest sense, an enriching movement back and forth between the fact of redemption and its process. Hence it is not simply a *past* event, since it figures in the constitution of our reality here and now, or rather, we figure in the constitution of ourselves by means of it:

> To understand the Paschal Mystery in terms of a soteriological-eschatological tension brings us face-to-face with the fact that the Paschal Mystery cannot be relegated to a past historical event. Hardly, for the Paschal Mystery has very much to do with our own relationship to God and to others in the concrete, everyday here and now. There is nothing "automatic" about Jesus' redemptive activity; that activity always demands an interaction with our own activity. . . . [O]ur ongoing appropriation of redemption is played out in the choices we make in our everyday lives. That is what we celebrate when we do Eucharist "in memory of me." The

structure of Jesus' death and Resurrection is not only interpretive of his
actions at the Lord's Supper, it is also a perfect analogue to our Christian
living. (Zimmerman, *Liturgy as Living Faith*, 69)

16. "In this volume we draw on the gains of specific linguistically based methods to support our thesis that the deep, dynamic structure of liturgy is identical to the deep, dynamic structure of Christian living. . . . What we celebrate in liturgy is none other than what we live as Christians committed to entering into the ongoing redemptive work of the Risen Christ" (Zimmerman, *Liturgy as Living Faith*, viii).

17. Chapter 1 offers a reading of Deuteronomy, drawing upon historical-critical findings to posit the intrinsic connection between the liturgical commemoration of the *magnalia Dei* wrought for Israel, and their being enjoined to execute justice on behalf of the "sojourner, the fatherless and the widow." Chapter 2 is an analogous reading of the subapostolic period wherein works of mercy (*diakonia*) were similarly integrated into worship. In particular, such activity—a response to the injunction of the Gospel to do good works so that others may glorify the Father in heaven—is directed toward Christ hidden in the poor, and realized in terms of fasting and almsgiving; the latter flows from the former as an expression of stewardship since the money saved from fasting was to be lavished upon the poor. Zimmerman treats the Eucharist, which engenders *diakonia*, under the figures of "unity," explicated according to the monoepiscopal theology of Ignatius of Antioch; "presence," i.e., the liturgical community's solidarity one with another as one Body in and through the celebration of the Eucharist, as recounted by Justin Martyr; "sacrifice," in terms of the early sources' attestation to a sacramental fulfillment in the Church of Old Testament sacrificial practice as well as to a conflation of the Eucharist and martyrdom (e.g., that of St. Polycarp); and finally, of "eschatology," the promise of the resurrection and eternal life heralded by the Eucharist: "Eucharist is a vertical movement of offering, praising and blessing God. It is a horizontal movement of unity, sharing and caring for others. Jesus is one with his community and at the same time he leads the community to the Father. We cannot reach the Father except through Jesus who is visible in his Body and shared in thanksgiving. There is a dynamic relationship between these movements . . ." (Zimmerman, *Liturgy as Living Faith*, 32).

18. "Distanciation is a distinct moment of interpretation directed toward the internal structure of the work in itself without any regard to the subject who produced the text or the one who interprets it. A text has its own 'world' of possibilities that opens up alternative ways for human living" (Zimmerman, *Liturgy as Living Faith*, 40). Zimmerman does not appear to consider the potential discrepancies between Ricoeur's hermeneutical and narrative arcs, nor the way such discrepancies may affect the applicability of Ricoeur's moments to the study of

liturgy. See the nuanced discussion in Dan R. Stiver, *Ricoeur and Theology* (London: Bloomsbury, 2012), 33–55.

19. Zimmerman, *Liturgy as Living Faith*, 42.

20. A case in point is Chapter 4, which strangely makes no mention of Ricoeur, even though it follows upon a highly technical presentation of participation-distanciation-appropriation and the theory of meaningful action in the preceeding chapter. Given that the burden of the chapter is to establish the nature of the Paschal Mystery, specifically interrogating the connection between past events and their meaning for us today, one might have expected the author to have adduced Ricoeur's reflections on the reality of the historical past or narrative identity. Zimmerman also fails to clarify the connection between the Lucan account of the Lord's Supper and present liturgical practice—i.e., why it should be seen as paradigmatic for our understanding of the Paschal Mystery, and not the narratives of the other Gospels, not to say the theology of the Epistles. Here, an incorporation of Ricoeur's insights into the polyphonicity of biblical genres, and an attempt to discern the modalities of the notion of Paschal Mystery (which term does not even arise in the Lucan narrative, or indeed elsewhere in the Scriptures) elsewhere in the Bible, would have proven beneficial. A similar discrepancy is evident in Chapter 5, where Zimmerman seeks to adumbrate the shape of participation in the Christian tradition by probing several "visages": Paschal Mystery, Baptism, Body of Christ, Ministry of the Assembly (Priesthood of the Faithful, Gifts of the Spirit), Community (Liturgical Community—Sociological Community) and Prayer (Liturgical and Devotional). Although claiming to have used the "methodological considerations presented in chapter 3 to interpret what we have called visages of Christian self-understanding," this chapter contains effectively no references to Ricoeur beyond the first paragraph and before the last, and no explanation of how the hermeneutical arc or theory of meaningful action applies specifically to the theological data discussed: One simply does not encounter the promised "innovative use of [Ricoeur's] insights" (Zimmerman, *Liturgy as Living Faith*, 87, 75). A Ricoeurian analysis would arguably proceed by regarding the "visages" as axial metaphors of the Christian tradition, and adducing Ricoeur's theory of metaphor to unpack their import.

21. Zimmerman, *Liturgy as Living Faith*, 53.

22. Zimmerman, *Liturgy as Living Faith*, 95.

23. Zimmerman's contention seems even less plausible since the Psalms as presented in the revised Liturgy of the Hours—the context under discussion—include not only Christological subtitles but the novel element of "Psalm prayers" (to be recited after the requisite trinitarian doxology), whose rationale is precisely a typological interpretation of the preceding text. In other words, the "new context" of Christian liturgy appears to make it all but impossible *not* to pray the Psalms Christologically. It is also worth noting that in the revised Roman offices

of Lauds and Vespers there are no "fixed psalms," and therefore any attempt to plumb their "deep structure" must attend rather to the ordinary elements (such as the trinitarian doxology) into which the variable elements (such as the Psalms themselves) are integrated.

24. The import of Zimmerman's discussion of Deuteronomy and the Lucan Last Supper was expressly to show that events of revelation are meaningful in the measure they come to fulfillment, in the midst of those who celebrate. This view, however, seems at odds with her suggestion that even when a psalm is attributed to David, it should be seen rather as the corporate voice of Israel, an expression of the latter's self-understanding, given the fact that it was incorporated into a volume destined for communal worship: "There is a dynamic in the psalms, then, that draws us into a larger framework" (Zimmerman, *Liturgy as Living Faith*, 95). Here one is at a loss to account for why she can approve of the Old Testament cult's reinterpretation of a psalm, but take issue with an analogous interpretation on the part of the early Church—especially when, as indicated in above, she countenances favorably the reinterpretation of Old Testament sacrifice effected in subapostolic eucharistic theology.

25. Zimmerman, *Liturgy as Living Faith*, 98.

26. Paul Ricoeur, *Essays on Biblical Interpretation*, ed. Lewis S. Mudge (Philadelphia: Fortress Press, 1980), 88–89.

27. It is also bears mentioning that although Zimmerman's presentation of Ricoeur's notion of "meaningful action" in Part One presents interesting possibilities, it is ultimately under-exploited in the course of Part Two's pastoral interpretations. Her resumé of Ricoeur's notion of meaningful action, with its fourfold taxonomy, does not carry over to her actual analysis of the rites under consideration. The treatment of given rites remains an exegesis of the respective liturgical texts, and even, of the nonrubrical elements therein. We do not find here, as in her earlier work, a demonstrable concern to attend to the nontextual dimensions of liturgical celebration, to its embodied character. She clarifies, on the one hand, that meaningful action—in this case ritual—can be construed as text, inasmuch as it is susceptible of interpretation in a manner analogous to that of text. On the other hand, this operative assumption does not lead to a consideration, for example, the musical, kinetic, tactile, olfactory, gustatory, iconographic or architectural aspects of celebration. It is not the case, of course, that these can be very easily categorized, but that they, rather than the verbal elements, are the dimensions of the liturgical "text" arguably most subject to modulation within a given tradition. It is somewhat confusing then, that Zimmerman oscillates between two meanings of text in this regard: the stricter sense of the liturgical script, and the wider, of its embodied celebration. She appears to have the latter sense in mind in asserting, "Liturgy differs from most kinds of other texts because liturgy is constantly being produced. Liturgy is never a fixed text as are, for example, classic

works of literature or art. The text of liturgy is necessarily fluid because its 'authors' are subjects who live through a tradition. We celebrate liturgy as part of a tradition that we, in turn, are helping to constitute" (Zimmerman, *Liturgy as Living Faith*, 89). But it is the former sense that guides her pastoral interpretations, which are based simply on the skeletal structure of the liturgical texts themselves. (Incidentally, one could contend that dramatic works of literature are, on the contrary, subject to a very similar dynamic as liturgy, inasmuch as the performers and spectators of a Shakespearean play, for example, "author" the "text" presented on any given occasion—but not in any substantial sense the Bard's script itself).

28. "The analytical, semiotic mode of explanation does not appear to allow for a configured narrative world of the text. The configuration of a fictive world is an act of the synthetic imagination. The critical analysis of such a world into its parts is quite a different process. Thus there seems to be a distinction between a configurative moment and an explanatory moment" (Dan R. Stiver, *Theology after Ricoeur: New Directions in Hermeneutical Theology* [Louisville, Ky.: Westminster John Knox Press, 2001], 71).

29. Zimmerman, *Liturgy as Living Faith*, 89. It is hard to understand how liturgy can provide for the critique of its own ideology—how, that is, one can simultaneously affirm belonging in and through the act of participating in a rite, and critique its legitimacy. If "liturgy functions as a kind of normative will that shapes the meaning of Christian living without hindering our own freedom of choice (arbitrary will)," nonetheless, the arbitrary will comes into focus rather outside of the liturgical context, when the corporate language of the "first-person plural" is replaced by the resumption of the first-person singular of ordinary discourse. (Zimmerman, *Liturgy as Living Faith*, 137).

30. Paul Ricoeur, *Critique and Conviction: Conversations with François Azouvi and Marc de Launay*, trans. Kathleen Blamey (New York: Columbia University Press, 1998), 144–45.

31. Ricoeur, *Critique and Conviction*, 145 Emphasis mine.

32. Paul Ricoeur, *Time and Narrative, Volume 1*, trans. Kathleen McLaughlin and David Pellauer (Chicago: University of Chicago Press, 1984).

33. Zimmerman, "Paschal Mystery," 304.

34. Zimmerman, "Paschal Mystery," 310.

35. Zimmerman, "Liturgical Assembly," 51.

36. Graham Hughes, *Worship as Meaning* (Cambridge University Press: Cambridge, 2003), 222.

37. Hughes, *Worship as Meaning*, 230–31.

38. "My discussion of the 'church' liturgical theologians should make it clear that it seems to me there is no future in an 'old' or 'first' naiveté that simply wishes modernity were not a factor. This seems to me to eviscerate everything we know . . . about the work of meaning-completion which readers of texts, recipients of signs

and interpreters of reality undertake in the construction of meanings. In our time, the recipients of liturgical signs are inhabitants of this modern culture and complete their meanings from within it" (Hughes, *Worship as Meaning*, 253). If Hughes undoubtedly does well to indicate the ruptures in thinking that can result from modern disenchantment, he arguably underestimates the resilience of the liturgy, taken as a compound symbol, and its remarkable potential to redeploy meaning in the face of doubt and indifference—its capacity to, as Ricoeur would say, "give rise to thought."

39. Hughes, *Worship as Meaning*, 253.

40. Bridget Nichols, *Liturgical Hermeneutics*, 15.

41. Bridget Nichols, *Liturgical Hermeneutics*, 18.

42. Bridget Nichols, *Liturgical Hermeneutics*, 26. Nichols approaches the Creed as a datum in itself, rather than as an element of the liturgy. In this respect, she neglects the performative quality of the Creed—i.e., the fact that it presents its propositions in the form of an attestation: "I believe in . . ." Not only for Byzantine-Rite Christians, who recite the Creed at every Divine Liturgy, Baptism, and Office of Compline, as well as in the course of their prescribed daily prayers; but also for Western Christians, who traditionally recite the Nicene Creed at Mass, and the Apostles' Creed devotionally (e.g., as part of the Rosary) and—in the Anglican tradition—at Evensong, the Creed serves as a *prayer*, rather than chiefly a referent for prayer. In the terminology of J. L. Austin that Nichols finds to be highly instructive, the Creed has both *illocutionary* as well as *perlocutionary* force, and thus is perhaps not to be taken as a decontextualized reference point, as Nichols does. Indeed, the Creed has veritable *perlocutionary* force as well, inasmuch as it is traditionally the act of reciting the Creed on the part of a catechumen (or his sponsors) that allows him to be admitted to Baptism. It is doubtful that Ricoeur would countenance this distinction, as he regards the encounter with "Faith" to be an encounter with the primary texts of Scripture, theology being taken as a second-order enterprise. He warns against abstraction from the originary word of revelation, and hence prefers to interpret the polyphonic discourse of the Bible rather than the works of theology.

43. Bridget Nichols, *Liturgical Hermeneutics*, 26–27.

44. Bridget Nichols, *Liturgical Hermeneutics*, 59.

45. Bridget Nichols, *Liturgical Hermeneutics*, 32.

46. Ricoeur, *Interpretation Theory*, 87–88.

47. Bridget Nichols, *Liturgical Hermeneutics*, 91.

48. Bridget Nichols, *Liturgical Hermeneutics*, 122.

49. Bridget Nichols, *Liturgical Hermeneutics*, 33.

50. Paul Ricoeur, *From Text to Action: Essays in Hermeneutics, II*, trans. Kathleen Blamey and John B. Thompson, foreword by Richard Kearney (Evanston, Ill.: Northwestern University Press, 2007), 144–67.

51. Nevertheless, Nichols persists in her critique, indicting Zimmerman for allegedly privileging the interpretation of the liturgical text rather than performance:

> Yet a clear priority of the written text over the liturgical performance emerges from her analytical premises. Thus Zimmerman treats the celebration of a written liturgical rite as the text's means of imprinting its status as "event" on the course of history. Under these conditions, the performance has its principal function in "lending [the text] an historical dimension [which is] part and parcel of its meaning". . . . Viewed thus, the performance does not propose a world to the worshippers or, better still, allow the worshippers to assist in proposing the world of the rite. On the contrary, its purpose is to demonstrate that there is a meaning to be extracted. (Bridget Nichols, *Liturgical Hermeneutics*, 32–33)

It is hard to sympathize with Nichols's objections in this connection: How else can the performance of the liturgical text allow for the proposing of a world, if not on account of the fact that there is meaning in said text, a meaning that is "extracted" through its dynamic realization as ritual—or at least, to use Gadamer's terms, a definite horizon that can fuse with that adduced by the worshipper?

52. Bridget Nichols, *Liturgical Hermeneutics*, 46.

53. Bridget Nichols, *Liturgical Hermeneutics*, 91–92. What makes Nichols's criticism of Zimmerman all the more astonishing in this regard is that the latter actually *does* endeavor to assess the significance of the performative dynamism of a liturgical text. This is after all the rationale for her synthesis of the communications theory of Roman Jakobson with the semantics of Ricoeur; by applying the Jakobsonian "codes" and "functions" to the rubrics of her chosen service, the Eucharist of the Roman Rite, Zimmerman seeks to elucidate the indicators of *action* represented by the rubrics.

54. "At all times, I have had to be content with a notion of the 'ideal performance'. This assumes a rite which follows the provisions of the written liturgy closely, and does not fluctuate according to the whim of the priest or the congregation. Such an assumption does not, of course, exactly reflect the procedures carried on day by day in Anglican churches. Equally, it does not seek a platonic liturgy on which all other liturgical rites are modelled" (Bridget Nichols, *Liturgical Hermeneutics*, 46).

55. Paul Ricoeur, *From Text to Action*, trans. Kathleen Blamey and John B. Thompson, Essays in Hermeneutics (Evanston, Ill.: Northwestern University Press, 1991), 99.

56. Bridget Nichols, *Liturgical Hermeneutics*, 39.

57. Bridget Nichols, *Liturgical Hermeneutics*, 35–36.

58. A question could also be raised with respect to the notion that faith is the "ground" of liturgy. It would perhaps be better, in a Ricoeurian perspective, to suggest that liturgy is grounded in anthropology, inasmuch as we are epistemologically predisposed to narration, on account of our natural faculty for grasping the world by configuring it. We must tell stories to make sense of our actions. Stiver discusses Ricoeur's view as follows: "Humans are a narrative in progress. . . . Until death, we are not finished works but are continually writing and rewriting our stories, stories that we have both constructed and deconstructed. The difference in narratives of our lives and fictional narratives is that we do not control the contingencies of nature and other people that constantly impinge upon us. We are being written as well as writing—which makes rewriting a necessity" (Stiver, *Ricoeur and Theology*, 103).

59. Hence the ambiguity of her hypothesis: "My founding premise is that, through the cognitive propositions of the Faith, worshippers find themselves placed in the prospect of the Kingdom in what I have defined as threshold positions. From these positions, the individuals who make up the congregation are empowered to make their personal appropriation, in faith, of the promises set out in the rite" (Bridget Nichols, *Liturgical Hermeneutics*, 87).

60. See, for example, Alexander Schmemann, *The Eucharist: Sacrament of the Kingdom* (Crestwood, NY: Saint Vladimir's Seminary Press, 1987), 40–43.

61. Bridget Nichols, *Liturgical Hermeneutics*, 37.

62. Derrida's concept of the "written performative" suggests that a text not ostensibly addressed to a given person will, by the very act of its being read, cause that one to interpret it as in some way addressed to him personally, and to unwittingly assume the role of the recipient. Accordingly, Nichols notes that a group of individuals becomes a congregation though mutually unsealing the "letter" enclosed in the liturgical rite: "The further the congregation proceeds in the action, the greater are the commitments they find themselves making in the dialogic responses, which, like the 'program' of Derrida's letter, do not seem to be overtly dictating any pattern of behaviour" (Bridget Nichols, *Liturgical Hermeneutics*, 105–6).

63. Bridget Nichols, *Liturgical Hermeneutics*, 128.

64. John Breck, *Scripture in Tradition: The Bible and Its Interpretation in the Orthodox Church* (Crestwood, N.Y.: St. Vladimir's Seminary Press, 2001), 76.

65. Bridget Nichols, *Liturgical Hermeneutics*, 256–57.

66. Nichols muses whether the very continuance of sacred vocabulary—for example, "pray" or "bless"—in the standard lexica of ordinary languages, in an age of alleged unbelief, does not witness to the irreducible presence of the numinous in the prefiguration of human action.

67. Bridget Nichols, *Liturgical Hermeneutics*, 264.

68. "Under the guidance of Ricoeur's practical sense that a realistic expectation of utopia can give rise to productive action, however, there is another possi-

bility to consider. Forms of worship which not only promise the Kingdom, but promise it as a model whose prospects can augment the existing resources of its users, can equally help to interpret secular experience" (Bridget Nichols, *Liturgical Hermeneutics*, 272).

69. Martin Stringer, "Text, Context and Performance: Hermeneutics and the Study of Worship," *Scottish Journal of Theology* 53, no. 3 (2000): 365–79.

70. Stringer, "Text, Context and Performance," 365.

71. Kieran Flanagan, *Sociology and Liturgy: Representations of the Holy* (London: Macmillan, 1991).

72. Stringer, "Text, Context and Performance," 366.

73. Stringer, "Text, Context and Performance," 371–72.

74. He cites, for example, way in which baptismal, ordination or marriage liturgies cause their candidates to acquire a new status that extends outside of the celebration (Stringer, "Text, Context and Performance," 376).

75. Stringer, "Text, Context and Performance," 376–77.

76. Stringer, "Text, Context and Performance," 377–78.

77. See, for example: Margaret Mary Kelleher, "Liturgical Theology: A Task and a Method," in *Foundations in Ritual Studies: A Reader for Students of Christian Worship*, ed. Paul Bradshaw and John Melloh (Grand Rapids, Mich.: Baker Academic, 2007), 201–22; and her "Hermeneutics in the Study of Liturgical Performance," *Worship* 67, no. 4 (July 1993): 292–318. See also Nathan D. Mitchell, *Liturgy and the Social Sciences* (Collegeville, Minn.: Liturgical Press, 1999).

78. Stringer, "Text, Context and Performance," 378.

79. Hughes, *Worship as Meaning*, 124 n20.

80. Stringer, "Text, Context and Performance," 378.

81. Hughes, *Worship as Meaning*, 212.

82. Stringer, "Text, Context and Performance," 378.

83. Kelleher, "Hermeneutics & Performance," 303.

84. Ethnography, in anthropological parlance, refers to fieldwork itself, as well as to the *documentation* of one's research—documentation that requires the work of configuration on the part of the author himself, as well as interpretation on the part of those who read his work. See Kelleher, "Hermeneutics & Performance," 293. Of course, in our day *videography* plays an increasingly important role in anthropology (a discipline that has been superseded or subsumed, in some quarters, by the new field of "cultural studies")—the documentary film eclipsing, perhaps, some of the conventional prerogatives of ethnography proper. But films also involve the act of configuration, and themselves give rise to varied interpretations; for its part the film review, as a genre, thus brings things full circle back to hermeneutics.

85. Kelleher, "Hermeneutics & Performance," 294.

86. It is in the cognitional theory of Bernard Lonergan that Kelleher finds the most comprehensive toolkit for arbitrating between objectivity and subjectivity in the empirical researching of liturgical performance.

87. As recent research in liturgical studies has contended, for instance, such celebrated "church orders" as the fourth- or fifth-century *Apostolic Tradition* of Hippolytus may attest to a liturgical tradition never actually in force. See, for example, Andrew B. McGowan, *Ancient Christian Worship: Early Church Practices in Social, Historical and Theological Perspective* (Grand Rapids, Mich.: Baker Academic, 2014), 12–13. Even here, however, a liturgical text arguably still witnesses to past action, to wit, the extant liturgical practice as it *should be* reformed/performed. For McGowan, the *Apostolic Tradition* is "a precious witness to some (probably) fourth-century compiler's highest liturgical and pastoral ideals, as well as to those of earlier writers or communities—some even as early as the elusive Hippolytus—who provided its sources."

88. Stiver, *Theology after Ricoeur*, 98.

89. Stiver, *Theology after Ricoeur*, 99.

90. Pelikan, *Credo*, 405.

91. Aidan Nichols, *The Shape of Catholic Theology*, 51.

92. There is a "subtle equilibrium" at work, Ricoeur says, expressed historically in the Church as "a dialectic of preaching and sacraments": "[In] preaching the kerygmatic element carries the day with its c oncern to 'apply' the word here and now both ethically and politically. In the sacrament, symbolism has the upper hand. We need only recall the correspondences Baptism awakens between the primordial waters, where all form is abolished, the flood, the water of death, and the water of purification. . . . The sacrament, we could say, is the mutation of sacred ritual into the kerygmatic realm" (Ricoeur, *Figuring the Sacred*, 67).

93. Peter Galadza, "Byzantine Christian Worship." http://religion.oxfordre .com/view/10.1093/acrefore/9780199340378.001.0001/acrefore-9780199340378 -e-56.

94. Kelleher, "Hermeneutics & Performance," 308, 316.

95. Nicholas Lash, *Theology on the Way to Emmaus* (London: SCM Press, 1986), 42.

96. Bridget Nichols, *Liturgical Hermeneutics*, 37.

97. Kelleher, "Liturgical Theology," 210–11. Note that words, for Kelleher, are a genre of symbols, alongside "objects, actions, relationships . . . gestures, and arrangements of space."

98. David M. Kaplan, ed., *Reading Ricoeur* (Albany: State University of New York Press, 2008), 3.

99. Roman Catholic liturgist David Stosur argues that Guardini was problematizing the postmodern, rather than the modern, condition. This, because a response to Guardini must transcend mere revision of ritual, or the fostering of a

present work, as a second-order discourse about liturgy, rather than a first-order instance of liturgical speech, is an example.

14. Clifford Geertz, "Deep Play: Notes on the Balinese Cockfight," in *Myth, Symbol and Culture*, ed. Clifford Geertz (New York: W.W. Norton & Co., 1971), 1–38; Ronald L. Grimes, *Ritual Criticism: Case Studies in Its Practice, Essays on Its Theory* (Columbia, S.C.: University of South Carolina Press, 1990).

15. Ricoeur, *Figuring the Sacred*, 218.

16. The mise-en-scène of the liturgy follows the indices of a script that both transcribes the tradition and prescribes it. Recall above, where Ugolnik contrasts the individualism of a reader-text paradigm with the communitarianism of an aural/oral liturgical celebration; what is obscured in this comparison, however, is the fact that this very celebration still proceeds on the basis of a text that must be interpreted. A rite enacts a text, albeit one displaying the sedimentation of past ritual action—a sedimentation so complex that it requires a special "eye" to examine it—i.e., the typikon. The typikon is often called the "eye of the Church." See Job Getcha, *The Typikon Decoded: An Explanation of Byzantine Liturgical Practice*, trans. Paul Meyendorff (Yonkers, N.Y.: St. Vladimir's Seminary Press, 2012). Schmemann wryly observes, with respect to the regulative character of the Orthodox typikon (i.e., the official *ordo* for worship), that it functions as the hermeneutical sine qua non for diametrically opposed liturgical camps (Alexander Schmemann, *For the Life of the World* [Crestwood, N.Y.: St. Vladimir's Seminary Press, 2002], 132–33).

17. Since liturgy is scripted, one must attend to particular scripts—in our case, that of the *GBW*—and not simply the performance, as if the performance obtained apart from the mediation of text. While ritual theory may, in the study of non-Christian rites, be able to identify examples wherein a scriptuary step has not been taken, this is manifestly not the case as concerns Christian liturgy. Ricoeur explains the "independence" of the text, and its importance, as follows: "The triple independence of the text with regard to its author, its context, and its initial audience explains why texts are open to innumerable 'recontextualizations' through listening and reading that are a reply to the 'decontextualization' already contained in the very act of writing or, more exactly, publication" (Ricoeur, *Figuring the Sacred*, 219).

18. For the seventh, see Paul Ricoeur, "The Self in the Mirror of the Scriptures," trans. David Pellauer, in *The Whole and Divided Self*, ed. David E. Aune and John McCarthy (New York: Crossroad Publishing Company, 1997), 201–20, as well as the *repetitio*, with a distinct introduction, "Experience and Language in Religious Discourse," in Dominique Janicaud, et al. *Phenomenology and the "Theological Turn": The French Debate* (New York: Fordham University Press, 2000), 127–46. For the eighth, see "The Summoned Subject in the School of the Narratives of the Prophetic Vocation," in *Figuring the Sacred*, 262–78. Ricoeur

was very concerned, throughout his career, to separate his philosophical from his exegetical, not to say theological, enterprises—a fact to which he often referred ambivalently himself and that has received thoughtful criticism from his readers. Stiver, for example, remarks: "Ricoeur's sometime view that his philosophy is separable from his religious beliefs seems naïve and curiously 'modern.' It is especially ironic since . . . the main tenor of his thought runs against such a separation" (Dan R. Stiver, *Theology after Ricoeur: New Directions in Hermeneutical Theology* [Louisville, Ky.: Westminster John Knox Press, 2001], 241).

19. Ricoeur, *Figuring the Sacred*, 217–18.

20. Ricoeur, *Figuring the Sacred*, 221. *Pace* Graham Ward's criticisms below ("Biblical Narrative and the Theology of Metonymy," *Modern Theology* 7, no. 4 [July 1991]: 335–49), Ricoeur does not in fact remain vague about what ordinary discourse is, even if one could question whether scientific discourse itself does not depend upon metaphors for its own intelligibility, à la Thomas Kuhn. This is precisely the drift of Sallie McFague in *Metaphorical Theology: Models of God in Religious Language* (Minneapolis, Minn.: Fortress Press, 1982).

21. Ricoeur, *Figuring the Sacred*, 222.

22. Ricoeur presumes that poetic discourse suspends first-order reference, whether ordinary or scientific. Several theorists, however, have demonstrated the essential metaphoricity of scientific models themselves—following the groundbreaking work of Thomas Kuhn in *The Structure of Scientific Revolutions*, 2nd ed. (Chicago: University of Chicago Press, 1970). Thus Ricoeur's argument only stands to gain from the assertion that metaphor is operative not only within but also beyond the bounds of poetic discourse (inclusive for Ricoeur of narrative fiction, lyricism and even the essay). A key if not sufficiently well-known text, in this connection, is Owen Barfield, *Saving the Appearances: A Study in Idolatry* (New York: Harcourt, Brace & World, Inc., 1965). Barfield's thesis is that in modernity, we have ceased to experience "participation"—equivalent to Ricoeur's notion of "our many ways of belonging to the world before we oppose ourselves to things understood as 'objects' that stand before a 'subject'"—since language has ceased to be encountered as providing "representations" of the "unrepresented." He challenges the ensuing loss of an "iconic" mode of perception.

23. Ricoeur, *Figuring the Sacred*, 223.

24. Paul Ricoeur, *From Text to Action*, trans. Kathleen Blamey and John B. Thompson, Essays in Hermeneutics (Evanston, Ill.: Northwestern University Press, 1991), 89–104.

25. Ricoeur will eventually qualify this distinction. In *Thinking Biblically*, he probes the "veritable event in thinking" displayed in the Septuagint's translation of Exodus 3:14: the encounter of Moses and the Burning Bush (André LaCoque and Paul Ricoeur, *Thinking Biblically: Exegetical and Hermeneutical Studies*, trans. David Pellauer [Chicago: University of Chicago Press, 1998], 331). In that instance,

he sees the originary biblical discourse already countenancing the ontotheologi-cal tradition, inasmuch as the history of Greek philosophical speculation on Being makes an entrée into the forum of God's self-revelation. The unnameable Name is thus irrevocably defined according to a heterogeneous frame of reference.

26. For a thoughtful engagement with this question by an author appreciative of Ricoeur, see Merold Westphal, *Overcoming Onto-Theology: Toward a Postmod-ern Christian Faith* (New York: Fordham University Press, 2001).

27. LaCoque and Ricoeur, *Thinking Biblically*, 332.

28. LaCoque and Ricoeur, *Thinking Biblically*, 342.

29. For Ricoeur, true listening requires a letting go of onto-theological "knowl-edge" no less than a disavowal of the narcissistic self-founding ego of Descartes and Kant: "This double renouncing of the absolute 'object' and the absolute 'sub-ject' is the price that must be paid to enter into a radically nonspeculative and prephilosophical mode of language" (*Figuring the Sacred*, 224).

30. Ricoeur, *Figuring the Sacred*, 227–28.

31. Ricoeur, *Figuring the Sacred*, 226.

32. Ricoeur argues, however, that the overarching schema of Scripture is nar-rative. God, named as the one who accomplishes wonders, both in Old Testa-ment and the New, grounds the interpretation of time itself:

> God is the God of Abraham, Isaac, and Jacob and is, therefore, the Actant of the great gesture of deliverance. And God's meaning as Actant is bound up with the founding events in which the community of interpretation recognizes itself as enrooted, set up, and established. It is these events that name God. . . . God is designated by the transcendence of the founding events in relation to the ordinary course of history. . . . To the extent that the narrative genre is primary, God's imprint is in history before being in speech. Speech comes second inasmuch as it confesses the trace of God in the event. (*Figuring the Sacred*, 225)

33. Ricoeur, *Figuring the Sacred*, 226.

34. Ricoeur, *Figuring the Sacred*, 228.

35. Ricoeur, *Figuring the Sacred*, 229.

36. Ricoeur, *Figuring the Sacred*, 230.

37. As we shall see, one of the features of Byzantine liturgical discourse is pre-cisely its tendency to do just this—namely, to give voice to a neo-Chalcedonian ethos, "a development in Byzantine Christology after the Council of Chalcedon which caused the Byzantines to disproportionately emphasize the divinity of Christ (at the expense of His humanity) in an attempt to win back the non-Chalcedonians" (Peter Galadza, "Canadian Ukrainian Catholic Worship: Towards a Framework for Analysis," *Logos: A Journal of Eastern Christian Studies*

34, no. 1–2 [1993]: 256n14). Of course, this aspect of the "world behind the text" is tangential to the dynamics of the "world in front of the text."

38. Ricoeur, *Figuring the Sacred*, 231–32.

39. Ricoeur, *Figuring the Sacred*, 232.

40. Ricoeur does not develop exactly what he intends by reference to this notoriously convoluted term of Kant. On the one hand, he seems to wish to accentuate the importance of the biblical figures, over and against a view that would categorize them as secondary or derivative; for Ricoeur, one does not go around Scripture but through it. As he elsewhere declares: "The literary genres of the Bible do not constitute a rhetorical façade which it would be possible to pull down in order to reveal some thought content that is indifferent to its literary vehicle" (Paul Ricoeur, *Essays on Biblical Interpretation*, ed. Lewis S. Mudge [Philadelphia: Fortress Press, 1980], 91). On the other hand, he is wary of attaching preeminence to any one figure or set of figures, as if such could be taken on their own rather than being set in dialectic with all others. According to Kant, the schema of a pure concept—such as "God" is, being by definition immune to empirical observation—serves as the model according to which images of said concept are represented to the mind (Howard Caygill, *A Kant Dictionary*, The Blackwell Philosopher Dictionaries [Malden, Mass.: Blackwell Publishing, 1995], 360–62). But in regard to God, Kant does not begin with Scripture, but rather with the exigencies of the ethical imperative (*A Kant Dictionary*, 215–16). By contrast, Ricoeur privileges originary discourse and thus accords primacy to *its* models.

41. Ricoeur, *Figuring the Sacred*, 45–46.

42. It should be noted that while Ricoeur, in "Naming God," only briefly refers to the terminology of the apophatic tradition, it will appear in his later work, and is certainly apropos. It would seem that he avoids developing it there because of the association with an a posteriori theological discourse, rather that with the originary discourse of Scripture itself.

43. Stiver, *The Philosophy of Religious Language*, 77.

44. "The combined interplay of models and their qualifiers continues in a wholly significant fashion in the practice that results in the transfer from texts to life." Such applications constitute a second result of understanding oneself "in front of the text": Beyond speculative engagement with the word, what is entailed is practical engagement with the world. While the Gospel does not promote a specific program, its limit-expressions open us up to "limit-experiences," to unlimited possibilities for action. Thus Ricoeur avers: "If language does not exist for itself, but in view of the world that it opens up and uncovers, then the interpretation of language is not distinct from the interpretation of the world. Hence self-understanding in the face of the text will have the same amplitude as the world of the text. Far, therefore, from being closed in upon a person or a dialogue, this

understanding will have the multidimensional character of biblical poetics. It will be cosmic, ethical, and political" (*Figuring the Sacred*, 234–35).

45. Paul Ricoeur, David Pellauer, and John McCarthy, "Conversation," in *The Whole and Divided Self*, ed. David E. Aune and John McCarthy (New York: The Crossroad Publishing Company, 1997), 228.

46. For an interesting comparison of how Orthodox and Protestant hymns interpret cardinal scriptural themes in their respective liturgical contexts, see Karen B. Westerfield Tucker, "The Liturgical Functioning of Orthodox Troparia and Wesleyan Hymns," in *In Orthodox and Wesleyan Scriptural Understanding and Practice*, ed. S. T. Kimbrough Jr. (Crestwood, N.Y.: St. Vladimir's Seminary Press, 2005), 293–304. A peculiarity of Byzantine liturgical language is that it functions as originary discourse—for Ricoeur identifies liturgical formularies as one such genre—but is nonetheless replete with theological terminology derived from the speculative works of the Church Fathers, which feature Ricoeur associates with secondary discourse. Ricoeur seems strangely indifferent to this feature of the liturgical idiom—i.e., its approximation to what he terms "mixed discourse." While it is plausible that Byzantine texts incorporate the greatest amount of philosophical *theologia*—in the patristic sense of speculative discourse about the inner life of the Holy Trinity—the conceptual formulae already evident in the New Testament epistles, and developed not only by the Fathers but also by the deliberations of the Ecumenical Councils, also appear in other classical liturgical traditions.

47. LaCoque and Ricoeur, *Thinking Biblically*, 277.

48. LaCoque and Ricoeur, *Thinking Biblically*, 280.

49. One might react to Ricoeur's hermeneutical confidence by questioning how *heresy* is then to be recognized. The celebrated anecdote from *Against the Heresies* by St. Irenaeus comes to mind: A miscreant extracts the tesserae of a mosaic depicting a king, shrewdly rearranges them to form the image of a fox or dog, and then proceeds to misinform innocent viewers as to the intention of the artist. St. Irenaeus's specific concern is with second-century Gnosticism and its lack of an orthodox "hypothesis" (or first principle) in accordance with which to (correctly) read and interpret the Scriptures. The interpretative problem he addresses, however, is perennial. See the nuanced discussion of the relevance of St. Irenaeus for contemporary Orthodox theology in John Behr, *The Mystery of Christ: Life in Death* (Crestwood, N.Y.: St. Vladimir's Seminary Press, 2006), 55–58.

50. "In other words, it is to the general phenomenon of intertextuality, as an effect of reading, rather than allegory, as allegedly immanent within Scripture, that we may appeal in order to generate theological readings of the Song of Songs, setting out, almost like sparks of new meaning, points of intersection among the texts that belong to the biblical canon. . . . Before any reuse of these texts there would be the intersecting reading that takes places [*sic*] within the canon"

(LaCoque and Ricoeur, *Thinking Biblically*, 295). Ricoeur does not seem to countenance the primacy of liturgical use, in the sense of its nascent intertextuality preceding the formation of the biblical canon as such. An Orthodox perspective would wish to affirm that the canon itself is the function of the liturgical practice of the Church—i.e., that the books that were eventually deemed canonical acquire and maintain their status as a result of having gained ecclesiastical approbation through public proclamation in the worshipping assembly. See John Anthony McGuckin, *The Orthodox Church: An Introduction to Its History, Doctrine, and Spiritual Culture* (Malden, Mass.: Wiley-Blackwell, 2011), 100–102.

51. Power writes:

> The heuristic within which both the breakdown and the emergence of creative expression may be appropriated is that of sacrament as a language-event. This indeed fits within a larger context in which the redemptive act itself is considered as a language-event. Jesus was manifested at his baptism and on the Cross as the Word coming forth from God, and those who believed gave testimony to this in their preaching, in their lives and in their writings. The written Word passes on the saying and teachings of Jesus, and the narratives of his passion and death. In the narratives of the resurrection in the Spirit, there is added the hope of the Second Coming, the assurance of the presence of Christ in his body the Church, and the gift of the Spirit to animate this body, enabling it to keep memory and interpret the truth, in word and in deed. It is in what is proclaimed as the Paschal Event that the redemptive operation of Word and spirit has its centre, and it is this which is at the heart of sacramental remembrance in the Church. (David N. Power, "The Language of Sacramental Memorial: Rupture, Excess and Abundance," in *Sacramental Presence in a Postmodern Context*, ed. L. Boeve and L. Leijssen [Leuven: Leuven University Press, 2001], 138–39)

52. Catherine Pickstock, *After Writing: On the Liturgical Consummation of Philosophy* (Oxford: Blackwell Publishers, 1998).

53. Power, "The Language of Sacramental Memorial," 137, 139.

54. We shall turn below to a consideration of the light to be shed on the temporal dynamics of liturgy by Ricoeur's account of time—and narrative. Suffice it to note here that, alongside the liturgical applications of his biblical hermeneutics adduced here, his treatment of "biblical time" is portentous, especially for a study of Byzantine liturgy. This is so, because of his appreciation of the unique mode of time expressed by the "today" of the hymn genre, preeminently evident in the Psalms. "Today" is a ubiquitous deictic in the Byzantine liturgical idiom, dramatically displayed, for example, in the *GBW*. Ricoeur traces a path for us to follow in interpreting it, by contrasting the temporality it expresses with several others extant in the several genres of the Old Testament (*Figuring the Sacred*, 167–80).

55. Power concedes that the Church may nevertheless be tempted to pretend to the erstwhile status of the Enlightenment metanarrative, in the wake of its current vicissitudes. If Christianity should advance such totalizing claims, however, it will suffer a like fate: "If the memorial of Christ is itself presented as meta-narrative, it too will be unable to integrate the realities of evil and the ethical challenge which arises from the convergence of the proclamation of the kerygma of love with this evil. After all, it does not take too much reflection to know that the Christian story and memory have in the past allowed complicity with the evil of the times and the victimisation of those who did not fit well into this narrative" (Power, "The Language of Sacramental Memorial," 141).

56. While at one level the unique narrative of Christ stands as a measure of our life projects, it may itself fall victim to the Zeitgeist, to the extent that ordinary life challenges it with "events, situations and conditions which in its given form it cannot accommodate." The liturgical celebration also, whether through the exigencies of intertextuality, or in respect of its vulnerability to the often antinomian dynamics of popular religiosity, can also strain the viability of said narrative; moreover, the ethical demands of the "other" may call into question its ability to accommodate novel circumstances and concerns. According to Power, even where a community responds to such effectively, its response must be integrated into the liturgy in some way, lest a double-think obtain, in which the ritual projection of Christian identity diverges from the community's actual self-understanding ("Language of Sacramental Memorial," 143).

57. If not legitimately posited in abstraction from the canonical micronarratives, therefore, a metastory can nonetheless be discerned in Scripture in the form of its plurivocal testimony to God's presence. As God is, one might say, contiguous but not coterminous with his naming, so the incommensurable "detail stories" of the Bible are the index to a metastory that paradoxically eludes telling: "The story of the partnership between God and Israel is, as such, not only open and ongoing but unfathomable and unspeakable. At that point the character of the metastory as that which cannot be told joins the theological theme of God's ineffability. Or rather the ineffability of the Name is the same thing as the inexhaustibility of the metastory" (Ricoeur, *Figuring the Sacred*, 242–43). Ricoeur returns here to one of his preferred pericopes, Ex. 3:14, to illustrate this parallel: The God who retreats into mystery by the very giving of his unnameable name— "I am who I am"—is also the God who affirms his presence to Israel, and his historic acts of presence to the Patriarchs. If the metastory, like the Name of God, can never be told directly, but only obliquely, by means of *petits récits*, Ricoeur reiterates that these themselves are nonetheless never purely narrative, but display a complex intertextuality that places them in dialectic with other modes of discourse (*Figuring the Sacred*, 245). Such a juxtaposition of genres causes texts to consequently be interpreted otherwise than if they stood alone:

Law becomes, through narrative, gift; narrative, through law, instruction; while both are transformed through sapiential literature into expressions of wisdom, through prophecy, into the unrealized beginning of something yet to come.

58. Ricoeur lauds Frye's discovery of a highly ramified network of correspondences, based on duality of the paradisiac/apocalyptic and the demonic, producing a battery of intersignifications. See Northrop Frye, *The Great Code: The Bible and Literature*, ed. Alvin A. Lee, *Collected Works of Northrop Frye* (Toronto: University of Toronto Press, 2006). He accepts that Frye is right to recognize an inner coherence to the biblical field of reference, a "'centripetal' structure that the Bible shares with all the great poetic texts." (Ricoeur, "Experience and Language," 137). Nevertheless, he is apprehensive lest this centripetal force lead to a homogenization of the biblical genres, most evident in the recurrent effort of theologians to construct a *Heilsgeschichte* that would reduce Scripture's poetic surplus to the prosaic univocity of a conceptual frame of reference.

59. Ricoeur, *Figuring the Sacred*, 242. Quoting Dietrich Ritschl and Hugh O. Jones (*"Story" als Rohmaterial der Theologie*, Theologische Existenz Heute 192 [Munich: Christian Kaiser Verlag, 1976]), he asserts that in liturgy "'the story and our story become one and the same.'"

60. Ricoeur, *Figuring the Sacred*, 245.

61. Ricoeur, *Figuring the Sacred*, 248.

62. Ricoeur has also commented on this tendency, to which he is favorable, in reflecting on ecumenism: "It seems to me that the problem of the split between Catholicism and Protestantism rests finally on the problem of authority, and it is true that here there is, for the moment, an unbridgeable gap. But I am not at all interested in institutional ecumenism because I believe in the originally plural destination of Christianity—it is, undoubtedly, for this reason that I am not Catholic" (Paul Ricoeur, *Critique and Conviction: Conversations with François Azouvi and Marc de Launay*, trans. Kathleen Blamey [New York: Columbia University Press, 1998], 167). Incidentally, Ricoeur seems to have had no acquaintance with the Eastern Catholic Churches, whose history and theology challenge the dichotomous stereotype he rehearses here. For Eastern Catholics, it is precisely because of a belief in the "plural destination of Christianity" that they are Catholic, seeing the Catholic communion as serving, in principle, to foster that very pluralism—even as it also serves for its theological arbitration and critique, in which process hierarchical authority plays a prominent, if differentiated, role. Peter Galadza, for instance, maps the "plural destination" of Catholicism charted by key documents of Vatican II such as *Lumen Gentium*, whose paragraph 23 reads: "By divine Providence it has come about that various churches, established in various places by the apostles and their successors, have in the course of time coalesced into several groups, organically united, which, preserving the unity of faith and the unique divine constitution of the universal Church, enjoy their own discipline, their own

liturgical usage, and their own theological and spiritual heritage. . . . This variety of local churches with one common aspiration is splendid evidence of the catholicity of the undivided Church." See "What is Eastern Catholic Theology? Some Ecclesial and Programmatic Dimensions," *Logos: A Journal of Eastern Christian Studies* 39, no. 1 (1998): 63–64.

63. Power, "The Language of Sacramental Memorial," 144.

64. Taft explains this distinction as follows:

> It is axiomatic in contemporary liturgical theology to distinguish between *theologia prima* and *theologia secunda*. *Theologia prima*, or first-level theology, is the faith expressed in the liturgical life of the church antecedent to speculative questioning of its theoretical implications, prior to its systematization in the dogmatic propositions of *theologia secunda* or systematic reflection on the lived mystery of the church. Liturgical language, the language of *theologia prima*, is typological, metaphorical, more redolent of Bible and prayer than of school and thesis, more patristic than scholastic, more impressionistic than systematic, more suggestive than probative. In a word, it is symbolic and evocative, not philosophical and ontological. ("Mass without Consecration? The Historic Agreement on the Eucharist between the Catholic Church and the Assyrian Church of the East Promulgated 26 October 2001," *Worship* 77, no. 6 [2003]: 495)

65. Taft, "Mass without Consecration?" 506–7.

66. Werner Jeanrond asks for a "more dialectical consideration of ongoing sacramental action and critical and self-critical theological theory," going on to contend that the fields of intrareligious dialogue and ecumenism both bring into relief the challenges that ensue where "rupture" is regarded as a constitutive process. Effectively, Jeanrond wonders whether "rupture" does not imply a continual iconoclasm that denies normativity to a tradition ("Response to David N. Power," in *Sacramental Presence in a Postmodern Context*, ed. L. Boeve and L. Leijssen [Leuven: Leuven University Press, 2001], 161–66).

4. At the Intersection of the *Via Positiva* and the *Via Negativa*

1. David Tracy, *Plurality and Ambiguity: Hermeneutics, Religion, Hope* (Chicago: University of Chicago Press, 1994), 28.

2. Tracy, *Plurality and Ambiguity*, 29.

3. Dan R. Stiver, *The Philosophy of Religious Language: Sign, Symbol and Story* (Malden, Mass.: Blackwell Publishers, 1996), 44.

4. John van den Hengel, "Naming the Unspeakable," in *Between Suspicion and Sympathy: Paul Ricoeur's Unstable Equilibrium*, ed. Andrzej Wierciński, Hermeneutic Series, Vol. 3 (Toronto: Hermeneutic Press [The International Institute for Hermeneutics], 2003), 244.

5. Paul Ricoeur, "Experience and Language in Religious Discourse," in Dominique Janicaud, et al. *Phenomenology and the "Theological Turn": The French Debate* (New York: Fordham University Press, 2000), 136.

6. Even so, Lewis has also been appreciated for his contribution to philosophy. See David Baggett, Gary R. Habermas, and Jerry L. Walls, eds., *C. S. Lewis as Philosopher: Truth, Goodness and Beauty* (Downers Grove, Ill.: IVP Academic, 2008). That Ricoeur and Lewis prove to be mutually illuminating has been demonstrated at length in Mara E. Donaldson, *Holy Places Are Dark Places: C. S. Lewis and Paul Ricoeur on Narrative Transformation* (Lanham, Md.: University Press of America, 1989).

7. C. S. Lewis, "Bluspels and Flalansferes," in *The Play of Language*, ed. Leonard F. Dean, Walker Gibson, and Kenneth G. Wilson (New York: Oxford University Press, 1971), 288–302.

8. The term is Mark Johnson's: "We are in the midst of a metaphormania. Only three decades ago the situation was just the opposite: poets created metaphors, everybody used them, and philosophers (linguists, psychologists, etc.) ignored them. Today we seem possessed by metaphor" (*Philosophical Perspectives on Metaphor* [Minneapolis: University of Minnesota Press, 1981], ix).

9. Lewis's distinction highlights the equivocity of the term "metaphor" itself. As Stiver explains, contemporary discussion of metaphoricity invokes the alternative terminology of "symbol" as well as "analogy," with a cumulative effect that is often confusing. The use of "analogy" typically reflects Lewis's magistral sense of metaphor—i.e., the adaptation of univocal language to new contexts on the basis of evident aptness, an adaptation that for Stiver can render the metaphor in question either a "stable" or "everyday" one—"well-known, familiar, but nonetheless still vital, metaphorical relations"—or else, eventually, one "dead," that is to say, a metaphor included in the lexicon whose very metaphoricity is forgotten through repeated use. The uniqueness of metaphor, as understood in contrast to analogy, however, is in the shock it occasions, which Ricoeur terms a "semantic impertinence": It cannot be reduced to univocal language, but only converted into the terms of yet another metaphor, if at all. For its part, "symbol" customarily has a nonlinguistic denotation that contours its linguistic connotations. Stiver concludes that "we can probably not overcome the disparity of definition. It is arguable that metaphor, analogy and symbol can be seen as very similar, and it is arguable that they are very different. What is important is always to be attentive to how thinkers are using their terms" (Dan. R. Stiver, *Philosophy of Religious Language*, 127).

10. Lewis, "Bluspels," 290.

11. Lewis, "Bluspels," 291. This distinction does not seem to be appreciated by Sallie McFague, who proposes that the path to theological emancipation is for all metaphors to be relativized (see her *Metaphorical Theology: Models of God in*

Religious Language [Minneapolis: Fortress Press, 1982]). She objects to the traditional hegemony of certain Scriptural metaphors, such as the use of Father for God, and suggests that new metaphors be coined to substitute for, or complement, those favored by tradition. C. S. Lewis also advocates, in the case of magistral metaphors, a creativity ordered to a greater comprehension of that referred to by metaphor; in other words, the production of new metaphors demonstrates that someone has adequately understood a phenomenon so as to be able to give an account of it from multiple perspectives. The catch, however, is that one must have independent access to such a phenomenon for the conventional metaphor to be deemed dispensable, or even ancillary. The problem with advocating an iconoclasm toward the metaphors used in the naming of God is that it is only through *them* that the distinctiveness of the Christian experience of God is constituted— excepting that mystical experience whose very rarity, ineffability, and individuality make it of limited value for interpreting a traditional, communal text such as the Bible. In attempting to transcend the metaphors of Scripture, does one not stake a claim to having had an experience equal or superior to the biblical authors, in virtue of which a *competence* for describing the divine has been acquired? McFague presumes that one can reduce the primary metaphors of Scripture to a common denominator (namely, that of personhood), and that therefore as long as *this* feature is respected, new or marginal metaphors may take the place of the former. Yet the abstract category of "personhood" seems artificial and plastic, favoring an insoluble perspectivism. In this connection, Ricoeur's adversion to the role of qualifiers—terms that make metaphors say more than they ordinarily would, rendering them "limit-expressions"—is pertinent, since such extend the metaphorical frontiers, so to speak, rather than erase them.

   12. Lewis notes that the "pupillary" metaphor works in two opposing ways: The pupil who never acquires the independent access to the matter originally perceived metaphorically may end up forgetting the metaphorical quality of the terms employed, deadening them through a literalism that risks degenerating into meaninglessness. (One wonders if Lewis is here acknowledging the potential critique of logical positivism.) A pupil who becomes a "master," however, would be unaffected by the career of the metaphor by which he first came to grasp an object, since his later, nonmetaphorical access to it has rendered the metaphor superfluous: "Our thought is independent of the metaphors we employ, in so far as these metaphors are optional: that is, in so far as we are able to have the same idea without them. . . . On the other hand, where the metaphor is our only method of reaching a given idea at all, there our thinking is limited by the metaphor so long as we retain the metaphor; and when the metaphor becomes fossilized, our 'thinking' is not thinking at all, but mere sound or mere incipient movements in the larynx" ("Bluspels," 294–95).

   13. Stiver, *Philosophy of Religious Language*, 117.

   14. This is, of course, the view advanced by Ricoeur in *The Symbolism of Evil*.

15. Lewis, "Bluspels," 300.

16. Lewis, "Bluspels," 300–1.

17. Ricoeur writes:

> The "it was and it was not" of the Majorca storytellers rules both the split reference of the metaphorical statement and the contradictory structure of fiction. Yet, we may say as well that the structure of the fiction not only reflects but completes the logical structure of the split reference. The poet is this genius who generates split references by creating fictions. It is in fiction that the "absence" proper to the power of suspending what we call "reality" in ordinary language concretely coalesces and fuses with the positive insight into the potentialities of our being in the world which our everyday transactions with manipulable objects tend to conceal. (Paul Ricoeur, "The Metaphorical Process as Cognition, Imagination, and Feeling," *Critical Inquiry* 5, no. 1 [Autumn 1978]: 155)

18. Paul Ricoeur, *Figuring the Sacred: Religion, Narrative and Imagination*, ed. Mark I. Wallace, trans. David Pellauer (Minneapolis, MN: Augsburg Fortress Press, 1995), 53.

19. Paul Ricoeur, "The Metaphorical Process as Cognition, Imagination, and Feeling," *Critical Inquiry* 5, no. 1 (Autumn 1978): 153.

20. David Pellauer, *Ricoeur: A Guide for the Perplexed* (New York: Continuum, 2007), 69.

21. Graham Ward, "Biblical Narrative and the Theology of Metonymy," *Modern Theology* 7, no. 4 (July 1991): 335–49.

22. Drawing on Umberto Eco's notion of "overcoding" in discourse, in which light he distinguishes metaphor from metonymy, Ward argues (following Jakobson and Jacques Lacan) that discourse is best understood as cruciform, with both a vertical, metaphorical axis, and a horizontal, metonymic one; as a result, the biblical text, for example, cannot be said to be purely metaphorical—the charge he brings against Ricoeur—since this would discount one of the axes. Ward concludes that Derrida's deconstructionism, with its admission of *différance*, provides the most balanced hermeneutic, since it does not attempt to determine meaning one way or another, but holds in tension the literal sense of a text, what Ward calls the *sensus rectus* together with an openness to an undetermined *sensus obliquus*.

23. Ward, "Biblical Narrative," 336–37.

24. Paul Ricoeur, *Memory, History, Forgetting*, trans. Kathleen Blamey and David Pellauer (Chicago: University of Chicago Press, 2004).

25. Ricoeur, *Figuring the Sacred*, 244–45. The "Yale School" is represented by the landmark work of Hans Frei, *The Eclipse of Biblical Narrative: A Study in Eighteenth and Nineteenth Century Hermeneutics* (New Haven, Conn.: Yale University Press, 1980).

26. While challenging the academic usurpation of the biblical text, Ricoeur nonetheless affirms that the critical function is concomitant in a specifically Christian approach to its "sacred text":

> Maybe in the case of Christianity there is no sacred text, because it is not the text that is sacred but the one about which it is spoken. For instance, there is no privilege of the language in which it was said for the first time. . . . There is already something that allows the critical act; the critical act is not forbidden by the nature of the text, because it is not a sacred text in the sense in which the Qur'an is sacred. . . . But in Christianity, translation is quite possible, for the Septuagint is a kind of desacralization of the original language. (Ricoeur, *Figuring the Sacred*, 68)

27. Ward provides his own version of Ricoeur's notion of distanciation in the following:

> We cannot use as a hermeneutic for a text a model of language and reference developed by speech-act theorists. Putnam is surely right in insisting that it is people who refer, not words, but only within certain restricted speech-acts. Within texts, it is words that "refer" the writer's work to the reader's, not people. Meaning issues from the perichoretic interplay of writer-language-reader; not simply the writer's intention, nor the reader's projection, nor the autonomous power of words, but all three critically examining each other. . . . A paradox ensues—there is, on the one hand, because of language's connative value, a surplus of meaning, while, on the other, no definite meaning at all. ("Biblical Narrative," 341)

Oddly, he does not seem to notice the similarity of his plea to Ricoeur's perpetual contention on behalf of the singularity of the act of inscription, in whose wake hermeneutics finds its purpose. Nor does he credit Ricoeur in speaking here of a "surplus of meaning" (see "The Hermeneutical Function of Distanciation" in *From Text to Action*, 75–88). Although Ward correctly observes that in *Time and Narrative* Ricoeur no longer speaks, as he did in *The Rule of Metaphor*, of "reference," per se, but rather of configuration, he does not appear to appreciate that this is due to the latter's intention to honor the active role of the reader in grasping a metaphor, following a narrative: The reader brings his or her own "world" into alignment with that of the text, and the "fusion of horizons" manifests a unique field of reference. This is all the more surprising since Ward concludes with a similar call for understanding reference or meaning as a joint enterprise of "writer-language-reader."

28. Ricoeur, *Figuring the Sacred*, 69.

29. Ricoeur defines his "nonreligious, nontheistic, nonbiblical" sense of revelation as follows: "Revelation, in this sense, designates the emergence of another

concept of truth than truth as adequation, regulated by the criteria of verification and falsification: a concept of truth as manifestation, in the sense of letting be what shows itself. What shows itself is each time the proposing of a world, a world wherein I can project my ownmost possibilities" (Ricoeur, *Figuring the Sacred*, 223).

30. "The idea of revelation that emerges in Ricoeur's essay, therefore, suffers from ill-defined terminology and oversimplification. It lacks the textual analysis that would have recognised the degrees of 'overcoding' [in the sense given the term by Umberto Eco] in a specific discourse and presented criteria for textual misreadings. The root of Ricoeur's error lies, I believe, in his understanding of the referential function of metaphor that results in what he variously describes in his work as the 'inversion of ordinary language'" (Ward, "Biblical Narrative," 338).

31. See Paul Ricoeur, *Essays on Biblical Interpretation*, ed. Lewis S. Mudge (Philadelphia: Fortress Press, 1980); *The Rule of Metaphor: Multi-Disciplinary Studies of the Creation of Meaning in Language*, trans. Robert Czerny, Kathleen McLaughlin, and John Costello (Toronto: University of Toronto Press, 1977).

32. Paul Ricoeur, *Time and Narrative, Volume 2*, trans. Kathleen McLaughlin and David Pellauer (Chicago: University of Chicago Press, 1985), 100–152. The novels at issue are Virginia Woolf's *Mrs. Dalloway*, Thomas Mann's *The Magic Mountain*, and Marcel Proust's *Remembrance of Things Past*.

33. Paul Ricoeur, "Biblical Hermeneutics," *Semeia* 4 (1975): 29–148.

34. Ricoeur, *On Biblical Interpretation*, 103.

35. Ricoeur, *Figuring the Sacred*, 223.

36. Ricoeur, *On Biblical Interpretation*, 104.

37. David Pellauer, "Paul Ricoeur on the Specificity of Religious Language," *The Journal of Religion* 61, no. 3 (July 1981): 278.

38. Arguably, the difficulty with Ward's Christological criterion—"The justification of Scripture being a sacred book must rest upon the fact that it testifies, or claims to testify, to an event [the Incarnation] set apart from other events, an ineffable event" (Ward, "Biblical Narrative," 336–37)—is that it ironically subverts the very point he wishes to make: to wit, that the Bible is unique. By Ward's reckoning, Scripture has to be justified on the basis of testifying to the Incarnation, but he does not specify by what criterion or by whom this justification is given. Certainly Jewish readers do not see the Tanakh as testifying to the Incarnation—but not for that reason failing to testify to the ineffable! Ricoeur's locating of ineffability in the naming of God, a leitmotif running through the course of the Bible with perhaps only a single exception (i.e., the Hebrew recension of Esther), seems a more reasonable means of positing the uniqueness of the biblical text. While the New Testament obviously takes the event of Christ as the object of its testimony, the Old Testament has prima facie (i.e., prescinding here from the typological reading of the Church) no such equivalent. It is therefore not to be considered Scripture? Perplexingly, although taking Ricoeur to

NOTES TO PAGES 95–96

task for allegedly not recognizing degrees of Eco's "overcoding" within a given pericope, Ward treats Scripture in the singular as "a sacred book," failing to comment upon Ricoeur's taxonomy of the different biblical genres and their disparate manners of naming God.

39. Ward, "Biblical Narrative," 338. Ward observes with consternation that Ricoeur makes use both of images of tension—the "suspension" or "eclipse" of reference—and those of what the former calls "tyrannical suppression," such as the latter's statement that metaphor involves the "abolition (or elimination) of reference." Ward asks for Ricoeur to specify whether he sees the primary and secondary references as possessing "equiprimordiality," or whether instead the one dominates the other. Lewis's distinction between "pupillary" and "magistral" metaphors may again be of assistance here, since in case of the latter the primary denotation is simply suspended—the terms used in the metaphor have been deliberately and temporarily combined to depict a reality independently accessed—while in the former, the primary denotation is "abolished" to the extent that it has no separate existence, serving only by its very incongruence to impel the imagination into a new mode of "seeing-as" and "being-as"—one unavailable for *direct* articulation.

40. Ricoeur, *On Biblical Interpretation*, 101.

41. It is intriguing that Ward suspects Ricoeur's view of poetic discourse of being Neoplatonic. Admittedly, the latter's view of symbols as "bound" to a preternatural meaning that shows itself opaquely and never fully, if yet truly, could be construed as constrained by a nostalgia for "participation," a nostalgia that Ricoeur often renders explicit. His theory of metaphor (and with it of the productive imagination), however, is framed by a conviction that it operates a "free invention of discourse"—i.e., not determined by a primary internal vision only given voice in a secondary, ancillary moment. Richard Kearney explains that Ricoeur adheres to the counterintuitive belief that metaphors are spoken before being seen: "For new meanings to come into being they need to be spoken or uttered in the form of new verbal images. And this requires that the phenomenological account of imagining as appearance be supplemented by its hermeneutic account as meaning. Imagination can be recognized accordingly as the act of responding to a demand for new meaning, the demand of emerging realities to be by being said in new ways" ("Paul Ricoeur and the Hermeneutic Imagination," in *The Narrative Path: The Later Works of Paul Ricoeur*, ed. Peter T. Kemp and David Rasmussen [Cambridge, Mass.: MIT Press, 1989], 5). Whether this is correct or not, it hardly seems appropriate to designate such a view as Neoplatonic, for which school of philosophy the imagination is typically regarded as "reproductive" rather than "productive," language, as derivative rather than originary. Dan Stiver's thoughts are apposite here: "In general, Ricoeur is such an 'incarnational' philosopher, in the sense of emphasizing how all our knowledge

and language is rooted in embodied and worldly beings (related to Martin Heidegger's understanding of *Dasein* as being-in-the-world), that he can hardly suppose a disembodied and transhuman, Platonic view of texts. Ricoeur makes it clear that texts are human works produced by humans and must be interpreted as such" (*Philosophy of Religious Language*, 133).

42. "It would seem that the enigma of metaphorical discourse is that it 'invents' in both senses of the word: what it creates, it discovers; and what it finds, it invents" (Ricoeur, *The Rule of Metaphor*, 239).

43. In *Divine Discourse: Philosophical Reflections on the Claim That God Speaks* (Cambridge: Cambridge University Press, 1995), Nicholas Wolterstoff also takes Ricoeur to task for an alleged reduction of theology to anthropology, a view of Scripture that betrays the divine prerogative of initiating speech to human beings—what Ward calls "the central tenet of Christian revelation in which God speaks of God through God and human beings are in the accusative not the nominative case" ("Biblical Narrative," 340). In a manner similar to Ward, Wolterstoff, according to Stiver's analysis, sees Ricoeur as not respecting the authorial intention embedded in the text. Stiver rejoins that for Ricoeur, "All of Scripture . . . refers back to God as the one who speaks in it," albeit mediated through the human agency producing it as a textual work (Dan R. Stiver, *Theology after Ricoeur: New Directions in Hermeneutical Theology* [Louisville, Ky.: Westminster John Knox Press, 2001], 132–33).

44. Ricoeur, *Time and Narrative, Vol. 1*, 64–68, 206–8.

45. Pellauer, "Ricoeur and Religious Language," 277.

46. As Zimmerman observes, "Liturgical language, in addition to the verbal, also takes into account the poetic, visual, aural, gustatory, tactile, olfactory, gestural: in effect, a whole linguistic gamut which cries out for interpretation especially in its textuality. As such, these liturgical texts require an interpretation that employs language-use and textual methods, areas . . . [which open up] a liturgical text's relationship to experience" (Joyce Ann Zimmerman, "Language and Human Experience," in *The New Dictionary of Sacramental Worship*, ed. Peter E. Fink [Collegeville, Minn.: A Michael Glazier Book, Liturgical Press, 1990], 649).

47. Ricoeur, "Biblical Hermeneutics," 135.

48. Here Ricoeur appropriates the thought of Professor Fred Streng from a lecture at American Association for the Study of Religion at Vanderbilt University, in the spring of 1973 (Ricoeur, "Biblical Hermeneutics," 135).

49. Hence he remarks, "Perhaps we would even go so far as to consider the closing of the canon as a fundamental structural act which delimits the space of the interplay of forms of discourse and determines the finite configuration within which each form and each pair of forms unfolds its signifying function" (*Philosophical Hermeneutics and Theological Hermeneutics: Ideology, Utopia and Faith; Protocol of the 17th Colloquy, 4 November 1975*, ed. Wilhelm Wuellner, Protocol

of the Colloquy of the Center for Hermeneutical Studies in Hellenistic and Modern Culture [Berkeley, Calif.: Center for Hermeneutical Studies in Hellenistic & Modern Culture, 1976], 22, cited in Pellauer, "Ricoeur and Religious Language," 282).

50. Ricoeur has on several instances outlined his taxonomy of scriptural genres. He identifies eight basic forms of discourse that correspond to originary expressions of faith: narrative, prophetic, prescriptive, sapiential and hymnic forms in Old Testament; parables, proverbs, and eschatological sayings in the New; sometimes he also mentions apocalyptic, but not as originary, dependent as it is on the genres of prophecy and wisdom. See Stiver, *Theology after Ricoeur*, 120–22.

51. If it has not by now become apparent, the Orthodox tradition undoubtedly considers liturgical texts as originary, even aboriginary in respect of their often being deemed immune to criticism and change. Prominent contemporary Russian churchman Metropolitan Hilarion Alfeyev provides a succinct defense of this outlook:

> In my view, liturgical texts are for Orthodox Christians an incontestable doctrinal authority, whose theological irreproachability is second only to Scripture. Liturgical texts are not simply the works of outstanding theologians and poets, but also the fruits of the prayerful experience of those who have attained sanctity and theosis. The theological authority of liturgical texts is, in my opinion, even higher than that of the works of the Fathers of the Church, for not everything in the works of the latter is of equal theological value and not everything has been accepted by the fullness of the Church. Liturgical texts, on the other hand, have been accepted by the whole Church as a "rule of faith" (*kanon pisteos*), for they have been read and sung everywhere in Orthodox churches over many centuries. Throughout this time, any erroneous ideas foreign to Orthodoxy that might have crept in either through misunderstanding or oversight were eliminated by Church Tradition itself, leaving only pure and authoritative doctrine clothed by the poetic forms of the Church's hymns. ("Orthodox Worship as a School for Theology." http://www.kiev-orthodox.org/site/english/682/)

52. Michael B. Aune, "Liturgy and Theology: Rethinking the Relationship [Part I]," *Worship* 81, no. 1 (2007), 65–68.

53. Aune, "Liturgy and Theology [Part I]," 65–66.

54. Paul Ricoeur, *The Symbolism of Evil*, trans. Emerson Buchanan (Boston: Beacon Press, 1967), 348.

55. This is ironically manifest in the second part of Aune's two-part article, where he quotes various Eastern liturgical texts *ad libitum* precisely in order to confute prevalent trends in contemporary Western liturgical theology: It is the Ethiopian version of the Sanctus, for example, whose theocentricity or "numinous

or epiphanic character" show the hymn to be "not so much about 'us' but about the incarnation—the divine activity among us and for us." Absent here is any concern with the historical context in which the Ethiopian Sanctus acquired its extant form, or any preoccupation with legitimating the antecedent theology brought to light in the text; where Prosper of Aquitaine's tag is bound to what he ostensibly intended by it, the meaning of the Ethiopian Sanctus is found in the way it corrects the allegedly outré musings of fellow Lutheran liturgist Gail Ramshaw ("Liturgy and Theology: Rethinking the Relationship [Part II]," *Worship* 81, no. 2 [2007]: 144, 145).

56. Aune, "Liturgy and Theology [Part II]," 142. Curiously, Aune appears to return, by the end of the second part of his article, to the very positions he critiqued at the outset. In praising the work of Reinhard Meßner, he observes that the same has been able to overcome the gap between dogma and liturgy through recourse to several scholars who "have sought to develop a theology of liturgy from liturgical texts themselves and to carry forward the implications of such theologizing for a renewed understanding of dogma/dogmatics and for ecumenical theology" (159). This statement, however, is surely a veritable précis of the methodology of Schmemann, whom Aune castigates for a naïveté concerning the historical normativity of the Byzantine tradition.

57. Ricoeur, *The Symbolism of Evil*, 348.

58. Aune, "Liturgy & Theology [Part II]," 154.

59. Aune wishes, simply put, to "have his cake and eat it too," by promoting an attentiveness to the fruits of historical scholarship—i.e., to the particularity of what the traditions actually say, as if such data is ipso facto theologically conclusive, while also maintaining that the authentic interpretation of such derives from a doctrinal a priori—doctrine that, oddly, he admits to be characteristic of traditions other than those whose liturgical texts actually figure in his presentation: "For some traditions such as Lutheranism or Calvinism, the primary action is always God's" ("Liturgy and Theology [Part II]," 156).

60. In Ricoeur's estimation, language preserves the orientation to transcendence that Rahner places at the heart of his anthropology; without language, we would be reduced to silence, but language gives a way to unname even as it names. Religious discourse, for its part, provides a link between theological discourse on God's incomprehensibility and anthropological discourse on man's "transcendentality."

61. Paul Ricoeur, "Response to Rahner," in *Celebrating the Medieval Heritage: A Colloquy on the Thought of Aquinas and Bonaventure*, ed. David Tracy (Chicago: University of Chicago Press, 1978), 128. Ricoeur would seem to have in mind such metaphorical statements as would be classified as "pupillary" by C. S. Lewis— i.e., such as serve as an index of realities to which we do not have independent, nonmetaphorical access.

62. Ricoeur is resistant to religious experience, to the extent that this is taken as an ineffable phenomenon: "I have vigorously resisted the word 'experience' throughout my career, out of a distrust of immediacy, effusiveness, intuitionism: I always favored, on the contrary, the mediation of language and scripture; this is even where my two affiliations confront one another" (*Critique and Conviction*, 139).

63. "The mediation of language preserves what Hegel calls, in the Preface to his *Phenomenology*, 'the seriousness, the pain and the patience and the work of the negative,' in spite of the temptation to yield to emotion, feeling, and sentiment. *Ignorantia* becomes *ignorantia* if it remains *docta*" (Ricoeur, "Response to Rahner," 128).

64. I speak here of Byzantine liturgical language as it is given in translation. It is all but impossible to reproduce in most other languages the Greek metres according to which Byzantine hymns were originally composed; even devices such as the acrostic, which are in principle transferable from one language to another typically make for awkward translations. Liturgical texts in translation are usually rendered in prosody, regardless of their original metre. There is considerable ecumenical interest in the philological, theological, and pastoral issues attaching to liturgical translation in the Eastern Churches. See the "Proceedings of the International Symposium on English Translations of Byzantine Liturgical Texts (Stamford, Conn.: June 17–20, 1998), Part 1," *Logos: A Journal of Eastern Christian Studies* 39, no. 2–4 (1998) and "Proceedings of the International Symposium on English Translations of Byzantine Liturgical Texts (Stamford, Conn.: June 17–20, 1998), Part 2," *Logos: A Journal of Eastern Christian Studies* 41–42 (2000–2001). Ricoeur has also given significant attention to the hermeneutics of translation. See *On Translation*, trans. Eileen Brennan (London: Routledge, 2004).

65. Pellauer summarizes:

> Revelation [for Ricoeur] is more an aspect of the world of the text conveyed by the interplay among the various forms of religious discourse than it is a comment on their author in the sense conveyed by theories of verbal inspiration that take a prophet's speech as their controlling paradigm. Yet each originary form of religious discourse does name God, thereby giving rise to theological reflection and speculation, just as the symbol gives rise to thought. So the interpreter's task is to discern what theology is implied by each of the various forms, then by their interrelations, and only then by some organizing perspective that partly stands over against them. ("Ricoeur and Religious Language," 271)

66. Ricoeur, "Response to Rahner," 129.

67. Elizabeth Theokritoff, "The Poet as Expositor in the Golden Age of Byzantine Hymnography and in the Experience of the Church," in *Orthodox and*

Wesleyan Scriptural Understanding and Practice, ed. S. T. Kimbrough Jr. (Crestwood, N.Y.: St. Vladimir's Seminary Press, 2005), 264. What the author neglects to mention is that not infrequently, in Byzantine hymnography, the event being interpreted typologically is not recounted in Scripture at all. In the case of Marian feasts, for example, it is indeed not a matter of understanding "the written word" as such but rather actions whose veracity is warranted by nonbiblical texts, if not solely by the oral memory of the Church. November 21's commemoration of the Entrance of the Theotokos into the Temple (an occasion whose narrative precedent is to be found in the noncanonical Protoevangelion of James) would be an instance of the former; her Dormition, of the latter—given that the earliest references to it in the sixth century are already hymnographic or homiletic. One recalls here Ricoeur's acknowledgment of the incorporation of Near Eastern mythology in the biblical text: "Another Logos besides that of the Jewish, Christian and Islamic Scriptures has always come between the believers and the living Word of their God. . . . [Thus] the words of Albert the Great: 'Scripture grows with those who read it'" ("Experience and Language," 134).

68. Theokritoff, "The Poet as Expositor," 273.

69. Ricoeur, "Experience and Language," 137.

70. Theokritoff, "The Poet as Expositor," 273.

71. David N. Power, "The Language of Sacramental Memorial: Rupture, Excess and Abundance," in *Sacramental Presence in a Postmodern Context*, ed. L. Boeve and L. Leijssen (Leuven: Leuven University Press, 2001), 144. I have explored this phenomenon in terms of the representation of marriage in the Byzantine liturgical tradition. See my *Married Saints in the Orthodox Tradition* (Saarbrücken: VDM Verlag, 2010).

72. Holy Transfiguration Monastery, trans., *The Pentecostarion* (Boston, Mass.: Holy Transfiguration Monastery, 1990), 420–21. This highlights what, in my opinion, is a further problem with the method of Sallie McFague in *Metaphorical Theology*. Convinced, along with Pseudo-Dionysius, that all the Old Testament names of God are metaphorical, she does not countenance, however, the possibility that God might in virtue of the Incarnation have *transcended* the metaphorical distance, and at the same time *laid claim* to it. Rather than assume that the naming of God in the Old Testament is arbitrary, its anthology of divine ascriptions the product of human machinations, ought we not to consider whether Jesus's approbation of "Moses and the Prophets" as having duly spoken of him does not place their "names" in a distinct category?

73. Most Reverend Joseph Raya and Baron José de Vinck, eds., *Byzantine Daily Worship* (Allendale, N.J.: Alleluia Press, 1969), 599. For the Divine Liturgy, consider the following: "It is fitting and right to sing to You, to bless You, to praise You, to give thanks to You, to worship You in every place of your dominion: for You are God, beyond description, beyond understanding, invisible, incomprehen-

sible, always existing, always the same" (Raya and de Vinck, *Byzantine Daily Worship*, 282).

74. Ricoeur, "Response to Rahner," 130.

75. "If the affirmative synthesis in the thought of man always and inevitably relates a 'what' to a 'something' in unresolvable difference, then in the point of relation of the predicating statement, *esse* itself is always simultaneously affirmed as not comprehended, and therefore the incomprehensibility of God is operatively present. Despite every possible insight into the predicated 'what,' all of man's knowing is rooted in an incomprehensibility which is the likeness of the incomprehensibility of God and in which even now God always appears as the nameless One" (Karl Rahner, S.J., "Thomas Aquinas on the Incomprehensibility of God," in *Celebrating the Medieval Heritage: A Colloquy on the Thought of Aquinas and Bonaventure*, ed. David Tracy [Chicago: University of Chicago Press, 1978], 115).

76. Rahner, "Aquinas on the Incomprehensibility of God," 122.

77. Ricoeur, "Response to Rahner," 130.

78. "In short, a good metaphor not only carries cognitive content but it also has attitudinal import" (Mark Searle, "Liturgy as Metaphor," *Worship* 55, no. 2 [1981]: 111). It leads, in other words, to a fruitful way of living, which is its "verification"— in Ricoeur's terminology, the validation of the metaphorical wager.

79. This process presupposes the notion of truth as disclosure, treated above; what is disclosed in metaphor, according to Searle, exerts a force upon us that compels existential transformation: "The most powerful metaphors in human language are those which touch on areas of experience which clearly engage our own mystery, opening up for us the wonder and ambiguity of human existence. . . . [M]etaphor requires the *engagement* of those who would understand it. . . . It requires an act of contemplation" (Searle, "Liturgy as Metaphor," 110). Such contemplation, in turn, binds us at the level of conviction: "Once inside, when a metaphor yields up its secret, it demands a second kind of commitment: that of loyalty to the insight offered" ("Liturgy as Metaphor," 111).

80. Searle, "Liturgy as Metaphor," 102.

81. Searle, "Liturgy as Metaphor," 103. Searle blames Thomistic-manual theology in this regard, alleging that it valorized real presence over epiphany; by an overemphasis on questions of the validity of matter/form, everything else was derogated as mere ceremony.

82. It is curious indeed that Searle does not advert to Ricoeur, especially in the context of such Ricoeuresque sentences as the following: "Reflection on the way metaphors allow themselves to be played out into a whole series of metaphors may also serve to remind us that it is properly the sentence rather than the word which is the true bearer of metaphorical meaning and that more often than not it is a whole opus, whether it be a poem or a novel or, indeed a liturgy, which

carries the overarching metaphor within which a whole series of otherwise literal references will be enabled to function metaphorically in their turn" (Searle, "Liturgy as Metaphor," 106–7). An interesting contrast to the foregoing similarity, however, is that Searle considers metaphor to arise from perception, and pass through the imagination into discourse, whereas Ricoeur emphasize the extent to which, counterintuitively, metaphors are construed on the basis of having first been spoken. Searle is following Ramsey, for whom the confrontation proffered by metaphor leads to "insight" rather than "knowledge"; the former is taken to be a gift, the latter, an object of mastery. Nonetheless, Searle and Ricoeur both agree that however metaphorical insight or disclosure is manifest, it constitutes a genuine mode of truth. Citing Max Black and Philip Wheelwright, Searle argues that the erstwhile regnant positivist view of language has been displaced by a recognition of its symbolic cast. Wheelwright contraposes "steno-language" and "tensive language"—paralleling Ricoeur's distinction between descriptive (ordinary) discourse and poetic discourse: "The shift in Western intellectual tradition . . . consists in the rejection of such a bias [one that privileges steno-language] and a recognition that whole areas of human experience can only be acknowledged through the legitimate use of tensive language, which expresses the constant outreach of the human mind and spirit beyond that which is already known and that which can be put into words already defined. The axiom of logical positivism, that statements incapable of empirical verification are a non-sense, has been replaced by the axiom that we know more than we can tell" (Searle, "Liturgy as Metaphor," 105).

83. P. Colin, "Phénoménologie et herméneutique du symbolisme liturgique," in *La liturgie après Vatican II*, ed. J-P. Jossua and Y. Congar, Unam Sanctam 66 (Paris: Éditions du Cerf, 1967), 226, cited in Searle, "Liturgy as Metaphor," 118.

84. Ricoeur, *Figuring the Sacred*, 235.

85. Kevin J. Vanhoozer makes drama the root metaphor for his recent systematic theology, *The Drama of Doctrine: A Canonical Linguistic Approach to Christian Theology* (Louisville, Ky.: Westminster John Knox Press, 2005). In his estimation, Scripture itself is like a script, in which the divine playwright speaks through various characters and scenarios; Christian doctrine in turn serves as the "director's notes," according to which the drama of Christian life is "performed"—i.e., lived out. It is not clear what the role of liturgy could be, following this analogy. It seems to me less confusing to portray the liturgy as the story within the story, the drama within the drama, wherein the plot of the latter is rehearsed. It is difficult to see how one can regard the disparate genres of Scripture as a unified "script." Perhaps a more coherent model could obtain if one took, with Vanhoozer, salvation history as the drama, but made the Bible the "director's notes," liturgy the "rehearsal" (outside of which we are to still remain "in character"?). Doctrine or theology might remain as the expression of dramaturgy—the critical review

of how the script (which includes Scripture, of course) is being interpreted. One may ask whether Vanhoozer's model does justice to the Incarnation? If one follows the adage of Pope St. Leo the Great—namely, that "what was visible in the life of the Redeemer has passed into the sacraments"—it seems that one may not simply see the Bible as the "script" for the divine drama, but must include the liturgy as the trace, to use Ricoeurian language, of God's action. A text, that is, is not equal to transcribing the divine drama: Both words and actions attest to the performance of God in history. This is a roundabout way of affirming the role of tradition, of which the liturgy is an integral expression; Vanhoozer's neglect of such is the burden of Hans Boersma's sympathetic but critical review, "On Baking Pumpkin Pie: Kevin Vanhoozer and Yves Congar on Tradition," *Calvin Theological Journal* 42, no. 2 (2007): 237–55.

86. Ricoeur, "Experience and Language," 143.

5. "The Summoned Subject"

1. Paul Ricoeur, "Experience and Language in Religious Discourse," in Dominique Janicaud, et al. *Phenomenology and the "Theological Turn": The French Debate* (New York: Fordham University Press, 2000), 144.

2. John Anthony McGuckin, *Standing in God's Holy Fire: The Byzantine Tradition* (Maryknoll, N.Y.: Orbis Books, 2001), 77–78.

3. According to Scott Holland, "Paul Ricoeur's work in biblical hermeneutics confirms Bakhtin's theory of intertextuality as it relates to the world of the biblical text. Ricoeur shows us that there is nothing pure or stable about the Bible; in fact, a variety of worlds exists in the biblical material." He explains this theory as follows:

> Bakhtin discovered the world of the text to be an intersection of textual surfaces rather than a fixed point of static meaning. For Bakhtin, every text represents a kind of dialogue among and between several writings. Each text is an intersection of texts where writings other than the plain sense of the text can be identified and read. He writes, "Each word tastes of the contexts in which it has lived its socially charged life." Bakhtin argued that all existence is dialogical in this sense and always in danger of being "monologized" by authoritarian political, moral, or religious discourses and interpretations. (*How Do Stories Save Us? An Essay on the Question with the Theological Hermeneutics of David Tracy in View* [Louvain: Peeters, 2006], 102)

4. Anton (Anthony) Ugolnik, *The Illuminating Icon* (Grand Rapids, Mich.: William B. Eerdman's Publishing Company, 1989), 167–69. Bakhtin's outlook seems eminently consonant with Ricoeur's: One sees in the following quote a marked parallel with the latter's understanding of how configuration in the world of the text leads to refiguration in the world of the reader. To quote Ugolnik again:

Textual liturgics is basic to [Bakhtin's] insight. For one, the text is a
product of many voices which the author selects and presents. Dialogue
takes place within the novel, just as, theologically, there is an "inner
economy" to the Trinity. But dialogue also takes place between the readers
and the text—just as, in the "outer economy" of the Trinity, God is seen to
engage us through the medium of the Word uttered toward us, God's
audience. The text is enacted, or realized, in the act of becoming, of
continually engaging the other. That is the task to which the text calls us,
and in that sense the text "transcends" itself. ("Textual Liturgics: Russian
Orthodoxy and Recent Literary Criticism," *Religion and Literature* 22,
no. 2–3 [1990]: 143)

5. Ugolnik, "Textual Liturgics," 142.
6. Ugolnik, *Illuminating Icon*, 169.
7. Ugolnik, "Textual Liturgics," 138–39.
8. One hears echoes of Ricoeur's *On Translation*, in Bakhtin's claim that
"heteroglossia" or polyphony is representative of both language and consciousness generally: "Heteroglossia also is a model, in a sense, for how language and
consciousness work. Each of us, after all, is a complex of many voices engaged in
continual encounter" ("Textual Liturgics," 144).
9. *Oneself as Another*, trans. Kathleen Blamey (Chicago: University of Chicago Press, 1992).
10. Charles E. Regan, *Paul Ricoeur: His Life and Work* (Chicago & London:
University of Chicago Press, 1996), 74. In his "Philosophical Essay: Personal Identity" (73–99), the author provides a précis of *OAA*.
11. The somewhat technical philosophical fray into which Ricoeur jumps in
the initial studies concerns the question of whether human action ought to be
regarded (as Donald Davidson maintains) as an "event" in the world; if so, then
the proper lens through which to view it is that of just *what* such an event is, and
why, i.e., *how* it comes about. Ricoeur is apprehensive at the loss of the human
subject in this relation; he is adamant that action cannot be made equivalent to
"event," because the latter does not countenance a *who*.
12. Regan, *Paul Ricoeur: His Life and Work*, 75.
13. John van den Hengel, "Paul Ricoeur's *Oneself as Another* and Practical Theology," *Theological Studies* 55 (1994): 459–60.
14. van den Hengel, "*OAA* and Practical Theology," 461.
15. "In *OAA* he proposes that narrated action mediates the descriptive and
prescriptive actions. The narrating of human action results in a *mimesis praxeos*,
a configuration of human action in a temporal mode. . . . Because the emplotment of human action is capable of describing the various possibilities of human
action but also of displaying how actions are imputed to individuals and can be-

come prescriptive, narrative is for Ricoeur like a propaedeutic to ethics" (van den Hengel, "*OAA* and Practical Theology," 463). One thinks here of Ricoeur's own summation of the connection between narrative and life, in "On Interpretation": "The models of action elaborated by narrative fiction are models for redescribing the practical field in accordance with the narrative typology resulting from the work of the productive imagination. Because it is a world, the world of the text necessarily collides with the real world in order to 'remake' it, either by confirming it or by denying it" (Paul Ricoeur, *From Text to Action: Essays in Hermeneutics, II*, trans. Kathleen Blamey and John B. Thompson, foreword by Richard Kearney [Evanston, Ill.: Northwestern University Press, 2007], 6).

16. van den Hengel, "*OAA* and Practical Theology," 464–65.

17. These borders are mapped through recourse to the "political theology" of Johannes Baptist Metz (van den Hengel, "*OAA* and Practical Theology," 474–75).

18. "If Christian faith is itself an experience of life, theology, as understanding of faith, must retain a form which does not dissolve this factical experience." The author holds the Bible to exemplify a performativity in keeping with such experience, to the extent that it is narrative; if narrative configures action, the biblical narratives show forth a configuration of divine-human interaction: "This primacy of the biblical narrative with its figure of the divine-human interaction means that no amount of theological conceptualization should be allowed to erase this underlying theme. The term 'practical' as applied to theology would insist that the primary analogue is action rather than substantive identity or being" ("*OAA* and Practical Theology," 475, 476).

19. van den Hengel, "*OAA* and Practical Theology," 478.

20. David Klemm eloquently captures the importance of narrative to a hermeneutic view of the self:

> For self-awareness to have content and therefore genuine meaning, the self must appropriate the expressions of its desire to be and effort to exist in the symbols, narratives, actions, and institutions that objectify it. Because for Ricoeur the symbolized self always precedes the "I think," we live deeper than we think. Thinking is always attempting to catch up to itself by recovering the meaning of the self in its acts of existing, and the meaning of the self that posits its being in thinking is finite (but not yet fallen) freedom. For Ricoeur, the thinking "I" freely appropriates itself as freedom by deciphering its own expressions in the linguistic world around it. ("Philosophy and Kerygma: Ricoeur as Reader of the Bible," in *Reading Ricoeur*, ed. David M. Kaplan [Albany: State University of New York Press, 2008], 48)

21. van den Hengel, "*OAA* and Practical Theology," 467.

22. As Ricoeur notes, anticipating what he will later argue in *OAA*:

To make a narrative of one's own life is, in a certain way, to posit a beginning, or several beginnings, a middle, with its highs and lows, and also an ending: one has completed a course of study, a project, a book. There is a kind of apprenticeship of beginning and ending and of beginning and continuing whose model is essentially narrative. But unlike a closed literary narrative, life is open at both ends—whether we think of the obscurity of our birth, which sends us back to the jungle of our ancestors, or that something that is not an ending but an interruption, our death, which is a kind of violence. (*Figuring the Sacred: Religion, Narrative and Imagination*, ed. Mark I. Wallace, trans. David Pellauer [Minneapolis, Minn.: Augsburg Fortress Press, 1995], 309).

23. Ricoeur, *Oneself as Another*, 121.

24. As Ricoeur succinctly explains elsewhere: "The *peripeteia*, the changes and reversals of fortune, in a narrative, which threaten concordance, are made significant by the plot. And if we apply this to characters, something I did not do in my previous work [i.e., *Time and Narrative*], we recognize, I believe, in ourselves and in others this work of the plot. We might term this the 'emplotment of character.' There is thus not just an emplotment of actions; there is also an emplotment of characters. And an emplotted character is someone seeking his or her or its identity" (Ricoeur, *Figuring the Sacred*, 309).

25. Ricoeur, *Oneself as Another*, 121.

26. Ricoeur, *Oneself as Another*, 123.

27. van den Hengel, "*OAA* and Practical Theology," 467.

28. van den Hengel, "*OAA* and Practical Theology," 477. Van den Hengel explains that for Ricoeur only a nonsubstantialist concept of being can account for selfhood as *ipse*, for the self as a projection into the future. This impels Ricoeur to reread the grand ontological tradition in search of resources hitherto underexploited or repressed, which may fund such a concept of being. He discovers such in Aristotle's treatment of action (*energeia*) and potency (*dynamis*) as modes of being that are amenable to the inclusion of otherness and passivity. Reading Aristotle through the lens of Heidegger, Ricoeur nonetheless substitutes the Spinozan concept of *conatus* (desire) for the Heideggerian translation of *energeia* as "facticity." One wonders whether Ricoeur might have availed himself in this respect of the notion of *epektasis* an (eternal) "stretching forth," prominent in the Orthodox tradition as illustrated in the thought of St. Gregory of Nyssa (circa 335–384 C.E.). For Gregory, *epektasis* means that we are called to make continual progress in the spiritual life and in virtue, not only on earth but even beyond. The inexhaustible perfection of God is not something that we can *ever* attain in its plenitude; our perfection obtains rather in moving toward the divine fullness, instead of being complacent with achieving a given pitch, or even aspiring to reach and remain

on some kind of summit. The term brings into relief the human capacity, as created according to the *imago Dei*, for an endless growth into God, a dynamic desire that never is sated because it is ordered, by grace, to the infinite proportions of its object. For a brief overview of Gregory's teaching within the context of the development of Byzantine spirituality, see Metropolitan Kallistos of Diokleia, "Hesychasm," in *The Encyclopedia of Eastern Orthodox Christianity, Vol. I (A-M)*, ed. John Anthony McGuckin (Malden, Mass.: Wiley-Blackwell, 2011), 299–306.

29. In liturgy, not only is a story rehearsed, but the participants are invited, compelled even, to appropriate the story as their own. Is it not this sense of ontological vehemence that engenders the conflict between observation and participation? If one participates in a liturgy, does it not bring to light the impossibility of pure observation to the extent that the act of being present already affects the phenomenon to be observed, and the observer him- or herself? Few people are reticent to play a new game, or again to read a book or watch a film recommended to them. But to pray in a tradition other than our own is always daunting, and often impossible, because such an act introduces elements into our personal history that challenge the consistency and coherence of our liturgical selfhood. The act of participation in a liturgy is already an incipient habit that affects the "character" pole of our identity. To enter into a liturgy, to cross the threshold of observation onto the floor of participation—as we suggest, a dubious distinction—is to subject one's selfhood to the mediation of the story that will unfold. The liturgical self, (dis)possessed by the exigencies of narrative identity, is "neither the inflated self of the Enlightenment nor the dissolved self of poststructuralism; it is a hermeneutical self who, in religious terms, is fragile enough to be haunted by sin and substantial enough to be redeemable by grace" (Dan R. Stiver, *Theology after Ricoeur: New Directions in Hermeneutical Theology* [Louisville, Ky.: Westminster John Knox Press, 2001], 175).

30. Nicholas Lash, *Theology on the Way to Emmaus* (London: SCM Press, 1986), 45–46.

31. Ricoeur, "Experience and Language," 146n4.

32. Ricoeur, "The Self in the Mirror of the Scriptures," trans. David Pellauer, in *The Whole and Divided Self*, ed. David E. Aune and John McCarthy (New York: Crossroad Publishing Company, 1997), 205.

33. Ricoeur, "Experience and Language," 137.

34. Ricoeur, "Experience and Language," 141.

35. Ricoeur, "Experience and Language," 143.

36. Ricoeur, "Experience and Language," 145. He elaborates:

> The Torah, inasmuch as it is indivisibly law and narrative tradition,
> establishes what could be called the ethico-narrative identity of the people;

and this identity is grounded in the security and the stability of a tradition. Prophecy, in turn, confronts this identity with the hazards of a strange and hostile history. . . . Opposite an identity that could be called well grounded, one finds an identity destabilized by prophetic speech, against the background of an agonizing question: Hasn't our God died with his people? It is to this serious question that Second Isaiah offered a passionate response; for it was necessary to call on the universality of a God of history and creation if one wanted to tear oneself away from the ghost of a vanquished God. As for the third form of Scripture, that of wisdom, it serves . . . as the hinge connecting historical singularity and universality. ("Experience and Language," 144–45)

37. In the rite of Holy Communion, there is not only a "return to the spoken word" on the part of the sacred text, but a veritable mutation of the word into gesture. For Ricoeur, the act of preaching—and, one may add, the liturgical celebration in which it is esconced—is more fundamental than textual inscription, since the latter serves only for a reconversion into word: "This is the impact of the fixation of liturgy, for in Christianity the liturgical kernel represents the Eucharist, as a kind of text that tells the story of the Last Supper; and it becomes a sacred text because it founds a sacred act, which is the Eucharist" (Ricoeur, *Figuring the Sacred*, 71).

38. For example, the following troparia from the first ode of the Great Canon of St. Andrew of Crete:

> [3] I have rivalled in transgression Adam the first-formed man, and I have found myself stripped naked of God, of the eternal Kingdom and its joy, because of my sins.

> [7] By my own free choice I have incurred the guilt of Cain's murder. I have killed my conscience, bringing the flesh to life and making war upon the soul by my wicked actions.

> [9] Like Cain, O miserable soul, we too have offered, to the Creator of all, defiled actions and a polluted sacrifice and a worthless life; and so we also are condemned.

> [20] From my youth, O Saviour, I have rejected Thy commandments. Ruled by the passions, I have passed my whole life in heedlessness and sloth. Therefore I cry to Thee, O Saviour, even now at the end: Save me.
> [21] As the Prodigal, O Saviour, I have wasted the substance of my soul in riotous living, and I am barren of the virtues of holiness. In my hunger I cry: O compassionate Father, come quickly out to meet me and take pity on me.

Mother Mary and Archimandrite Kallistos Ware, trans., *The Lenten Triodion: Translated from the Original Greek*, The Service Books of the Orthodox Church (London: Faber & Faber, 1978), 378–80.

39. Monday evening Vespers, for the week of Tone 5; from the stichera at Psalm 140. *The Office of Vespers* (Uniontown, Pa.: The Liturgical Commission of the Sisters of St. Basil the Great, 1987), 102–3. Or again the following from Tuesday evening Vespers, for the same week; from the stichera at Psalm 140 ("Hail, of ascetics"):

> Stop the assaults of the demons, which are launched against me, O Lover of mankind, as they seek to put my lowly soul to death and to bring me down to destruction; bring their plans and plots each day by night and day to nothing and rescue me from them, Master; stop the raging tempest of life, deliver me from Gehenna and eternal darkness, I beg, O Christ, when you come with glory to judge the world as supremely good.

> When the books are opened on the day of your fearful coming, O Christ, and all are standing at the judgement seat and awaiting the sentence, as the fire flows before the tribunal and the trumpet loudly sounds, what shall I do, a wretch examined by my conscience and condemned to the unquenchable fire? I beg, therefore, to find release from my faults before the end, Christ my God, who grant the world your great mercy.

> You took your Cross on your shoulders, O Christ, as you went to your passion, and granted an example to us who wish to live in you, how we might be glorified with you and live; grant that we may also become partakers of your sufferings and of your glory, bearing your death around with themselves; slay the stirrings of my flesh, O Lover of mankind, and nail down its limbs from your divine fear, making me dead to the world and alive only to your commandments.

Archimandrite Ephrem Lash, "Weekday Vespers." https://web.archive.org/web /20160424054806/http://anastasis.org.uk/weekday_vespers4.htm.

40. As we will see below, the *GBW* invokes what in David Klemm's estimation is one of the guiding themes of Ricoeur's thought—namely, the notion that freedom allows for evil, but is recuperated to a limited degree through the avowal of sinfulness ("the bound will that claims its freedom by admitting its personal responsibility for evil"). Klemm asserts: "It is important to understand that consciousness of fault as my own also sets in motion a temporal dynamism to the guilty conscience. In remorseful contemplation of the past, the guilty conscience recollects itself in repentance; yet in hopeful anticipation of the future, the penitent projects the possibility of regeneration, reconciliation, and redemption in eschatological fulfillment. Within these limits, humanity is 'the Joy of Yes in the

sadness of the finite.'" (Klemm, "Philosophy and Kerygma" 56; the Ricoeur quote is from *Fallible Man*, trans. Charles A. Kelbley [New York: Fordham University Press, 1986], 140). To be sure, the apparent despair of the hymnography cited above is counterbalanced not only by the hope for mercy articulated intercalated between its laments but also, as in the Psalms themselves, by the fact that one may yet speak to God: All is not lost so long as one retains the power to *speak* one's suffering.

41. Ricoeur, "Experience and Language," 134.

42. One of the stichera for Pentecost Vespers (at Psalm 140, Tone 2), also sung in the Byzantine Divine Liturgy after the completion of the distribution of Communion. See Peter Galadza, ed., *The Divine Liturgy: An Anthology for Worship* (Ottawa: Metropolitan Andrey Sheptytsky Institute of Eastern Christian Studies, 2004), 453.

43. Ricoeur, *Figuring the Sacred*, 67.

44. For a consideration of the import of Ricoeur's thought for interreligious dialogue, see my "Naming the Unnameable(?) Liturgical (Un)Translatability and the Challenge of Interreligious Dialogue," in *Proceedings of the North American Academy of Liturgy: Annual Meeting, Houston, Texas, 7–9 January, 2016* (July 2017), 67–76. See also the probative contributions of Marianne Moyaert, from which I have greatly profited, including the following: "The (Un-)Translatability of Religions? Ricoeur's Linguistic Hospitality as a Model for Inter-Religious Dialogue," *Exchange* 37 (2008): 337–64, and "Recent Developments in the Theology of Interreligious Dialogue: From Soteriological Openness to Hermeneutical Openness," *Modern Theology* 28, no. 1 (January 2012): 25–52. Moyaert's recent work (inspired by the pioneering research of Francis Clooney, S.J., progenitor of the nascent discipline known as Comparative Theology) has sought to approach interreligious dialogue through the matrix of "inter-riting." See Marianne Moyaert and Joris Geldhof, eds., *Ritual Participation and Interreligious Dialogue: Boundaries, Transgressions and Innovations* (London & New York: Bloomsbury Academic, 2016).

45. Ricoeur, indeed, describes it as the latter:

> Two factors, I believe, have facilitated this surpassing of the linguistic turn: on the one hand, the recognition that discourse is an action; on the other hand, and in a contrary sense, the recognition that human action is speaking action. I have the impression that this is taken for granted today and that we are no longer caught in the quarrel between praxis and discourse. We know that every form of practice is discursive and that, conversely, practices are always articulated by norms, symbols, signs, not to speak of the unsaid (prejudices, for example), which is still a kind of discourse in action. (*Figuring the Sacred*, 305)

46. Scott Holland points to the work of George Lakoff and Mark Johnson (*Philosophy in the Flesh: The Embodied Mind and Its Challenge to Western Thought* [New York: Basic Books, 1999]), summarizing their conclusions as follows: "First, most thought is unconscious. Second, abstract concepts are largely metaphorical. The richness of life is found in the rule of metaphor. Third, the mind is inherently embodied. Thought requires a body—not in the trivial sense that you need a physical brain with which to think, but in the profound sense that the very structure of our thoughts comes from the nature of the body. The mind is inherently embodied" (Holland, *How Do Stories Save Us?*, 135).

47. Holland, *How Do Stories Save Us?*, 133.

48. Stiver, *Theology after Ricoeur*, 164.

49. Matt 26:41

50. For example:

> For I do not understand my own actions. For I do not do what I want, but I do the very thing I hate. . . . So now it is no longer I who do it, but sin that dwells within me. For I know that nothing good dwells in me, that is, in my flesh. For I have the desire to do what is right, but not the ability to carry it out. For I do not do the good I want, but the evil I do not want is what I keep on doing. Now if I do what I do not want, it is no longer I who do it, but sin that dwells within me. So I find it to be a law that when I want to do right, evil lies close at hand. For I delight in the law of God, in my inner being, but I see in my members another law waging war against the law of my mind and making me captive to the law of sin that dwells in my members. Wretched man that I am! Who will deliver me from this body of death? (Rom 7:15; 17–24)

51. George Maloney, ed., *Pilgrimage of the Heart: A Treasury of Eastern Christian Spirituality* (San Francisco: Harper & Row, Publishers, 1983), 21–22.

52. Fergus Kerr, *Theology after Wittgenstein* (Oxford: Basil Blackwell Ltd, 1986), 5.

53. Ricoeur, *Oneself as Another*, 48.

54. Ricoeur, *Oneself as Another*, 49.

55. Ricoeur, *Oneself as Another*, 54–55.

56. From the first "mystagogical catechesis" of St. Cyril of Jerusalem. Presented *in toto* along with the other four belonging to the set in Edward Yarnold, S.J., *The Awe-Inspiring Rites of Initiation: The Origins of the R.C.I.A.*, 2nd ed. (Collegeville, Minn.: Liturgical Press, 1994), 70.

57. Paul Bradshaw, "The Use of the Bible in Liturgy: Some Historical Perspectives," *Studia Liturgica* 22 (1992): 51–52.

58. Holland, *How Do Stories Save Us?*, 134.

59. John Donne, "Meditation XVII." http://www.online-literature.com/donne /409/.

60. Stiver, *Theology after Ricoeur*, 168.

61. Ricoeur, *Oneself as Another*, 124.

62. Ricoeur, *Oneself as Another*, 160, 161.

63. Ricoeur, *Oneself as Another*, 165.

64. Ricoeur, *Figuring the Sacred*, 262–78.

65. Ricoeur, *Oneself as Another*, 166.

66. Ricoeur, *Oneself as Another*, 168.

67. Galadza, *The Divine Liturgy*, 447, 449.

68. Zimmerman, "Liturgical Assembly," 47.

69. Zimmerman, "Liturgical Assembly," 48.

70. Zimmerman, "Liturgical Assembly," 51.Evocatively, Zimmerman proposes that liturgy, in virtue of its narrative structure, can be what Ricoeur calls a "bearer of hope." If, following his reading of Augustine, the present-of-the-future is held in the present-of-the-present, then liturgy as present action can be the effective means whereby the eschatological destiny of the Church is already disclosed— even "remembered," we might add, given the summons of the Divine Liturgy of St. John Chrysostom; "Remembering . . . all that was done for us: the cross, the tomb, the resurrection on the third day, the ascension into heaven, the sitting at the right hand, and the second and glorious coming" (Galadza, *The Divine Liturgy*, 435).

71. Also problematic is Zimmerman's interesting suggestion that it is the continuity of liturgical tradition that provides said assembly with the assurance of being liturgical in nature. One may ask, however, whether Ricoeur's understanding of narrative identity as *ipse*, characterized as this is by change rather than continuity, is not more apt. For the Church's liturgical practice has certainly varied throughout its history; while there is indeed a fidelity to a commissive, namely, to "do this in memory of me," one does not find identity as *idem*, since there has always been variety within and between Rites. Indeed, it is arguably a lack of appreciation for *ipse* identity, and an insistence on its *idem* dimension, that has caused the Churches to prove so intolerant of one another, on so many an occasion. That is, the idea that the Church has always worshiped according to a specific liturgical form has led to a triumphalism by which many an "other" has been anathematized. For thoughtful commentary on this issue, see Robert F. Taft, "The Problem of 'Uniatism' and the 'Healing of Memories': Anamnesis not Amnesia," *Logos: A Journal of Eastern Christian Studies* 41–42 (2000–2001): 155–96.

72. Peter Galadza notes that even Schmemann was wont to mistranslate this suggestive text, excerpted from Psalm 118:126 (LXX). See "Schmemann between Fagerberg and Reality: Towards an Agenda for Byzantine Christian Pastoral Liturgy," *Bollettino Della Badia Greca Di Grottaferrata* 4 (2007), 23.

73. The *Catechism of the Catholic Church* states:

> The prayer and offering of the Church are inseparable from the prayer and offering of Christ, her head; it is always the case that Christ worships in and through his Church. The whole Church, the Body of Christ, prays and offers herself "through him, with him, in him," in the unity of the Holy Spirit, to God the Father. The whole Body, *caput et membra*, prays and offers itself, and therefore those who in the Body are especially his ministers are called ministers not only of Christ, but also of the Church. It is because the ministerial priesthood represents Christ that it can represent the Church. (Ottawa: Canadian Conference of Catholic Bishops, 1994, ¶1553)

This teaching is reiterated in an Orthodox "key" by Schmemann:

> When our gifts, our offering, are brought to the altar, the Church affirms that this offering is accomplished by Christ ("Thou are the Offerer") and that it is an offering of the sacrifice that was offered by him once and is eternally being offered ("and the Offered"). . . . [The priest] can fulfil this service only because the priesthood of the priest is not "his," not "other" in relation to the priesthood of Christ, which eternally lives and is eternally fulfilled in the Church, the body of Christ. And in what is the priesthood of Christ constituted, if not in the unity in him of all who believe in him, if not in the gathering and the creation of his body, if not in the offering of all in him and in all of him? (*The Eucharist: Sacrament of the Kingdom* [Crestwood, N.Y.: St. Vladimir's Seminary Press, 1987], 115).

74. Klemm, "Philosophy and Kerygma," 60.
75. Klemm, "Philosophy and Kerygma," 61.
76. van den Hengel, "*OAA* and Practical Theology," 468.
77. van den Hengel, "*OAA* and Practical Theology," 468–69.
78. Klemm, "Philosophy and Kerygma," 65.
79. For Klemm, one must reckon with the power of the Bible to open up a space for encounter with God that can be surveyed, but not bordered, by means of philosophical terminology. It is irrational, on this view, to deny that there are phenomena that are essentially nonrational. Ambiguities remain, however, as to whether this hermeneutic ultimately equates to an apologia for all religious texts; is not the limit-expression/limit-experience dynamic also to be found in the religious reading of the Qur'an or Vedas, for example, which like Scripture "intend the infinite source and goal of any possible mode of being because they possess a reference to God within them"? (Klemm, "Philosophy and Kerygma," 62). These texts also initiate a refiguration of life in their reading communities based on the figures of the ineffable represented therein. If the Bible does not hold a monopoly on limit-expressions, therefore, theology must presumably honor the testimony

to limit-experience issuing from other quarters. The question that then arises is the following: Does the specificity of the limit-expression determine the content of its corollary experience, or does the same experience surge forth from diverse sources? And how, indeed, is the affair to be arbitrated?

80. Louis-Marie Chauvet, "The Broken Bread as Theological Figure of Eucharistic Presence," in *Sacramental Presence in a Postmodern Context*, ed. L. Boeve and L. Leijssen (Leuven: Leuven University Press, 2001), 253. There can never be a complete synthesis, moreover, of these categories: "Would not the keeping of a distance between the confession of faith and the result of phenomenological mediation be in fact the condition for the eucharist not to become an idol?" ("Broken Bread as Theological Figure," 256).

81. Chauvet, "The Broken Bread as Theological Figure," 257.

82. Ricoeur, *Oneself as Another*, 329.

83. McGuckin writes eloquently of "the strange and paradoxical ways of a God who, with the world's salvation in the balance, chose a simple and innocent heart which was ready to say to him: 'Let it be done in me, as I am your servant.'" The Theotokos, he continues, is "glorious in her virginity, but even more glorious in that virginity of her faith whereby she had moved the heart of God himself to intervene for the salvation of Israel and the whole world" (*The Orthodox Church: An Introduction to Its History, Doctrine, and Spiritual Culture*, 217).

84. Ugolnik, "Textual Liturgics," 138–39.

85. Ricoeur, *Oneself as Another*, 330. David Klemm explains this dynamic, in discussing how biblical reading transforms the reader: the naming of God inverts the normal pattern of reading, since instead of my interpreting him, he ends up interpreting me. What I feel in the process, moreover, also bears upon how I act post factum, since metaphor effects both affective and cognitive disclosure: "In the act of appropriating the specifically metaphorical level of meaning—in which the 'I' claims the emergent meaning as its own and is restructured affectively accordingly—the real possibility for a positive change of heart appears" (Klemm, "Philosophy and Kerygma," 64).

86. Ricoeur, *Oneself as Another*, 351–55.

87. *Oration XXVII (First Theological Oration)*, ¶ 285, in Philip Schaff and Henry Wace, eds., *Cyril of Jerusalem, Gregory Nazianzen*, Nicene and Post-Nicene Fathers: Second Series (Peabody, Mass.: Hendrickson Publishers, 2004), 579.

6. Truth as Attestation

1. While postmodern philosophy is often accused of fomenting a dangerous "perspectivism" with regard to truth claims, Dan R. Stiver argues that this is in fact not the case. Rather, the idea that the only alternative to a total knowledge is utter relativism, is itself a modern and not a postmodern assumption. Postmod-

ernism instead presumes that agreement on truth can be obtained, but never comprehensively or definitively: never with an objectivity that is not subjectively situated. Contemporary truth-claims thus operate in a different mode than their modern predecessors in that they pass through traditions rather than around them. (*The Philosophy of Religious Language: Sign, Symbol and Story* [Malden, Mass.: Blackwell Publishers, 1996], 211–12).

2. Dan R. Stiver, *Theology after Ricoeur: New Directions in Hermeneutical Theology* (Louisville, Ky.: Westminster John Knox Press, 2001), 197.

3. Paul Ricoeur, *Oneself as Another*, trans. Kathleen Blamey (Chicago: University of Chicago Press, 1992), 21.

4. John van den Hengel, "Paul Ricoeur's *Oneself as Another* and Practical Theology," *Theological Studies* 55 (1994), 471. On the same page the author remarks further: "But in attestation the self expresses the assurance that, in spite of suspicion, meaning and the self are possible. Truth here is not necessarily verifiable truth. Attestation is the self in its commitment to the world. Attestation is the self as Care."

5. Jean Ladrière, "Meaning and Truth in Theology," in *The Linguistic Turn and Contemporary Theology: Essays on the Theme with an Introduction by Michael J. Scanlon*, ed. George Kilcourse, Current Issues in Theology 2 (Macon, Ga.: Catholic Theological Society of America, 1987), 9.

6. Friedrich Nietzsche, *The Portable Nietzsche*, trans. and ed. Walter Kaufmann (New York: Penguin, 1977), 458.

7. David Novak, "Talking with Christians: Musings of a Jewish Theology," in *Talking with Christians: Musings of a Jewish Theologian* (Grand Rapids, Mich.: Wm B. Eerdmans, 2005), 232.

8. Ladrière, "Meaning and Truth in Theology," 11.

9. Ladrière, "Meaning and Truth in Theology," 11.

10. Paul Ricoeur, *From Text to Action: Essays in Hermeneutics, II*, trans. Kathleen Blamey and John B. Thompson, foreword by Richard Kearney (Evanston, Ill.: Northwestern University Press, 2007), 89–104.

11. Ladrière, "Meaning and Truth in Theology," 15.

12. C. S. Lewis, *The Collected Letters of C. S. Lewis, Volume 2*, ed. Walter Hooper (San Francisco: Harper, 2004), 176.

13. We should add, however, that for Ladrière even the descriptive language of theology has ontological vehemence, to the extent that constative utterances themselves have illocutionary force and therefore imply a commitment on the part of the utterer: there is no pure distinction between such utterances and obviously performative utterances since assertions imply the existential commitment, "I believe this." He writes, "And so it appears that in the case of the most simple statement, as well in the cases of overt self-implications, there is some form of implication of the subject, who compromises himself, so to speak, by the way in

which he interprets the state of affairs to which his assertion refers. The speaker is not neutral with respect to the situation which he describes" (Ladrière, "Meaning and Truth in Theology," 3).

14. Paul Ricoeur, *Essays on Biblical Interpretation*, ed. Lewis S. Mudge (Philadelphia: Fortress Press, 1980), 129–30.

15. Possibly because of Ricoeur's wish to make OAA an autonomous philosophical discourse, there is no reprise there of this important theme. Van den Hengel remarks, apropos of the specificity of the religious witness: "Attestation links the witness and the conviction: it is the self enjoined and challenged to be the bearer of a promise or hope. But philosophy cannot cross the broad ditch from the idea of the absolute to the investment of a moment of history with an absolute character. Christian theology does" (van den Hengel, "*OAA* and Practical Theology," 474).

16. Stiver, *Theology after Ricoeur*, 217.

17. Paul Ricoeur, *Figuring the Sacred: Religion, Narrative and Imagination*, ed. Mark I. Wallace, trans. David Pellauer (Minneapolis, Minn.: Augsburg Fortress Press, 1995), 222. DavidKlemm neatly summarizes Ricoeur's claim:

> Literary or poetic texts overturn the reference of descriptive texts to an actual world and manifest in its place a possible world as a redescription of the actual world. They do so through the metaphorical process at the level of the text: the "is not" of the literal meaning evokes an "is like" of figurative meaning, which projects a network of meaningful connections—a "world of the text"—as horizon for a possible "mode of being." In other words, through the metaphorical process the poetic text is a model of the imagination that has the capacity to redescribe reality in the mode of possibility through semantic innovation. ("Philosophy and Kerygma: Ricoeur as Reader of the Bible," in *Reading Ricoeur*, ed. David M. Kaplan [Albany: State University of New York Press, 2008], 62)

18. Stiver, *Theology after Ricoeur*, 225.

19. van den Hengel, "*OAA* and Practical Theology," 471.

20. Stiver, *Theology after Ricoeur*, 205.

21. Anselm's own dictum was "*credo ut intelligam*"—"I *believe* in order to understand." See the illuminating discussion of his legacy in Paul Vincent Spade, "Medieval Philosophy," in *The Oxford Illustrated History of Western Philosophy*, ed. Anthony Kenny (Oxford: Oxford University Press, 1993), 76–82.

22. Paul Ricoeur, *The Course of Recognition*, trans. David Pellauer (Cambridge, Mass.: Harvard University Press, 2006), 248.

23. Ricoeur, *The Course of Recognition*, 251.

24. Ricoeur, *The Course of Recognition*, 219.

25. "The paradox of the gift and the gift in return will constitute in this regard the polemical site par excellence where the unilateralness of agape will be

able to exercise its critical function with regard to a logic of reciprocity that transcends the discrete acts of individuals in the situation of an exchange of gifts. In this way the ground will be cleared for an interpretation of the mutuality of the gift founded on the idea of symbolic recognition" (Ricoeur, *The Course of Recognition*, 219–20).

26. Christina Gschwandtner, *Postmodern Apologetics? Arguments for God in Contemporary Philosophy* [New York: Fordham University Press, 2013], 119.

27. Gschwandtner, *Postmodern Apologetics*, 120.

28. Martin Blanchard, review of *The Course of Recognition*, by Paul Ricoeur, trans. David Pellauer, *Ethics* 117, no. 2 (January 2007): 375.

29. David Bentley Hart, *The Beauty of the Infinite: The Aesthetics of Christian Truth* (Grand Rapids, Mich.: Eerdmans, 2003), 132. In this connection Hart observes that "the Christian understanding of God as Trinity, without need of the world even for his determination as difference, relatedness, or manifestation, for the first time confronted Western thought with a genuine discourse of transcendence. . . . The event of being, for beings, is a gift in an absolute sense, into whose mysteries no *scala naturae* by itself grants us proper entry" (Hart, *Beauty of the Infinite*, 130–31).

30. Ricoeur, *The Course of Recognition*, 251.

31. Ricoeur, *The Course of Recognition*, 243.

32. Thus the Byzantine Rite Liturgy of the Presanctified Gifts boldly exclaims, "[You] have revealed to us the service of this liturgy" (Most Reverend Joseph Raya and Baron José de Vinck, eds., *Byzantine Daily Worship* [Allendale, N.J.: Alleluia Press, 1969], 381).

33. John Anthony McGuckin, ed., *The Encyclopedia of Eastern Orthodox Christianity, Vol. II (N-Z)* (Malden, Mass.: Wiley-Blackwell, 2011), 444.

34. Ricoeur, *Figuring the Sacred*, 262–75.

35. Ricoeur, *The Course of Recognition*, 261, 263.

36. See the helpful overview of the importance of the face to Lévinas, in Gschwandtner, *Postmodern Apologetics*, 44–45.

37. Ricoeur, *The Course of Recognition*, 256.

38. Ricoeur, *The Course of Recognition*, 256–57.

39. Raya and de Vinck, *Byzantine Daily Worship*, 601.

7. Liturgical Time, Narrative, Memory, and History

1. In this, we hopefully are not far from the approach of Ricoeur himself, who similarly—for example, in his rehearsal of recent conversations in "Ordinary Language Philosophy" in the opening studies of *Oneself as Another*, trans. Kathleen Blamey (Chicago: University of Chicago Press, 1992)—seeks to root his own reflections in an intellectually hospitable climate. Of course, the reader will have to judge the extent to which the debate described presently is, in point of fact, favorable to the Ricoeurian intervention I propose.

2. Michael B. Aune, "Liturgy and Theology: Rethinking the Relationship [Part I]," *Worship* 81, no. 1 (2007), 47–48.

3. Robert F. Taft, *Beyond East and West: Problems in Liturgical Understanding* (Rome: Pontifical Oriental Institute, 1997), x.

4. Aune, "Liturgy and Theology [Part I]," 48.

5. Donald Marshall's consideration is that "it would be premature to 'review,' still less to judge a book that addresses as many complex problems and carries through as subtle an argumentation as this one. I have read through it carefully, but time and study are needed for its insights to sink in, to weave themselves into one's way of thinking—or rather one's whole spiritual comportment. One must expect that much of what he says will initially elude one's grasp" (review of *Memory, History, Forgetting*, by Paul Ricoeur, trans. Kathleen Blamey and David Pellauer, *Christianity and Literature* 56, no. 2 [2007]: 373). One may hope for the eventual emergence of a companion anthology, such as those published in the wake of Ricoeur's *Time and Narrative* and *Oneself as Another*, which will mine this text's rich and varied veins of argumentation. See, for example, Joy Morny, ed., *Paul Ricoeur and Narrative: Context and Contestation* (Calgary: University of Calgary Press, 1997), and Richard A. Cohen and James L. Marsh, eds., *Ricoeur as Another: The Ethics of Subjectivity* (Albany: State University of New York Press, 2002), respectively.

6. Michael Johnson, review of *Memory, History, Forgetting*, by Paul Ricoeur, trans. Kathleen Blamey and David Pellauer, *Anglican Theological Review* 89, no. 1 (Winter 2007): 112.

7. Paul Ricoeur, *Memory, History, Forgetting*, trans. Kathleen Blamey and David Pellauer (Chicago: University of Chicago Press, 2004), 36.

8. Ricoeur, *MHF*, 41.

9. Ricoeur, *MHF*, 41.

10. Ricoeur, *MHF*, 43.

11. George Lakoff and Mark Johnson, *Philosophy in the Flesh: The Embodied Mind and Its Challenge to Western Thought* (New York: Basic Books, 1999).

12. Taft, *Beyond East and West*, 23–24.

13. Brouria Bitton-Ashkelony, *Encountering the Sacred: The Debate on Christian Pilgrimage in Late Antiquity*, Transformation of the Classical Heritage (Berkeley: University of California Press, 2005), 4.

14. Egeria, *Egeria: Diary of a Pilgrimage*, Ancient Christian Writers, George E. Gingras (Mahwah, N.J.: Paulist Press, 2002).

15. See the helpful overview of fourth-century hagiopolite topography, pilgrimage, practice and stational liturgy in the third chapter of Daniel Galadza, "Worship of the Holy City in Captivity: The Liturgical Byzantinization of the Orthodox Patriarchate of Jerusalem after the Arab Conquest (8th–13th C.)" (Rome: Pontificium Institutum Orientale, 2013).

16. Bitton-Ashkelony, *Encountering the Sacred*, 51.

17. Taft, *Beyond East and West*, 17.

18. Ricoeur, *MHF*, 44.

19. For one of a myriad of personal accounts, see Thomas A. Idinopulos, "Holy Fire in Jerusalem," *Christian Century* 99 (No. 12, Ap 7 1982): 407–9.

20. Taft, *Beyond East and West*, 19.

21. *The Office of Vespers* (Uniontown, Pa.: The Liturgical Commission of the Sisters of St. Basil the Great, 1987), 31.

22. As Vasiliki Limberis notes, even someone who had himself been on pilgrimage to the Holy Land, like St. Gregory of Nyssa, could speak of the practice as unnecessary and even perhaps counterproductive: "Gregory argued that visiting these holy places was not commanded in the Gospel: 'The Lord does not include a pilgrimage to Jerusalem amongst [the apostles'] good deeds' (*Letters 17*). Needless to say, Gregory's censure had little effect on this popular practice" ("The Cult of the Martyrs and the Cappadocian Fathers," in *Byzantine Christianity*, ed. Derek Krueger, A People's History of Christianity, Volume 3 [Minneapolis, Minn.: Fortress Press, 2010], 53).

23. Ricoeur, *MHF*, 57.

24. Ricoeur, *MHF*, 60.

25. Ricoeur, *MHF*, 61.

26. Ciszek writes:

> After breakfast, I would say Mass by heart—that is, I would say all the prayers, for of course I had no way actually to celebrate the Holy Sacrifice. I said the Angelus morning, noon, and night as the Kremlin clock tolled the hours over Red Square a few blocks from Lubianka Street. At noon, I would make an examination of conscience. . . . I would make another examen before going to bed at night, and also prepare the points for my next morning's meditation. Each afternoon, I said three rosaries—one in Polish, one in Latin, and one in Russian—as a substitute for my breviary. (Walter Ciszek, S.J., and Daniel Flaherty, *He Leadeth Me* [Garden City, N.Y.: Doubleday & Company, Inc., 1973], 59)

27. Ciszek, *He Leadeth Me*, 139.

28. See ¶ 14 of the Second Vatican Council's *Sacrosanctum Concilium* (The Constitution on the Sacred Liturgy), in Austin Flannery, O.P., *Vatican Council II: The Basic Sixteen Documents* (Northport, N.Y.: Costello Publishing Company, 2007), 124.

29. Ricoeur, *MHF*, 502.

30. Vladimir Lossky, *In the Image and Likeness of God* (Crestwood, N.Y.: St. Vladimir's Seminary Press, 1974), 196.

31. Ricoeur, *MHF*, 81.

32. Lossky, *In the Image and Likeness of God*, 199.

33. Ricoeur, *MHF*, 120.

34. It would perhaps be important to further explore the analogy between the role of close relations, "those who approve of my existence and whose existence I approve of in the reciprocity and equality of esteem," and that of the Church constituted as a community of liturgical "attestation." Ricoeur declares, "What I expect from my close relations is that they approve of what I attest: that I am able to speak, act, recount, impute to myself the responsibility for my actions. . . . I include among my close relations those who disapprove of my actions, but not of my existence" (*MHF*, 132). In this vein, one could probe the role of the "domestic church" as mediating between the individual and the "family of God." Given that the family acts as the primary organ of the formation of children's identity generally, laying the groundwork for the way in which they will, in adulthood, appropriate for themselves the collective memory of larger social units, how does family life interpret to children the phenomenon of the Church, which latter presents itself as subsisting in typological relation to the family?

35. Ricoeur, *MHF*, 163–64.

36. Ricoeur, *MHF*, 153.

37. Ricoeur, *MHF*, 175.

38. Ricoeur, *MHF*, 254.

39. Ricoeur, *MHF*, 228–29.

40. Ricoeur, *MHF*, 242.

41. This analysis dovetails with the work of Hayden White regarding the shared rhetorical quality of history and fiction. Ricoeur applauds the general tenor of White's argument to the end that history and fiction are both fictive from the perspective of their mutual exploitation of the "deep structures of the imagination." A typology of these structures suggests that the very form of a story— beginning, middle, end—has an explanatory effect, communicating a sense of order and coherence. Thus again, "the contours of the story prevail over the distinct meanings of the events recounted" (*MHF*, 252). Consequently, the force of argument in historiography obtains through persuasion rather than logical demonstration. The "truth" of history, that is, cannot be said to present itself according to a strict model of correspondence. Rather, the emplotment operative in historical narrative aligns with the various genres of literature, such as romance, tragedy, comedy or satire, and this in turn highlights the ineluctable ideological bias of the historian. For White there can be no stable perspective, no nonrelative discourse; all narratives maintain an opacity with regard to the reality they claim to transcribe.

42. Ricoeur, *MHF*, 244.

43. Ricoeur, *MHF*, 258.

44. Ricoeur, *MHF*, 283–84.

45. Ricoeur, *MHF*, 298. An uncritical use of the term "history" fosters a temporal naïveté, a perception that the past recounted is the past *tout court*. The particularly modern expression of this naïveté is the drive to unify all discrete memories in an all-encompassing world history, of which humanity is the "total object" as well as the "unique subject." In this modern view, engendered by the Enlightenment, humanity is seen to progress from what is lower to what is higher, from the local to universal, in a constant evolution whereby reason outstrips religion as the determining factor of the present and future. Furthermore, "the idea of progress is not confined to suggesting an a priori superiority of the future—or, more precisely, of things to come—over things of the past. The idea of novelty attached to that of modernity . . . implies at the minimum a depreciation of earlier times struck with obsolescence, at the maximum a denial amounting to a rupture" (Ricoeur, *MHF*, 302).

46. Ricoeur, *MHF*, 302.

47. Ricoeur, *MHF*, 304.

48. Andrew Louth, "Is Development of Doctrine a Valid Category for Orthodox Theology?" in *Orthodoxy and Western Culture: A Collection of Essays Honoring Jaroslav Pelikan on His Eightieth Birthday*, ed. Valerie Hotchkiss and Patrick Henry (Crestwood, N.Y.: St. Vladimir's Seminary Press, 2005), 55.

49. Louth, "Development of Doctrine," 57–58.

50. Louth refers to St. Basil's *On the Holy Spirit,* and its inventory of the Church's "unwritten traditions [which] are liturgical—the use of the sign of the cross, facing east for prayer, the epiclesis in the Eucharist, blessings of water for baptism and oil for unction [and] the Trinitarian doxology" ("Development of Doctrine," 58).

51. Louth, "Development of Doctrine," 61.

52. Ricoeur, *MHF*, 392–93.

53. While this is originally assimilated cognitively, as something coming from the outside, it is gradually adopted through social "familiarization" as the mnemonic matrix for one's own experiences: through the "phenomenon of transgenerational memory," there obtains a "transition from learned history to living memory" (Ricoeur, *MHF*, 394). A key attribute of "living memory" is its sense of continuity, versus the "periodization proper to historical knowledge—a discontinuity that underscores the past as over and done with, no longer in existence" (Ricoeur, *MHF*, 396). Alternatively, one can consider this in terms of the preoccupation of written history with difference and oppositions (albeit ones that it typically presumes to reconcile in a unitary narrative), versus the assurance of living or collective memory, namely, that it is situated within a continuum that it also serves to extend.

54. Ricoeur, *MHF*, 397.

55. Ricoeur, *MHF*, 398.

56. Ricoeur, *MHF*, 400.

57. Maxwell E. Johnson, "Can We Avoid Relativism in Worship? Liturgical Norms in the Light of Contemporary Scholarship," *Worship* 74, no. 2 (2000): 135–36.

58. Maxwell E. Johnson, "Can We Avoid Relativism in Worship?," 155. One wonders here if liturgical research must defer to the "history" of those who are possessors of Yerushalmi's "living memory." Ought not a canonical historiography, which endeavors to inscribe "collective memory" for the sake of its transmission from one generation to the next, be assisted rather than subverted by a critical historiography? To adapt two of Ricoeur's favored terms, must not "critique" serve as the handmaiden of "conviction"? This is certainly not to cast aspersions on the value of critique; Taft insists that "if our understanding of liturgy is to advance, we too must constantly seek to bend and negate our frameworks, create new systems that will yield new understanding. I am convinced that one cannot do this while ignoring history." Ricoeur would concur with this, and his own oeuvre displays a remarkable facility with numerous scholarly methodologies, the genealogy of which he is ever careful to trace. Nonetheless, the "our" in Taft's comment is significant: while excavating the past, Taft intends to speak to a community whose solicitude for the welfare of the Church's liturgy he presumes—a community that regards its history, that is to say "tradition," as "a genetic vision of the present" (Taft, *Beyond East and West*, 153).

59. Thus Aune states: "The problem [with Schmemann's vision of liturgy and of liturgical theology] is this—the sort of unity and synthesis in theology, worship, and life that Schmemann believed to be exemplified in the patristic period simply did not exist. . . . What we do know is that variant traditions lived alongside one another" ("Liturgy and Theology [Part I]," 51–52).

60. "[Fagerberg's] use of liturgical commentaries does not mean that this genre is objective in its point of view. Rather, they are an insider's 'take' on the experience of the faith of the church as this experience is found in the church's actual liturgical celebrations. As such they are particular, not universal" (Aune, "Liturgy and Theology [Part I]," 55). Aune's dismissal of classical liturgical commentaries like that of St. Germanus of Constantinople, on the charge that such represent the views of an "insider" is somewhat baffling, given that Aune throughout his article reprimands the status quo of liturgical theology, supposedly the result of the "Schmemann-Kavanaugh-Fagerberg-Lathrop line['s]" hegemony, for not grasping "the centrality of Christ, and thus God's activity in liturgy," for not seeing it "as an event of the divine, grace-filled initiative of God" (Aune, "Liturgy and Theology [Part I]," 61, 64, 65). Such an opinion surely betrays Aune's own "insider" bias.

61. Aune, "Liturgy and Theology [Part I]," 58. Schmemann, for his part, was certainly well aware of the existence of variant traditions in the patristic period

and beyond. But this is the point: A unified ritual expression of Christian worship did obtain in the different geographic regions of the Church. Taft explains that unification in the liturgical families of the first millennium, from the Peace of Constantine on, was "centripetal, leading to greater standardization among families" (*Beyond East and West*, 160). Moreover, the Byzantine Rite to which Schmemann constantly refers increased its influence far and wide throughout the first millennium and nearly monopolized the conversion of Slavs from around the turn of the millennium on; finally, it is today the liturgy of over four hundred million people, for whom it indeed serves as a "synthesis in theology, worship and life." Thus Schmemann would appear, despite Aune's reservations, to be prudent, in basing his theology on this Rite—clearly an expression of the "living memory" discussed above.

62. Aune, "Liturgy and Theology [Part I]," 48.

63. Aune writes:

> In my judgment, the greater need in liturgical theology is not for an ecclesiology—liturgical or otherwise . . . but rather for a theology which, by implication, is a way of speaking of God by speaking to God. For some traditions such as Lutheranism or Calvinism, the primary action is always God's. Moreover, the question of where the emphasis is to be placed has always been, at least until the past generation, an important part of Lutheran theology. To shift the emphasis toward "church" and/or "assembly" can leave one vulnerable or susceptible to a different kind of theology where God no longer appears to be the initiator of the action of worship. ("Liturgy and Theology [Part II]," 156–57)

Ironically, having excoriated the four liturgical theologians mentioned above for allegedly predetermining the meaning of liturgy apart from the witness of history, Aune concludes by doing the exact same thing, only in this instance it is the Lutheran presuppositions that are to govern the interrogation of the liturgy's historical *Bausteine*. What is fascinating, moreover, is that the "building blocks" selected for examination, and put forward as evidence in favor of what Aune deems to be a characteristic hermeneutic of his own confession, are all drawn from Eastern sources (Byzantine, Ethiopian, and Armenian). It is hard to not regard this approach as tendentiousness: One cannot critique Schmemann for attempting to elaborate a theology on the basis of the received Byzantine tradition; or Fagerberg, for consulting a classical Byzantine liturgical commentary like that of Germanus; or Lathrop, for discerning an *ordo* amidst the classical liturgical families, and in the same breath proof-text an eclectic set of liturgical sources, all drawn from the *textus receptus* of their respective traditions, to highlight the salience of a given theological principle espoused by a heterogeneous confession.

8. Manifestation and Proclamation

1. Given that there are, in point of fact, several recensions of the *GBW*, proper to specific Churches (e.g., the Vatican-issued *Recensio Ruthena* for Ukrainian, Ruthenian, Slovak, and Hungarian Greco-Catholics), I am using this term in the broad sense. As Nicholas Denysenko makes clear in *The Blessing of Waters and Epiphany: The Eastern Liturgical Tradition* (Surrey, England: Ashgate, 2012), the only significant differences between the majority Greek and Slavic traditions concern the prescription to repeat the blessing on the day of the feast, and the recitation of the prologue to the "Great are You" prayer, both omitted in the ritual books of the Slavic Churches. One must qualify Denysenko's distinction, however, by mentioning that the Greco-Churches adhering to the *Recensio Ruthena*—as well as the Russian Old Believers—actually follow Greek usage in both respects, with the addition of a significant ritual element not treated by Denysenko, and generally unknown to both modern Greek and Russian practice, namely, the immersion of three triple-branched candlesticks during the respective recitations of the first line of "Great are You." Because this book does not address the historical-critical concerns of Denysenko, but rather appropriates his research in the service of a hermeneutical inquiry, we have chosen to refer to the English translations of the late Archimandrite Ephrem Lash, generally well respected for their literalness, theological accuracy and sensitivity to patristic allusions. His rendering of the *GBW* ("Service of the Great Blessing of the Waters") is provided in full in the appendix below, and available online: "The Menaia." http://newbyz.org/lashmenaion.html#_Toc102863613. Alternatively, see Mother Mary and Kallistos Ware, trans., *The Festal Menaion*, The Service Books of the Orthodox Church (London: Faber & Faber, 1977), 348–59.

2. According to the Greek rubrics: "During the singing of the sticheron, *The voice of the Lord upon the waters*, the clergy and people proceed in procession to a nearby river or spring, or to the sea shore, and the Blessing is held there in the open air" (Mother Mary and Kallistos Ware, *The Festal Menaion*, 387).

3. Kallistos Ware notes: "If there is a permanent font in the church, the Blessing takes place there. In normal practice today, a large vessel of water is prepared on a special table in the centre of the church" (Mother Mary and Kallistos Ware, *The Festal Menaion*, 348n1).

4. There is also a lesser blessing of water, traditionally celebrated on Aug. 1 and throughout the year whenever there is a need to replenish the church's reserve of holy water—monthly or even more frequently (especially in a domestic context). See the illuminating study by Bert Groen, "Curative Holy Water and the Small Water Blessing in the Orthodox Church of Greece," in *Rites and Rituals of the Christian East: Proceedings of the Fourth International Congress of the Society of Oriental Liturgy, Lebanon, 10–15 July 2012*, ed. Bert Groen, et al. (Leuven: Peeters, 2014), 387–404.

5. Nicholas E. Denysenko, *The Blessing of Waters*.

6. Stefano Parenti and Elena Velkovska, eds., *L'Eucologio Barberini Gr. 336, 2nd Edition*, BELS (Rome: Edizioni liturgiche, 2000).

7. Namely, "Lord Jesus Christ," "Great are You" (with varying prologue, if any), "Incline Your ear"—all still present in the rite—and the following, supplemental "courtyard prayer," absent from it: "God our God, who in the days of Moses changed the bitter water into sweet for the people, and healed the dangerous waters by salt in the days of Elisha, and sanctified the streams of the Jordan by your unblemished manifestation, now yourself, master, sanctify this water, and make it a spring of blessing, the healing of passions, the sanctification of dwellings, a protection from all visible and invisible attack for all who draw from it and partake of it. For yours is the dominion, and yours is the kingdom, and the power, and the glory, of the Father."

8. Denysenko, *The Blessing of the Waters*, 77.

9. Denysenko, *The Blessing of the Waters*, 75.

10. Denysenko, *The Blessing of the Waters*, 77.

11. Denysenko, *The Blessing of the Waters*, 103.

12. "The blessings received from drawing and partaking correspond to those received at Baptism. Participants use the water for growth in the spiritual life, leading to the rejection of sin, which explains the language of the healing of passions and purification of soul and body. Divine activity penetrates into participants' homes, as the water is used to sanctify daily life, and has the versatility to be used for expedient purposes" (Denysenko, *The Blessing of the Waters*, 129).

13. Denysenko, *The Blessing of the Waters*, 197.

14. For instance, David W. Fagerberg, "Liturgy, Signs, and Sacraments," in *Oxford Handbook of Sacramental Theology*, ed. Hans Boersman and Matthew Levering (Oxford: Oxford University Press, 2016), 455–65.

15. Denysenko, *The Blessing of the Waters*, 8.

16. For recent debates on this question, see the excellent collection of essays in Bryan D. Spinks, ed. *The Place of Christ in Liturgical Prayer: Trinity, Christology, and Liturgical Theology* (Collegeville, Minn.: Liturgical Press, 2008).

17. Denysenko, *The Blessing of the Waters*, 11.

18. Paul Ricoeur, *Figuring the Sacred: Religion, Narrative and Imagination*, ed. Mark I. Wallace, trans. David Pellauer (Minneapolis, Minn.: Augsburg Fortress Press, 1995), 230.

19. Denysenko, *The Blessing of the Waters*, 195. And earlier he observes:

> It is not unusual to understand all liturgy as representative of Christ's saving work, but a liturgical celebration that so closely aligns Christ's activity in salvation history with his initiating activity in blessing waters for

our salvation today is noteworthy. . . . Contextually, the "Great are You" prayer . . . directly addresses Christ as the author, initiator, and chief celebrant of the liturgical event. The language of the prayer understands the unfolding of the event and the grace it bestows as an act of the entire Holy Trinity, with the Father bearing witness to Christ as the divine son of God, and the Holy Spirit manifesting Christ. (*The Blessing of the Waters*, 124)

20. John Meyendorff acknowledges, and seeks to quell, the apprehension represented by this epithet in Chapter 12 of *Byzantine Theology: Historical Trends and Doctrinal Themes* (New York: Fordham University Press, 1979), 151–67.

21. Jaroslav Pelikan, *The Emergence of the Catholic Tradition (100–600)*, The Christian Tradition: A History of the Development of Doctrine (Chicago: University of Chicago Press, 1971), 177.

22. Ricoeur, *Figuring the Sacred*, 225.

23. Ricoeur, *Figuring the Sacred*, 179.

24. Ricoeur, *Figuring the Sacred*, 54.

25. Paul Ricoeur, "Experience and Language in Religious Discourse," in Dominique Janicaud, et al. *Phenomenology and the "Theological Turn": The French Debate* (New York: Fordham University Press, 2000), 145.

26. Ricoeur, *Figuring the Sacred*, 176. Earlier he explains:

The [narrative] tradition also looks toward the future. In founding the identity of the people, it projects itself toward the future in the form of an unuprootable confidence in a security that cannot fail. But it is precisely this assurance, transformed into a possession, that the prophet Amos denounces when he proclaims vehemently that the Day of Yahweh will not be a day of joy but one of terror and mourning. Hence it is in relation to this illusory projection of the tradition about the future that the prophet takes his stand. And he does so in opposing to this fallacious assurance the true reading of the present situation. It is in this sense that we can say the first temporal structure of prophecy is not foresight but the irruption of real history, or, to put it in another way, the confrontation of an ideological use of the tradition with a truthful discernment of historical actuality. (Ricoeur, *Figuring the Sacred*, 174)

27. Ricoeur, *Figuring the Sacred*, 176.

28. "Pour Schmemann, le Royaume est inauguré et il viendra encore, mais il est évident que c'est la même réalité qui se manifeste à chaque fois. Au lieu de 'déjà mais *pas encore*' Schmemann semble dire 'déjà *et* maintenant *et* encore'" [translation mine] (Stig Simeon Frøyshov, "Symbole et symbolisme liturgiques chez Alexandre Schmemann," in *La joie du royaume. Actes du colloque international*

"*L'héritage du Père Alexandre Schmemann*" *[Paris 11–14 décembre 2008]*, ed. André Lossky, Cyrille Sollogoub, and Daniel Struv [Paris: YMCA Press, 2012], 167).

29. Denysenko, *The Blessing of the Waters*, 20.

30. Ricoeur, *Figuring the Sacred*, 175–76.

31. See "To the Reader of the Psalms" in *A New English Translation of the Septuagint and Other Greek Translations Traditionally Included under That Title*, trans. Albert Pietersma (New York & Oxford: Oxford University Press, 2000), xix–xxvii.

32. Ricoeur, "Experience and Language," 136.

33. Ricoeur, "Experience and Language," 560.

34. Denysenko notes the development of a rite of quasi-eucharistic "Communion of the Epiphany Waters," in Slavonic sources of fifteenth to seventeenth centuries, the exaggerated culmination of a much older custom of offering penitents the consumption of blessed water as a surrogate for reception of the Eucharist, in the process of their reconciliation (*The Blessing of the Waters*, 149–53).

35. Respectively, "Today you have appeared to the inhabited world; and your light, O Lord, has been marked upon us; who with knowledge sing your praise. You have come, you have appeared, the unapproachable Light"; and, "Let us the faithful praise the greatness of God's dispensation concerning us. For in our transgression he, alone clean and undefiled, becoming man, is cleansed in Jordan, sanctifying me and the waters, and crushing the heads of the dragons on the waters. Let us therefore draw water with gladness, brethren. For the grace of the Spirit is being given invisibly to those who draw with faith by Christ, God and the Saviour of our souls."

36. Especially germane to the imminent action of the rite is the reference in the text to the descent of the Holy Spirit upon Christ as he comes up out of the water. The invocation of the Holy Spirit, or epiclesis, is a persistent feature of Eastern sacramental rites; it is through the Holy Spirit that things of this world realize their potential to serve as loci for the encounter with the ineffable God. As we see in the general intentions, or Great Litany, which follow the Gospel, there are several petitions invoking a descent of the Spirit analogous to that experienced by Christ in his Baptism and, *mutatis mutandis*, to that rehearsed in the Eucharist: "For this water to be sanctified by the power and operation and visitation of the Holy Spirit, let us pray to the Lord. For there to come down upon these waters the cleansing operation of the Trinity beyond all being, let us pray to the Lord. For there to be given them the grace of redemption, the blessing of Jordan, let us pray to the Lord." The text supplicates, unreservedly and unashamedly, that the matter lying before the community, the quotidian element of water, itself the substance most necessary to physical life on the planet, become the place wherein God will salvifically act. It does so with a naïve sacramental realism, adhering to

the scriptural paradigm according to which water repeatedly occasions hierophany.

37. Colm Luibheid, trans., *Pseudo-Dionysius: The Complete Works* (New York & Mahwah, N.J.: Paulist Press, 1987), 135. Curiously, Denysenko makes no mention of this connection in his discussion of the prayer (*The Blessing of the Waters*, 118–19).

38. Gorazd Kocijančič, "He Who Is and Being: On the Postmodern Relevance of Eastern Christian Apophaticism," in *The Christian East: Its Institutions and Thought*, ed. Robert F. Taft, S.J. (Rome: Orientalia Christiana Analecta 251, 1996), 646–47.

39. While attending at length to the theme of creation in the *GBW* (its revelation in the liturgy as beautiful, transfigured by Theophany), Denysenko offers only a modest treatment of its remarkable dragon motif (which he takes as a synonym for "evil spirits"). This motif is potentially an important node whereby sacramental theology may intersect with theodicy. Certainly, in the wake of the tsunami of December 2004, and indeed of any water-related disaster, affirmation of the beauty of creation cannot proceed apart from consideration of its proclivity to sponsor unmitigated disaster. On this theme, see the poignant ruminations of David Bentley Hart in *The Doors of the Sea: Where Was God in the Tsunami?* (Grand Rapids, Mich.: Wm. B. Eerdmans Publishing Co., 2005).

40. Denysenko writes:

> In conclusion, the plunging of the cross constitutes a symbolic action allowing a multivalence of interpretation which ultimately refers to God's salvation of his people in the continuum of history. Christ's historic entrance into the Jordan remains the paradigmatic action that blesses the waters, as illustrated by a variety of liturgical prayers and hymns drawn from the Eastern liturgies. As the epiclesis requests that Christ would come forward again, the plunging of the cross can also be understood as an action that completes the Christological trajectory of the blessing of the waters, as the cross conveys the presence of Christ himself. The plunging of the cross became the symbolic ritual expressing Christ's historical entrance into the Jordan, a tangible epicletic action completing the anamnesis of the Jordan event. (*The Blessing of the Waters*, 165–66)

41. Kevin Vanhoozer, *The Drama of Doctrine: A Canonical Linguistic Approach to Christian Theology* (Louisville, Ky.: Westminster John Knox Press, 2005), 381. The author refers to Ricoeur's commentary on this "myth" in *The Symbolism of Evil*, trans. Emerson Buchanan (Boston: Beacon Press, 1967). See also the incisive reading of Ricoeur's Christology (and its corollary soteriology) in "Passion of Jesus, power of Christ: the possibility of human freedom," Chapter 9 of Vanhoozer's revised doctoral dissertation, *Biblical Narrative in the Philosophy of Paul*

Ricoeur: A Study in Hermeneutics and Theology (Cambridge: Cambridge University Press, 1990), 224–72.

42. John van den Hengel, "Naming the Unspeakable," in Andrzej Wierciński, ed. *Between Suspicion and Sympathy: Paul Ricoeur's Unstable Equilibrium*, Hermeneutic Series, Volume 3 (Toronto: Hermeneutic Press [The International Institute for Hermeneutics], 2003), 244. See Ricoeur's "Evil: A Challenge to Philosophy and Theology" in *Figuring the Sacred*, 249–61.

43. Ricoeur, *Figuring the Sacred*, 249.

44. "However, evil as wrongdoing and evil as suffering belong to two heterogeneous categories, that of blame and that of lament. . . . [W]hereas blame makes culprits of us, lament reveals us as victims." Blame, that is, reflects culpability on our part; lament, that we undergo suffering. Yet Ricoeur concedes that it is part of the mystery of evil that we do encounter these two phenomena to be inextricably bound together: "This strange experience of passivity, at the very heart of evildoing, makes us feel ourselves to be victims in the very act that makes us guilty" (*Figuring the Sacred*, 250).

45. According to Ricoeur's definition, theodicy requires three univocal propositions (God is omnipotent; God is good; evil exists), an apologetic goal, and a logically coherent method. Its legacy matures in "ontotheology" but expires to the extent that it can never garner sufficient proof of the ultimate triumph of good.

46. Ricoeur, *Figuring the Sacred*, 260.

47. Ricoeur cites Augustine's redefinition of evil, as a negation or absence of the good (*privatio boni*), as seminal: "The most important corollary of this negating of the substantiality of evil is that the confession of evil grounds an exclusively moral vision of evil. If the question *Unde malum?* loses all ontological meaning, the question that replaces it— *Unde malum faciamus?* (From whence comes wrongdoing?)—shifts the problem of evil into the sphere of action, of willing, of free will" (*Figuring the Sacred*, 253). The doctrine of original sin is the price to pay for this rationalization, according to Ricoeur—one that he finds exorbitant, since sin is seen as not simply preceding, but corrupting us all. Nevertheless, it testifies persuasively to the undeniable fact of evil's prevenience.

48. Ricoeur, *Figuring the Sacred*, 251.

49. "One fundamental aspect of the experience of evil [is] the both individual and communal sense of human impotence in the face of the demonic power of evil already there, long before any bad initiative may be assigned to some deliberate intention" (Ricoeur, *Figuring the Sacred*, 254).

50. "On the Exegesis of Genesis 1:1–2:4a" in *Figuring the Sacred*, 129–43.

51. Alexander Schmemann, *Of Water and the Spirit* (Crestwood, N.Y.: St. Vladimir's Seminary Press, 1974), 47.

52. See also Psalm 88:9 (LXX).

53. Ricoeur, *Figuring the Sacred*, 131.

54. The troparion of the feast also reflects this emphasis, making no mention whatsoever of a sanctification of the waters, much less privileging such as the axial meaning of Christ's baptism: "As you were baptised in the Jordan, Lord, the worship of the Trinity was made manifest, for the voice of the Father bore witness to you, naming you the Beloved Son; and the Spirit, in the form of a dove, confirmed the sureness of the word. Christ God, who appeared and enlightened the world, glory to you."

55. It seems appropriate, in light of the foregoing, to qualify somewhat the view of creation put forward by David Bentley Hart, as discussed in Chapter 6. Recall that he argued, with respect to the Genesis narrative, that a Christian cosmogony ought to perceive nature as gratuitous, its coming into being as an essentially irenic process. While it is true that the rite's thematizing of light is generally harmonious with such strains, the bellicose history of the waters sounds a note of dissonance, as it were—responding to Ricoeur's appraisal of evil as an unresolvable enigma. The beauty of creation displayed in the *GBW* is tempered by the sober awareness of its (and our) need for redemption.

56. Thus the "Lord Jesus Christ" prayer declares:

> Lord Jesus Christ, only-begotten Son, who are in the bosom of the Father, true God, source of life and immortality, Light from Light, who came into the world to enlighten it, *flood our mind with light* by your Holy Spirit and accept us as we bring you praise and thanksgiving for your wondrous mighty works from every age. . . . As we celebrate the memory of this divine Mystery, we entreat you, Master, lover of mankind: *Sprinkle on us, your unworthy servants, cleansing water,* in accordance with your divine promise, the gift of your compassion, that the request of us sinners over this water may become acceptable by your goodness and that through it your blessing to be granted to us and to all your faithful people, to the glory of your holy, venerated Name.

57. Similarly, Denysenko draws attention to the combination of imagery, with its compound baptismal allusions, in one of the variant chants historically sung during the plunging of the Cross: "Great is the cross that shined in the pool; slaves of sin are going down and coming up children of incorruption, receiving a second light and having been clothed in Christ, the pearl" (*The Blessing of Waters and Epiphany*, 72). He also adroitly surveys the striking confluence of fire and water symbolism in other Eastern liturgical traditions. Many of these have, or have had, some form of the practice of immersing fire (candles, charcoal) into the waters; incidentally, and surprisingly unnoted by Denysenko, this custom is also extant among some Byzantine-Rite Christians—such as the Russian Old Believers and Ukrainian Greco-Catholics.

58. Pope Benedict writes:

He inaugurated his public activity by stepping into the place of sinners. His inaugural gesture is an anticipation of the Cross. He is, as it were, the true Jonah who said to the crew of the ship, "Take me and throw me into the sea" (Jon. 1:12). The whole significance of Jesus' Baptism, the fact that he bears "all righteousness," first comes to light on the Cross: The Baptism is an acceptance of death for the sins of humanity, and the voice that calls out "This is my beloved Son" over the baptismal waters is an anticipatory reference to the Resurrection. This also explains why, in his own discourses, Jesus uses the word baptism to refer to his death (cf. Mk. 10:38; Lk. 12:50). (Joseph Ratzinger [Pope Benedict XVI], *Jesus of Nazareth* [New York: Doubleday, 2007], 18)

59. Ratzinger (Pope Benedict XVI), *Jesus of Nazareth*, 19.

60. Pope Benedict XVI also suggests that there is a parallel between the hymnography prescribed for the days leading up to Theophany, and that for the latter days of Holy Week, although he unfortunately does not give any specific examples or cite sources. Certainly, one discovers a series of references to atonement, to cleansing of sin and deliverance from the curse of Adam, in the prefestive hymns of Theophany, along with a consistent avowal of the renewal of human (and cosmic) nature it portends.

61. Ricoeur credits Karl Barth (1886–1968) for appreciating how evil is "not just a nothingness of deficiency and privation, but one of corruption and destruction. In this way we do justice to the protest of suffering humanity that refuses to allow itself to be included within the cycle of moral evil in terms of the doctrine of retribution, or even to allow itself to be enrolled under the banner of providence, another name for the goodness of creation" (*Figuring the Sacred*, 257).

62. van den Hengel, "Naming the Unspeakable," 259–60.

63. Ricoeur, *Figuring the Sacred*, 53.

64. Ricoeur, *Figuring the Sacred*, 52.

65. Ricoeur, *Figuring the Sacred*, 54.

66. Ricoeur, *Figuring the Sacred*, 53.

67. Ricoeur, *Figuring the Sacred*, 54.

68. It is worth mentioning that this has traditionally also been the case in the West. For a critical comparison of the traditional Roman Rite and post–Vatican II forms for the blessing of water, see Dominic E. Serra, "The Blessing of Baptismal Water at the Paschal Vigil: Ancient Texts and Modern Revisions," *Worship* 64, no. 2 (March 1990): 142–56; as well as, Alex Stock, "The Blessing of the Font in the Roman Liturgy," in *Blessing and Power*, ed. Mary Collins, David Noel Power, and Marcus Lefébure (Edinburgh: T & T Clark Ltd., 1985), 43–52.

69. Concerning the comprehensiveness of this blessing, Orthodox theologian Sergei Bulgakov remarks: "Man also needs the communion with holy water in order to receive communion with the Holy Spirit, in order to receive the Jordan blessing. In this is contained the power of deification, the union of the divine and creaturely essences, divine condescension and the human reception of God. And not only does man himself receive this water in communion, but he also sanctifies with it his entire life, his dwelling, his garments, and all his things, in order to repulse the assault of foes visible and invisible." Intriguingly, he also attests that "those who partake of the holy water of the Epiphany remark that it usually preserves its taste and freshness for a long period of time" (*Churchly Joy: Orthodox Devotions for the Church Year*, trans. Boris Jakim [Grand Rapids, Mich.: Eerdmans, 2008], 54).

70. Ricoeur, *Figuring the Sacred*, 54.

71. "Thus we have to be attentive to preserving both terms of the metaphor and the logical gap between them. If the gap closes and one meaning assumes the other meaning into itself, we are back to literal statements and prosaic actions. At that point, they have either become totally secularized, or else they have become mere stenosymbols for otherworldly realities. While the Church has always been conscious of the danger of secularization, she has not always recognized that the opposite tendency is equally damaging to the disclosure-function of liturgical words and actions" (Mark Searle, "Liturgy as Metaphor" in *Worship* 55, no. 2 [1981], 119).

72. Searle, "Liturgy as Metaphor," 117–18.

73. Searle, "Liturgy as Metaphor," 108.

74. David Power, "The Language of Sacramental Memorial: Rupture, Excess and Abundance" in L. Boeve and L. Leijssen, eds. *Sacramental Presence in a Postmodern Context* (Leuven: Leuven University Press, 2001), 145.

75. Power, "The Language of Sacramental Memorial," 145.

76. He summarizes his method as follows: "Without a keenly developed ritualdramatic sense our narratives are at best intellectual ideals and at worst sources of heteronomously imposed, introjected images. . . . If we are serious about overcoming [the Enlightenment's spirit/matter dualism], we must 1) learn to perceive narrating in relation to enacting, 2) not sever temporality from spatiality, and 3) discern the spatial and ritual possibilities of narrative" (Ronald L. Grimes, "Of Words the Speaker, of Deeds the Doer," *Journal of Religion* 66, no. 1 [January 1986]: 8, 15).

77. Ricoeur, *Figuring the Sacred*, 67.

78. "Contextually, the 'Great are You' prayer . . . constitutes the apogee of the entire liturgical rite, and directly addresses Christ as the author, initiator and chief celebrant of the liturgical event. The language of the prayer understands the unfolding of the event and the grace it bestows as an act of the entire Holy Trinity,

with the Father bearing witness to Christ as the divine son of God, and the Holy Spirit manifesting Christ" (Denysenko, *The Blessing of the Waters*, 124).

79. van den Hengel, "From Text to Action," 132.

80. Ricoeur, *Figuring the Sacred*, 271.

81. Ricoeur, "Experience and Language," 128–29.

82. Denysenko, *The Blessing of the Waters*, 196.

83. Denysenko, *The Blessing of the Waters*, 118.

84. Denysenko, *The Blessing of the Waters*, 196.

85. One may easily miss the persistent tone of *supplication* in the prayers of the liturgy, which continually hold forth the possibility of remaining unfulfilled. As the *GBW* has it: "Incline your ear and hear us, Lord, who accepted to be baptised in Jordan and to sanctify the waters, and bless us all, who signify our calling as servants by the bending of our necks. And count us worthy to be filled with your sanctification through the partaking and sprinkling of this water. And let it be for us, Lord, for healing of soul and body."

86. Schmemann, *For the Life of the World*, 14–15.

87. Schmemann, *For the Life of the World*, 15.

88. Elena Velkova Velkovska, "Blessings in the East," in *Handbook for Liturgical Studies, Volume IV: Sacraments and Sacramentals*, ed. Anscar J. Chupungo (Collegeville, Minn.: Liturgical Press, 2000), 383. According to the author, blessings other than the Eucharist itself, however, do not appear in the liturgical tradition until the end of the fourth century. For the early Christians, the Eucharist seems to have represented the blessing of ordinary matter par excellence. Even today, in both East and West, many blessings are imparted within the eucharistic context, celebrated "like an appendix"—or in some cases, a prefix—to the Divine Liturgy. Velkovska observes that while some of the blessing-prayers in current Byzantine-Rite usage are ancient, going back to the fourth-century *Apostolic Constitutions*, most are from the medieval Byzantine period or even later. The use of holy water as the ritual action accompanying blessings is common, yet an even more ubiquitous action is the sign of the cross made by the hand of the priest (with or without the actual use of a hand-cross). The cross-blessing originated in the Divine Liturgy and became a standard, even constitutive part of all blessings. On the Jewish origins of the eucharistic blessing, and the connection of blessing with *thanksgiving*, see Andrew B. McGowan, *Ancient Christian Worship: Early Church Practices in Social, Historical, and Theological Perspective* (Grand Rapids, Mich.: Baker Academic, 2014), 25–29, 184–86.

89. Certain other blessings have become part and parcel of a given feast's observance, such as the blessing of candles on the feast of the Encounter (Feb. 2); palms/pussy-willows on Flowery (Palm) Sunday; first-fruits at Transfiguration (Aug. 6); or flowers and herbs on the Dormition (Aug. 15). Aside from these notable instances, however, many blessings remain buried in the depths of larger

collections, until some competent authority decides to insert them into a given edition of such pastoral hand-books as are more frequently used on the ground. These, in turn, depending on the particular Church and even eparchy, contain different prayers and even different versions of the same kind of blessing. Such variety reflects the relatively decentralized manner in which the Byzantine liturgical tradition has evolved, with given prayers being composed, used and discarded or replaced over time (and others remaining on the books long after they cease to be actually employed, due to the obviation of the practical need that originally occasioned them). While the Roman Rite regards the *Rituale Romanum* to be an integral part of the official liturgy of the Church, i.e., not a para-liturgical devotional resource, it is debatable whether the Eastern tradition is similarly amenable to such distinctions. In the absence of a central organ responsible for the codification (and standardization) of liturgical books, it becomes more difficult to say if and when a given blessing may be considered normative for the Byzantine Rite as a whole.

90. Velkovska,"Blessings in the East," 389.

91. Joseph Haggar, trans., *Byzantine Melkite Euchologion* (Newton, Mass.: Eparchy of Newton, 1999), 145.

92. The American Heritage Dictionary states:

> The verb bless comes from Old English *blǣdsian, blēdsian, blētsian,* "to bless, wish happiness, consecrate." Although the Old English verb has no cognates in any other Germanic language, it can be shown to derive from the Germanic noun **blōdan,* "blood." *Blǣdsian* therefore literally means "to consecrate with blood, sprinkle with blood." The Angles, Saxons, and Jutes, the early Germanic migrants to Britain, used *blǣdsian* for their pagan sacrifices. After they converted to Christianity, *blǣdsian* acquired new meanings as a result of its use in translations of the Latin Bible, but it kept its pagan Germanic senses as well. (The American Heritage Dictionary of the English Language, 4th ed. [Houghton Mifflin Company, 2004]. On-line: http://dictionary.reference.com/browse/bless)

93. For Christian tradition, it is the blood of Christ that is the life of the world: "For through Christ God was pleased to reconcile to himself all things, whether on earth or in heaven, by making peace through the blood of his cross" (Col 1:20). To bless—to "redden with blood"—in this connection to apply the blood of Christ; the *GBW* announces obliquely, in this respect, the confluence of blood and water pouring forth from Christ's side onto the Cross. To build on the speculations of Orthodox theologian Sergei Bulgakov, the *GBW* celebrates the latent glory of the earth that has received Christ's life-blood into herself, and has been unwittingly transformed as a result:

The idea that Christ's sacrificial blood which . . . flowed out of His side belongs to and abides in our world, this idea is further elucidated . . . with reference to the mystery of the whole of human life, the whole of human history, with reference to "liturgy" (the common work)—both inside the temple and outside the temple, the liturgy of the world. . . . But Christ's power abides in humankind also naturally, immanently, by the very fact of the Incarnation, through the adoption by Him of human nature and the abiding in the world of this humanity in the blood and water that flowed out of Christ's side. If, after Christ's coming into the world, "the great Pan died" and all of nature changed, having become a participant in Christ's humanity, then humanity too changed, precisely in its naturalness. (Sergei Bulgakov, *The Holy Grail and the Eucharist*, trans. and ed. Boris Jakim [Hudson, N.Y.: Lindisfarne Books, 1997], 50, 56–57)

94. Reiner Kaczynski, "Blessings in Rome and the Non-Roman West," in *Handbook for Liturgical Studies, Vol. IV: Sacraments and Sacramentals*, ed. Anscar J. Chupungco (Collegeville, Minn.: Liturgical Press, 2000), 395.

95. Margaret Visser, *The Rituals of Dinner: The Origins, Evolution, Eccentricities, and Meaning of Table Manners* (New York: Penguin Books, 1991).

96. A little-known Vatican document summarizes well this sacramental Weltanschauung, in its treatment of creation as sacrament:

The sacraments thus communicate, above all, the mysteries of Christ, which means all that he accomplished on earth to carry out the plan hidden from ages past in God who created the universe (cf. Eph. 3:9–11), "to sum up all things in Christ, in heaven and on earth" (Eph. 1:10), and render us "holy and without blemish before him in love" (Eph. 1:4–5). The mysteries of Christ are communicated to us through visible signs. The sacraments are, therefore, the place in which created things are assumed in order to give thanks to God and thus reach the fullness of their meaning. The economy of divine grace dispensed to mankind is accomplished by deeds and words (cf. Acts 1:1), increasing the value of the 'cosmic elements': the human body above all; then water, oil, bread, and wine [etc.] Such elements are taken up by the Lord Jesus through the Holy Spirit, recapitulated by him and entrusted to the Church as instruments of salvific sacramentality. In fact, the grace of the Holy Spirit makes use of these for the redemption and sanctification of mankind and the cosmos (cf. Rom. 8:16–25) and for rendering the Father worship that is worthy. It is in this context that the liturgical gestures and benedictions acquire all their meaning. (Congregation for the Eastern Churches, *Instruction for Applying the Liturgical Prescriptions of the Code of Canons of the Eastern Churches* [Vatican: Libreria Editrice Vaticana, 1996], §41)

97. "Quod itaque Redemptoris nostri conspicuum fuit, in sacramenta transivit" (*Sermo 74 [De ascens. 2] 2,* Patrologia Latina 54, 398). Cited in Taft, *Beyond East and West,* 28.

98. St. Gregory of Nazianzus writes:

> If anyone has put his trust in Him as a Man without a human mind, he is really bereft of mind, and quite unworthy of salvation. For that which He has not assumed He has not healed; but that which is united to His Godhead is also saved. If only half Adam fell, then that which Christ assumes and saves may be half also; but if the whole of his nature fell, it must be united to the whole nature of Him that was begotten, and so be saved as a whole. Let them not, then, begrudge us our complete salvation, or clothe the Saviour only with bones and nerves and the portraiture of humanity. (*Ep. Cl.,* ¶ 440, in Philip Schaff and Henry Wace, eds. *Cyril of Jerusalem, Gregory Nazianzen.* Nicene and Post-Nicene Fathers: Second Series [Peabody, Mass.: Hendrickson Publishers, 2004], 861)

99. Anscar J. Chupungco, "Sacraments and Sacramentals," in *Handbook for Liturgical Studies, Vol. IV: Sacraments and Sacramentals,* ed. Anscar J. Chupungco (Collegeville, Minn.: Liturgical Press, 2000), xxiii.

100. Thus we see, for example, in the blessing of travelers, an anamnesis of "God, the true and living Way, who accompanied your servants Joseph and Tobias on their way and who sailed with your holy disciples and apostles in the ship"; in that of a new house, of "God our Saviour [who] willed to enter the house of Zaccheus for his salvation and the salvation of all who were in the house"; and in that of a car, of the "Lord our God . . . [who] travel on the wings of the wind [and] sent to your servant Elijah a fiery chariot as a means of conveyance" (Haggar, *Byzantine Melkite Euchologion,* 144, 147, 148). The God who was present to these personages in their own unique situations is summoned to manifest his presence anew to participants in the blessing, that the latter may experience the same combination of temporal and spiritual welfare. In this way, the biblical events are taught and celebrated simultaneously, worshippers educated ("led out") to exercise, through implication in the rite, the very faith they profess.

101. The blessing of an icon, for example, is extant in several versions. In one, we have the account of Christ's sending a handkerchief, with which he wiped his face, to King Abgar in Edessa; the so-called "Made without Hands" is interpreted as a warrant for the Church's own making and veneration of icons. In another, the referent is Moses's "sketch[ing] a picture of a Cherub in the holy Tent," an action taken to have identical ramifications. One episode, therefore, is apocryphal, and the other canonical. Does it really matter? A third version of the prayer actually includes both incidents in a veritable string of precedents. The common "Prayer for the Blessing of Fleshmeat on the Holy and Great Sunday of Pascha"

displays a similar insouciance toward the diverse genres recruited for narrative service. Here, rolled into a compound precedent, are the "ram which the faithful Abraham brought unto Thee . . . the lamb which [Abel] offered unto Thee as a whole-offering [and] the fatted calf which Thou didst command to be slain for Thy prodigal son when he returned again unto Thee" (St. Tikhon's Monastery, trans., *The Great Book of Needs, Volume II: The Sanctification of the Temple and Other Ecclesiastical and Liturgical Blessings* [South Canaan, Pa.: St. Tikhon's Seminary Press, 1998], 336). The prayer appears oblivious, that is, to the potential imprudence of imputing a like historicity to such a motley crew of personages (rendered as equally valid precedents for the present blessing of meat!). At face value, the prayer gives the impression that there actually was *a* particular prodigal son who returned to God, on whose behalf a fatted calf was slain. Incidentally, there is a further, theological problem with this prayer, namely, that Christians offer something like ham or sausages for the remission of sins. For if its precedent is the sacrifice of animals offered in worship, then arguably the only appropriate fulfillment of such a type is the Lamb of God himself, slain for the world, and the Christian faithful inasmuch as they, in Christ, are living sacrifices. Indeed, the references to Abraham and Abel's offerings in the traditional Roman *Canon Missae*, are given as foreshadowing Calvary. Do we not then trivialize their import by making them also foreshadowings of the Easter indulgence in meat?

102. Ricoeur, *Figuring the Sacred*, 317.

103. Richard Kearney, *On Paul Ricoeur: The Owl of Minerva* (Burlington, Vt.: Ashgate, 2004), 101, 103.

104. van den Hengel, "Naming the Unspeakable," 261.

105. Kearney, *On Paul Ricoeur*, 101.

106. In discussing Ricoeur's view of the naming of evil, van den Hengel explains: "The incapacity of language is overtaken by the opaqueness of the event. What is left is a feeling before an event in which language is at first silenced. . . . Before [such events at the limits], Ricoeur admits, one experiences a crisis of testimony because the experience is so extremely strange. And until the strangeness is appropriated it cannot be received" (van den Hengel, "Naming the Unspeakable," 262). For Ricoeur, feelings "nourish and educate" the lamentation and complaint occasioned by the experience of evil. But inverting this consideration and applying it to the subject matter of liturgy, one perceives a rationale for why the celebration of Christian mysteries has typically drawn upon the full range of aesthetic resources in a given culture. The "feeling" elicited by the experience of transcendence similarly nourishes and educates the response of faith, and assists in its appropriation. One cannot without consequence dispense, therefore, with the ritual "externals" whose extravagance—in the Byzantine Rite, gold vestments, incense, continual singing etc.—serves for a "reorientation by disorientation" toward the strangeness of the festal event at issue.

107. Richard Kearney, "On the Hermeneutics of Evil," in *Reading Ricoeur*, ed. David M. Kaplan (Albany: State University of New York Press, 2008), 78 (emphasis mine).

108. Robert Taft asserts: "Liturgical feasts, therefore, have the same purpose as the Gospel: to present this new reality [i.e., the life in Christ] in '*anamnesis*,' memorial, as a continual sign to us not of a past history, but of the present reality of our lives in him. As St. Paul says in 2 Cor 6:2: 'Behold *now* is the acceptable time; behold *now is* the day of salvation'" ("What Is a Christian Feast? A Reflection," *Worship* 83, no. 1 [2009]: 17).

109. Taft, "What Is a Christian Feast? A Reflection," 17.

110. Mother Mary and Kallistos Ware, *The Festal Menaion*, 354.

111. Paul Ricoeur, *Memory, History, Forgetting*, trans. Kathleen Blamey and David Pellauer (Chicago: University of Chicago Press, 2004), 153.

Conclusion

1. Schmemann, "Symbols and Symbolism," 125.

2. Terence Cuneo, *Ritualized Faith: Essays on the Philosophy of Liturgy* (Oxford: Oxford University Press, 2016).

3. http://www.ricoeursociety.org/

4. http://ricoeur.pitt.edu/ojs/index.php/ricoeur

Bibliography

Alfeyev, Metropolitan Hilarion. "Orthodox Worship as a School for Theology." http://www.kiev-orthodox.org/site/english/682/.

Allen, Diogenes, and Eric O. Springsted. Philosophy for Understanding Theology. 2nd ed. Louisville, Ky.: Westminster John Knox Press, 2007.

Aune, Michael B. "Liturgy and Theology: Rethinking the Relationship [Part I]." *Worship* 81, no. 1 (2007): 46–68.

———. "Liturgy and Theology: Rethinking the Relationship [Part II]." *Worship* 81, no. 2 (2007): 141–69.

———. Review of *Liturgy as a Language of Faith: A Liturgical Methodology in the Mode of Paul Ricoeur's Textual Hermeneutics*, by Joyce Ann Zimmerman. *Journal of the American Academy of Religion* 58, no. 4 (Winter 1990): 733–35.

Austin, J. L. *How to Do Things with Words: The William James Lectures Delivered at Harvard University in 1955*. Oxford: Clarendon Press, 1963.

Baggett, David, Gary R. Habermas, and Jerry L. Walls, eds. *C. S. Lewis as Philosopher: Truth, Goodness and Beauty*. Downers Grove, Ill.: IVP Academic, 2008.

Barfield, Owen. *Saving the Appearances: A Study in Idolatry*. New York: Harcourt, Brace & World, Inc., 1965.

Behr, John. *The Mystery of Christ: Life in Death*. Crestwood, N.Y.: St. Vladimir's Seminary Press, 2006.

Bitton-Ashkelony, Brouria. *Encountering the Sacred: The Debate on Christian Pilgrimage in Late Antiquity*. Transformation of the Classical Heritage. Berkeley: University of California Press, 2005.

Blanchard, Martin. Review of *The Course of Recognition*, by Paul Ricoeur, translated by David Pellauer. *Ethics* 117, no. 2 (January 2007): 373–77.

Bobrinskoy, Boris. "God in Trinity." In *The Cambridge Companion to Orthodox Christian Theology*, edited by Mary B. Cunningham and Elizabeth Theokritoff, 49–62. Cambridge: Cambridge University Press, 2008.

Boersma, Hans. "On Baking Pumpkin Pie: Kevin Vanhoozer and Yves Congar on Tradition." *Calvin Theological Journal* 42, no. 2 (2007): 237–55.

Bornert, René. *Les Commentaires Byzantins de la Divine Liturgie Du VIIe Au XVe Siècle.* Paris: Archives de l'Orient Chrétien, 1966.

Bradshaw, Paul. "The Use of the Bible in Liturgy: Some Historical Perspectives." *Studia Liturgica* 22 (1992): 35–52.

Breck, John. *Scripture in Tradition: The Bible and Its Interpretation in the Orthodox Church.* Crestwood, N.Y.: St. Vladimir's Seminary Press, 2001.

Bulgakov, Sergei (Sergius). *Churchly Joy: Orthodox Devotions for the Church Year.* Translated by Boris Jakim. Grand Rapids, Mich.: Eerdmans, 2008.

———. *The Holy Grail and the Eucharist.* Translated and edited by Boris Jakim. Hudson, N.Y.: Lindisfarne Books, 1997.

Butcher, Brian A. *Married Saints in the Orthodox Tradition.* Saarbrücken: VDM Verlag, 2010.

———. "Naming the Unnameable(?) Liturgical (Un)Translatability and the Challenge of Interreligious Dialogue." In *Proceedings of the North American Academy of Liturgy: Annual Meeting, Houston, Texas, 7–9 January, 2016* (July 2017): 67–76.

———. "Orthodox Sacramental Theology: Sixteenth–Nineteenth Centuries." In *Oxford Handbook of Sacramental Theology*, edited by Hans Boersman and Matthew Levering, 329–47. Oxford: Oxford University Press, 2016.

———. "Orthodox Tradition." In *Encyclopedia of Christianity in the United States*, vol. 4: N-S, edited by George Thomas Kurian and Mark A. Lamport, 1711–18. London: Rowman & Littlefield, 2016.

Catechism of the Catholic Church. Ottawa: Canadian Conference of Catholic Bishops, 1994.

Caygill, Howard. *A Kant Dictionary.* Blackwell Philosopher Dictionaries. Malden, Mass.: Blackwell Publishing, 1995.

Charlesworth, Max. *Philosophy and Religion: From Plato to Postmodernism.* Oxford: Oneworld Publications, 2002.

Chauvet, Louis-Marie. "The Broken Bread as Theological Figure of Eucharistic Presence." In *Sacramental Presence in a Postmodern Context*, edited by L. Boeve and L. Leijssen, 236–64. Leuven: Leuven University Press, 2001.

Chupungco, Anscar J. "Sacraments and Sacramentals." In *Handbook for Liturgical Studies, Vol. IV: Sacraments and Sacramentals*, edited by Anscar J. Chupungco, xxi–xxvi. Collegeville, Minn.: Liturgical Press, 2000.

Ciszek, Walter, S.J. and Daniel Flaherty. *He Leadeth Me*. Garden City, N.Y.: Doubleday & Company, Inc., 1973.

Cohen, Richard A., and James L. Marsh, eds. *Ricoeur as Another: The Ethics of Subjectivity*. Albany: State University of New York Press, 2002.

Congregation for the Eastern Churches. *Instruction for Applying the Liturgical Prescriptions of the Code of Canons of the Eastern Churches*. Vatican: Libreria Editrice Vaticana, 1996.

Cummings, Naomi. *The Sonic Self: Musical Subjectivity and Signification*. Bloomington: Indiana University Press, 2000.

Cuneo, Terence. *Ritualized Faith: Essays on the Philosophy of Liturgy*. Oxford: Oxford University Press, 2016.

Denysenko, Nicholas E. *The Blessing of Waters and Epiphany: The Eastern Liturgical Tradition*. Surrey, England: Ashgate, 2012.

Donaldson, Mara E. *Holy Places Are Dark Places: C. S. Lewis and Paul Ricoeur on Narrative Transformation*. Lanham, Md.: University Press of America, 1989.

Donne, John. "Meditation XVII." http://www.online-literature.com/donne/409/.

Egeria. *Egeria: Diary of a Pilgrimage*. Ancient Christian Writers. George E. Gingras. Mahwah, N.J.: Paulist Press, 2002.

Fagerberg, David W. "Liturgy, Signs, and Sacraments." In *Oxford Handbook of Sacramental Theology*, edited by Hans Boersman and Matthew Levering, 455–65. Oxford: Oxford University Press, 2016.

———. *Theologia Prima: What Is Liturgical Theology?* Chicago: Hillenbrand Books, 2004.

Flanagan, Kieran. *Sociology and Liturgy: Representations of the Holy*. London: Macmillan, 1991.

Flannery, Austin, O.P. *Vatican Council II: The Basic Sixteen Documents*. Northport, N.Y.: Costello Publishing Company, 2007.

Frei, Hans. *The Eclipse of Biblical Narrative: A Study in Eighteenth and Nineteenth Century Hermeneutics*. New Haven, Conn.: Yale University Press, 1980.

Frøyshov, Stig Simeon. "Symbole et symbolisme liturgiques chez Alexandre Schmemann." In *La joie du royaume. Actes du colloque international "L'héritage du Père Alexandre Schmemann" (Paris 11–14 décembre 2008)*, edited by André Lossky, Cyrille Sollogoub, and Daniel Struv, 157–84. Paris: YMCA Press, 2012.

Frye, Northrop. *The Great Code: The Bible and Literature*. Edited by Alvin A. Lee. *Collected Works of Northrop Frye*. Toronto: University of Toronto Press, 2006.

Gadamer, Hans-Georg. *Truth and Method*. New York: Seabury Press, 1975.

Galadza, Daniel. "Worship of the Holy City in Captivity: The Liturgical Byzantinization of the Orthodox Patriarchate of Jerusalem after the Arab Conquest (8th–13th C.)." Rome: Pontificium Institutum Orientale, 2013.

Galadza, Peter. "Byzantine Christian Worship." http://religion.oxfordre.com/view
/10.1093/acrefore/9780199340378.001.0001/acrefore-9780199340378-e-56.

———. "Canadian Ukrainian Catholic Worship: Towards a Framework for
Analysis." *Logos: A Journal of Eastern Christian Studies* 34, no. 1–2 (1993):
248–69.

———, ed. *The Divine Liturgy: An Anthology for Worship*. Ottawa: Metropolitan
Andrey Sheptytsky Institute of Eastern Christian Studies, 2004.

———"Schmemann between Fagerberg and Reality: Towards an Agenda for
Byzantine Christian Pastoral Liturgy." *Bollettino Della Badia Greca Di Grottaferrata* 4 (2007): 7–32.

———. "Twentieth-Century and Contemporary Orthodox Sacramental Theology." In *Oxford Handbook of Sacramental Theology*, edited by Hans Boersman
and Matthew Levering, 433–52. Oxford: Oxford University Press, 2016.

———. "What is Eastern Catholic Theology? Some Ecclesial and Programmatic
Dimensions." *Logos: A Journal of Eastern Christian Studies* 39, no. 1 (1998):
59–70.

Geertz, Clifford. "Deep Play: Notes on the Balinese Cockfight." In *Myth, Symbol
and Culture*, edited by Clifford Geertz, 1–38. New York: W. W. Norton & Co.,
1971.

Geldhof, Joris. "Liturgy as Theological Norm: Getting Acquainted with 'Liturgical Theology'." *Neue Zeitschrift für systematische Theologie und Religionsphilos-
ophie* 52, no. 2 (2010): 155–76.

Getcha, Job. *The Typikon Decoded: An Explanation of Byzantine Liturgical Practice*. Translated by Paul Meyendorff. Yonkers, N.Y.: St. Vladimir's Seminary
Press, 2012.

Grimes, Ronald L. "Of Words the Speaker, of Deeds the Doer." *Journal of Religion*
66, no. 1 (January 1986): 1–17.

———. *Ritual Criticism: Case Studies in Its Practice, Essays on Its Theory*. Columbia, S.C.: University of South Carolina Press, 1990.

Grisbrooke, W. Jardine. *Liturgy and Tradition: Theological Reflections of Alexander
Schmemann*. In *Liturgy and Tradition*. Edited by Thomas J. Fisch. Crestwood,
N.Y.: St. Vladimir's Seminary Press, 1990.

Groen, Bert. "Curative Holy Water and the Small Water Blessing in the Orthodox Church of Greece." In *Rites and Rituals of the Christian East: Proceedings
of the Fourth International Congress of the Society of Oriental Liturgy, Lebanon,
10–15 July 2012*, edited by Bert Groen, Daniel Galadza, Nina Glibetić, and
Gabriel Radle, 387–404. Leuven: Peeters, 2014.

Gschwandtner, Christina M. *Postmodern Apologetics? Arguments for God in Contemporary Philosophy*. New York: Fordham University Press, 2013.

Haggar, Joseph, trans. *Byzantine Melkite Euchologion*. Newton, Mass.: Eparchy
of Newton, 1999.

Hahn, Lewis Edwin. *The Philosophy of Paul Ricoeur*. Chicago: Open Court, 1996.

Hart, David Bentley. "Response from David Bentley Hart to McGuckin and Murphy." *Scottish Journal of Theology* 60, no. 1 (2007): 95–101.

―――. *The Beauty of the Infinite: The Aesthetics of Christian Truth*. Grand Rapids, Mich.: Eerdmans, 2003.

―――. *The Doors of the Sea: Where Was God in the Tsunami?* Grand Rapids, Mich.: Eerdmans, 2005.

Hauser, Alan J., and Duane F. Watson. *A History of Biblical Interpretation, Vol. 2: The Medieval through the Reformation Periods*. Grand Rapids, Mich.: Eerdmans, 2009.

Heaney, Maeve Louise. *Music as Theology: What Music Says about the Word*. Eugene, Ore.: Pickwick Publications, 2012.

Holland, Scott. *How Do Stories Save Us? An Essay on the Question with the Theological Hermeneutics of David Tracy in View*. Louvain: Peeters, 2006.

Holy Transfiguration Monastery, trans. *The Pentecostarion*. Boston, Mass.: Holy Transfiguration Monastery, 1990.

Hughes, Graham. *Worship as Meaning*. Cambridge University Press: Cambridge, 2003.

Idinopulos, Thomas A. "Holy Fire in Jerusalem." *Christian Century* 99, no. 12 (April 7 1982): 407–9.

Jeanrond, Werner. "Response to David N. Power." In *Sacramental Presence in a Postmodern Context*, edited by L. Boeve and L. Leijssen, 161–66. Leuven: Leuven University Press, 2001.

Johnson, Mark, ed. *Philosophical Perspectives on Metaphor*. Minneapolis: University of Minnesota Press, 1981.

Johnson, Maxwell E. "Can We Avoid Relativism in Worship? Liturgical Norms in the Light of Contemporary Scholarship." *Worship* 74, no. 2 (2000): 135–55.

Johnson, Michael. Review of *Memory, History, Forgetting*, by Paul Ricoeur, trans. Kathleen Blamey and David Pellauer. *Anglican Theological Review* 89, no. 1 (Winter 2007): 105–12.

Kaczynski, Reiner. "Blessings in Rome and the Non-Roman West." In *Handbook for Liturgical Studies, Vol. IV: Sacraments and Sacramentals*, edited by Anscar J. Chupungco, 393–410. Collegeville, Minn.: Liturgical Press, 2000.

Kalaitzidis, Pantelis. "From the 'Return to the Fathers' to the Need for a Modern Orthodox Theology." *St. Vladimir's Theological Quarterly* 54, no. 1 (2010): 5–36.

Kaplan, David M., ed. *Reading Ricoeur*. Albany: State University of New York Press, 2008.

Kearney, Richard. *On Paul Ricoeur: The Owl of Minerva*. Burlington, Vt.: Ashgate, 2004.

―――. "On the Hermeneutics of Evil." In *Reading Ricoeur*, edited by David M. Kaplan, 71–88. Albany: State University of New York Press, 2008.

————. "Paul Ricoeur and the Hermeneutic Imagination." In *The Narrative Path: The Later Works of Paul Ricoeur*, edited by Peter T. Kemp and David Rasmussen. Cambridge, Mass.: MIT Press, 1989.

Kelleher, Margaret Mary. "Hermeneutics in the Study of Liturgical Performance." *Worship* 67, no. 4 (July 1993): 292–318.

————. "Liturgical Theology: A Task and a Method." In *Foundations in Ritual Studies: A Reader for Students of Christian Worship*, edited by Paul Bradshaw and John Melloh, 201–22. Grand Rapids, Mich.: Baker Academic, 2007.

Kerr, Fergus. *Theology after Wittgenstein*. Oxford: Basil Blackwell Ltd, 1986.

Kilcourse, George, ed. *The Linguistic Turn and Contemporary Theology: Essays on the Theme with an Introduction by Michael J. Scanlon*. Current Issues in Theology. Macon, Ga.: Catholic Theological Society of America, 1987.

Klemm, David E. "Philosophy and Kerygma: Ricoeur as Reader of the Bible." In *Reading Ricoeur*, edited by David M. Kaplan, 47–70. Albany: State University of New York Press, 2008.

Kocijančič, Gorazd. "He Who Is and Being: On the Postmodern Relevance of Eastern Christian Apophaticism." In *The Christian East: Its Institutions and Thought*, edited by Robert F. Taft, S.J., 631–49. Rome: Orientalia Christiana Analecta 251, 1996.

Kuhn, Thomas. *The Structure of Scientific Revolutions*. Second ed. Chicago: University of Chicago Press, 1970.

LaCoque, André, and Paul Ricoeur. *Thinking Biblically: Exegetical and Hermeneutical Studies*. Translated by David Pellauer. Chicago: University of Chicago Press, 1998.

Ladrière, Jean. "Meaning and Truth in Theology." In *The Linguistic Turn and Contemporary Theology: Essays on the Theme with an Introduction by Michael J. Scanlon*, edited by George Kilcourse. Current Issues in Theology 2, 1–15. Macon, Ga.: Catholic Theological Society of America, 1987.

Lakoff, George, and Mark Johnson. *Philosophy in the Flesh: The Embodied Mind and Its Challenge to Western Thought*. New York: Basic Books, 1999.

Lash, Archimandrite Ephrem. "The Menaia." http://newbyz.org/lashmenaion .html#_Toc102863613.

————. "Weekday Vespers on Sunday Evening." https://web.archive.org/web /20160424054806/http://anastasis.org.uk/weekday_vespers4.htm.

Lash, Nicholas. *Theology on the Way to Emmaus*. London: SCM Press, 1986.

Lawlor, Leonard. *Imagination and Chance: The Difference between the Thought of Ricoeur and Derrida*. Albany: State University of New York Press, 1992.

Lewis, C. S. "Bluspels and Flalansferes." In *The Play of Language*, edited by Leonard F. Dean, Walker Gibson, and Kenneth G. Wilson, 288–302. New York: Oxford University Press, 1971.

———. *The Collected Letters of C. S. Lewis, Volume 2.* Edited by Walter Hooper. San Francisco: Harper, 2004.

Limberis, Vasiliki. "The Cult of the Martyrs and the Cappadocian Fathers." In *Byzantine Christianity*, edited by Derek Krueger. A People's History of Christianity, Volume 3, 39–58. Minneapolis, Minn.: Fortress Press, 2010.

Lossky, Vladimir. *In the Image and Likeness of God.* Crestwood, N.Y.: St. Vladimir's Seminary Press, 1974.

Louth, Andrew. *Discerning the Mystery: An Essay on the Nature of Theology.* Oxford: Clarendon Press, 1983.

———. *Introducing Eastern Orthodox Theology.* Downers Grove, Ill.: IVP Academic, 2013.

———. "Is Development of Doctrine a Valid Category for Orthodox Theology?" In *Orthodoxy and Western Culture: A Collection of Essays Honoring Jaroslav Pelikan on His Eightieth Birthday*, edited by Valerie Hotchkiss and Patrick Henry, 45–63. Crestwood, N.Y.: St. Vladimir's Seminary Press, 2005.

———. *Modern Orthodox Thinkers: From the* Philokalia *to the Present.* Downers Grove, Ill.: IVP Academic, 2015.

Luibheid, Colm, trans. *Pseudo-Dionysius: The Complete Works.* New York: Paulist Press, 1987.

Maloney, George, ed. *Pilgrimage of the Heart: A Treasury of Eastern Christian Spirituality.* San Francisco: Harper & Row, Publishers, 1983.

Marshall, Donald. Review of *Memory, History, Forgetting*, by Paul Ricoeur, trans. Kathleen Blamey and David Pellauer. *Christianity and Literature* 56, no. 2 (2007): 373–76.

McFague, Sallie. *Metaphorical Theology: Models of God in Religious Language.* Minneapolis, Minn.: Fortress Press, 1982.

McGowan, Andrew B. *Ancient Christian Worship: Early Church Practices in Social, Historical and Theological Perspective.* Grand Rapids, Mich.: Baker Academic, 2014.

———. *Ancient Christian Worship: Early Church Practices in Social, Historical, and Theological Perspective.* Grand Rapids, Mich.: Baker Academic, 2014.

McGrath, Alister E. *Reformation Thought: An Introduction.* Second ed. Oxford: Blackwell Publishers, 1993.

McGuckin, John Anthony. Review of *The Beauty of the Infinite: The Aesthetics of Christian Truth*, by David Bentley Hart. *Scottish Journal of Theology* 60, no. 1 (2007): 90–94.

———, ed. *The Encyclopedia of Eastern Orthodox Christianity, Vol. II (N–Z).* Malden, Mass.: Wiley-Blackwell, 2011.

———. *The Orthodox Church: An Introduction to Its History, Doctrine, and Spiritual Culture.* Malden, Mass.: Wiley-Blackwell, 2011.

———. *Standing in God's Holy Fire: The Byzantine Tradition.* Maryknoll, N.Y.: Orbis Books, 2001.

Metropolitan Kallistos of Diokleia. "Hesychasm." In *The Encyclopedia of Eastern Orthodox Christianity, Vol. I (A-M),* edited by John Anthony McGuckin, 299–306. Malden, Mass.: Wiley-Blackwell, 2011.

Meyendorff, John. *Byzantine Theology: Historical Trends and Doctrinal Themes.* New York: Fordham University Press, 1979.

Mitchell, Nathan D. *Liturgy and the Social Sciences.* Collegeville, Minn.: Liturgical Press, 1999.

Morny, Joy, ed. *Paul Ricoeur and Narrative: Context and Contestation.* Calgary: University of Calgary Press, 1997.

Mother Mary, and Archimandrite Kallistos Ware, trans. *The Festal Menaion.* The Service Books of the Orthodox Church. London: Faber & Faber, 1977.

———, trans. *The Lenten Triodion: Translated from the Original Greek.* The Service Books of the Orthodox Church. London: Faber & Faber, 1978.

Moyaert, Marianne. "Recent Developments in the Theology of Interreligious Dialogue: From Soteriological Openness to Hermeneutical Openness." *Modern Theology* 28, no. 1 (January 2012): 25–52.

———. "The (Un-)Translatability of Religions? Ricoeur's Linguistic Hospitality as a Model for Inter-Religious Dialogue." *Exchange* 37 (2008): 337–64.

Moyaert, Marianne, and Joris Geldhof, eds. *Ritual Participation and Interreligious Dialogue: Boundaries, Transgressions and Innovations.* London: Bloomsbury Academic, 2016.

Myers, Jacob D. "Toward an Erotic Liturgical Theology: Schmemann in Conversation with Contemporary Philosophy." *Worship* 87, no. 5 (September 2013): 387–413.

A New English Translation of the Septuagint and Other Greek Translations Traditionally Included under That Title. Translated by Albert Pietersma. New York: Oxford University Press, 2000.

Nichols, Aidan. *Light from the East: Authors and Themes in Orthodox Theology.* London: Sheed & Ward Limited, 1999.

———. *Rome and the Eastern Churches: A Study in Schism.* San Francisco: Ignatius Press, 1992.

———. *The Shape of Catholic Theology.* Collegeville, Minn.: Liturgical Press, 1991.

———. *Theology in the Russian Diaspora: Church, Fathers, Eucharist in Nikolai Afanas'ev (1893–1966).* Cambridge: Cambridge University Press, 2008.

Nichols, Bridget. *Liturgical Hermeneutics: Interpreting Liturgical Rites in Performance.* Frankfurt: Peter Lang, 1996.

Nietzsche, Friedrich. *The Portable Nietzsche.* Translated and edited by Walter Kaufmann. New York: Penguin, 1977.

Novak, David. "Talking with Christians: Musings of a Jewish Theology." In *Talking with Christians: Musings of a Jewish Theologian*. Grand Rapids, Mich.: Eerdmans, 2005.

The Office of Vespers. Uniontown, Pa.: The Liturgical Commission of the Sisters of St. Basil the Great, 1987.

Paffenroth, Kim, and Robert P. Kennedy, eds. *A Reader's Companion to Augustine's* Confessions. Louisville, Ky.: Westminster John Knox Press, 2003.

Parenti, Stefano, and Elena Velkovska, eds. *L'Eucologio Barberini Gr. 336, Second Edition*. BELS. Rome: Edizioni liturgiche, 2000.

Pelikan, Jaroslav. *Credo: Historical and Theological Guide to Creeds and Confessions of Faith in the Christian Tradition*. New Haven: Yale University Press, 2003.

———. *The Emergence of the Catholic Tradition (100–600)*. The Christian Tradition: A History of the Development of Doctrine. Chicago: University of Chicago Press, 1971.

Pellauer, David. "Paul Ricoeur on the Specificity of Religious Language." *The Journal of Religion* 61, no. 3 (July 1981): 264–84.

———. *Ricoeur: A Guide for the Perplexed*. New York: Continuum, 2007.

Pickstock, Catherine. *After Writing: On the Liturgical Consummation of Philosophy*. Oxford: Blackwell Publishers, 1998.

Plekon, Michael. "The Russian Religious Revival and Its Theological Legacy." In *The Cambridge Companion to Orthodox Christian Theology*, edited by Mary B. Cunningham and Elizabeth Theokritoff, 203–17. Cambridge: Cambridge University Press, 2008.

Power, David N. "The Language of Sacramental Memorial: Rupture, Excess and Abundance." In *Sacramental Presence in a Postmodern Context*, edited by L. Boeve and L. Leijssen, 135–60. Leuven: Leuven University Press, 2001.

"Proceedings of the International Symposium on English Translations of Byzantine Liturgical Texts (Stamford, Conn.: June 17–20, 1998), Part 1." *Logos: A Journal of Eastern Christian Studies* 39, no. 2–4 (1998).

"Proceedings of the International Symposium on English Translations of Byzantine Liturgical Texts (Stamford, Conn.: June 17–20, 1998), Part 2." *Logos: A Journal of Eastern Christian Studies* 41–42 (2000–2001).

Pseudo-Dionysius. *The Complete Works*. The Classics of Western Spirituality. Edited by Paul Rorem. Translated by Colm Luibheid. New York: Paulist Press, 1987.

Rahner, Karl, S.J. "Thomas Aquinas on the Incomprehensibility of God." In *Celebrating the Medieval Heritage: A Colloquy on the Thought of Aquinas and Bonaventure*, edited by David Tracy, 107–25. Chicago: University of Chicago Press, 1978.

Ratzinger, Joseph (Pope Benedict XVI). *Jesus of Nazareth*. New York: Doubleday, 2007.

Raya, Most Reverend Joseph, and Baron José de Vinck, eds. *Byzantine Daily Worship*. Allendale, N.J.: Alleluia Press, 1969.

Regan, Charles E. *Paul Ricoeur: His Life and Work*. Chicago: University of Chicago Press, 1996.

Ricoeur, Paul. "Biblical Hermeneutics." *Semeia* 4 (1975): 29–148.

———. *The Conflict of Interpretations: Essays in Hermeneutics*. New ed. Edited by Don Ihde. Evanston, Ill.: Northwestern University Press, 2007.

———. *The Course of Recognition*. Translated by David Pellauer. Cambridge, Mass.: Harvard University Press, 2006.

———. *Critique and Conviction: Conversations with François Azouvi and Marc de Launay*. Translated by Kathleen Blamey. New York: Columbia University Press, 1998.

———. *Essays on Biblical Interpretation*. Edited by Lewis S. Mudge. Philadelphia: Fortress Press, 1980.

———. "Experience and Language in Religious Discourse." In *Phenomenology and the "Theological Turn": The French Debate*, Dominique Janicaud, Jean-François Courtine, Jean-Louis Chrétien, Michel Henry, Jean-Luc Marion, and Paul Ricoeur, 127–46. New York: Fordham University Press, 2000.

———. *Figuring the Sacred: Religion, Narrative and Imagination*. Edited by Mark I. Wallace. Translated by David Pellauer. Minneapolis, Minn.: Augsburg Fortress Press, 1995.

———. *From Text to Action*. Translated by Kathleen Blamey and John B. Thompson. Essays in Hermeneutics. Evanston, Ill.: Northwestern University Press, 1991.

———. *From Text to Action: Essays in Hermeneutics, II*. Translated by Kathleen Blamey and John B. Thompson, with a foreword by Richard Kearney. Evanston, Ill.: Northwestern University Press, 2007.

———. *Hermeneutics and the Human Sciences*. Edited and translated by John B. Thompson. Cambridge: Cambridge University Press, 1981.

———. *Interpretation Theory: Discourse and the Surplus of Meaning*. Fort Worth, Tex.: Texas Christian University Press, 1976.

———. "Liberating the Core of Goodness." http://www.taize.fr/en_article102.html.

———. *Memory, History, Forgetting*. Translated by Kathleen Blamey and David Pellauer. Chicago: University of Chicago Press, 2004.

———. "The Metaphorical Process as Cognition, Imagination, and Feeling." *Critical Inquiry* 5, no. 1 (Autumn 1978): 143–59.

———. *On Translation*. Translated by Eileen Brennan. London: Routledge, 2004.

———. *Oneself as Another*. Translated by Kathleen Blamey. Chicago: University of Chicago Press, 1992.

————. *Philosophical Anthropology: Writings and Lectures, Volume 3*. Edited by Johann Michel and Jérôme Porée. Translated by David Pellauer. Cambridge: Polity Press, 2016.

————. *Philosophical Hermeneutics and Theological Hermeneutics: Ideology, Utopia and Faith; Protocol of the 17th Colloquy, 4 November 1975*. Edited by Wilhelm Wuellner. Protocol of the Colloquy of the Center for Hermeneutical Studies in Hellenistic and Modern Culture. Berkeley, Calif.: Center for Hermeneutical Studies in Hellenistic & Modern Culture, 1976.

————. "Postface." In *Taizé et l'Église de Demain*, Jean-Marie Paupert, 247–51. Paris: Fayard, 1967.

————. "Response to Rahner." In *Celebrating the Medieval Heritage: A Colloquy on the Thought of Aquinas and Bonaventure*, edited by David Tracy, 126–34. Chicago: University of Chicago Press, 1978.

————. *The Rule of Metaphor: Multi-Disciplinary Studies of the Creation of Meaning in Language*. Translated by Robert Czerny, Kathleen McLaughlin, and John Costello. Toronto: University of Toronto Press, 1977.

————. "The Self in the Mirror of the Scriptures." Translated by David Pellauer. In *The Whole and Divided Self*, edited by David E. Aune and John McCarthy, 201–20. New York: Crossroad Publishing Company, 1997.

————. *The Symbolism of Evil*. Translated by Emerson Buchanan. Boston: Beacon Press, 1967.

————. *Time and Narrative, Volume 1*. Translated by Kathleen McLaughlin and David Pellauer. Chicago: University of Chicago Press, 1984.

————. *Time and Narrative, Volume 2*. Translated by Kathleen McLaughlin and David Pellauer. Chicago: University of Chicago Press, 1985.

Ricoeur, Paul, David Pellauer, and John McCarthy. "Conversation." In *The Whole and Divided Self*, edited by David E. Aune and John McCarthy, 221–43. New York: Crossroad Publishing Company, 1997.

Roberson, Ronald. *The Eastern Christian Churches: A Brief Survey*. 7th edition. Rome: Edizioni "Orientalia Christiana," 2008.

Schaff, Philip, and Henry Wace, eds. *Cyril of Jerusalem, Gregory Nazianzen*. Nicene and Post-Nicene Fathers: Second Series. Peabody, Mass.: Hendrickson Publishers, 2004.

Schmemann, Alexander. *The Eucharist: Sacrament of the Kingdom*. Crestwood, N.Y.: St. Vladimir's Seminary Press, 1987.

————. *For the Life of the World*. Crestwood, N.Y.: St. Vladimir's Seminary Press, 2002.

————. *Introduction to Liturgical Theology*. Translated by Asheleigh E. Moorhouse. Bangor, Maine: Faith Press, 1970.

———. "Liturgical Theology, Theology of Liturgy, and Liturgical Reform." In *Liturgy and Tradition: Theological Reflections of Alexander Schmemann*, edited by Thomas J. Fisch. Crestwood, N.Y.: St. Vladimir's Seminary Press, 1990.

———. *Of Water and the Spirit*. Crestwood, N.Y.: St. Vladimir's Seminary Press, 1974.

———. "Symbols and Symbolism in the Byzantine Liturgy: Liturgical Symbols and Their Theological Interpretation." In *Liturgy and Tradition: Theological Reflections of Alexander Schmemann*, edited by Thomas J. Fisch, 115–28. Crestwood, N.Y.: St. Vladimir's Seminary Press, 1990.

Schultz, Hans-Joachim. *Byzantine Liturgy: Symbolic Structure and Faith Expression*. Translated by Matthew J. O'Connell. New York: Pueblo Publishing Company, 1986.

Searle, Mark. "*Fons Vitae*: A Case Study in the Use of Liturgy as a Theological Source." In *Fountain of Life*, edited by Gerard Austin, 217–42. Washington, DC: Pastoral Press, 1991.

———. "Liturgy as Metaphor." *Worship* 55, no. 2 (1981): 98–120.

Serra, Dominic E. "The Blessing of Baptismal Water at the Paschal Vigil: Ancient Texts and Modern Revisions." *Worship* 64, no. 2 (March 1990): 142–56.

Spade, Paul Vincent. "Medieval Philosophy." In *The Oxford Illustrated History of Western Philosophy*, edited by Anthony Kenny, 55–105. Oxford: Oxford University Press, 1993.

Spinks, Bryan D., ed. *The Place of Christ in Liturgical Prayer: Trinity, Christology, and Liturgical Theology*. Collegeville, Minn.: Liturgical Press, 2008.

St. Tikhon's Monastery, trans. *The Great Book of Needs, Volume II: The Sanctification of the Temple and Other Ecclesiastical and Liturgical Blessings*. South Canaan, Pa.: St. Tikhon's Seminary Press, 1998.

Stiver, Dan R. *The Philosophy of Religious Language: Sign, Symbol and Story*. Malden, Mass.: Blackwell Publishers, 1996.

———. *Ricoeur and Theology*. London: Bloomsbury, 2012.

———. *Theology after Ricoeur: New Directions in Hermeneutical Theology*. Louisville, Ky.: Westminster John Knox Press, 2001.

Stock, Alex. "The Blessing of the Font in the Roman Liturgy." In *Blessing and Power*, edited by Mary Collins, David Noel Power, and Marcus Lefébure, 43–52. Edinburgh: T & T Clark Ltd., 1985.

Stosur, David A. "Liturgy and (Post)Modernity: A Narrative Response to Guardini's Challenge." *Worship* 77, no. 1 (January 2003): 22–41.

Stringer, Martin. "Text, Context and Performance: Hermeneutics and the Study of Worship." *Scottish Journal of Theology* 53, no. 3 (2000): 365–79.

Taft, Robert F. *Beyond East and West: Problems in Liturgical Understanding*. Rome: Pontifical Oriental Institute, 1997.

———. *The Byzantine Rite: A Short History*. American Essays in Liturgy Series. Collegeville, Minn.: Liturgical Press, 1992.

———. *The Great Entrance: A History of the Transfer of Gifts and Other Pre-Anaphoral Rites of the Liturgy of St. John Chrysostom*. Rome: Orientalia Christiana Periodica, 1975.

———. "The Liturgical Enterprise Twenty-Five Years after Alexander Schmemann (1921–1983): The Man and His Heritage." *St. Vladimir's Theological Quarterly* 53, no. 2–3 (2009): 139–63.

———. "Mass without Consecration? The Historic Agreement on the Eucharist between the Catholic Church and the Assyrian Church of the East Promulgated 26 October 2001." *Worship* 77, no. 6 (2003): 482–509.

———. "The Problem of 'Uniatism' and the 'Healing of Memories': Anamnesis not Amnesia." *Logos: A Journal of Eastern Christian Studies* 41–42 (2000–2001): 155–96.

———. "What Is a Christian Feast? A Reflection." *Worship* 83, no. 1 (2009): 2–18.

Theokritoff, Elizabeth. "The Poet as Expositor in the Golden Age of Byzantine Hymnography and in the Experience of the Church." In *Orthodox and Wesleyan Scriptural Understanding and Practice*, edited by S. T. Kimbrough Jr., 259–76. Crestwood, N.Y.: St. Vladimir's Seminary Press, 2005.

Tracy, David. *Plurality and Ambiguity: Hermeneutics, Religion, Hope*. Chicago: University of Chicago Press, 1994.

Ugolnik, Anton (Anthony). *The Illuminating Icon*. Grand Rapids, Mich.: William B. Eerdman's Publishing Company, 1989.

———. "An Orthodox Hermeneutic in the West." *St. Vladimir's Theological Quarterly* 27, no. 2 (1983): 93–118.

———(Anthony). "Textual Liturgics: Russian Orthodoxy and Recent Literary Criticism." *Religion and Literature* 22, no. 2–3 (1990): 133–54.

———. "Tradition as Freedom from the Past: Eastern Orthodoxy and the Western Mind." *Journal of Ecumenical Studies* 21, no. 2 (Spring 1984): 278–94.

Valdés, Mario, ed. *A Ricoeur Reader: Reflection and Imagination*. Toronto: University of Toronto Press, 1991.

van den Hengel, John. "Can There Be a Science of Human Action?" In *Ricoeur as Another: The Ethics of Subjectivity*, edited by Richard A. Cohen and James L. Marsh, 71–92. Albany: State University of New York, 2002.

———. "From Text to Action in Theology." In *Memory, Narrativity, Self and the Challenge to Think God*, edited by Maureen Junker-Kenny and Peter Kenny, 117–33. Münster: Lit Verlag, 2004.

———. *The Home of Meaning*. Lanham, Md.: University Press of America, 1982.

———. "Jesus Between Fiction and History." In *Meanings in Texts and Actions: Questioning Paul Ricoeur*, edited by David E. Klemm and William Schweiker, 133–56. Charlottesville: University Press of Virginia, 1993.

———. "Naming the Unspeakable." In *Between Suspicion and Sympathy: Paul Ricoeur's Unstable Equilibrium*, edited by Andrzej Wierciński. Hermeneutic Series, Volume 3, 244–65. Toronto: Hermeneutic Press (The International Institute for Hermeneutics), 2003.

———. "Paul Ricoeur's *Oneself as Another* and Practical Theology." *Theological Studies* 55 (1994): 458–80.

Vanhoozer, Kevin J. *Biblical Narrative in the Philosophy of Paul Ricoeur: A Study in Hermeneutics and Theology*. Cambridge: Cambridge University Press, 1990.

———. *The Drama of Doctrine: A Canonical Linguistic Approach to Christian Theology*. Louisville, Ky.: Westminster John Knox Press, 2005.

Velkovska, Elena Velkova. "Blessings in the East." In *Handbook for Liturgical Studies, Volume IV: Sacraments and Sacramentals*, edited by Anscar J. Chupungo, 383–92. Collegeville, Minn.: Liturgical Press, 2000.

Visser, Margaret. *The Rituals of Dinner: The Origins, Evolution, Eccentricities, and Meaning of Table Manners*. New York: Penguin Books, 1991.

von Balthasar, Hans Urs. *Cosmic Liturgy*. Translated by Brian E. Daley. San Francisco: Ignatius Press, 2003.

Ward, Graham. "Biblical Narrative and the Theology of Metonymy." *Modern Theology* 7, no. 4 (July 1991): 335–49.

Westerfield Tucker, Karen B. "The Liturgical Functioning of Orthodox Troparia and Wesleyan Hymns." In *In Orthodox and Wesleyan Scriptural Understanding and Practice*, edited by S. T. Kimbrough Jr., 293–304. Crestwood, N.Y.: St. Vladimir's Seminary Press, 2005.

Westphal, Merold. *Overcoming Onto-Theology: Toward a Postmodern Christian Faith*. New York: Fordham University Press, 2001.

Williams, Rowan. "Eastern Orthodox Theology." In *The Modern Theologians: An Introduction to Christian Theology since 1918*, edited by David Ford and Rachel Muers, 572–88. Malden, Mass.: Blackwell Publishing, 2005.

———. *The Edge of Words: God and the Habits of Language*. London: Bloomsbury, 2014.

Wybrew, Hugh. *The Orthodox Liturgy: The Development of the Eucharistic Liturgy in the Byzantine Rite*. Crestwood, N.Y.: St. Vladimir's Seminary Press, 1989.

Yarnold, Edward, S.J. *The Awe-Inspiring Rites of Initiation: The Origins of the R.C.I.A.* Second ed. Collegeville, Minn.: Liturgical Press, 1994.

Zimmerman, Joyce Ann. "Language and Human Experience." In *The New Dictionary of Sacramental Worship*, edited by Peter E. Fink, 644–51. Collegeville, Minn.: A Michael Glazier Book, Liturgical Press, 1990.

———. "Liturgical Assembly: Who is the Subject of Liturgy?" *Liturgical Ministry* 3 (Spring 1994): 41–51.

———. *Liturgy and Hermeneutics*. Collegeville, Minn.: Liturgical Press, 1999.

————. *Liturgy as a Language of Faith: A Liturgical Methodology in the Mode of Paul Ricoeur's Textual Hermeneutics*. Lanham, Md.: University Press of America, 1988.

————. *Liturgy as Living Faith: A Liturgical Spirituality*. Scranton: University of Scranton Press, 1993.

————. "Paschal Mystery—Whose Mystery? A Post-Critical Methodological Reinterpretation." In *Primary Sources of Liturgical Theology: A Reader*, edited by Dwight W. Vogel, 302–12. Collegeville, Minn.: Liturgical Press, 2000.

————. Review of *Christian Hermeneutics: Paul Ricoeur and the Refiguring of Theology*, by James Fodor. *International Philosophical Quarterly* 38 (1998): 86–88.

Zizioulas, John. *Being as Communion*. Crestwood, N.Y.: St. Vladimir's Seminary Press, 1985.

INDEX

Ambrose, St., 78
Anaphora of Addai and Mari, 83
Anselm of Canterbury, St., 143, 298n21
apophatic, 5, 63, 71, 76, 77, 85, 97, 101, 103, 104, 105, 112, 128, 131, 133, 134, 148, 176, 186, 187, 215, 266n42
Aquinas, St. Thomas, 19, 20, 71, 101, 105
Aristotle, 26, 64, 138, 152, 288n28; *phronēsis*, 64
Arranz, Miguel, 176
ars memoriae, 156, 158
Assyrian Church of the East, 83, 237n18
Augustine, St., 27, 93, 147, 191, 199, 247n73, 294n70, 311n47
Aune, Michael, 99, 100, 150–52, 160, 169, 170, 279n55, 304nn59–61, 305nn61,63
Austin, J. L., 45, 47, 49, 65, 256n42

Bakhtin, Mikhail, 112–13, 130, 135, 285nn3–4, 286nn4,8
baptism, 4, 35, 42, 78, 79, 104, 162, 173, 174, 176, 177, 183, 185, 186, 190, 191, 197, 199, 200, 207, 208, 210, 211, 217, 224, 253n20, 256n42, 260n92, 307n12, 309n36, 312n57, 313n58
Barfield, Owen, 195, 264n22
Basil the Great, St., 175, 303n50
Benedict XVI, Pope, 191, 202, 313n60
Bible, 5, 9, 46, 48, 68, 69, 77, 81, 83, 86, 91, 92, 93, 94, 95, 98, 104, 108, 112, 148, 185, 248n81, 253n20, 256n42, 266n40, 269n57, 271n64, 273n11, 276n38, 284–85n85, 285n3, 287nn18,20, 295n79, 316n92
Bitton-Ashkelony, Brouria, 154
Bobrinskoy, Boris, 200, 238n2

Bradshaw, Paul, 126, 169
Breck, John, 48
Butcher, Brian, 237n18, 239n12
Byzantine Rite, 4, 16, 27, 108, 129, 155, 156, 169, 175, 246n66, 248n81, 299n32, 305n61, 319n106

Cabasilas, Nicholas, 10
Chalcedon, Council of, 21, 265n37
Charlesworth, Max, 18–20
Chauvet, Louis-Marie, 133–34
Chomsky, Noam, 65
Ciszek, Walter, S.J., 158, 301n26
Codex Barberini 336, 174
commissive, 115, 294
Constantinople, 26, 174
Cuneo, Terence, 215
Cyril of Jerusalem, St., 78, 125

Denysenko, Nicholas, 174–80, 185, 199, 200, 202, 215, 306n1, 309n34, 310n37, 310nn39–40, 312n57
Derrida, Jacques, 22, 45, 48, 258n62, 274n22
Descartes, René, 64, 114, 123, 124, 138, 265n29
Divine Liturgy, 12, 13, 27, 32, 56, 57, 108, 158, 173, 239n12, 240n18, 256n42, 282n73, 292n42, 294n70, 315n88; Little Entrance, 13, 15, 16, 17; Liturgy of the Presanctified Gifts, 299n32
Dix, Dom Gregory, 42
docta ignorantia, 101–2
Donne, John, 126
doxa, 26, 138, 149, 159

337

Latin Rite, 33, 36, 80, 134, 257n53, 313n68, 316n89
Lawlor, Leonard, 22
Leo the Great, Pope St., 204, 285n85
Lévinas, Emmanuel, 19, 147, 235n10, 299n36
Lewis, C. S., 87–89, 96, 114, 141, 186, 214, 272n6, 272n9, 273nn11–12, 277n39, 280n61
lex orandi, lex credendi, 2, 3, 6, 10, 13, 30, 99, 100, 151, 159, 160, 234nn5–6, 238n2
limit-experiences, 97, 133, 147, 208, 266n44
limit-language, 95, 97
linguistic turn, 63–66, 153, 292n45
Little Entrance. *See* Divine Liturgy: Little Entrance
liturgical theology, 2, 6, 9, 11, 18, 23, 30, 35, 41, 47, 50, 58, 63, 64, 68, 80, 100, 116, 150, 151, 157, 165, 169, 170, 178, 213, 215, 233n5, 234n6, 236n15, 238n2, 239n9, 241n20, 243n41, 271n64, 279n55, 304nn59–69, 305n63
liturgiology, 170, 234, 236n15
logos, 17, 145
Logos, 122, 185, 204, 282n67
Lossky, Vladimir, 11, 159, 160
Louth, Andrew, 166, 231, 236n15, 239n9, 245n58, 303n50

MacIntyre, Alisdair, 204
magnalia Dei, 105, 112, 133, 163, 207, 252n17
Maloney, George, 124
Marion, Jean-Luc, 145, 234n6
Mary, St. *See* Mother of God
Maximus the Confessor, St., 20–23, 244n56
McFague, Sallie, 90, 264n20, 272–73n11, 282n72
McGowan, Andrew B., 260n87
McGrath, Alister, 241n23
McGuckin, John, 24, 112, 296n83
Merleau-Ponty, Maurice, 148
metaphor, 2, 15, 19, 22, 34, 44, 60, 63, 65, 66, 67, 69, 74, 75, 82–83, 85–91, 94, 96, 97, 101, 106, 107, 123, 131, 143, 145, 157, 185, 187, 192, 193, 195, 205, 210, 211, 216, 242n28, 244n47, 245n64, 253n20, 262n6, 264n22, 272nn8–9, 273nn11–12, 274n22, 275n27, 276n30, 277nn39,41, 283nn78–79, 284nn82,85 293n46, 296n85, 314n71
metonymy, 90, 96, 97, 274n22
Meyendorff, Paul, 27, 308n20
mimesis, 40, 56, 78, 204, 286n15
Mink, Louis, 163
Mother of God, 127, 135, 159, 160, 222, 282n67, 296n83
mystagogy, 9, 16, 78, 125, 242n35

Nicene Creed, 138, 256n42
Nichols, Aidan, 19, 56, 243n44
Nichols, Bridget, 41–52, 57, 213, 256n42
Nietzsche, Friedrich, 114, 138, 139
Novak, David, 139

ontotheology, 71, 73, 118, 185, 195, 311n45
Origen, 21, 22

Paschal Mystery, 35, 37, 40, 188, 190, 207, 251n15, 253n20
Paul, St., 184, 210, 229, 320n108
Pelikan, Jaroslav, 25–27, 32, 56, 138, 180
Pellauer, David, 90, 95, 97
Pentecost, 104, 292n42
performance, 33, 34, 42, 45–47, 49–57, 66–68, 80, 85, 106, 108, 116, 118–19 158, 257nn51,54, 260n86, 262n13, 263n17, 285n85
perichoresis, 146
perlocutionary force, 52, 256n42
petits récits, 82, 196, 205, 269n57
philosophy, 1, 3, 18–24, 64, 65, 75, 100, 114, 123, 139, 141, 213, 243n41, 277n41, 296n1, 298n15; *ancilla theologiae*, 19; Ordinary Language Philosophy, 115, 299n1; *philosophia perennis*, 20, 244n47
Pickstock, Catherine, 80
Plato, 68, 152, 161
Plekon, Michael, 2
poesis, 80
Power, David, 80–84, 104, 112, 113, 165, 195, 205, 214, 268n51, 269nn55–56
pravoslavie, 25, 26
preaching, 67, 68, 77, 78–79, 236n14, 260n92, 268n51, 290n37
promissive, 115, 242
prophetic literature, 81, 120, 121, 182, 183, 197, 279n50, 282n72, 290n36
Prosper of Aquitaine, 99, 280n55
Pseudo–Dionysius the Areopagite, 5, 16, 21, 23, 104, 105, 112, 237n20, 282n72

Quadriga, 14

Rahner, Karl, 101, 105, 280n60
Ramsey, Ian T., 76, 284n82
Regan, Charles, 114
Ricoeur, Paul: appropriation, 31, 35, 36, 39, 40, 46, 196, 197, 236n14, 249n3, 250n4, 251n15, 253n20; attestation, 116, 136, 137, 138, 141, 142, 143, 146, 148, 214, 242n34, 256n42, 297n4, 302n34; "bound" symbolism, 122, 182; configuration, 38, 40, 46, 48, 54, 56, 119, 122, 194, 197, 203,

ORTHODOX CHRISTIANITY AND CONTEMPORARY THOUGHT

George E. Demacopoulos and Aristotle Papanikolaou, series editors

George E. Demacopoulos and Aristotle Papaniklaou (eds.), *Orthodox Constructions of the West.*

John Chryssavgis and Bruce V. Foltz (eds.), *Toward an Ecology of Transfiguration: Orthodox Christian Perspectives on Environment, Nature, and Creation.* Foreword by Bill McKibben. Prefatory Letter by Ecumenical Patriarch Bartholomew.

Lucian N. Leustean (ed.), *Orthodox Christianity and Nationalism in Nineteenth-Century Southeastern Europe.*

John Chryssavgis (ed.), *Dialogue of Love: Breaking the Silence of Centuries.* Contributions by Brian E. Daley, S.J., and Georges Florovsky.

George E. Demacopoulos and Aristotle Papaniklaou (eds.), *Christianity, Democracy, and the Shadow of Constantine.*

Brian A. Butcher, *Liturgical Theology after Schmemann: An Orthodox Reading of Paul Ricoeur.* Foreword by Andrew Louth.

Ecumenical Patriarch Bartholomew, *In the World, Yet Not of the World: Social and Global Initiatives of Ecumenical Patriarch Bartholomew.* Edited by John Chryssavgis. Foreword by Jose Manuel Barroso.

Ecumenical Patriarch Bartholomew, *Speaking the Truth in Love: Theological and Spiritual Exhortations of Ecumenical Patriarch Bartholomew.* Edited by John Chryssavgis. Foreword by Dr. Rowan Williams, Archbishop of Canterbury.

Ecumenical Patriarch Bartholomew, *On Earth as in Heaven: Ecological Vision and Initiatives of Ecumenical Patriarch Bartholomew.* Edited by John Chryssavgis. Foreword by His Royal Highness, the Duke of Edinburgh.